WEST-E
005

Elementary Education
Teacher Certification Exam

By: Sharon Wynne, M.S.
Southern Connecticut State University

"And, while there's no reason yet to panic, I think it's only prudent that we make preparations to panic."

XAMonline, INC.
Boston

XAMonline, Inc.
25 First Street, Suite 106
Cambridge, MA 02141
Toll Free 1-800-509-4128
Email: info@xamonline.com
Web www.xamonline.com
Fax: 1-781-662-9268

Library of Congress Cataloging-in-Publication Data

Wynne, Sharon A.
Elementary Education 005 Teacher Certification / Sharon A. Wynne. -3rd ed.
ISBN 978-1-60787-138-5
1. Elementary Education 005   2. Study Guides.   3. WEST-E
4. Teachers' Certification & Licensure.   5. Careers

Disclaimer:

The opinions expressed in this publication are the sole works of XAMonline and were created independently from the National Education Association, Educational Testing Service, or any State Department of Education, National Evaluation Systems or other testing affiliates.

Between the time of publication and printing, state specific standards as well as testing formats and website information may change that is not included in part or in whole within this product. Sample test questions are developed by XAMonline and reflect similar content as on real tests; however, they are not former tests. XAMonline assembles content that aligns with state standards but makes no claims nor guarantees teacher candidates a passing score. Numerical scores are determined by testing companies such as NES or ETS and then are compared with individual state standards. A passing score varies from state to state.

Printed in the United States of America   œ-1

WEST-E Elementary Education
-ISBN: 978-1-60787-138-5

TABLE OF CONTENTS

DOMAIN I.   **MATHEMATICS**

COMPETENCY 0001   UNDERSTAND PRINCIPLES, CONCEPTS, AND PROCEDURES RELATED TO MATHEMATICAL REPRESENTATION AND COMMUNICATION.

Skill 1.1   Extracting mathematical information from a variety of sources (e.g., pictures, diagrams, text, graphs)..1

Skill 1.2   Using textual, graphic, numeric, and symbolic representations to communicate mathematical concepts 5

Skill 1.3   Translating between textual, graphic, numeric, and symbolic representations..7

Skill 1.4   Using mathematical language to communicate ideas and information, including interpreting mathematical terminology, symbols, and representations......................................9

COMPETENCY 0002   UNDERSTAND PRINCIPLES, CONCEPTS, AND PROCEDURES RELATED TO MATEMATICAL REASONING, PROOF, AND CONNECTIONS.

Skill 2.1   Applying knowledge of formal and informal mathematical reasoning processes (e.g., using logical reasoning to draw and justify conclusions)..14

Skill 2.2   Developing and evaluating conjectures and informal proofs..15

Skill 2.3   Recognizing and applying mathematics in real-world contexts and applying connections among mathematical ideas............20

Skill 2.4   Demonstrating knowledge of the historical development of mathematics, including contributions from many cultures.....25

COMPETENCY 0003   UNDERSTAND PRINCIPLES, CONCEPTS, AND PROCEDURES RELATED TO MATHEMATICAL PROBLEM SOLVING AND THE USE OF TECHNOLOGY.

Skill 3.1   Applying knowledge of appropriate mathematical concepts, procedures, tools, and technologies to solve problems 27

Skill 3.2   Making use of pictures, models, charts, graphs, and symbols as tools of mathematical problem solving 28

Skill 3.3   Applying, analyzing, and evaluating mathematical thinking and strategies 28

Skill 3.4   Recognizing the appropriate use of tools and technology to visualize mathematical concepts and to perform mathematical experiments and explore conjectures 30

COMPETENCY 0004   UNDERSTAND PRINCIPLES, CONCEPTS, AND PROCEDURES RELATED TO NUMBERS, NUMBER SENSE, AND NUMERATION.

Skill 4.1   Demonstrating knowledge of the characteristics of whole numbers, integers, rational numbers, and real numbers 32

Skill 4.2   Identifying equivalent forms of fractions, decimals, percents, roots and powers, including using scientific notation to represent small and large numbers 32

Skill 4.3   Comparing and ordering numbers 36

Skill 4.4   Applying fundamental concepts of number theory, including prime and composite numbers, place value, factors and multiples, and divisibility rules 37

COMPETENCY 0005   UNDERSTAND PRINCIPLES, CONCEPTS, AND PROCEDURES RELATED TO MATHEMATICAL OPERATIONS, CALCULATION, AND ESTIMATION.

Skill 5.1   Using a variety of models, methods, and algorithms to represent operations with integers and whole and rational numbers 43

Skill 5.2   Demonstrating knowledge of the properties of the rational number system (e.g., commutative, associative) 45

Skill 5.3   Identifying situations in which estimation is an appropriate problem-solving strategy 47

Skill 5.4   Making use of estimation to predict results and determine the reasonableness of answers 48

Skill 5.5   Solving problems involving integers, fractions, decimals, ratios, proportions, percents, powers, and roots using a variety of algorithms, procedures, and strategies, including mental math 49

COMPETENCY 0006   APPLY PRINCIPLES, CONCEPTS, AND PROCEDURES RELATED TO ALGEBRA

Skill 6.1   Recognizing, representing, and extending patterns, relationships, and functions using numbers, graphs, symbols, variables, and rules 52

Skill 6.2   Simplifying and evaluating algebraic expressions and formulas, and solving algebraic equations and inequalities ...54

Skill 6.3   Making use of algebraic functions to plot points and describe graphs, and analyzing change in various contexts 57

Skill 6.4   Translating word problems into mathematical terms using algebraic concepts such as variables and equations 63

Skill 6.5   Using mathematical models to represent quantitative relationships (e.g., proportional relationships, linear relationships) 66

Skill 6.6   Solving problems using a variety of algebraic concepts, models, and methods 66

COMPETENCY 0007   APPLY PRINCIPLES, CONCEPTS, AND PROCEDURES RELATED TO GEOMETRY

Skill 7.1   Analyzing various representations (e.g., diagrams, perspective drawings, projections, nets) of two- and three-dimensional objects 71

Skill 7.2   Analyzing properties and relationships of various geometric shapes and structures 73

Skill 7.3   Applying core concepts and principles of Euclidean geometry (e.g., symmetry, similarity, congruence) in two and three dimensions (e.g., points, lines, planes) to solve problems 74

Skill 7.4   Applying knowledge of coordinate grids to represent basic geometric figures and analyze transformations 79

COMPETENCY 0008   APPLY PRINCIPLES, CONCEPTS, AND PROCEDURES RELATED TO MEASUREMENT.

Skill 8.1   Identifying and measuring component parts (e.g., angles, lines, segments) and properties (e.g., area, volume) of geometric figures and recognizing the relationships between two- and three-dimensional figures 82

Skill 8.2   Demonstrating knowledge of the relationship of units within the U.S. and metric systems 89

Skill 8.3   Recognizing appropriate uses of standard measurement units, selecting appropriate measurement tools, measuring objects and events, and calculating rates and determining units 94

Skill 8.4   Applying knowledge of the concepts of precision, accuracy, and estimation 101

COMPETENCY 0009   APPLY PRINCIPLES, CONCEPTS, AND PROCEDURES REALTED TO STATISTICS AND PROBABILITY.

Skill 9.1   Identifying various methods (e.g., surveys, tables, graphs) of systematically collecting, organizing, and displaying data ... 106

Skill 9.2   Applying knowledge of statistical methods and technological tools to analyze data and describe shape, spread, and center (e.g., mean, median, mode, range) 106

Skill 9.3   Making inferences based on analysis of experimental results, statistical data, and graphic representations 109

Skill 9.4   Applying knowledge of how statistics can be used to support different points of view and identifying misuses of statistics and invalid conclusions 110

Skill 9.5   Applying counting procedures to determine probabilities 112

Skill 9.6   Applying properties of dependent and independent events to calculate probabilities 117

Skill 9.7   Demonstrating knowledge of the use of tools (e.g., spinners, number cubes) and technology-based simulations to estimate probable outcomes 120

DOMAIN II.   **SCIENCE**

COMPETENCY 0010   UNDERSTAND MATTER AND ENERGY AND
                       THEIR INTERACTION IN PHYSICAL SYSTEMS

Skill 10.1   Identifying the physical and chemical properties of matter .. 122

Skill 10.2   Distinguishing physical and chemical changes in matter 123

Skill 10.3   Demonstrating knowledge of how energy is transformed from
                 one form into another and methods of energy transfer (e.g.,
                 conduction, convection, radiation) 124

Skill 10.4   Recognizing properties, characteristics, and behaviors of
                 sound, water, and light waves 128

Skill 10.5   Demonstrating knowledge of basic concepts related to
                 electricity and magnetism 129

Skill 10.6   Comparing and contrasting characteristics of elements,
                 atoms, molecules, mixtures, and compounds 131

Skill 10.7   Recognizing that energy and matter are conserved in chemical
                 and physical systems 135

COMPETENCY 0011   UNDERSTAND THE INTERACTION OF FORCE,
                       MASS, AND MOTION IN PHYSICAL SYSTEMS.

Skill 11.1   Applying knowledge of Newton's three laws of motion and
                 solving problems involving the force, mass, and motion of
                 objects in everyday phenomena 137

Skill 11.2   Analyzing graphs that represent the motion of objects in terms
                 of distance, time, velocity, and acceleration.......................... 138

Skill 11.3   Identifying the kinds of forces (e.g., frictional, gravitational)
                 that act on objects in everyday situations 140

Skill 11.4   Recognizing the role that the force of gravity plays in tides and
                 the solar system 140

Skill 11.5   Demonstrating knowledge of the use of simple machines (i.e.,
                 lever, pulley, wedge, wheel and axle, screw) in everyday life
                 and the mechanical advantage they provide 140

COMPETENCY 0012   UNDERSTAND FUNDAMENTAL CONCEPTS AND PRINCIPLES RELATED TO EARTH AND SPACE SYSTEMS.

Skill 12.1   Demonstrating knowledge of the processes that change the surface of the earth (e.g., soil formation, weathering, erosion, volcanism, tectonic activity) and the causes and effects of those processes 142

Skill 12.2   Recognizing the characteristics and processes of the rock cycle and physical and chemical properties of earth materials 148

Skill 12.3   Recognizing how fossils and other evidence are used to document life and environmental changes over time 149

Skill 12.4   Recognizing the components, structure, and interconnections among the earth's crust, atmosphere, and hydrosphere 149

Skill 12.5   Demonstrating knowledge of the water cycle and weather patterns and factors that influence weather and climate 149

Skill 12.6   Demonstrating knowledge of the structure of the solar system and of the characteristics, interactions, and motions of its components 152

Skill 12.7   Demonstrating knowledge of renewable and nonrenewable resources and of the effects of human activities on the environment 155

COMPTENCY 0013   UNDERSTAND FUNDAMENTAL CONCEPTS AND PRINCIPLES OF LIFE SCIENCE AND LIVING SYSTEMS.

Skill 13.1   Recognizing basic structures and functions of cells 165

Skill 13.2   Recognizing the characteristics, processes, and classification of living things 168

Skill 13.1   Demonstrating knowledge of the basic structures and functions of human body systems 171

Skill 13.4   Recognizing the processes by which organisms obtain matter and energy for life processes 178

Skill 13.5   Analyzing how organisms interact with one another and with their environment, including the effects of human activities on the environment...178

Skill 13.6   Demonstrating knowledge of characteristics of the life cycles of common plants and animals...182

Skill 13.7   Recognizing the principles of the transmission of genetic information and of biological evolution 184

COMPETENCY 0014   UNDERSTAND THE NATURE, SKILLS, AND PROCESSES OF SCIENTIFIC INQUIRY

Skill 14.1   Recognizing the nature of scientific inquiry, including how scientific theories explain facts using inferential logic and the role of curiosity, honesty, skepticism, observation, and openness in the scientific process..192

Skill 14.2   Identifying controlled, manipulated (i.e., independent), and responding (i.e., dependent) variables in scientific investigations 194

Skill 14.3   Demonstrating knowledge of the skills and processes of scientific inquiry, including planning scientific investigations, collecting and presenting data in different contexts, and drawing conclusions from data and evidence.......................194

Skill 14.4   Recognizing appropriate procedures for making scientific investigations reliable and valid 195

Skill 14.5   Recognizing potential safety hazards, sources of information, and appropriate protocols for maintaining safety and responding to emergencies in laboratory situations.............195

Skill 14.6   Demonstrating knowledge of appropriate tools, equipment, and procedures to collect, record, measure, and represent data in scientific investigations 200

COMPETENCY 0015   UNDERSTAND PROBLEM-SOLVING STRATEGIES AND MATHEMATICAL THINKING USED IN SCIENTIFIC INVESTIGATIONS.

Skill 15.1   Recognizing appropriate use of charts, tables, and graphs for data display and analysis in different contexts 203

Skill 15.2   Applying basic mathematical procedures (e.g., averaging, estimating, using ratios and proportions) to interpret scientific data 204

Skill 15.3   Recognizing the appropriate use of fractions, percents, and decimals to represent data 205

Skill 15.4   Recognizing how physical models (e.g., relating electric current to flowing water, using a globe and lamp to demonstrate changing seasons) and computer simulations (e.g., weather forecasting, earthquake analysis) are used to explain systems and processes 206

Skill 15.5   Demonstrating knowledge of the appropriate metric units and levels of precision used in scientific investigations 207

COMPETENCY 0016   UNDERSTAND THE HISTORICAL DEVELOPMENT OF SCIENCE AND THE INTERCONNECTIONS AMONG SCIENCE, TECHNOLOGY, AND SOCIETY

Skill 16.1   Recognizing the contributions of individuals from diverse cultures to the development of science and technology 209

Skill 16.2   Analyzing how science and technology have affected individuals, cultures, and societies throughout history 210

Skill 16.3   Demonstrating knowledge of how science and technology are used to develop solutions to economic, societal, and environmental problems 212

Skill 16.4   Recognizing the integration and interdependence of science, technology, society, the workplace, and the environment 213

DOMAIN III.   **HEALTH/FITNESS**

COMPETENCY 0017   UNDERSTAND TYPICAL FACTORS, PRINCIPLES, AND PRACTICES RELATED TO THE DEVELOPMENT OF PERSONAL HEALTH AND SAFETY.

Skill 17.1   Recognizing patterns and stages of child growth and development and factors that affect growth and development, including the ways in which health and fitness choices and habits affect quality of life, health, and life span 215

Skill 17.2   Demonstrating knowledge of nutritional principles and the influence of nutritional practices on health and development.... 220

Skill 17.3   Identifying principles, practices, and skills for maintaining personal health and safety and for reducing health risks (e.g., using health-care products safely, recognizing risky situations, demonstrating injury-prevention techniques) 221

Skill 17.4   Applying knowledge of how to use social skills to respond to peer pressure, to express opinions and resolve conflicts constructively, and to maintain safe and respectful relationships 223

Skill 17.5   Identifying types and effects of stress, factors that affect family life and mental and emotional health, and strategies for managing stress and for maintaining healthy family relationships and positive mental, emotional, physical, and sexual health...226

Skill 17.6   Recognizing the physical, emotional, and legal consequences of using alcohol, tobacco, and other drugs, and identifying techniques and strategies for resisting pressures and unhealthy messages related to drug use 230

Skill 17.7   Demonstrating knowledge of practices and skills that prevent and reduce the risk of contracting and transmitting communicable diseases and that help prevent and control non-communicable diseases...232

COMPETENCY 0018   DEMONSTRATE KNOWLEDGE OF BASIC MOVEMENT CONCEPTS, MOTOR SKILLS, RHYTHMIC ACTIVITIES, FITNESS ACTIVITIES, AND GAMES AND SPORTS.

Skill 18.1   Demonstrating knowledge of movement concepts related to body awareness, spatial awareness, and direction, and of the ways in which children grow and develop kinesthetically 234

Skill 18.2   Recognizing types and elements of basic motor skills (e.g., locomotor, nonlocomotor, manipulative) and techniques, cues, and prompts for developing fundamental and specialized motor skills (e.g., run, throw, kick) 235

Skill 18.3 Demonstrating knowledge of appropriate strategies, activities, games, and sports for various purposes and for various developmental, age, and ability levels....................................240

Skill 18.4 Recognizing appropriate principles, techniques, cues, prompts, and feedback for promoting skill development and safe participation in rhythmic activities, games, and sports.......
....241

Skill 18.5 Demonstrating knowledge of physical fitness principles and activities for developing healthy levels of cardio respiratory fitness, muscular strength and endurance, flexibility, and body composition...243

Skill 18.6 Recognizing the health-related benefits of movement and fitness activities and the role of physical activities in promoting social skills such as cooperation, support, respect, inclusion, and understanding and appreciation of similarities and differences 247

DOMAIN IV.   ENGLISH LANGUAGE ARTS

COMPETENCY 0019   UNDERSTAND THE NATURE OF FIRST- AND SECOND-LANGUAGE ACQUISITION AND DEVELOPMENT.

Skill 19.1 Demonstrating knowledge of the grammar of Standard American English, including semantics, syntax, morphology, and phonology...249

Skill 19.2 Recognizing the interrelationship between first- and second-language acquisition and literacy 252

Skill 19.3 Identifying examples of diversity in language use (e.g., grammar, patterns, dialects) 254

Skill 19.4 Recognizing ways in which linguistic and rhetorical patterns affect written and oral expression 255

Skill 19.5 Identifying skills that promote respectful communication and factors that affect intercultural communication 255

COMPETENCY 0020   UNDERSTAND THE DEVELOPMENT PROCESSES OF READING AND READING COMPREHENSION.

Skill 20.1 Recognizing concepts of print (e.g., holding a book, directionality, tracking of print)..257

Skill 20.2   Demonstrating knowledge of phonemic awareness and its
              importance to reading development..260

Skill 20.3   Demonstrating knowledge of the basic principles of phonics....
             261

Skill 20.4   Identifying strategies for monitoring and facilitating
              comprehension before, during, and after reading..................261

Skill 20.5   Recognizing the components of reading fluency, factors that
              affect fluency, and the relationship between fluency and
              reading comprehension...265

Skill 20.6   Recognizing ways in which speaking, listening, spelling, and
              writing are essential components of reading development ..274

COMPETENCY 0021   UNDERSTAND WORD RECOGNITION SKILLS
                      AND THE DEVELOPMENT OF VOCABLARY
                      SKILLS AND KNOWLEDGE.

Skill 21.1   Identifying decoding and word identification strategies,
              including the use of structural analysis, spelling patterns, and
              syllabication...275

Skill 21.2   Recognizing methods of direct and indirect vocabulary
              instruction (e.g., specific word instruction, context clues) ...277

Skill 21.3   Recognizing ways to help students identify and use references
              (e.g., dictionary, thesaurus) for various purposes 279

Skill 21.4   Demonstrating an understanding of how prior knowledge,
              context clues, and graphic features of text can be used to
              predict, clarify, and expand word meanings..........................279

COMPETENCY 0022   UNDERSTAND STRATEGIES FOR
                      COMPREHENDING
                      INFORMATIONAL/EXPOSITORY AND
                      PERSUASIVE TEXTS.

Skill 22.1   Identifying characteristics of informational/expository and
              persuasive writing 281

Skill 22.2   Demonstrating knowledge of strategies for analyzing,
              interpreting, and evaluating a variety of
              informational/expository and persuasive texts 284

Skill 22.3 Recognizing how tone, bias, and point of view influence meaning in informational/expository and persuasive texts......... 285

Skill 22.4 Recognizing how to apply comprehension strategies before, during, and after reading to promote understanding of informational/expository and persuasive texts 286

COMPETENCY 0023   **UNDERSTAND STRATEGIES FOR COMPREHENDING LITERARY TEXTS.**

Skill 23.1 Recognizing authors of literature written for children and young adults and characteristics of their works 290

Skill 23.2 Identifying characteristics of genres and recognizing themes of literature written for children and young adults................294

Skill 23.3 Analyzing story elements in works of fiction.........................298

Skill 23.4 Recognizing literary and narrative devices and historical contexts of literary works and analyzing their relationship to the meaning of the text 301

Skill 23.5 Analyzing a variety of literary texts, including how elements such as tone, style, and point of view influence meaning 305

Skill 23.6 Recognizing the structural elements and essential attributes of poetic forms (e.g., rhyme scheme, meter, stanza)..................306

COMPETENCY 0024   **UNDERSTAND THE PROCESS OF WRITING.**

Skill 24.1 Demonstrating knowledge of the developmental stages of emergent writing (e.g., scribbling, letter strings, inventive spelling)..310

Skill 24.2 Identifying strategies for generating topics and developing ideas and for using organizational structures in writing 311

Skill 24.3 Identifying strategies for prewriting, drafting, revising, editing, proofreading, and publishing materials 313

Skill 24.4 Analyzing and identifying revisions of written work in relation to organization, unity, clarity, and style 316

Skill 24.5 Recognizing factors to consider when writing for various audiences and purposes 317

Skill 24.6   Demonstrating knowledge of how form (e.g., research paper, editorial, memoir) and mode (e.g., expository, persuasive, narrative) shape writing 318

COMPETENCY 0025   APPLY KNOWLEDGE OF GRAMMAR, USAGE, AND MECHANICS.

Skill 25.1   Applying knowledge of grammar and punctuation conventions for Standard American English 320

Skill 25.2   Applying knowledge of orthographic patterns and usage rules for Standard American English 327

Skill 25.3   Recognizing a variety of sentence structures and their uses 328

Skill 25.4   Recognizing a variety of paragraph formats and their uses 329

COMPETENCY 0026   UNDERSTAND THEINTERRELATIONSHIPS AMONG READING, WRITING, SPEAKING, LISTENING, VIEWING, AND THINKING.

Skill 26.1   Demonstrating knowledge of the role of metacognition in reading and writing and in listening and speaking 333

Skill 26.2   Analyzing ways in which the integration of reading, writing, speaking, listening, viewing, and thinking is necessary for constructing knowledge and communicating effectively 337

Skill 26.3   Recognizing how features of spoken language and nonverbal cues affect communication 338

Skill 26.4   Identifying strategies for planning, organizing, delivering, and evaluating oral presentations for a variety of audiences and purposes 340

Skill 26.5   Analyzing the influence of media on culture and on people's actions and communications 344

COMPETENCY 0027   UNDERSTAND INQUIRY AND
                   RESEARCHMETHODS IN LANDGUAGE ARTS.

Skill 27.1   Identifying strategies for locating information from a variety of sources (e.g., table of contents, indexes, newspaper, the Internet) 345

Skill 27.2   Demonstrating knowledge of appropriate source citations for bibliographies, footnotes, and endnotes 346

Skill 27.3   Identifying effective note-taking strategies...........................347

Skill 27.4   Demonstrating knowledge of the appropriate use of quotations as well as methods for summarizing and paraphrasing source information...348

Skill 27.5   Identifying methods for formulating research topics and essential questions 349

DOMAIN V.   SOCIAL STUDIES

COMPETENCY 0028   DEMONSTRATE KNOWLEDGE OF CONCEPTS
                   RELATED TO CITIZENSHIP AND GOVERNMENT.

Skill 28.1   Recognizing basic purposes and concepts of government and laws, the organization of federal, state, and local government in the United States, and how stakeholders influence public policy 350

Skill 28.2   Demonstrating knowledge of the core values and democratic principles of the United States as set forth in foundational documents, including the Constitution and the Declaration of Independence, and of key ideals of U.S. democracy 351

Skill 28.3   Demonstrating knowledge of the principles of democratic civic involvement and the roles, rights, and responsibilities of citizenship at the federal, state, local, and neighborhood levels 354

Skill 28.4   Demonstrating knowledge of the political organization of the world, characteristics of past and present forms of government, and factors that affect international relationships and the development of foreign policy...................................355

COMPETENCY 0029   DEMONSTRATE KNOWLEDGE OF ECONOMIC CONCEPTS AND SYSTEMS.

Skill 29.1   Recognizing basic terminology and concepts related to economics..357

Skill 29.2   Recognizing characteristics of economic systems and that economic choices involve costs and consequences.............360

Skill 29.3   Demonstrating knowledge of the purposes and functions of currency and financial institutions and the role of government as participant in the economy through taxation, spending, and policy...361

Skill 29.4   Demonstrating knowledge of the economic issues that all societies face...363

COMPETENCY 0030   UNDERSTAND MAJOR PRINCIPLES, CONCEPTS, AND PHENOMENA OF GEOGRAPHY.

Skill 30.1   Demonstrating knowledge of major geographic concepts and themes..365

Skill 30.2   Recognizing major geographic features of the United States and the world and their historical and contemporary significance...366

Skill 30.3   Deriving information from maps, charts, and other geographic tools...367

Skill 30.4   Demonstrating knowledge of settlement patterns around the world and the natural processes and human activities that create them 373

Skill 30.5   Analyzing the cultural and physical characteristics that define specific areas as regions..376

COMPETENCY 0031   UNDERSTAND MAJOR FORMS OF INTERATCTION BETWEEN PEOPLE, ENVIRONMENTS, AND CULTURES.

Skill 31.1   Recognizing basic concepts related to the structure and organization of human societies.................................381

Skill 31.2   Recognizing basic concepts related to the transmission and diffusion of culture, interactions among cultures, and the global interdependence of societies......................................383

Skill 31.3   Analyzing the nature and implications of the effects of human activities on the environment...384

Skill 31.4   Analyzing the nature and implications of the effects of the environment and environmental changes on people............387

COMPETENCY 0032   UNDERSTAND MAJOR CONCEPTS, ISSUES, PEOPLE, EVENTS, AND DEVELOPMENTS IN THE HISTORY OF THE UNITED STATES.

Skill 32.1   Identifying and comparing the characteristics and interactions of cultures during different periods of U.S. history...............388

Skill 32.2   Demonstrating knowledge of major issues, people, events, and cause-and-effect relationships during different periods of U.S. history, their influence on the present, and how they affect planning for the future 404

Skill 33.3   Analyzing various perspectives and interpretations of issues and events in the history of the United States........................404

Skill 33.4   Recognizing the influence of individuals, movements, culture, cultural groups, ideas, and technology on history and social change in the United States 405

COMPETENCY 0033   UNDERSTAND MAJOR CONCEPTS, ISSUES, PEOPLE, EVENTS, AND DEVELOPMENTS IN WORLD HISTORY.

Skill 33.1   Recognizing ways in which historical events are organized into time periods and eras, the chronological relationships within those periods and eras, and the ways in which different cultures perceive and record the passage of time 406

Skill 33.2   Demonstrating knowledge of early civilizations and cultures and their lasting influence 408

Skill 33.3   Demonstrating knowledge of major issues, people, events, and cause-and-effect relationships in historical periods of the world, their influence on the present, and how they affect planning for the future 422

Skill 33.4 Recognizing the causes and consequences of major world conflicts...425

Skill 33.5 Analyzing various perspectives and interpretations of issues and events in world history 426

Skill 33.6 Recognizing the influence of individuals, movements, culture, cultural groups, ideas, and technology on history and social change in the world..426

COMPETENCY 0034 UNDERSTAND INQUIRY AND INFORMATION SKILLS IN SOCIAL STUDIES.

Skill 34.1 Demonstrating knowledge of strategies for locating information from a variety of social studies resources and of creating graphic representations of textual information 431

Skill 34.2 Identifying time, place, audience, purpose, and form of a source and distinguishing between primary and secondary sources...431

Skill 34.3 Recognizing stereotypes, clichés, bias, and propaganda techniques and distinguishing between fact and opinion.....432

Skill 34.4 Demonstrating knowledge of strategies for evaluating the accuracy and reliability of information, including identifying the message and target audience of narrative documents ...434

DOMAIN VI. **THE ARTS**

COMPETENCY 0035 UNDERSTAND THE CONCEPTS, TECHNIQUES, MATERIALS, FUNCTIONS, METHODS, AND PROCESSES OF MUSIC AND THE VISUAL ARTS.

Skill 35.1 Demonstrating knowledge of basic elements, techniques, concepts, skills, and foundations in music and basic elements, principles of design, concepts, and skills in the visual arts 437

Skill 35.2 Recognizing types and characteristics of musical instruments, including the human voice, and methods, processes, and philosophies of creating music..439

Skill 35.3 Recognizing types and characteristics of materials, tools, techniques, methods, and processes used to create a variety of visual arts (e.g., painting, drawing, sculpting) 441

Skill 35.4   Recognizing methods and processes of creating, performing, and responding to music and to the visual arts 442

Skill 35.5   Demonstrating knowledge of how music and the visual arts are used to communicate and to express ideas and feelings for specific purposes and of how aesthetic and cultural diversity are reflected in music and in the visual arts 445

Skill 35.6   Recognizing vocal and instrumental musical styles and visual arts styles and achievements from various artists, cultures, and periods of history and how music and the visual arts shape and reflect culture and history......................................447

Skill 35.7   Demonstrating knowledge of how music and the visual arts make connections within and across the arts and to other disciplines, life, cultures, and work 453

COMPETENCY 0036   UNDERSTAND THE CONCEPTS, TECHNIQUES, MATERIALS, METHODS, AND PROCESSES RELATED TO DANCE AND THEATRE.

Skill 36.1   Demonstrating knowledge of basic elements, techniques, and principles of composition in dance 456

Skill 26.2   Demonstrating knowledge of basic concepts, skills, foundations, and techniques in theatre................................457

Skill 36.3   Demonstrating knowledge of dance forms (e.g., ballet, folk, modern) and their characteristic forms of movement, expressive qualities, and cultural origins 458

Skill 36.4   Demonstrating knowledge of dramatic and theatrical forms and their characteristics (e.g., pantomime, improvisation) ...459

Skill 36.5   Recognizing methods and processes of creating, performing, and responding to dance and theatre................................461

Skill 36.6   Demonstrating knowledge of how dance and theatre are used to communicate and to express ideas and feelings for specific purposes and of how aesthetic and cultural diversity are reflected in dance and theatre..462

Skill 36.7   Recognizing dance and theatre styles and achievements from various artists, cultures, and periods of history and how dance and theatre shape and reflect culture and history.................463

Skill 36.8   Demonstrating knowledge of how dance and theatre make connections within and across the arts and to other disciplines, life, cultures, and work 465

Sample Test 466

Answer Key 493

Rigor Table 494

Rationales 495

Great Study and Testing Tips!

What to study in order to prepare for the subject assessments is the focus of this study guide, but equally important is *how* you study.

You can increase your chances of truly mastering the information by taking some simple but effective steps.

Study Tips:

1. <u>Some foods aid the learning process</u>. Foods such as milk, nuts, seeds, rice, and oats help your study efforts by releasing natural memory enhancers called CCKs (*cholecystokinin*) composed of *tryptopha*n, *choline*, and *phenylalanine*. All of these chemicals enhance the neurotransmitters associated with memory. Before studying, try a light, protein-rich meal of eggs, turkey, and fish. All of these foods release the memory enhancing chemicals. The better the connections, the more you comprehend.

Likewise, before you take a test, stick to a light snack of energy boosting and relaxing foods. A glass of milk, a piece of fruit, or some peanuts will release various memory-boosting chemicals and help you to relax and focus on the subject at hand.

2. <u>Learn to take great notes</u>. A by-product of our modern culture is that we have grown accustomed to getting our information in short doses (e.g., TV news sound bites or newspaper articles styled after USA Today).

Consequently, we've subconsciously trained ourselves to assimilate information in <u>neat little packages</u>. If your notes are scrawled all over the paper, it fragments the flow of the information. Strive for clarity. Newspapers use a standard format to achieve clarity. Your notes can be much clearer through the use of proper formatting. A very effective format is called the <u>*"Cornell Method."*</u>

Take a sheet of loose-leaf lined notebook paper and draw a line all the way down the paper about 1-2" from the left-hand edge.

Draw another line across the width of the paper about 1-2" up from the bottom. Repeat this process on the reverse side of the page.

Look at the highly effective result. You have ample room for notes, a left hand margin for special emphasis items or inserting supplementary data from the textbook, a large area at the bottom for a brief summary, and a little rectangular space for just about anything you want.

3. **Get the concept then the details.** Too often we focus on the details and don't gather an understanding of the concept. However, if you simply memorize only dates, places, or names, you may well miss the whole point of the subject.

A key way to understand things is to put them in your own words. If you are working from a textbook, automatically summarize each paragraph in your mind. If you are outlining text, don't simply copy the author's words.

Rephrase them in your own words. You remember your own thoughts and words much better than someone else's, and subconsciously tend to associate the important details with the core concepts.

4. **Ask Why?** Pull apart written material paragraph by paragraph and don't forget the captions under the illustrations.

Example: If the heading is "Stream Erosion," flip it around to read "Why do streams erode?" Then answer the questions.

If you train your mind to think in a series of questions and answers, not only will you learn more, but it will also help to lessen test anxiety because you are used to answering questions.

5. **Read for reinforcement and future needs.** Even if you only have 10 minutes, put your notes or a book in your hand. Your mind is similar to a computer; you have to input data in order to have it processed. *By reading, you are creating the neural connections for future retrieval.* The more times you read something, the more you reinforce the learning of ideas.

Even if you don't fully understand something on the first pass, *your mind stores much of the material for later recall.*

6. **Relax to learn; go into exile.** Our bodies respond to an inner clock called biorhythms. Burning the midnight oil works well for some people, but not everyone.

If possible, set aside a particular place to study that is free of distractions. Shut off the television, cell phone, and pager and exile your friends and family during your study period.

If you really are bothered by silence, try background music. Light classical music at a low volume has been shown to aid in concentration over other types of music. Music that evokes pleasant emotions without lyrics is highly suggested. Try just about anything by Mozart. It relaxes you.

7. Use arrows not highlighters. At best, it's difficult to read a page full of yellow, pink, blue, and green streaks. Try staring at a neon sign for a while and you'll soon see that the horde of colors obscure the message.

A quick note, a brief dash of color, an underline, or an arrow pointing to a particular passage is much clearer than a horde of highlighted words.

8. Budget your study time. Although you shouldn't ignore any of the material, *allocate your available study time in the same ratio that topics may appear on the test.*

By setting your personal study topics in much the same way that the test will be patterned, you will be better equipped to answer all of the test questions.

Testing Tips:

1. Get smart, play dumb. *Don't read anything into the question.* Don't make an assumption that the test writer is looking for something else than what is asked. Stick to the question as written and don't read extra things into it.

2. Read the question and all the choices *twice* before answering the question. You may miss something by not carefully reading and re-reading both the question and the answers.

If you really don't have a clue as to the right answer, leave it blank on the first time through. Go on to the other questions, as they may provide a clue as to how to answer the skipped questions.

If later on, you still can't answer the skipped ones . . . *guess.* The only penalty for guessing is that you *might* get it wrong. Only one thing is certain; if you don't put anything down, you will get it wrong!

3. Turn the question into a statement. Look at the way the questions are worded. The syntax of the question usually provides a clue. Does it seem more familiar as a statement rather than as a question? Does it sound strange?

By turning a question into a statement, you may be able to spot if an answer sounds right, and it may also trigger memories of material you have read.

4. Look for hidden clues. It's actually very difficult to compose multiple-choice questions without giving away part of the answer in the options presented.

In most questions you can often readily eliminate one or two of the potential answers. This leaves you with only two real possibilities; automatically, your odds go to fifty-fifty for very little work.

5. Trust your instincts. For every fact that you have read, you subconsciously retain something of that knowledge. On questions that you aren't really certain about, go with your basic instincts. *Your first impression on how to answer a question is usually correct.*

6. Mark your answers directly on the test booklet. Don't bother trying to fill in the optical scan sheet on the first pass through the test.

Just be very careful not to mis-mark your answers when you eventually transcribe them to the scan sheet.

7. Watch the clock! You have a set amount of time to answer the questions. Don't get bogged down trying to answer a single question at the expense of ten questions you can more readily answer.

THIS PAGE BLANK

DOMAIN I.   MATHEMATICS

COMPETENCY 0001   UNDERSTAND PRINCIPLES , CONCEPTS, AND
                         PROCEDURES RELATED TO REPRESENTATION
                         AND COMMUNICATION.

Skill 1.1   Extracting mathematical information from a variety of sources
              (e.g., pictures, diagrams, text, graphs)

Often data is made more readable and user-friendly by consolidating the
information in the form of a graph.

Bar graphs are used to compare various quantities using bars of different
lengths. A **pictograph** shows comparison of quantities using symbols. Each
symbol represents a number of items. To make a **bar graph** or a **pictograph**,
determine the scale to be used for the graph. Then determine the length of each
bar on the graph or determine the number of pictures needed to represent each
item of information. Be sure to include an explanation of the scale in the legend.

Example: A class had the following grades:
             4 A's, 9 B's, 8 C's, 1 D, 3 F's.
             Graph these on a bar graph and a pictograph.

Pictograph

Bar graph

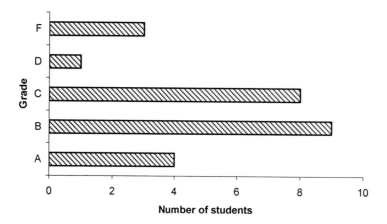

Line graphs are used to show trends, often over a period of time.

To make a line graph, determine appropriate scales for both the vertical and horizontal axes (based on the information to be graphed). Describe what each axis represents and mark the scale periodically on each axis. Graph the individual points of the graph and connect the points on the graph from left to right.

<u>Example:</u>   Graph the following information using a line graph.

Height of Two Pea Plants for Six Days

Day	1	2	3	4	5	6
Plant 1 Height (in.)	1.2	1.4	1.4	1.8	2.3	2.4
Plant 2 Height (in.)	0.7	0.9	1.2	1.5	1.6	1.7

Height of Two Pea Plants for Six Days

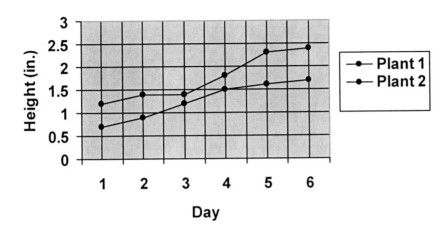

Circle graphs show the relationship of various parts of a data set to each other and the whole. Each part is shown as a percentage of the total and occupies a proportional sector of the circular area. To make a circle graph, total all the information that is to be included on the graph. Determine the central angle to be used for each sector of the graph using the following formula:

$$\frac{\text{information}}{\text{total information}} \times 360^\circ = \text{degrees in central } \square$$

Lay out the central angles according to these sizes, label each section and include its percentage.

<u>Example:</u>　　Graph this information on a circle graph:

Monthly expenses:

Rent, $400
Food, $150
Utilities, $75
Clothes, $75
Church, $100
Misc., $200

Scatter plots compare two characteristics of the same group of things or people and usually consist of a large body of data. They show how much one variable is affected by another. The relationship between the two variables is their **correlation**. The closer the data points come to making a straight line when plotted, the closer the correlation.

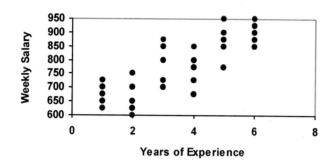

Stem-and-leaf plots are visually similar to histograms. The **stems** are the digits in the greatest place value of the data values, and the **leaves** are the digits in the next greatest place values. Stem and leaf plots are best suited for small sets of data and are especially useful for comparing two sets of data.

Example: Make a stem-and-leaf plot to display the following test scores: 49, 54, 59, 61, 62, 63, 64, 66, 67, 68, 68, 70, 73, 74, 76, 76, 76, 77, 77, 77, 77, 78, 78, 78, 78, 83, 85, 85, 87, 88, 90, 90, 93, 94, 95, 100, 100.

stem leaves

4	9
5	4 9
6	1 2 3 4 6 7 8 8
7	0 3 4 6 6 6 7 7 7 8 8 8 8
8	3 5 5 7 8
9	0 0 3 4 5
10	0 0

Histograms are used to summarize information from large sets of data that can be naturally grouped into intervals. The vertical axis indicates **frequency** (the number of times any particular data value occurs), and the horizontal axis indicates data values or ranges of data values. The number of data values in any interval is the **frequency of the interval**.

Example: The human resources department of a small company surveyed workers on their weekly salaries. Ten workers earned between $600 and $624 per week. Twenty workers earned between $625–$649/week. Twenty workers earned between $650–$674/week. Fifteen workers earned between $675–$699/week. Twenty-five workers earned between $700–$724/week. Five workers earned $725 or more each week. Draw a histogram to display the results.

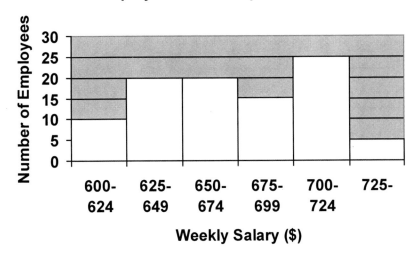

Example: Justin surveyed his classmates on their favorite magazines. What is the best graph to show his data?

Since Justin is using counting data, so a bar graph or pictograph would be the best format to display his data.

Example: Lakeisha recorded the amount of rain that fell in Augusta, GA, for 6 weeks. What is the best graph to show her data?

Since Lakeisha is displaying a change over time, a line graph would be the best format to show her data.

Skill 1.2   Using textual, graphic, numeric, and symbolic representations to communicate mathematical concepts

Displaying data in graphical format can reveal a lot of information about the data set. An **inference** is a statement that is derived from reasoning. When reading a graph, inferences help with interpretation of the data that is being presented. From this information, a **conclusion** and even **predictions** about what the data actually means is possible.

A **trend** line on a line graph shows the correlation between two sets of data. A trend may show positive correlation (both sets of data get greater together) negative correlation (one set of data increases while the other decreases), or no correlation.

Example: Katherine and Tom were both doing poorly in math class. Their teacher had a conference with each of them in November. The following graph shows their math test scores during the school year.

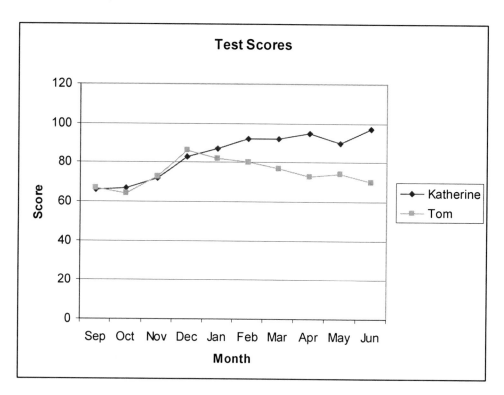

What kind of trend does this graph show?

This graph shows that there is a positive trend in Katherine's test scores and a negative trend in Tom's test scores.

What inferences can you make from this graph?

We can infer that Katherine's test scores rose steadily after November. Tom's test scores spiked in December but then began a negative trend.

What conclusion can you draw based upon this graph?

We can conclude that Katherine took her teacher's meeting seriously and began to study in order to do better on the exams. It seems as though Tom tried harder for a bit but his test scores eventually slipped back down to the level where he began.

Skill 1.3   Translating between textual, graphic, numeric, and symbolic representations

Mathematics is, in some ways, a formalization of language that concerns such concepts as quantity and organization. Mathematics often involves symbolic representations, which can help alleviate the ambiguities found in common language. Naturally, then, communication of mathematical ideas requires conversion back and forth from verbal and symbolic forms. These two forms can often help to elucidate one another when an attempt is made to understand an idea that they represent. Other representations of mathematical concepts can involve graphs and numerals.

Mathematical ideas and expressions can sometimes be easily translated into language; for instance, basic arithmetic operations are usually fairly easy to express in everyday language (although complicated expressions may be less so). In some cases, common language more easily expresses certain ideas than does symbolic language (and sometimes vice versa). Much of the translation process is learned through practicing expression of mathematical ideas in verbal (or written) form and by translating verbal or written expressions into a symbolic form.

Likewise, the use of graphic or numeric representations may offer a more lucid presentation. For instance, although a function can be represented symbolically using a polynomial of some degree, the polynomial may be so complex that a graph of the function provides a better and simpler description. Likewise, numbers—especially those with decimals—are more easily expressed using numerals (1, 2, 3...) than using words (one, two, three...). As such, translation among these various representations can help improve and simplify mathematical communication.

The material throughout this guide attempts to present mathematical ideas both in a variety of formats. Thus, practicing by carefully following the text and example problems and by attempting to articulate the various concepts using English, using mathematical symbols (including numerals), and using graphs should help the student (and teacher) of mathematics gain mastery of this skill.

Example: Express the following in written language (textual) form:
{..., –2, –1, 0, 1, 2,...}.

This symbolic expression, in written language form, is simply "the set of integers."

Throughout this guide, mathematical operations and situations are represented through words, algebraic symbols, geometric diagrams and graphs. A few commonly used representations are discussed below.

The basic mathematical operations include addition, subtraction, multiplication and division. In word problems, these are represented by the following typical expressions.

Operation	Descriptive Words
Addition	"plus", "combine", "sum", "total", "put together"
Subtraction	"minus", "less", "take away", "difference"
Multiplication	"product", "times", "groups of"
Division	"quotient", "into", "split into equal groups",

Some verbal and symbolic representations of basic mathematical operations include the following:

7 added to a number	$n + 7$
a number decreased by 8	$n - 8$
12 times a number divided by 7	$12n \div 7$
28 less than a number	$n - 28$
the ratio of a number to 55	$\dfrac{n}{55}$
4 times the sum of a number and 21	$4(n + 21)$

Multiplication can be shown using arrays. For instance, 3×4 can be expressed as 3 rows of 4 each

In a similar manner, addition and subtraction can be demonstrated with symbols.

$\psi\,\psi\,\psi\,\xi\,\xi\,\xi\,\xi$
$3 + 4 = 7$
$7 - 3 = 4$

Fractions can be represented using pattern blocks, fraction bars, or paper folding.

Diagrams of arithmetic operations can present mathematical data in visual form. For example, a number line can be used to add and subtract, as illustrated below.

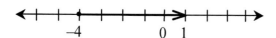

Five added to negative four on the number line or $-4 + 5 = 1$.

Pictorial representations can also be used to explain the arithmetic processes.

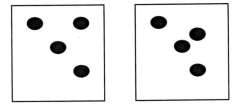

The diagram above shows two groups of four equal eight, or 2 x 4 = 8. The next diagram illustrates addition of two objects to three objects, resulting in five objects.

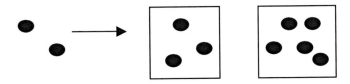

SEE also Skills 1.1 and 1.2

Skill 1.4 Using mathematical language to communicate ideas and information, including interpreting mathematical terminology, symbols, and representations

Examples, illustrations, and symbolic representations are useful tools in explaining and understanding mathematical concepts. The ability to create examples and alternative methods of expression allows students to solve real world problems and better communicate their thoughts. Many different kinds of graphs, diagrams, symbols and tables have been used throughout this guide.

Concrete examples are real world applications of mathematical concepts. For example, measuring the shadow produced by a tree or building is a real world application of trigonometric functions; acceleration or velocity of a car is an application of derivatives; and finding the volume or area of a swimming pool is a real world application of geometric principles.

Pictorial illustrations of mathematic concepts help clarify difficult ideas and simplify problem solving.

Example: Rectangle R represents the 300 students in School A. Circle P represents the 150 students that participated in band. Circle Q represents the 170 students that participated in a sport. 70 students participated in both band and a sport.

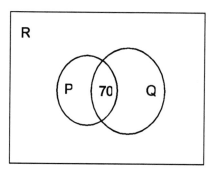

Pictorial representation of above situation.

Example: A marketing company surveyed 200 people and found that 145 people subscribed to at least one magazine, 26 people subscribed to at least one book-of-the-month club, and 19 people subscribed to at least one magazine and one book club. How many people did not subscribe to either a magazine or book club?

Draw a Venn diagram.

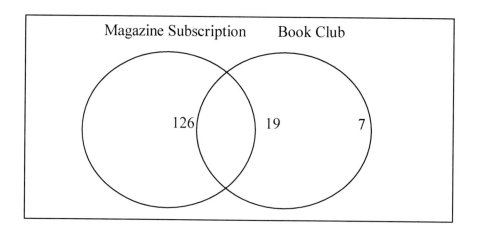

200 – (126 + 19 + 7) = 48 people do not subscribe to either.

Symbolic representation is the basic language of mathematics. Converting data to symbols allows for easy manipulation and problem solving. Students should have the ability to recognize what the symbolic notation represents and convert information into symbolic form. For example, from the graph of a line, students should have the ability to determine the slope and intercepts and derive the line's equation from the observed data. Another possible application of symbolic representation is the formulation of algebraic expressions and relations from data presented in word problem form.

Mathematical concepts and procedures can take many different forms. Students of mathematics must be able to recognize different forms of equivalent concepts.

For example, we can represent the slope of a line graphically, algebraically, verbally, and numerically. A line drawn on a coordinate plane will show the slope. In the equation of a line, $y = mx + b$, the term m represents the slope. We can define the slope of a line several different ways. The slope of a line is the change in the value of the y divided by the change in the value of x over a given interval. Alternatively, the slope of a line is the ratio of "rise" to "run" between two points. Finally, we can calculate the numeric value of the slope by using the verbal definitions and the algebraic representation of the line.

Most mathematical concepts can be expressed in multiple ways. For example a parabola can be expressed as an equation or a graph. A function can be rewritten as a table. Each way is an equally accurate method of representing the concept, but different techniques may be useful in different situations. It is therefore important to be able to translate any concept into the most appropriate form for addressing any given problem.

$y = (x - 1)^2 - 3$ *is equivalent*
to

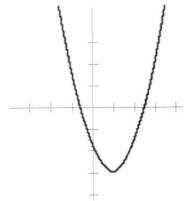

One example of a mathematical idea that can be presented in multiple ways is any group of numbers that is a subset of the real number line. There are three common ways to denote such a set of numbers: graphically on the real number line, in interval notation, and in set notation. For example, the set of numbers consisting of all values greater than negative 2 and less than or equal to 4 could be written in the following three ways:

Graphically:
In this type of notation, open circles exclude an endpoint while closed circles include it.

Interval Notation: $(-2, 4]$. Interval notation uses round brackets to exclude the endpoint of a set, and square brackets to include it.

Set Notation: $\{-2 < x \leq 4\}$

Depending on why you need to represent this group of numbers, each form of notation has its advantages. Set notation is the most flexible, since finite sets can be written as lists within the brackets. However, it is often far more cumbersome than interval notation, and in some circumstances graphical notation may be the most clear.

An algebraic formula is an equation that describes a relationship among variables. While it is not often necessary to derive the formula, one must know how to rewrite a given formula in terms of a desired variable.

Example: Given that the relationship of voltage, V, applied across a material with electrical resistance, R, when a current, I, is flowing through the material is given by the formula $V = IR$. Find the resistance of the material when a current of 10 milliamps is flowing, when the applied voltage is 2 volts.

$V = IR$. Solve for R.
$IR = V$; $R = V/I$ Divide both sides by I.
When $V = 2$ volts; $I = 10 \times 10^{-3}$ amps;

$R = \dfrac{2}{10^1 \times 10^{-3}}$

$R = \dfrac{2}{10^{-2}}$ Substituting in $R = V/I$, we get,

$R = 2 \times 10^2$

$R = 200$ ohms

Another example of translating between mathematical language and everyday language is the conversion of recipes to different serving sizes. The conversion factor, the number we multiply each ingredient by, is:

$$\text{Conversion Factor} = \frac{\text{Number of Servings Needed}}{\text{Number of Servings in Recipe}}$$

<u>Example:</u> Consider the following recipe.

3 cups flour
½ tsp. baking powder
2/3 cups butter
2 cups sugar
2 eggs

If the above recipe serves 8, how much of each ingredient do we need to serve only 4 people?
First, determine the conversion factor.

$$\text{Conversion Factor} = \frac{4}{8} = \frac{1}{2}$$

Next, multiply each ingredient by the conversion factor.

3 x ½ =	1 ½ cups flour
½ x ½ =	¼ tsp. baking powder
2/3 x ½ = 2/6 =	1/3 cups butter
2 x ½ =	1 cup sugar
2 x ½ =	1 egg

COMPETENCY 0002   **UNDERSTAND PRINCIPLES, CONCEPTS, AND PROCEDURES RELATED TO MATHEMATICAL REASONING, PROOF, AND CONNECTIONS.**

Skill 2.1   **Applying knowledge of formal and informal mathematical reasoning processes (e.g., using logical reasoning to draw and justify conclusions)**

Deductive reasoning

Deductive thinking is the process of arriving at a conclusion based on other statements that are all known to be true, such as theorems, axioms, or postulates. Conclusions found by deductive thinking based on true statements will *always* be true.

Inductive reasoning

Inductive thinking is the process of finding a pattern from a group of examples. The pattern is the conclusion that a set of examples seemed to indicate. It may be a correct conclusion or it may be an incorrect conclusion, as other examples may not follow the predicted pattern.

<u>Example:</u>

Suppose:
On Monday Mr.Peterson eats breakfast at McDonalds.
On Tuesday Mr.Peterson eats breakfast at McDonalds.
On Wednesday Mr.Peterson eats breakfast at McDonalds.
On Thursday Mr.Peterson eats breakfast at McDonalds again.

Conclusion: On Friday Mr. Peterson will eat breakfast at McDonalds again.

This is a conclusion based on inductive reasoning. Based on several days' observations, you conclude that Mr. Peterson will eat at McDonalds. This may or may not be true, but it is a valid inductive conclusion.

Adaptive reasoning

A **valid argument** is a statement made about a pattern or relationship between elements, thought to be true, which is subsequently justified through repeated examples and logical reasoning. Another term for a valid argument is a **proof**.

For example, the statement that the sum of two odd numbers is always even could be tested through actual examples.

Two Odd Numbers	Sum	Validity of Statement
1+1	2 (even)	Valid
1+3	4 (even)	Valid
61+29	90 (even)	Valid
135+47	182 (even)	Valid
253+17	270 (even)	Valid
1,945+2,007	3,952 (even)	Valid
6,321+7,851	14,172 (even)	Valid

Adding two odd numbers always results in a sum that is even. It is a valid argument based on the justifications in the table above.

Consider another example. The statement that a fraction of a fraction can be determined by multiplying the numerator by the numerator and the denominator by the denominator can be proven through logical reasoning. For example, one-half of one-quarter of a candy bar can be found by multiplying ½ x ¼. The answer would be one-eighth. The validity of this argument can be demonstrated as valid with a model.

The entire rectangle represents one whole candy bar. The top half section of the model is shaded in one direction to demonstrate how much of the candy bar remains from the whole candy bar. The left quarter, shaded in a different direction, demonstrates that one-quarter of the candy bar has been given to a friend. Since the whole candy bar is not available to give out, the area that is double-shaded is the fractional part of the ½ candy bar that has been actually given away. That fractional part is one-eighth of the whole candy bar, as shown in both the sketch and the algorithm.

Skill 2.2   Developing and evaluating conjectures and informal proofs

Conditional statements are frequently written in "**if-then**" form. The "if" clause of the conditional is known as the **hypothesis**, and the "then" clause is called the **conclusion**. In a proof, the hypothesis is the information that is assumed to be true, while the conclusion is what is to be proven true. A conditional is considered to be of the form:

If p, then q
p is the hypothesis and q is the conclusion.

Conditional statements can be diagrammed using a **Venn diagram**. This is done when a diagram is drawn with one circle inside another circle. The inner circle represents the hypothesis. The outer circle represents the conclusion. If the hypothesis is taken to be true, then you are located inside the inner circle. If you are located in the inner circle then you are also inside the outer circle, so that proves the conclusion is true.

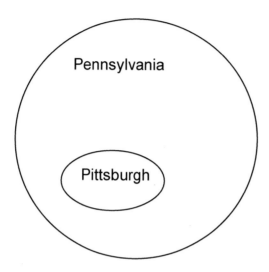

Example:
If you are in Pittsburgh, then you are in Pennsylvania.
In this statement "you are in Pittsburgh" is the hypothesis.
In this statement "you are in Pennsylvania" is the conclusion.

Example:
If an angle has a measure of 90 degrees, then it is a right angle.

In this statement "an angle has a measure of 90 degrees" is the hypothesis.
In this statement "it is a right angle" is the conclusion.

Conditional: If p, then q
p is the hypothesis and q is the conclusion.

Inverse: If ~p, then ~q.
Negate both the hypothesis (If not p) and the conclusion (then not q) from the original conditional.

Converse : If q, then p.
Reverse the two clauses. The original hypothesis (p) becomes the conclusion. The original conclusion (q) then becomes the new hypothesis.

Contrapositive: If ~q, then ~p.
Reverse the two clauses. The original hypothesis (p) becomes the conclusion. The original conclusion (q) then becomes the new hypothesis. THEN negate both the new hypothesis and the new conclusion.

Example:

Given the **conditional**:
If an angle measures 60°, then it is an acute angle.

Its **inverse**, in the form "If ~p, then ~q", would be:
If an angle doesn't measure 60°, then it is not an acute angle
NOTICE that the inverse is not true, even though the conditional statement was true.

Its **converse**, in the form "If q, then p", would be:
If an angle is an acute angle, then it has 60°.
NOTICE that the converse is not necessarily true, even though the conditional statement was true. It is a very common logical mistake to assume that the converse of a given statement is true. There are times (see below) where the converse is true, but in general it does not have to be true.

Its **contrapositive**, in the form "If q, then p", would be:
If an angle isn't an acute angle, then it doesn't have 60°.
NOTICE that the contrapositive is true, assuming the original conditional statement was true.

TIP: If you are asked to pick a statement that is logically equivalent to a given conditional, look for the contrapositive. The inverse and converse are not always logically equivalent to every conditional. The contrapositive is ALWAYS logically equivalent.

Example:
Find the inverse, converse, and contrapositive of the following conditional statement. Also determine if each of the four statements is true or false.

Conditional: If $x = 5$, then $x^2 - 25 = 0$.   TRUE
Inverse: If $x \neq 5$, then $x^2 - 25 \neq 0$.   FALSE, x could be ‾5
Converse: If $x^2 - 25 = 0$, then $x = 5$.   FALSE, x could be ‾5
Contrapositive: If $x^2 - 25 \neq 0$, then $x \neq 5$.   TRUE

Conditional: If $x = 5$, then $6x = 30$.   TRUE
Inverse: If $x \neq 5$, then $6x \neq 30$.   TRUE
Converse: If $6x = 30$, then $x = 5$.   TRUE
Contrapositive: If $6x \neq 30$, then $x \neq 5$. TRUE

Sometimes, as in this example, all four statements can be logically equivalent; however, the only statement that will always be logically equivalent to the original conditional is the contrapositive.

Conditional statements can also be diagrammed using a Venn diagram.

Suppose that these statements are given to you, and you are asked to try to reach a conclusion. The statements are:

All swimmers are athletes.
    All athletes are scholars.

In "if-then" form, these would be:

If you are a swimmer, then you are an athlete.
    If you are an athlete, then you are a scholar.

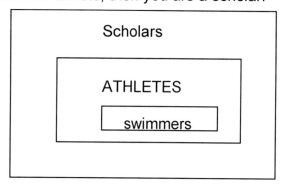

Clearly, if you are a swimmer, then you are also an athlete. This includes you in the group of scholars.

Suppose that these statements are given to you, and you are asked to try to reach a conclusion. The statements are:

    All swimmers are athletes.
    All wrestlers are athletes.

In "if-then" form, these would be:

If you are a swimmer, then you are an athlete.
　　If you are a wrestler, then you are an athlete.

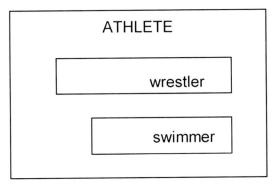

Clearly, if you are a swimmer or a wrestler, then you are also an athlete. This does NOT allow you to come to any other conclusions.

A swimmer may or may NOT also be a wrestler. Therefore, NO CONCLUSION IS POSSIBLE.

Suppose that these statements are given to you, and you are asked to try to reach a conclusion. The statements are:

　　All rectangles are parallelograms.
　　Quadrilateral ABCD is not a parallelogram.

In "if-then" form, the first statement would be:

If a figure is a rectangle, then it is also a parallelogram.
The contrapositive of this statement, "if a figure is not a parallelogram, then it is not a rectangle" is also true. So we can conclude in the original question that Quadrilateral ABCD is not a rectangle. Looking at the Venn diagram below, if all rectangles are parallelograms, then rectangles are included as part of the parallelograms. Since quadrilateral ABCD is not a parallelogram, it is excluded from being placed anywhere inside the parallelogram box. This allows you to conclude that ABCD can not be a rectangle either.

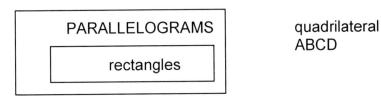

quadrilateral
ABCD

Try These:

What conclusion, if any, can be reached? Assume each statement is true, regardless of any personal beliefs. (Hint: always create a contrapositive statement from the statement you are given, since you know that the contrapositive statement is always true.)

1. If the Red Sox win the World Series, I will die.
   I died.

2. If an angle's measure is between 0° and 90°, then the angle is acute.
   Angle B is not acute.

3. Students who do well in geometry will succeed in college.
   Annie is doing extremely well in geometry.

4. Left-handed people are witty and charming.
   You are left-handed.

Skill 2.3   Recognizing and applying mathematics in real-world contexts and applying connections among mathematical ideas

Numbers are everywhere, at the gas station, in the weather forecast, in the ups and downs of the stock market. Shopping is the most common real-world situation in which mathematical skills are needed. Following are several examples of the application of mathematics to everyday activities.

To find the amount of sales tax on an item, change the percent of sales tax into an equivalent decimal number by moving the decimal point two places to the left. Then multiply the decimal number by the price of the object to find the sales tax. The total cost of an item will be the price of the item plus the sales tax.

Example: A guitar costs $120 plus 7% sales tax. How much are the sales tax and the total bill?

7% = 0.07 in decimal form
(0.07)($120) = $8.40 sales tax
$120 + $8.40 = $128.40 ← total cost

An alternative method to find the total cost is to multiply the price times the factor 1.07 (price + sales tax):

$120 × 1.07 = $128.40

This gives you the total cost in fewer steps.

Example: A suit costs $450 plus 6½% sales tax. How much are the sales tax and the total bill?

6½% = 0.065 in decimal form
(0.065)(450) = $29.25 sales tax
$450 + $29.25 = $479.25 ← total cost

Using the alternative method to find total cost, multiply the price times the factor 1.065 (price + sales tax):

$$\$450 \times 1.065 = \$479.25$$

This gives you the total cost in fewer steps.

Another kind of real-world mathematical calculation involves time. Elapsed time problems are usually one of two types. One type of problem is the elapsed time between two times given in hours, minutes and seconds. The other common type of problem is between two times given in months and years.

For any time of day past noon, change to military time by adding 12 hours. For instance, 1:15 p.m. would be 13:15. Remember when you borrow a minute or an hour in a subtraction problem that you have borrowed 60 more seconds or minutes.

Example: Find the time from 11:34:22 a.m. until 3:28:40 p.m.

Convert 3:28:40 p.m. to military time
```
   3:28:40
+12:00:00
 15:28:40
```
Now subtract
```
 15:28:40
−11:34:22
      :18
```
Borrow an hour and add 60 more minutes. Subtract.
```
 14:88:40
−11:34:22
  3:54:18   ↔ 3 hours, 54 minutes, 18 seconds
```

Example: John lived in Arizona from September 1991 until March 1995. How long is that?

	year	month
March 1995	= 95	03
September 1991	= −91	09

Borrow a year and convert it into 12 more months,

subtract.

	year	month
March 1995	= 94	15
September 1991	= −91	09
	3 yrs	6 months

Example: A race took the winner 1 hr. 58 min. 12 sec. on the first half of the race and 2 hr. 9 min. 57 sec. on the second half of the race. How much time did the entire race take?

```
    1 hr.  58 min.  12 sec.
  + 2 hr.   9 min.  57 sec.  Add
    3 hr.  67 min.  69 sec.
              + 1 min. −60 sec.  Convert 60 sec. to 1 min.
    3 hr.  68 min.   9 sec.
  + 1 hr.−60 min.
    4 hr.   8 min.   9 sec. ← Final answer   Convert 60 min. to 1 hr.
```

Number relations can be found in a variety of real-world situations. A **relation** is any set of ordered pairs.

For example, the Drama Club is washing cars for a fundraiser. The club earns $10 for each car the group washes. Thus, the drama club will earn $10 after washing one car, $20 after washing two cars, $30 after washing three cars, etc. The relation can also be represented graphically.

Money Earned at Car Wash

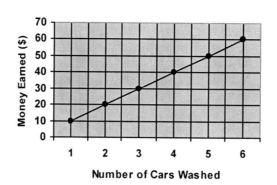

<u>Example:</u>   The cost of making a call on a particular cell phone is $0.15 per minute. Describe and graph this relation. How much will it cost to make a 5-minute phone call?

The relation states that for every minute someone talks on this cell phone, he or she will be charged $0.15. So, a 5-minute call will cost $0.75. The relation is shown in the graph below.

Cell Phone Cost per Min

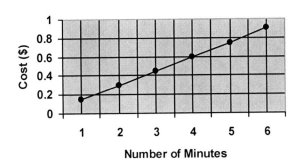

Number of Minutes

More examples

The unit rate for purchasing an item is its price divided by the number of pounds (or ounces, etc.) in the item. The item with the lower unit rate is the lower price.

<u>Example:</u>   Find the item with the best unit price:

$1.79 for 10 ounces
$1.89 for 12 ounces
$5.49 for 32 ounces

$\frac{1.79}{10} = .179$ per ounce $\frac{1.89}{12} = .1575$ per ounce $\frac{5.49}{32} = .172$ per ounce

$1.89 for 12 ounces is the best price.

A second way to find the better buy is to make a proportion with the price over the number of ounces, etc. Cross multiply the proportion, writing the products above the numerator that is used. The better price will have the smaller product.

<u>Example:</u>   Find the better buy:

$8.19 for 40 pounds or $4.89 for 22 pounds
Find the unit price.

$$\frac{40}{8.19} = \frac{1}{x}$$ $$\frac{22}{4.89} = \frac{1}{x}$$

$40x = 8.19$ $22x = 4.89$

$x = .20475$ $x = .22\overline{227}$

Since $.20475 < .22\overline{227}$, $8.19 is less and is a better buy.

To find the amount of sales tax on an item, change the percent of sales tax into an equivalent decimal number. Then multiply the decimal number times the price of the object to find the sales tax. The total cost of an item will be the price of the item plus the sales tax.

<u>Example:</u>   A guitar costs $120 plus 7% sales tax. How much are the sales tax and the total bill?

7% = .07 as a decimal
(.07)(120) = $8.40 sales tax
$120 + $8.40 = $128.40 ← total price

<u>Example:</u>   A suit costs $450 plus 6½% sales tax. How much are the sales tax and the total bill?

6½% = .065 as a decimal
(.065)(450) = $29.25 sales tax
$450 + $29.25 = $479.25 ← total price

Examining the change in area or volume of a given figure requires you first to find the existing area given the original dimensions and then the new area given the increased dimensions.

<u>Example:</u>   Given the rectangle below, determine the change in area if the length is increased by 5 and the width is increased by 7.

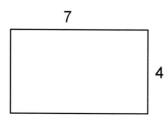

7

4

Draw and label a sketch of the new rectangle.

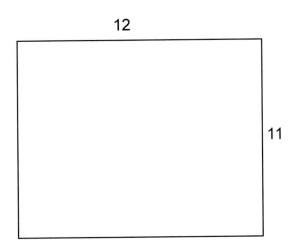

12

11

Find the areas.

Area of original = LW   Area of enlarged shape = LW
$\quad$ = (7)(4) $\qquad\qquad$ = (12)(11)
$\quad$ = 28 units^2 $\qquad\quad$ = 132 units^2

The change in area is $132 - 28 = 104$ units^2

Skill 2.4 Demonstrating knowledge of the historical development of mathematics, including contributions from many cultures

Noted mathematicians from early times include Pythagoras (born 580 B.C.) and Theano (the wife of Pythagoras who was born 546 B.C.), who was a mathematician and physician who wrote the significant piece on the principle of the "Golden Mean." Euclid (300 B.C.) is considered the father of geometry; Archimedes (born 287 B.C.) made the first real progress on the estimation of π, and Apollonius and Ptolemy (85 A.D.) also made significant contributions to the development of mathematics.

During the 3rd century in China, Tsu Ch'ung-Chih estimated π, as Archimedes did, using circumscribed and inscribed polygons. In India, Brahmagupta made valuable contributions to geometry during the 6th century A.D., and Arabs played an important role in preserving the work of the Greeks through translations and expansion of that knowledge.

Archeological digs in Babylonia and Greece have uncovered counting boards. These include the Chinese abacus, whose current form dates from approximately 1200 A.D. Prior to the development of the concept of zero, a counting board or abacus was the common method used for all types of calculations. In fact, the abacus is still taught in Asian schools and is used by some Asian proprietors. Blind children learn to use the abacus, which is an equivalent method of learning basic mathematical calculations.

Islamic culture from the 6th through 12th centuries drew knowledge from areas ranging from Africa and Spain to India. Al-Khowarizmi introduced Hindu numerals to the West for the first time during the 9th century, and wrote a significant article on algebra. At the beginning of the 15th century, notable Muslim mathematician Al-Kashi wrote the book *Key to Arithmetic* in which he used decimals instead of fractions. Fibonacci made important contributions to algebra and geometry during the 1200's.

It was after the Renaissance era, however, that some of the most significant contributions were made (during the 17th century). Newton, along with Leibniz, developed calculus, and Descartes formulated analytical geometry. Maria Gaetana Agnesi is known for the "Witch of Agnesi": the modern version of the curve called the Cartesian equation. Also during this period, John Napier developed a theory of logarithms and Pascal and Fermat broadened knowledge of number theory. The 18th century saw contributions by Gauss in arithmetic, algebra and number theory. Gauss insisted that every area of mathematics must apply rigorous proofs, and this influenced Cauchy in the 19th century to develop a more comprehensible theory of limits, the definite integral, continuity and the derivative. David Hilbert laid the foundations of geometry in the 19th century.

During the 20th century, increasingly abstract mathematics broadened the definitions of system operations, thereby connecting the areas of topology, algebra and geometry. A number of present-day individuals have also made significant contributions to the field of mathematics. David Blackwell was the first African-American to be named to the National Academy of Sciences, and he won the von Neumann Theory Prize in 1979 for his contributions to the field of statistics. African-American Etta Falconer (1933 – 2002) received numerous awards and recognitions (from 1967 to 1995) during her lifetime for her contributions to furthering the opportunities for minorities and women in the fields of mathematics and science. Margaret Wright is well known in such fields as linear algebra and numerical and scientific computing. She has received several awards recognizing her contributions to mathematics. Sijue Wu received two awards in 2001 for her part in finding a solution to a long-standing problem in the water-wave equation.

This mix of cultures, gender and ethnicities have culminated in substantial developments in many areas of mathematics, including algebra, our current numbering system, geometry, trigonometry, calculus, statistics and discrete mathematics.

COMPETENCY 0003   **UNDERSTAND PRINCIPLES, CONCEPTS, AND PROCEDURES RELATED TO MATHEMATICAL PROBLEM SOLVING AND THE USE OF TECHNOLOGY.**

Skill 3.1   Applying knowledge of appropriate mathematical concepts, procedures, tools, and technologies to solve problems

There are many forms of **technology** available to math teachers. For example, students can test their understanding of math concepts by working on skill specific computer programs and websites. Graphing calculators can help students visualize the graphs of functions. Teachers can also enhance their lectures and classroom presentations by creating multimedia presentations.

Technology is increasingly important in schools today. Knowing what each item is, how to use each item and the importance of each item beyond the walls of the school is extremely important for teachers and students. We will cover some of the most important technology tools below:

Computers: Personal computing, word processing, research, and multi-media devices that utilize hard drive or "memory" in order to save, transform, and process information. It is easy to look past the importance of the computer, itself, in the wake of internet technology. However, many children from low socioeconomic backgrounds throughout the country lack access to computers and may not have basic computing skills. Indeed, many teachers must be taught to utilize some of the more advanced features that could help them with their daily work. In general, the computer is viewed as a tool for storage and efficient processing.

Internet: Platform for the sharing and organization of information throughout the world. It began with simple phone connections between dozens of computers in the 70s and 80s. In the 90s, it became a standard feature on virtually every computer. Through websites, the internet allows people to view, post, and find anything that is available for public viewing. This is helpful when it comes to classroom research; however, there is plenty of material that is inappropriate for children and irrelevant to school. Care should be given to filtering out websites that are inappropriate for students.

Video Projection: Video in the classroom is a common tool to enhance the learning of students. Indeed, video has become a "text" in itself, much like literature. While the internet has been a good source for information, video continues to be a great source of refined, carefully structured information for teachers and students. In addition, it is a great way for students to express themselves, as they develop and present multi-media presentations, for example.

CDs or DVDs: Data discs that are inserted into computers. Usually, CDs and DVDs are discs contain computer programs. It used to be that they contained information, such as encyclopedic information. Now, that material is typically stored on a computer hard drives or servers.

While computers cannot replace teachers, they can be used to enhance the curriculum. Computers may be used to help students practice basic skills. Many excellent programs exist to encourage higher-order thinking skills, creativity and problem solving. Learning to use technology appropriately is an important preparation for adulthood. Computers can also show the connections between mathematics and the real world.

Calculators: Calculators are important tools. They should be encouraged in the classroom and at home. They do not replace basic knowledge, but they can relieve the tedium of mathematical computations, assuming that the requisite basic knowledge is already present.

Students will be able to use calculators more intelligently if they are taught how. Students need to always check their work by estimating. The goal of mathematics is to prepare the child to survive in the real world, and technology is a reality in today's society.

Skill 3.2   **Making use of pictures, models, charts, graphs, and symbols as tools of mathematical problem solving**

SEE Skills 1.1 and 1.2

Skill 3.3   **Applying, analyzing, and evaluating mathematical thinking and strategies**

The process of problem solving in mathematics is similar to that of other areas. One of the first steps is to identify what is known about the problem. Each problem for which a solution can be found should provide enough information to form a starting point; from this point, a valid sequence of reasoning leads to the desired conclusion: a solution to the problem. Between identification of known information and identification of a solution to the problem is a somewhat gray area that, depending on the problem, could potentially involve myriad different approaches. Two potential approaches that do not involve a "direct" solution method are discussed below.

The **guess-and-check** strategy calls for making an initial guess of the solution, checking the answer, and using the outcome of this check to inform the next guess. With each successive guess, one should get closer to the correct answer. Constructing a table from the guesses can help organize the data.

<u>Example:</u> There are 100 coins in a jar: 10 are dimes, and the rest are pennies and nickels. If there are twice as many pennies as nickels, how many pennies and nickels are in the jar?

Based on the given information, there are 90 total nickels and pennies in the jar (100 coins − 10 dimes = 90 nickels and pennies). Also, there are twice as many pennies as nickels. Using this information, guess results that fulfill the criteria and then adjust the guess in accordance with the result. Continue this iterative process until the correct answer is found: 60 pennies and 30 nickels. The table below illustrates this process.

Number of Pennies	Number of Nickels	Total Number of Pennies and Nickels
40	20	60
80	40	120
70	35	105
60	30	90

Another non-direct approach to problem solving is **working backwards**. If the result of a problem is known (for example, in problems that involve proving a particular result), it is sometimes helpful to begin from the conclusion and attempt to work backwards to a particular known starting point. A slight variation of this approach involves both working backwards and working forwards until a common point is reached somewhere in the middle. The following example from trigonometry illustrates this process.

<u>Example:</u> Prove that $\sin^2 \theta = \dfrac{1}{2} - \dfrac{1}{2}\cos 2\theta$.

If the method for proving this result is not clear, one approach is to work backwards and forwards simultaneously. The following two-column approach organizes the process. Judging from the form of the result, it is apparent that the Pythagorean identity is a potential starting point.

$$\sin^2 \theta + \cos^2 \theta = 1$$

$$\sin^2 \theta = 1 - \cos^2 \theta$$

$$\sin^2 \theta = \dfrac{1}{2} - \dfrac{1}{2}\cos 2\theta$$

$$\sin^2 \theta = \dfrac{1}{2} - \dfrac{1}{2}\left(2\cos^2 \theta - 1\right)$$

$$\sin^2 \theta = \dfrac{1}{2} - \cos^2 \theta + \dfrac{1}{2}$$

$$\sin^2 \theta = 1 - \cos^2 \theta$$

Thus, a proof is apparent based on the combination of the reasoning in these two columns.

Selection of an appropriate problem-solving strategy depends largely on the type of problem being solved and the particular area of mathematics with which the problem deals. For instance, problems that involve proving a specific result often require different approaches than do problems that involve finding a numerical result.

Skill 3.4   Recognizing the appropriate use of tools and technology to visualize mathematical concepts and to perform mathematical experiments and explore conjectures

The use of supplementary materials in the classroom can greatly enhance the learning experience by stimulating student interest and satisfying different learning styles. Manipulatives, models, and technology are examples of tools available to teachers.

Manipulatives are materials that students can physically handle and move. Manipulatives allow students to understand mathematic concepts by allowing them to see concrete examples of abstract processes, and they are attractive to students because they appeal to the students' visual and tactile senses. Available for all levels of math, manipulatives are useful tools for reinforcing operations and concepts. They are not, however, a substitute for the development of sound computational skills. An example of a manipulative is a spinner with pie-piece-shaped areas marked around the center. Such a device can be used to perform probability experiments and to illustrate the theory of probability in certain contexts.

Models are another means of representing mathematical concepts by relating the concepts to real-world situations. Teachers must choose wisely when devising and selecting models because, to be effective, models must be applied properly. For example, a building with floors above and below ground is a good model for introducing the concept of negative numbers. It would be difficult, however, to use the building model in teaching subtraction of negative numbers.

Finally, there are many forms of **technology** available to math teachers. For example, students can test their understanding of math concepts by working on specific computer programs and websites. Graphing calculators can help students visualize the graphs of functions. Teachers can also enhance their lectures and classroom presentations by creating multimedia presentations.

Although each type of tool or technology can be helpful when studying mathematics, whether for visualization of mathematical concepts, performing experiments, or exploring conjectures, teachers and students must recognize the limitations of each. Computers, for instance, can be extremely helpful tools for aiding in complicated calculations and for visualizing mathematical concepts. A computer has numerous limitations, however, including its inability to deal with certain types of numbers (such as numbers with many decimal places) and the tendency of students (and teachers) to rely too heavily on it.

COMPETENCY 0004   UNDERSTAND PRINCIPLES, CONCEPTS, AND PROCEDURES RELATED TO NUMBERS, NUMBER SENSE, AND NUMERATION.

Skill 4.1   Demonstrating knowledge of the characteristics of whole numbers, integers, rational numbers, and real numbers

In order to effectively solve equations, it is important to acquaint yourself with the definitions of various mathematical terms.

Natural numbers–the counting numbers: 1,2,3…

Whole numbers–the counting numbers along with zero: 0,1,2…

Integers–the counting numbers, their opposites, and zero: … -1,0,1…

Rationals–all of the fractions that can be formed from the whole numbers. *Zero cannot be the denominator.* In decimal form, these numbers will either be terminating or repeating decimals.

Irrationals–real numbers that cannot be written as a fraction. The decimal forms of these numbers are neither terminating nor repeating: $\pi, e, \sqrt{2}$, etc.

Real numbers–the set of numbers obtained by combining the rationals and irrationals. Complex numbers (i.e., numbers that involve i or $\sqrt{-1}$) are not real numbers.

Skill 4.2   Identifying equivalent forms of fractions, decimals, percents, roots, and powers, including using scientific notation to represent small and large numbers

Roots and **exponents** are frequently used in finance and science.

Examples of situations where roots and exponents are used:

    Amortization of loans
    Describing acid rain, measuring pH
    Earthquakes (Richter scale)
    The decibel level of sound
    Brightness of stars

Scientific notation uses exponents to express very large numbers easily.

Scientific notation is a more convenient method for writing very large and very small numbers. It employs two factors. The first factor is a number between -10 and 10. The second factor is a power of 10. This notation is a shorthand way to express large numbers (like the weight of 100 freight cars in kilograms) or small numbers (like the weight of an atom in grams).

$10^n = (10)^n$	Ten multiplied by itself n times.
$10^6 = 1,000,000$	(mega)
$10^3 = 10 \times 10 \times 10 = 1000$	(kilo)
$10^2 = 10 \times 10 = 100$	(hecto)
$10^1 = 10$	(deca)
$10^0 = 1$	Any nonzero number raised to power of zero is 1.
$10^{-1} = 1/10$	(deci)
$10^{-2} = 1/100$	(centi)
$10^{-3} = 1/1000$	(milli)
$10^{-6} = 1/1,000,000$	(micro)

Scientific notation format. Convert a number to a form of $b \times 10^n$ where -$10 < b < 10$ and n is an integer.

Example: Write 356.73 in various forms.

$$356.73 = 3567.3 \times 10^{-1} \qquad (1)$$
$$= 35673 \times 10^{-2} \qquad (2)$$
$$= 35.673 \times 10^1 \qquad (3)$$
$$= 3.5673 \times 10^2 \qquad (4)$$
$$= 0.35673 \times 10^3 \qquad (5)$$

Only (4) is written in proper scientific notation format.

Example: Write 46,368,000 in scientific notation.

1. Introduce a decimal point. 46,368,000 = 46,368,000.0

2. Move the decimal place to **left** until only one nonzero digit is in front of it, in this case between the 4 and 6.

3. Count the number of digits the decimal point moved, in this case 7. This is the nth power of ten and is **positive** because the decimal point moved **left**.

Therefore, $46{,}368{,}000 = 4.6368 \times 10^7$

Example: Write 0.00397 in scientific notation.

1. The decimal point is already in place.

2. Move the decimal point to the **right** until there is only one nonzero digit in front of it, in this case between the 3 and 9.

3. Count the number of digits the decimal point moved, in this case 3. This is the nth power of ten and is **negative** because the decimal point moved **right**.

Therefore, $0.00397 = 3.97 \times 10^{-3}$.

Example: Evaluate $\dfrac{3.22\times10^{-3}\times736}{0.00736\times32.2\times10^{-6}}$

Since we have a mixture of large and small numbers, convert each number to scientific notation:

$$736 = 7.36\times10^2$$

$$0.00736 = 7.36\times10^{-3}$$

$$32.2\times10^{-6} = 3.22\times10^{-5} \quad \text{thus we have,}$$

$$\dfrac{3.22\times10^{-3}\times7.36\times10^2}{7.36\times10^{-3}\times3.22\times10^{-5}}$$

$$= \dfrac{3.22\times7.36\times10^{-3}\times10^{2}}{7.36\times3.22\times10^{-3}\times10^{-5}}$$

$$= \dfrac{3.22\times7.36}{7.36\times3.22}\times\dfrac{10^{-1}}{10^{-8}}$$

$$= \dfrac{3.22\times7.36}{3.22\times7.36}\times10^{-1}\times10^{8}$$

$$= \dfrac{23.6992}{23.6992}\times10^7$$

$$= 1\times10^7 = 10,000,000$$

COMMON EQUIVALENTS

- $\frac{1}{2} = 0.5 = 50\%$
- $\frac{1}{3} = 0.33\frac{1}{3} = 33\frac{1}{3}\%$
- $\frac{1}{4} = 0.25 = 25\%$
- $\frac{1}{5} = 0.2 = 20\%$
- $\frac{1}{6} = 0.16\frac{2}{3} = 16\frac{2}{3}\%$
- $\frac{1}{8} = 0.12\frac{1}{2} = 12\frac{1}{2}\%$
- $\frac{1}{10} = 0.1 = 10\%$
- $\frac{2}{3} = 0.66\frac{2}{3} = 66\frac{2}{3}\%$
- $\frac{5}{6} = 0.83\frac{1}{3} = 83\frac{1}{3}\%$
- $\frac{3}{8} = 0.37\frac{1}{2} = 37\frac{1}{2}\%$
- $\frac{5}{8} = 0.62\frac{1}{2} = 62\frac{1}{2}\%$
- $\frac{7}{8} = 0.87\frac{1}{2} = 87\frac{1}{2}\%$
- $1 = 1.0 = 100\%$

Skill 4.3   Comparing and ordering numbers

When comparing and ordering numbers in different representations, it is convenient to manipulate the numbers so that they are all the same representation. For example, if a student is asked to compare three numbers: a fraction, a decimal, and a square root, encourage the child to convert the numbers to decimals and then compare.

<u>Example:</u>   Complete the number sentence.

$$\frac{7}{8} \_\_\_\_\_ 0.88$$

To solve, convert $\frac{7}{8}$ to a decimal. $\frac{7}{8} = 0.875$

Now compare the two decimals: $0.875 < 0.88$.

So, $\frac{7}{8} < 0.88$

<u>Example:</u>   Order the following numbers: $8, \sqrt{60}, \frac{125}{16}, 8.008$.

$$\sqrt{60} \approx 7.746, \quad \frac{125}{16} = 7.8125$$

$$\sqrt{60}, \frac{125}{16}, 8, 8.008$$

When rounding to a given place value, it is necessary to look at the number in the next smaller place value. If that number is 5 or greater, the number being rounded is increased by one and all numbers to the right are changed to zero. If the number is less than 5, the number being rounded stays the same and all numbers to the right are changed to zero.

One method of rounding measurements can require an additional step. First, the measurement must be converted to a decimal number. Then the rules for rounding applied.

Example: Round the measurements to the given units.

1 foot 7 inches → feet
5 pound 6 ounces → pounds
$5\dfrac{9}{16}$ inches → inches

Convert each measurement to a decimal number. Then apply the rules for rounding.

1 foot 7 inches = $1\dfrac{7}{12}$ ft = 1.58333 ft, round up to 2 ft

5 pounds 6 ounces = $5\dfrac{6}{16}$ pounds = 5.375 pound, round to 5 pounds

$5\dfrac{9}{16}$ inches = 5.5625 inches, round up to 6 inches

Skill 4.4   **Applying fundamental concepts of number theory, including prime and composite numbers, place value, factors and multiples, and divisibility rules**

Prime numbers are whole numbers greater than 1 that have only two factors – 1 and the number itself. Examples of prime numbers are 2, 3, 5, 7, 11, 13, 17, and 19. Note that 2 is the only even prime number.

Composite numbers are whole numbers that have factors other than 1 and the number itself. For example, 9 is composite because 3 is a factor in addition to 1 and 9. The number 70 is also composite because, besides the factors of 1 and 70, the numbers 2, 5, 7, 10, 14, and 35 are also all factors.

Remember that the number 1 is neither prime nor composite.

Divisibility Rules:

a. A number is divisible by 2 if that number is even (which means it ends in 0, 2, 4, 6, or 8).

Example: 1,354 ends in 4, so it is divisible by 2. 240,685 ends in a 5, so it is not divisible by 2.

b. A number is divisible by 3 if the sum of its digits is evenly divisible by 3.

Example: The sum of the digits of 964 is 9 + 6 + 4 = 19. Since 19 is not divisible by 3, neither is 964. The sum of the digits of 86,514 is 8 + 6 + 5 + 1 + 4 = 24. Since 24 is divisible by 3, 86,514 is also divisible by 3.

c. A number is divisible by 4 if the number in its last 2 digits is divisible by 4.

Example: The number 113,336 ends with the number 36 in the last 2 places. Since 36 is divisible by 4, then 113,336 is also divisible by 4.

The number 135,627 ends with the number 27 in the last 2 places. Since 27 is not divisible by 4, then 135,627 is also not divisible by 4.

d. A number is divisible by 5 if the number ends in either a 5 or a 0.

Example: 225 ends with a 5 so it is divisible by 5. 2,358 is not divisible by 5 because its last digit is an 8, not a 5 or a 0.

e. A number is divisible by 6 if the number is even and the sum of its digits is evenly divisible by 3.

Example: 4,950 is an even number and its digits add to 18. (4 + 9 + 5 + 0 = 18) Since the number is even and the sum of its digits is 18 (which is divisible by 3), then 4,950 is divisible by 6. 326 is an even number, but its digits add up to 11. Since 11 is not divisible by 3, then 326 is not divisible by 6.

f. A number is divisible by 8 if the number in its last 3 digits is evenly divisible by 8.

Example: The number 113,336 ends with the 3-digit number 336 in the last three places. Since 336 is divisible by 8, then 113,336 is also divisible by 8.

The number 465,627 ends with the number 627 in the last three places. Since 627 is not evenly divisible by 8, then 465,627 is also not divisible by 8.

g. A number is divisible by 9 if the sum of its digits is evenly divisible by 9.

Example: The sum of the digits of 874 is 8 + 7 + 4 = 19. Since 19 is not divisible by 9, neither is 874. The digits of 116,514 are 1 + 1 + 6 + 5 + 1 + 4 = 18. Since 18 is divisible by 9, 116,514 is also divisible by 9.

h. A number is divisible by 10 if the number ends in the digit 0.

Example: 305 ends with a 5 so it is not divisible by 10. The number 2,030,270 is divisible by 10 because its last digit is a 0.

Example: Is the number 387 prime or composite? If the number is composite, list the factors.

The number 387 is composite. Its factors are 1, 3, 9, 43, 129, 387.

Place Value

Decimals = deci = part of ten. To find the decimal equivalent of a fraction, use the denominator to divide the numerator as shown in the following example.

Example: Find the decimal equivalent of $\dfrac{7}{10}$.

Since 10 cannot divide into 7 evenly,

$$\frac{7}{10} = 0.7$$

A number in standard form is represented by a number of digits separated by a decimal point. Each digit to the left of the decimal point increases progressively in powers of ten. Each digit to the right of the decimal point decreases progressively in powers of ten.

Factors and Multiples

GCF is the abbreviation for the **greatest common factor**. The GCF is the largest number that is a factor of all the numbers given in a problem. The GCF can be no larger than the smallest number given in the problem. If no other number is a common factor, then the GCF will be the number 1.

To find the GCF, list all possible factors of the smallest number given (include the number itself). Starting with the largest factor (which is the number itself), determine if it is also a factor of all the other given numbers. If so, that is the GCF. If that factor doesn't work, try the same method on the next smaller factor. Continue until a common factor is found. That is the GCF.

Note: There can be other common factors besides the GCF.

Example: Find the GCF of 12, 20, and 36.

The smallest number in the problem is 12. The factors of 12 are 1,2,3,4,6, and 12. 12 is the largest factor, but it does not divide evenly into 20. Neither does 6, but 4 will divide into both 20 and 36 evenly. Therefore, 4 is the GCF.

Example: Find the GCF of 14 and 15.

Factors of 14 are 1,2,7, and 14. 14 is the largest factor, but it does not divide evenly into 15. Neither does 7 or 2. Therefore, the only factor common to both 14 and 15 is the number 1, the GCF.

LCM is the abbreviation for **least common multiple**. The least common multiple of a group of numbers is the smallest number that all of the given numbers will divide into. The least common multiple will always be the largest of the given numbers or a multiple of the largest number.

Example: Find the LCM of 20, 30, and 40.

The largest number given is 40, but 30 will not divide evenly into 40. The next multiple of 40 is 80 (2 x 40), but 30 will not divide evenly into 80 either. The next multiple of 40 is 120. 120 is divisible by both 20 and 30, so 120 is the LCM (least common multiple).

Example: Find the LCM of 96, 16, and 24.

The largest number is 96. 96 <u>is</u> divisible by both 16 and 24, so 96 is the LCM.

Example: 12345.6789 occupies the following powers of ten positions:

10^4	10^3	10^2	10^1	10^0	.	10^{-1}	10^{-2}	10^{-3}	10^{-4}
1	2	3	4	5	.	6	7	8	9

Names of power-of-ten positions:

10^0 = ones　　　　　　　　　　(note that any **non-zero** base raised to power zero is 1)

10^1 = tens　　　　　　　　　　(number 1 and 1 zero or 10)

10^2 = hundred　　　　　　　　(number 1 and 2 zeros or 100)

10^3 = thousand　　　　　　　(number 1 and 3 zeros or 1000)

10^4 = ten thousand　　　　　(number 1 and 4 zeros or 10000)

$10^{-1} = \dfrac{1}{10^1} = \dfrac{1}{10}$ = tenths　　　(1st digit after decimal point or 0.1)

$10^{-2} = \dfrac{1}{10^2} = \dfrac{1}{100}$ = hundredth　　(2nd digit after decimal point or 0.01)

$10^{-3} = \dfrac{1}{10^3} = \dfrac{1}{1000}$ = thousandth　　(3rd digit after decimal point or 0.001)

$10^{-4} = \dfrac{1}{10^4} = \dfrac{1}{10000}$ = ten thousandth　(4th digit after decimal point or 0.0001)

Example:　　Write 73169.00537 in expanded form.

We start by listing all the powers of ten positions.

$$10^4 \quad 10^3 \quad 10^2 \quad 10^1 \quad 10^0 \quad . \quad 10^{-1} \quad 10^{-2} \quad 10^{-3} \quad 10^{-4} \quad 10^{-5}$$

Multiply each digit by its power of ten. Add all the results.

Thus $73169.00537 = (7 \times 10^4) + (3 \times 10^3) + (1 \times 10^2) + (6 \times 10^1)$

$$+ (9 \times 10^0) + (0 \times 10^{-1}) + (0 \times 10^{-2}) + (5 \times 10^{-3})$$

$$+ (3 \times 10^{-4}) + (7 \times 10^{-5})$$

Example:　　Determine the place value associated with the underlined digit in 3.16<u>9</u>5.

$$10^0 \quad . \quad 10^{-1} \quad 10^{-2} \quad 10^{-3} \quad 10^{-4}$$
$$3 \quad . \quad 1 \quad 6 \quad 9 \quad 5$$

The place value for the digit 9 is 10^{-3} or $\dfrac{1}{1000}$.

Example: Find the number that is represented by

$$(7 \times 10^3) + (5 \times 10^0) + (3 \times 10^{-3}).$$
$$= 7000 + 5 + 0.003$$
$$= 7005.003$$

Example: Write 21×10^3 in standard form.

$$= 21 \times 1000 = 21,000$$

Example: Write 739×10^{-4} in standard form.

$$= 739 \times \frac{1}{10000} = \frac{739}{10000} = 0.0739$$

COMPETENCY 0005   **UNDERSTAND PRINCIPLES, CONCEPTS AND ELATED TO MATHEMATICAL OPERATIONS, CALCULATION AND ESTIMATION.**

Skill 5.1   **Using a variety of models, methods, and algorithms to represent operations with integers and whole and rational numbers**

Mathematical Operations

Mathematical operations include addition, subtraction, multiplication, and division.

Addition can be indicated by the expressions: sum, greater than, and, more than, increased by, added to.

Subtraction can be expressed by: difference, fewer than, minus, less than, decreased by.

Multiplication is shown by: product, times, multiplied by, twice.

Division is used for: quotient, divided by, ratio.

Examples:

7 added to a number	$n + 7$
a number decreased by 8	$n - 8$
12 times a number divided by 7	$12n \div 7$
28 less than a number	$n - 28$
4 times the sum of a number and 21	$4(n + 21)$

The **Order of Operations** are to be followed when evaluating algebraic expressions. Follow these steps in order:

1. Simplify inside grouping characters such as parentheses, brackets, square root, fraction bar, etc.
2. Multiply out expressions with exponents.
3. Do multiplication or division, from left to right.
4. Do addition or subtraction, from left to right.

Samples of simplifying expressions with exponents:

$(-2)^3 = -8$

$(-2)^4 = 16$

$\left(\frac{2}{3}\right)^3 = \frac{8}{27}$

$5^0 = 1$

$4^{-1} = \frac{1}{4}$

Arithmetic Sequences

When given a set of numbers where the common difference between the terms is constant, use the following formula:

$$a_n = a_1 + (n-1)d$$
where a_1 = the first term
n = the nth term (general term)
d = the common difference

Example: Find the 8th term of the arithmetic sequence 5, 8, 11, 14, ...

$a_n = a_1 + (n-1)d$	
$a_n = 5$	identify the 1st term
$d = 8 - 5 = 3$	find d
$a_n = 5 + (8-1)3$	substitute
$a_n = 26$	

Example: Given two terms of an arithmetic sequence, find a_1 and d.

$a_4 = 21$	$a_6 = 32$
$a_n = a + (n-1)d$	$a_4 = 21, n = 4$
$21 = a_1 + (4-1)d$	$a_6 = 32, n = 6$
$32 = a_1 + (6-1)d$	

$21 = a_1 + 3d$	solve the system of equations
$32 = a_1 + 5d$	

$21 = a_1 + 3d$	
$\underline{-32 = -a_1 - 5d}$	multiply by -1
$-11 = -2d$	add the equations
$5.5 = d$	

$21 = a_1 + 3(5.5)$	substitute d = 5.5, into one of the equations
$21 = a_1 + 16.5$	
$a_1 = 4.5$	

The sequence begins with 4.5 and has a common difference of 5.5 between numbers.

Geometric Sequences

When using geometric sequences, consecutive numbers are compared to find the common ratio.

$$r = \frac{a_{n+1}}{a_n}$$

where r = common ratio
a = the nth term

The ratio is then used in the geometric sequence formula:
$$a_n = a_1 r^{n-1}$$

Skill 5.2 Demonstrating knowledge of the properties of the rational number system (e.g., commutative, associative)

Commutative
$a + b = b + a$

Example:　　$5 + {}^-8 = {}^-8 + 5 = {}^-3$

　　　　　　$ab = ba$

Example:　　${}^-2 \times 6 = 6 \times {}^-2 = {}^-12$

The order of the addends or factors does not affect the sum or product.

Associative
$(a + b) + c = a + (b + c)$

Example:　　$({}^-2 + 7) + 5 = {}^-2 + (7 + 5)$
　　　　　　$5 + 5 = {}^-2 + 12 = 10$

　　　　　　$(ab)\,c = a\,(bc)$

Example:　　$(3 \times {}^-7) \times 5 = 3 \times ({}^-7 \times 5)$
　　　　　　${}^-21 \times 5 = 3 \times {}^-35 = {}^-105$

The grouping of the addends or factors does not affect the sum or product.

Distributive
$a\,(b + c) = ab + ac$

Example:　　$6 \times ({}^-4 + 9) = (6 \times {}^-4) + (6 \times 9)$
　　　　　　$6 \times 5 = {}^-24 + 54 = 30$

To multiply a sum by a number, multiply each addend by the number, then add the products.

Additive and multiplicative inverses

Additive Identity (Property of Zero)
$a + 0 = a$

Example: $17 + 0 = 17$

The sum of any number and zero is that number.

Multiplicative Identity (Property of One)
$a \cdot 1 = a$

Example: $^-34 \times 1 = {}^-34$

The product of any number and one is that number.

Additive Inverse (Property of Opposites)
$a + {}^-a = 0$

Example: $25 + {}^-25 = 0$

The sum of any number and its opposite is zero.

Multiplicative Inverse (Property of Reciprocals)
$a \times \frac{1}{a} = 1$

Example: $5 \times \frac{1}{5} = 1$

The product of any number and its reciprocal is one.

Field Properties

Real numbers exhibit the following addition and multiplication properties, where a, b, and c are real numbers.

Note: Multiplication is implied when there is no symbol between two variables. Thus, $a \times b$ can be depicted as ab. Multiplication can also be indicated by a raised dot: $a \cdot b$

Closure

a + b is a real number

Example: Since 2 and 5 are both real numbers, 7 is also a real number.

ab is a real number

Example: Since 3 and 4 are both real numbers, 12 is also a real number.

The sum or product of two real numbers is a real number.

Skill 5.3   Identifying situations in which estimation is an appropriate problem-solving strategy

In order to estimate measurements, it is helpful to have a familiar reference with a known measurement. For instance, you can use the knowledge that a dollar bill is about six inches long or that a nickel weighs about 5 grams to make estimates of weight and length without actually measuring with a ruler or a balance.

Some common equivalents include:

ITEM	APPROXIMATELY EQUAL TO	
	METRIC	Customary
large paper clip	1 gram	1 ounce
capacity of sports bottle	1 liter	1 quart
average sized adult	75 kilograms	170 pounds
length of an office desk	1 meter	1 yard
math textbook	1 kilogram	2 pounds
length of dollar bill	15 centimeters	6 inches
thickness of a dime	1 millimeter	0.1 inches
area of football field		6,400 sq. yd
temperature of boiling water	100°C	212°F
temperature of ice	0°C	32°F
1 cup of liquid	240 mL	8 fl oz
1 teaspoon	5 ml	

<u>Example:</u>   Estimate the measurement of the following items:

a)   The length of an adult cow = _____meters
b)   The thickness of a compact disc = _____millimeters
c)   Your height = _____meters
d)   length of your nose = _____centimeters
e)   weight of your math textbook = _____kilograms
f)   weight of an automobile = _____kilograms
g)   weight of an aspirin = _____grams

a) $\frac{3}{2}$
b)
c)   1.5
d)   4
e)   1
f)   1,000
g)   1

Depending on the degree of accuracy needed, an object may be measured to different units.

For example, a pencil may be 6 inches to the nearest inch, or 6-3/8 inches to the nearest eighth of an inch. Similarly, it might be 15 cm to the nearest cm or 154 mm to the nearest mm.

Skill 5.4   Making use of estimation to predict results and determine the reasonableness of answers

Estimation and approximation may be used to check the reasonableness of answers.

<u>Example:</u>   Estimate the answer.

$$\frac{58 \times 810}{1989}$$

58 becomes 60, 810 becomes 800 and 1989 becomes 2000.

$$\frac{60 \times 800}{2000} = 24$$

Word problems: An estimate may sometimes be all that is needed to solve a problem.

Example: Janet goes into a store to purchase a CD on sale for $13.95. While shopping, she sees two pairs of shoes, prices $19.95 and $14.50. She only has $50. Can she purchase everything, assuming no sales tax?

Solve by rounding:
$19.95 → $20.00
$14.50 → $15.00
$13.95 → $14.00
$49.00   Yes, she can purchase the CD and the shoes.

Skill 5.2   Solving problems involving integers, fractions, decimals, ratios, proportions, percents, powers, and roots using a variety of algorithms, procedures, and strategies, including mental math.

Rational numbers include integers, fractions and mixed numbers, and terminating and repeating decimals. Every rational number can be expressed as a repeating or terminating decimal and can be shown on a number line.

Ratios, Proportions and Percents

Proportions can be used to solve word problems whenever relationships are compared. Some situations include scale drawings and maps, similar polygons, speed, time and distance, cost, and comparison shopping.

Example: Which is the better buy, 6 items for $1.29 or 8 items for $1.69? Find the unit price.

$6x = 1.29$ $8x = 1.69$
$x = 0.215$ $x = 0.21125$

Thus, 8 items for $1.69 is the better buy.

Example: A car travels 125 miles in 2.5 hours. How far will it go in 6 hours?

Write a proportion comparing the distance and time.

Let x represent distance in miles. Then,

$\frac{125}{2.5} = \frac{x}{6}$ set up the proportion

$2.5x = 6 \cdot 125$ cross-multiply

$2.5x = 750$ simplify

$x = {}^{750}/_{2.5}$ divide both sides of the equation by 2.5

$x = 300$ miles   simplify

<u>Example:</u>   The scale on a map is inch = 6 miles. What is the actual distance between two cities if they are 2 inches apart on the map?

Write a proportion comparing the scale to the actual distance.

$$
\begin{array}{rl}
\text{scale} & \text{actual} \\
x = & 1 \times 6 \\
x = & 6 \\
2x = & 12
\end{array}
$$

Thus, the actual distance between the cities is 12 miles.

Word problems involving percents can be solved by writing the problem as an equation, then solving the equation. Keep in mind that **"of" means "multiplication"** and **"is" means "equals."**

<u>Example:</u>   The Ski Club has 85 members. 80% of the members are able to attend the meeting. How many members attended the meeting?

Restate the problem.   What is 80% of 85?
Write an equation. $n = 0.8 \times 85$
Solve. $n = 68$

Sixty-eight members attended the meeting.

<u>Example:</u>   There are 64 dogs in the kennel. 48 are collies. What percent are collies?

Restate the problem.   48 is what percent of 64?
Write an equation. $48 = n \times 64$
Solve. $48 \div 64 = n$
      $n = 75\%$

75% of the dogs are collies.

<u>Example:</u>   The auditorium was filled to 90% capacity. There were 558 seats occupied. What is the capacity of the auditorium?

Restate the problem.   90% of what number is 558?
Write an equation. $0.9n = 558$
Solve. $n = {}^{558}/_{.09}$
      $n = 620$

The capacity of the auditorium is 620 people.

Example: Shoes cost $42.00. Sales tax is 6%. What is the total cost of the shoes?

Restate the problem.   What is 6% of 42?
Write an equation. $n = 0.06 \times 42$
Solve. $n = 2.52$
Add the sales tax. $42.00 + $2.52 = $44.52

The total cost of the shoes, including sales tax, is $44.52.

SEE also Skill 4.2.

Mental math practice
Give students regular practice in doing mental math. The following website offers many mental calculation tips and strategies:
http://mathforum.org/k12/mathtips/mathtips.html

Because frequent calculator use tends to deprive students of a sense of numbers, they will often approach a sequence of multiplications and divisions the hard way. For instance, asked to calculate 770 x 36/ 55, they will first multiply 770 and 36 and then do a long division with the 55. They fail to recognize that both 770 and 55 can be divided by 11 and then by 5 to considerably simplify the problem. Give students plenty of practice in multiplying and dividing a sequence of integers and fractions so they are comfortable with canceling top and bottom terms.

COMPETENCY 0006   **APPLY PRINCIPLES, CONCEPTS, AND PROCEDURES RELATED TO ALGEBRA.**

Skill 6.1   **Recognizing, representing, and extending patterns, relationships, and functions using numbers, graphs, symbols, variables, and rules**

Algebraic methods and representations

A relationship between two quantities can be shown using a table, graph or rule. In this example, the rule y= 9x describes the relationship between the total amount earned, y, and the total amount of $9 sunglasses sold, x.

A table using this data would appear as:

number of sunglasses sold	1	5	10	15
total dollars earned	9	45	90	135

Each *(x,y)* relationship between a pair of values is called the **coordinate pair**, and can be plotted on a graph. The coordinate pairs *(1,9)*, *(5,45)*, *(10,90)*, and *(15,135)*, are plotted on the graph below.

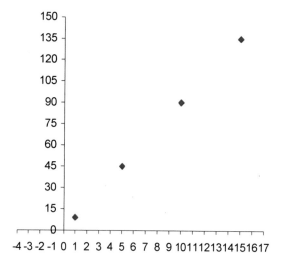

The graph above shows a linear relationship. A **linear relationship** is one in which two quantities are proportional to each other. Doubling x also doubles y. On a graph, a straight line depicts a linear relationship.

Another type of relationship is a **nonlinear relationship**. This is one in which change in one quantity does not affect the other quantity to the same extent. Nonlinear graphs have a curved line, such as the graph below.

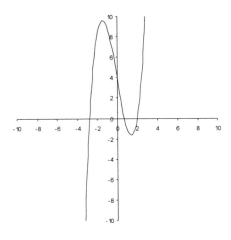

Functions

The function or relationship between two quantities may be analyzed to determine how one quantity depends on the other. For example, the function below shows a relationship between y and x:

$$y=2x+1$$

The relationship between two or more variables can be analyzed using a table, graph, written description, or symbolic rule. The function, y=2x+1, is written as a symbolic rule. The same relationship is also shown in the table below:

x	0	2	3	6	9
y	1	5	7	13	19

A relationship could be written in words by saying "the value of y is equal to two times the value of x, plus one." This relationship could be shown on a graph by plotting given points, such as the ones shown in the table above.

Another way to describe a function is as a process in which one or more numbers are input into an imaginary machine that produces another number as the output. If 5 is input, (x), into a machine with a process of x +1, the output, (y), will equal 6.

In real situations, relationships can be described mathematically. The function, y=x+1, can be used to describe the idea that people age one year on their birthdays. To describe the relationship in which a person's monthly medical costs are 6 times a person's age, we could write y=6x. The monthly cost of medical care could be predicted using this function. A 20 year-old person would spend $120 per month (120=20*6). An 80 year-old person would spend $480 per month (480=80*6). Therefore, one could analyze the relationship to say: as you get older, medical costs increase $6.00 each year.

Skill 6.2 Simplifying and evaluating algebraic expressions and formulas, and solving algebraic equations and inequalities

Rational expressions can be simplified into equivalent expressions by reducing. When dividing any number of terms by a single term, divide or reduce their coefficients. Then subtract the exponent of a variable in the denominator from the exponent of the same variable in the numerator.

Example: Simplify

$$\frac{24x^3y^6z^3}{8x^2y^2z} = 3xy^4z^2$$

To reduce a rational expression with more than one term in the denominator, the expression must be factored first. Factors that are exactly the same will cancel and each becomes 1. Factors that have exactly the opposite signs of each other, such as $(a - b)$ and $(b - a)$, will cancel and one factor becomes 1 and the other becomes $a - 1$.

Example: Simplify

$$\frac{3x^2 - 14xy - 5y^2}{x^2 - 25y^2} = \frac{(3x + y)(x - 5y)}{(x + 5y)(x - 5y)} = \frac{3x + y}{x + 5y}$$

Solving algebraic equations
The procedure for solving algebraic equations is demonstrated using the example below.

Example: $3(x+3) = {}^-2x + 4$ Solve for x.

  1) Expand to eliminate all parentheses.
  $3x + 9 = {}^-2x + 4$

  2) Multiply each term by the LCD to eliminate all denominators (there are none here).

  3) Combine like terms on each side when possible (there is no need to do that here).

  4) Use real number properties to put all variables on one side and all constants on the other.

  $\rightarrow 3x + 9 - 9 = {}^-2x + 4 - 9$ (subtract nine from both sides)

  $\rightarrow 3x = {}^-2x - 5$
  $\rightarrow 3x + 2x = {}^-2x + 2x - 5$ (add $2x$ to both sides)
  $\rightarrow 5x = {}^-5$
  $\rightarrow \dfrac{5x}{5} = \dfrac{{}^-5}{5}$ (divide both sides by 5)
  $\rightarrow x = {}^-1$

Example: Solve $3(2x+5) - 4x = 5(x+9)$

  $6x + 15 - 4x = 5x + 45$
  $2x + 15 = 5x + 45$
  ${}^-3x + 15 = 45$
  ${}^-3x = 30$
  $x = {}^-10$

Absolute value equations
If a and b are real numbers, and k is a non-negative real number, the solution of $|ax + b| = k$ is $ax + b = k$ and $ax + b = {}^-k$

<u>Example:</u> $|2x + 3| = 9$ solve for x.

$2x + 3 = 9$	and	$2x + 3 = {}^-9$
$2x + 3 - 3 = 9 - 3$	and	$2x + 3 - 3 = {}^-9 - 3$
$2x = 6$	and	$2x = {}^-12$
$\dfrac{2x}{2} = \dfrac{6}{2}$	and	$\dfrac{2x}{2} = \dfrac{{}^-12}{2}$
$x = 3$	and	$x = {}^-6$

Therefore, the solution is $x = \{3, {}^-6\}$

Algebraic equations are often used to model and solve real life problems.

<u>Example:</u>   Mark and Mike are twins. Three times Mark's age plus four equals four times Mike's age minus 14. How old are the boys?

Since the boys are twins, their ages are the same. "Translate" the English into algebra.

Let x = their age
$3x + 4 = 4x - 14$
$18 = x$

The boys are each 18 years old.

<u>Example:</u>   The YMCA wants to sell raffle tickets to raise $32,000. If they must pay $7,250 in expenses and prizes out of the money collected from the tickets, how many tickets worth $25 each must they sell?

Let x = number of tickets sold
Then $25x$ = total money collected for x tickets

Total money minus expenses must be equal to $32,000.
$25x - 7,250 = 32,000$
$25x = 39,250$
$x = 1,570$

If they sell 1,570 tickets, they will raise $32,000.

Example: The Simpsons went out for dinner. All 4 of them ordered the aardvark steak dinner. Bert paid for the 4 meals and included a tip of $12 for a total of $84.60. How much was an aardvark steak dinner?

Let $x =$ the price of one aardvark dinner

So $4x =$ the price of 4 aardvark dinners

$4x = 84.60 - 12$

$4x = 72.60$

$x = \dfrac{72.60}{4} = \$18.15$ The price of one aardvark dinner.

An **inequality** is a statement that orders two expressions. The symbols used are < (less than), > (greater than), ~ (less than or equal to), ~ (greater than or equal to) and ~(not equal to). Most inequalities have an infinite number of solutions. Methods for solving inequalities are similar to those used for solving equations, with this exception--when both sides of an inequality are multiplied or divided by a <u>negative</u> real number, the inequality sign in reversed.

Example: $3x - 2 > 13$
            $(3x - 2) + 2 > 13 + 2$ Add 2.
            $3x > 15$ Simplify.
            $\dfrac{3}{3} \quad \dfrac{}{3}$ Divide by 3.
            $x > 5$ Simplify.

Thus the solution set is all real numbers greater than 5.

Skill 6.3   Making use of algebraic functions to plot points and describe graphs, and analyzing change in various contexts

A relationship between two quantities can be shown using a table, graph, written description or symbolic rule. In the following example, the rule $y = 9x$ describes the relationship between the total amount earned, y, and the number of sunglasses sold, x.

A table using this data would appear as:

number of sunglasses sold	1	5	10	15
total dollars earned	9	45	90	135

Each *(x,y)* relationship between a pair of values is called the coordinate pair and can be plotted on a graph. The coordinate pairs (1, 9), (5, 45), (10, 90), and (15, 135), are plotted on the graph below.

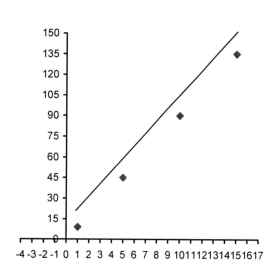

[JF1]
The graph shows a linear relationship. A linear relationship is one in which two quantities are proportional to each other. On a graph, a straight line depicts a linear relationship.

The function or relationship between two quantities may be analyzed to determine how one quantity depends on the other.

For example, the function below shows a linear relationship between *y* and *x*: $y = 2x + 1$. The function $y = 2x + 1$, is written as a symbolic rule. The same relationship is also shown in the table below:

x	0	2	3	6	9
y	1	5	7	13	19

The function can also be graphed, as shown:

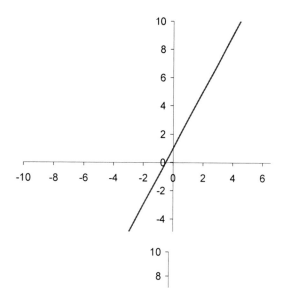

A relationship could be written in words by saying "The value of y is equal to two times the value of x, plus one." This relationship could be shown on a graph by plotting given points such as the ones shown in the table above.

Another way to describe a function is as a process in which one or more numbers are input into an imaginary machine that produces another number as the output. If 5 is input (x) into a machine with a process of $x + 1$, the output (y) will equal 6.

In real situations, relationships can be described mathematically. The function, $y = x + 1$, can be used to describe the idea that people age one year on their birthday. To describe the relationship in which a person's monthly medical costs are 6 times a person's age, we could write $y = 6x$. The monthly cost of medical care could be predicted using this function. A 20 year-old person would spend $120 per month ($120 = 20 \times 6$). An 80 year-old person would spend $480 per month ($480 = 80 \times 6$). Therefore, one could analyze the relationship to say: as you get older, medical costs increase $6.00 per month each year.

Linear inequalities are solved following a procedure similar to that used for solving linear equations. There is however one important point that must be noted while solving inequalities: **dividing or multiplying by a negative number will reverse the direction of the inequality sign.**

The solution to an inequality with one variable is represented in graphical form on the number line or in interval form. In identifying word problems that can be represented by inequalities watch for words like greater than, less than, at least, or no more than.

<u>Example:</u> Solve the inequality. Show its solution using interval form and graph the solution on the number line.

$$\frac{5x}{8} + 3 \geq 2x - 5$$

$$8\left(\frac{5x}{8}\right) + 8(3) \geq 8(2x) - 5(8)$$ Multiply by LCD = 8.

$$5x + 24 \geq 16x - 40$$

$$5x + 24 - 24 - 16x \geq 16x - 16x - 40 - 24$$ Subtract 16x and 24 from both sides of the equation.

$$^-11x \geq ^- 64$$

$$\frac{^-11x}{^-11} \leq \frac{^-64}{^-11}$$

$$x \leq \frac{64}{11} \quad ; \quad x \leq 5\frac{9}{11}$$

Note the change in direction of the equality with division by a negative number.

Solution in interval form: $\left(^-\infty, 5\frac{9}{11}\right]$

Note: "] " means $5\frac{9}{11}$ is included in the solution.

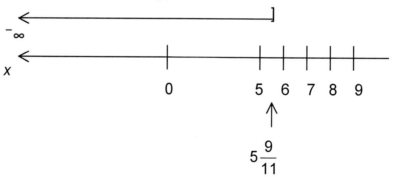

Example: Solve the following inequality and express your answer in both interval and graphical form.

$$3x - 8 < 2(3x - 1)$$
$$3x - 8 < 6x - 2 \qquad \text{Distributive property.}$$
$$3x - 6x - 8 + 8 < 6x - 6x - 2 + 8$$

Add 8 and subtract $6x$ from both sides of the equation.

$$^-3x < 6$$
$$\frac{^-3x}{^-3} > \frac{6}{^-3} \qquad x > ^-2$$

Graphical form:

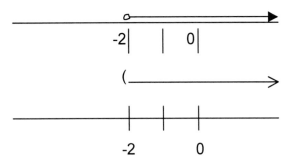

or

Interval form: $(^-2, \infty)$

Recall: a) Using a parentheses or an open circle implies the point in not included in the answer.

b) Using a bracket or a closed circle implies the point is included in the answer.

Example: Solve $6x + 21 < 8x + 31$
$$^-2x + 21 < 31$$
$$^-2x < 10$$
$$x > ^-5$$

Note that the inequality sign has changed.

To graph an inequality involving two variables x and y, solve the inequality for y. This puts the inequality in the **slope-intercept form**, (for example: $y < mx + b$). The point $(0, b)$ is the y-intercept and m is the line's slope.

When graphing a linear inequality, the line will be dashed if the inequality sign is $<$ or $>$. If the inequality signs are either $\geq$ or $\leq$, the line on the graph will be a solid line. Shade above the line when the inequality sign is $\geq$ or $>$. Shade below the line when the inequality sign is $<$ or $\leq$.

<u>Example:</u>   Graph the following inequality.

$$3x - 2y \geq 6$$
$$y \leq 3/2\, x - 3$$

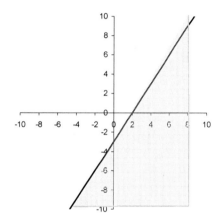

If the inequality solves to x $>$, $\geq$, $<$ **or** $\leq$ **any number**, then the graph includes a **vertical line**.

If the inequality solves to y $>$, $\geq$, $<$ **or** $\leq$ **any number**, then the graph includes a **horizontal line**.

For inequalities of the forms $x >$ number, $x \leq$ number, $x <$ number, or $x \geq$ number, draw a vertical line (solid or dashed). Shade to the right for $>$ or $\geq$. Shade to the left for $<$ or $\leq$.

Example: Graph the following inequality:

$$3x + 12 < -3$$
$$x < {}^-5$$

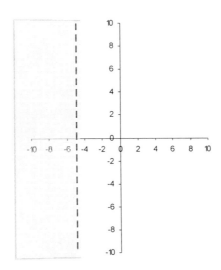

Skill 6.4 Translating word problems into mathematical terms using algebraic concepts such as variables and equations

Word problems can sometimes be solved by using a system of two equations in two unknowns. This system can then be solved using substitution, the addition-subtraction method, or graphing.

Example: Mrs. Winters bought 4 dresses and 6 pairs of shoes for $340. Mrs. Summers went to the same store and bought 3 dresses and 8 pairs of shoes for $360. If all the dresses were the same price and all the shoes were the same price, find the price charged for a dress and for a pair of shoes.

Let x = price of a dress
Let y = price of a pair of shoes

Mrs. Winters' equation would be: $4x + 6y = 340$
Mrs. Summers' equation would be: $3x + 8y = 360$

To solve by addition-subtraction:
Multiply the first equation by 4: $4(4x + 6y = 340)$
Multiply the other equation by $^-3$: $^-3(3x + 8y = 360)$

By doing this, the equations can be added to each other to eliminate one variable and to solve for the other variable.

$$16x + 24y = 1360$$
$$-9x - 24y = {}^-1080$$
$$7x = 280$$
$$x = 40 \leftarrow \text{the price of a dress was \$40}$$

Solving for y, $y = 30 \leftarrow$ the price of a pair of shoes, $30

Example: The YMCA wants to sell raffle tickets to raise at least $32,000. If they must pay $7,250 in expenses and prizes out of the money collected from the tickets, how many tickets worth $25 each must they sell?

Since they want to raise **at least $32,000**, that means they would be happy to get 32,000 **or more**. This requires an inequality.

Let $x =$ number of tickets sold
Then $25x =$ total money collected for x tickets

Total money minus expenses is greater than $32,000.

$$25x - 7250 \geq 32000$$
$$25x \geq 39250$$
$$x \geq 1570$$

If they sell **1,570 tickets or more**, they will raise AT LEAST $32,000.

Example: The Simpsons went out for dinner. All 4 of them ordered the aardvark steak dinner. Bert paid for the 4 meals and included a tip of $12 for a total of $84.60. How much was an aardvark steak dinner?

Let $x =$ the price of one aardvark dinner.
So $4x =$ the price of 4 aardvark dinners.
$$4x + 12 = 84.60$$
$$4x = 72.60$$
$$x = \$18.50 \text{ for each dinner.}$$

Example: Sharon's Bike Shoppe can assemble a 3 speed bike in 30 minutes or a 10 speed bike in 60 minutes. The profit on each bike sold is $60 for a 3 speed or $75 for a 10 speed bike. How many of each type of bike should they assemble during an 8 hour day (480 minutes) to make the maximum profit? Total daily profit must be at least $300.

Let x = number of 3 speed bikes.
y = number of 10 speed bikes.

Since there are only 480 minutes to use each day,
$30x + 60y \leq 480$ is the first inequality.

Since the total daily profit must be at least $300,
$60x + 75y \geq 300$ is the second inequality.

$32x + 65y \leq 480$ solves to $y \leq 8 - 1/2\,x$
$60x + 75y \geq 300$ solves to $y \geq 4 - 4/5\,x$

Graph these two inequalities:

$y \leq 8 - 1/2\,x$
$y \geq 4 - 4/5\,x$

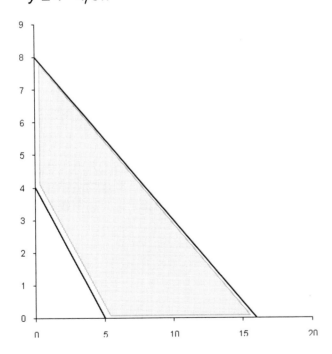

Realize that $x \geq 0$ and $y \geq 0$, since the number of bikes assembled can not be a negative number. Graph these as additional constraints on the problem.

The number of bikes assembled must always be an integer value, so points within the shaded area of the graph must have integer values. The maximum profit will occur at or near a corner of the shaded portion of this graph. Those points occur at (0,4), (0,8), (16,0), or (5,0).

Since profits are \$60/3-speed or \$75/10-speed, the profit would be:

(0,4) $60(0) + 75(4) = 300$

(0,8) $60(0) + 75(8) = 600$

(16,0) $60(16) + 75(0) = 960 \leftarrow$ Maximum profit

(5,0) $60(5) + 75(0) = 300$

The maximum profit would occur if sixteen 3-speed bikes are made daily.

Skill 6.5   Using mathematical models to represent quantitative relationships (e.g., proportional relationships, linear relationships)

SEE Skill 6.1

Skill 6.6   Solving problems using a variety of algebraic concepts, models, and methods

Many of the example problems throughout this guide illustrate various algebraic concepts, models, and methods for obtaining a correct solution. The following discussion highlights some of the main ideas in this regard and illustrates them with a number of example problems.

Many word problems can be modeled and solved using **linear systems of equations and inequalities**. Some examples are given below.

Example: Farmer Greenjeans bought 4 cows and 6 sheep for \$1,700. Mr. Ziffel bought 3 cows and 12 sheep for \$2,400. If all the cows were the same price and all the sheep were another price, find the price charged for a cow or for a sheep.

Let x = price of a cow
Let y = price of a sheep

Then Farmer Greenjeans' equation would be $4x + 6y = 1700$
Mr. Ziffel's equation would be $3x + 12y = 2400$

To solve by **addition-subtraction**:

Multiply the first equation by $^-2$: $^-2(4x + 6y = 1700)$
Keep the other equation the same : $(3x + 12y = 2400)$

By doing this, the equations can be added to each other to eliminate one variable and solve for the other variable.

$$^-8x - 12y = {}^-3400$$
$$\underline{3x + 12y = 2400}$$
$$^-5x \qquad = {}^-1000$$

Add these equations.

$x = 200 \leftarrow$ the price of a cow was \$200.

Solving for y, $y = 150 \leftarrow$ the price of a sheep—\$150.
(This problem can also be solved by substitution or determinants.)

<u>Example:</u>   Mrs. Allison bought 1 pound of potato chips, a 2-pound beef roast, and 3 pounds of apples for a total of \$8.19. Mr. Bromberg bought a 3-pound beef roast and 2 pounds of apples for \$9.05. Kathleen Kaufman bought 2 pounds of potato chips, a 3-pound beef roast, and 5 pounds of apples for \$13.25. Find the per pound price of each item.

To solve by **substitution**:

Let x = price of a pound of potato chips
Let y = price of a pound of roast beef
Let z = price of a pound of apples

Mrs. Allison's equation is $\qquad 1x + 2y + 3z = 8.19$
Mr. Bromberg's equation is $\qquad 3y + 2z = 9.05$
K. Kaufman's equation is $\qquad 2x + 3y + 5z = 13.25$

Take the first equation and solve for x. (This equation was chosen because x is the easiest variable to get alone in this set of equations.) This equation becomes

$$x = 8.19 - 2y - 3z$$

Substitute this expression into the other equations in place of x:

$$3y + 2z = 9.05 \leftarrow \text{ equation 2}$$
$$2(8.19 - 2y - 3z) + 3y + 5z = 13.25 \leftarrow \text{ equation 3}$$

Simplify the equation by combining like terms:

$$3y + 2z = 9.05 \leftarrow \text{equation 2}$$
$$-1y - 1z = -3.13 \leftarrow \text{equation 3}$$

Solve equation 3 for either y or z:

$$y = 3.13 - z \quad (*)$$

Substitute this into equation 2 for y:

$$3(3.13 - z) + 2z = 9.05 \leftarrow \text{equation 2}$$
$$-1y - 1z = -3.13 \leftarrow \text{equation 3}$$

Combine like terms in equation 2:

$$9.39 - 3z + 2z = 9.05$$
$$z = \$0.34 \text{ per pound (price of apples)}$$

Substitute .34 for z in the equation marked with an asterisk (*) above to solve for y:

$$y = 3.13 - z$$
$$y = 3.13 - .34$$
$$y = \$2.79 = \text{per pound price of roast beef}$$

Substituting .34 for z and 2.79 for y in one of the original equations, solve for x:

$$1x + 2y + 3z = 8.19$$
$$1x + 2(2.79) + 3(.34) = 8.19$$
$$x + 5.58 + 1.02 = 8.19$$
$$x + 6.60 = 8.19$$
$$x = \$1.59 \text{ per pound of potato chips}$$
$$(x, y, z) = (\$1.59, \$2.79, \$0.34)$$

<u>Example:</u> Aardvark Taxi charges $4 initially plus $1 for every mile traveled. Baboon Taxi charges $6 initially plus $.75 for every mile traveled. Determine the mileage at which it becomes cheaper to ride with Baboon Taxi than it is to ride Aardvark Taxi.

Aardvark Taxi's equation:	$y = 1x + 4$
Baboon Taxi's equation:	$y = .75x + 6$
Use substitution:	$.75x + 6 = x + 4$
Multiply both sides by 4:	$3x + 24 = 4x + 16$
Solve for x:	$8 = x$

This result tells us that, at 8 miles, the total charge for the two companies is the same. If you compare the charge for 1 mile, Aardvark charges $5 and Baboon charges $6.75. Therefore, Aardvark Taxi is cheaper for distances up to 8 miles, but Baboon is cheaper for distances greater than 8 miles. This problem can also be solved by graphing both equations.

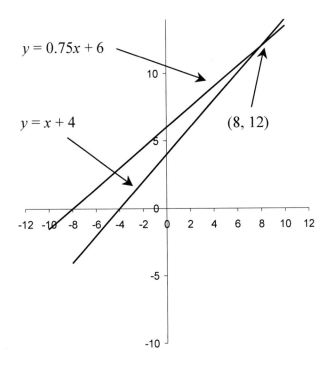

The lines intersect at (8, 12); therefore, at 8 miles both companies charge $12. For distances less than 8 miles, Aardvark Taxi charges less (the corresponding line is below that of Baboon). For distances greater than 8 miles, Aardvark charges more (the corresponding line is above that of Baboon).

Other word problems can be modeled using **quadratic equations or inequalities**. Examples of this type of problem follow.

Example: A family is planning to add a new room to their house. They would like the room to have a length that is 10 ft more than the width and a total area of 375 sq. feet. Find the length and width of the room.

Let x be the width of the room. The length of the room is then $x + 10$. Thus,

$$x(x+10) = 375$$
$$x^2 + 10x - 375 = 0$$

Factor the quadratic expression to solve the equation:

$$x^2 + 25x - 15x - 375 = 0 \quad \text{Break up the middle}$$
$$x(x+25) - 15(x+25) = 0 \quad \text{term using factors of 375}$$
$$(x+25)(x-15) = 0$$
$$x = -25 \text{ or } x = 15$$

Since the dimension of a room cannot be negative, we choose the positive solution x=15. Thus, the width of the room is 15 ft and the length of the room is 25ft.

Example: The height of a projectile fired upward at a velocity of v meters per second from an original height of h meters is $y = h + vx - 4.9x^2$. If a rocket is fired from an original height of 250 meters with an original velocity of 4800 meters per second, find the approximate time the rocket would drop to sea level (a height of 0).

Substituting the height and velocity into the equation yields:
$y = 250 + 4800x - 4.9x^2$. If the height at sea level is zero, then $y = 0$ so $0 = 250 + 4800x - 4.9x^2$. Solving for x could be done by using the quadratic formula.

$$x = \frac{-4800 \pm \sqrt{4800^2 - 4(-4.9)(250)}}{2(-4.9)}$$

$$x \approx 979.53 \text{ or } x \approx -0.05 \text{ seconds}$$

Since the time has to be positive, it will be approximately 980 seconds until the rocket reaches sea level.

COMPETENCY 0007   APPLY PRINCIPLES, CONCEPTS, AND PROCEDURES RELATED TO GEOMETRY.

Skill 7.1   **Analyzing various representations (e.g., diagrams, perspective drawings, projections, nets) of two- and three-dimensional objects**

Mathematical operations can be shown using manipulatives, or drawings.

Multiplication can be shown using arrays.

3×4

Addition and subtractions can be demonstrated with symbols.

$\psi \, \psi \, \psi \, \xi \, \xi \, \xi \, \xi$

$3 + 4 = 7$

$7 - 3 = 4$

Fractions can be clarified using pattern blocks, fraction bars, or paper folding.

To read a bar graph or a pictograph, read the explanation of the scale that was used in the legend. Compare the length of each bar with the dimensions on the axes and calculate the value each bar represents. On a pictograph, count the number of pictures used in the chart and calculate the value of all the pictures.

To read a circle graph, find the total of the amounts represented on the entire circle graph. To determine the actual amount that each sector of the graph represents, multiply the percent in a sector times the total amount number. To read a chart, read the row and column headings on the table. Use this information to evaluate the given information in the chart.

We refer to three-dimensional figures in geometry as **solids**. A solid is the union of all points on a simple closed surface and all points in its interior. A **polyhedron** is a simple closed surface formed from planar polygonal regions. Each polygonal region is called a **face** of the polyhedron. The vertices and edges of the polygonal regions are called the **vertices** and **edges** of the polyhedron.

We may form a cube from three congruent squares. However, if we tried to put four squares about a single vertex, their interior angle measures would add up to 360° (i.e., four edge-to-edge squares with a common vertex lie in a common plane and therefore cannot form a corner figure of a regular polyhedron).

There are five ways to form corner figures with congruent regular polygons[SAA3]:

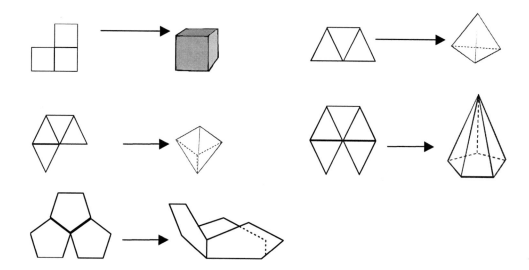

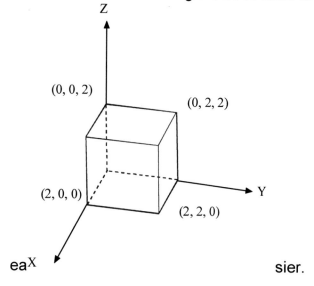

In order to represent three-dimensional figures, we need three coordinate axes (X, Y, and Z) that are all mutually perpendicular to each other. Since we cannot draw three mutually perpendicular axes on a two-dimensional surface, we use oblique representations.

Example: Represent a cube with sides of 2.

We draw three sides along the three axes to make things

eaX   sier.

Each point has three coordinates (x, y, z).

Skill 7.2   Analyzing properties and relationships of various geometric shapes and structures

The union of all points on a simple closed surface and all points in its interior form a space figure called a **solid**. The five regular solids, or **polyhedra**, are the cube, tetrahedron, octahedron, icosahedron, and dodecahedron. A **net** is a two-dimensional figure that can be cut out and folded up to make a three-dimensional solid. Below are models of the five regular solids with their corresponding face polygons and nets.

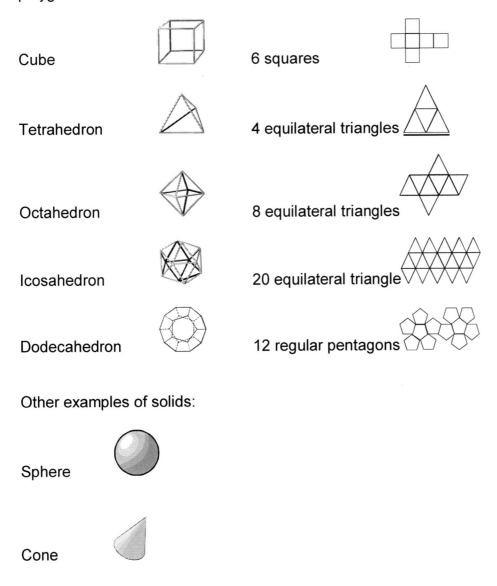

Cube   6 squares

Tetrahedron   4 equilateral triangles

Octahedron   8 equilateral triangles

Icosahedron   20 equilateral triangle

Dodecahedron   12 regular pentagons

Other examples of solids:

Sphere

Cone

Geometric Sequences

When using geometric sequences, consecutive numbers are compared to find the common ratio.

$$r = \frac{a_{n+1}}{a_n}$$

where r = common ratio
a = the nth term

The ratio is then used in the geometric sequence formula:

$$a_n = a_1 r^{n-1}$$

<u>Example:</u>   Find the 8th term of the geometric sequence 2, 8, 32, 128 ...

$r = \frac{a_{n+1}}{a_n}$ use common ratio formula to find ratio

$r = 8/2$ substitute $a_n = 2$ $a_{n+1} = 8$
$r = 4$

$a_n = a_1 \times r^{n-1}$ use r = 4 to solve for the 8th term
$a_n = 2 \times 4^{8-1}$
$a_n = 32{,}768$

Skill 7.3   **Applying core concepts and principles of Euclidean geometry (e.g., symmetry, similarity, congruence) in two and three dimensions (e.g., points, lines, planes) to solve problems**

When creating a three-dimensional figure, if we know any two values of the vertices, faces, and edges, we can find the remaining value by using **Euler's Formula**: $V + F = E + 2$.

For example:

We want to create a pentagonal pyramid, and we know it has six vertices and six faces. Using Euler's Formula, we compute:

$$V + F = E + 2$$
$$6 + 6 = E + 2$$
$$12 = E + 2$$
$$10 = E$$

Thus, we know that our figure should have 10 edges.

Pythagorean Theorem

The Pythagorean theorem states that *in a right triangle*, the square of the length of the hypotenuse is equal to the sum of the squares of the lengths of the legs. Symbolically, this is stated as:

$$c^2 = a^2 + b^2$$

Given the right triangle below, find the missing side.

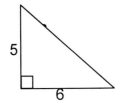

$c^2 = a^2 + b^2$	1. write formula
$c^2 = 5^2 + 6^2$	2. substitute known values
$c^2 = 61$	3. take square root
$c = \sqrt{61}$ or 7.81	4. solve

The converse of the Pythagorean theorem states that if the square of one side of a triangle is equal to the sum of the squares of the other two sides, then the triangle is a right triangle.

<u>Example:</u>　Given ΔXYZ, with sides measuring 12, 16, and 20 cm, determine if this is a right triangle.

$$c^2 = a^2 + b^2$$
$$20^2\ \underline{?}\ 12^2 + 16^2$$
$$400\ \underline{?}\ 144 + 256$$
$$400 = 400$$

Yes, the triangle is a right triangle.

This theorem can be expanded to determine if triangles are obtuse or acute.

If the square of the longest side of a triangle is greater than the sum of the squares of the other two sides, then the triangle is an obtuse triangle.

and

If the square of the longest side of a triangle is less than the sum of the squares of the other two sides, then the triangle is an acute triangle.

<u>Example:</u>   Given $\triangle$LMN with sides measuring 7, 12, and 14 inches, is the triangle right, acute, or obtuse?

$14^2 \; \underline{?} \; 7^2 + 12^2$
$196 \; \underline{?} \; 49 + 144$
$196 > 193$

Therefore, the triangle is obtuse.

<u>Example:</u>   Find the area and perimeter of a rectangle if its length is 12 inches and its diagonal is 15 inches.

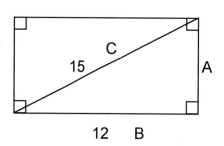

1. Draw and label sketch.
2. Since the height is still needed find the missing leg of the triangle

$$A^2 + B^2 = C^2$$
$$A^2 + 12^2 = 15^2$$
$$A^2 = 15^2 - 12^2$$
$$A^2 = 81$$
$$A = 9$$

Now use this information to find the area and perimeter.

$A = LW$ $P = 2(L + W)$ 1. write formula
$A = (12)(9)$ $P = 2(12 + 9)$ 2. substitute
$A = 108 \text{ in}^2$ $P = 42$ inches   3. solve

<u>Example:</u>   Given the figure below, find the area by dividing the polygon into smaller shapes.

1. divide the figure into two triangles and a rectangle

2. find the missing lengths

3. find the area of each part

4. find the sum of all areas

Find base of both right triangles using the Pythagorean formula:

$$a^2 + b^2 = c^2$$
$$a^2 + 12^2 = 15^2$$
$$a^2 = 225 - 144$$
$$a^2 = 81$$
$$a = 9$$

$$a^2 + b^2 = c^2$$
$$a^2 + 12^2 = 20^2$$
$$a^2 = 400 - 144$$
$$a^2 = 256$$
$$a = 16$$

Area of triangle 1   Area of triangle 2   Area of rectangle

$$A = \frac{1}{2}bh$$

$$A = \frac{1}{2}(9)(12)$$

$A = 54$ sq. units

$$A = \frac{1}{2}bh$$

$$A = \frac{1}{2}(16)(12)$$

$A = 96$ sq. units

$$A = LW$$

$$A = (15)(12)$$

$A = 180$ sq. units

Find the sum of all three figures.

$54 + 96 + 180 = 330$ square units

Given the special right triangles below, we can find the lengths of other special right triangles.

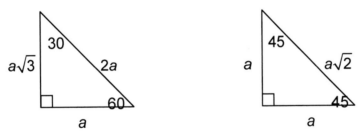

Sample problems:

1.

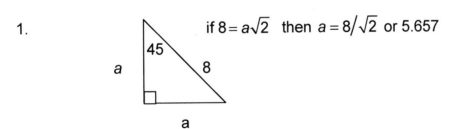

if $8 = a\sqrt{2}$ then $a = 8/\sqrt{2}$ or 5.657

2.

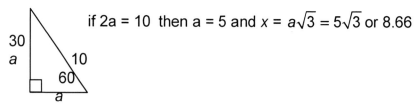

if $7=a$ then $c = a\sqrt{2} = 7\sqrt{2}$ or 9.899

3.

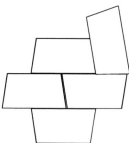

if $2a = 10$ then $a = 5$ and $x = a\sqrt{3} = 5\sqrt{3}$ or 8.66

Tesselations

A **tessellation** is an arrangement of closed shapes that completely covers the plane without overlapping or leaving gaps. Unlike **tilings**, tessellations do not require the use of regular polygons. In art, the term is used to refer to pictures or tiles—mostly in the form of animals and other life forms—that cover the surface of a plane in a symmetrical way without overlapping or leaving gaps. M. C. Escher is known as the "father" of modern tessellations. Tessellations are used for tiling, mosaics, quilts, and art.

If you look at a completed tessellation, you will see that the original motif repeats in a pattern. There are seventeen possible ways that a pattern can be used to tile a flat surface or "wallpaper."

The tessellation below is a combination of the four types of transformational symmetry we have discussed:

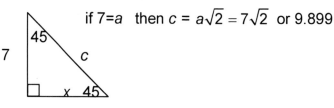

Skill 7.4   Applying knowledge of coordinate grids to represent basic geometric figures and analyze transformations

We can represent any two-dimensional geometric figure in the **Cartesian** or **rectangular coordinate system**. The Cartesian or rectangular coordinate system is formed by two perpendicular axes (coordinate axes): the x-axis and the y-axis. If we know the dimensions of a two-dimensional, or planar, figure, we can use this coordinate system to visualize the shape of the figure.

Example: Represent an isosceles triangle with two sides with a length of 4.

Draw the two sides along the x- and y- axes and connect the points (vertices).

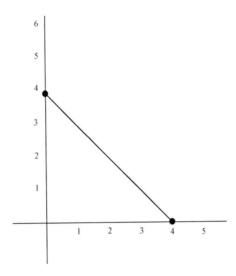

A **transformation** is a change in the position, shape, or size of a geometric figure. **Transformational geometry** is the study of manipulating objects by flipping, twisting, turning, and scaling them. **Symmetry** is exact similarity between two parts or halves, as if one were a mirror image of the other.

A **translation** is a transformation that "slides" an object a fixed distance in a given direction. The original object and its translation have the same shape, the same size, and they face in the same direction.

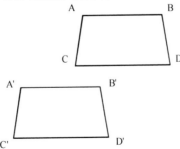

An example of a translation in architecture would be stadium seating. The seats are the same size, the same shape, and they face in the same direction.

A **rotation** is a transformation that turns a figure about a fixed point called the center of rotation. An object and its rotation are the same shape and size, but the figures may be turned in different directions. Rotations can occur in either a clockwise or a counterclockwise direction.

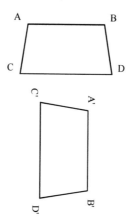

Rotations can often be seen in wallpaper and art. A Ferris wheel is an example of rotation.

An object and its **reflection** have the same shape and size, but the figures face in opposite directions.

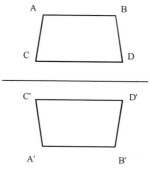

The line (where a mirror may be placed) is called the **line of reflection**. The distance from a point to the line of reflection is the same as the distance from the point's image to the line of reflection.

A **glide reflection** is a combination of a reflection and a translation.

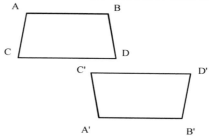

Another type of transformation is **dilation**. Dilation is a transformation that "shrinks" an object or makes it bigger.

Example: Use dilation to transform a diagram.

Starting with a triangle whose center of dilation is point P,

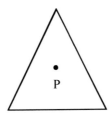

we dilate the lengths of the sides by the same factor to create a new triangle.

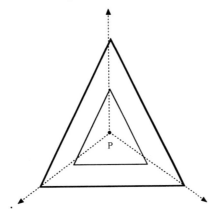

SEE also Skills 6.1 and 7.1

COMPETENCY 0008   APPLY PRINCIPLES, CONCEPTS, AND PROCEDURES RELATED TO MEASUREMENT.

Skill 8.1   Identifying and measuring component parts (e.g., angles, lines, segments) and properties (e.g., area, volume) of geometric figures and recognizing the relationships between two- and three-dimensional figures

Angles

The classifying of angles refers to the angle measure. The naming of angles refers to the letters or numbers used to label the angle.

Sample Problem:

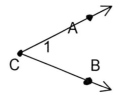

$\overrightarrow{CA}$ (read ray CA) and $\overrightarrow{CB}$ are the sides of the angle.
The angle can be called $\angle ACB$, $\angle BCA$, $\angle C$ or $\angle 1$.

Angles are classified according to their size as follows:

  acute: greater than 0 and less than 90 degrees.
  right: exactly 90 degrees.
  obtuse: greater than 90 and less than 180 degrees.
  straight: exactly 180 degrees

Angles can be classified in a number of ways. Some of those classifications are outlined here.

Adjacent angles have a common vertex and one common side but no interior points in common.

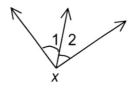

Complementary angles add up to 90 degrees.

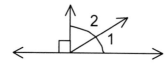

Supplementary angles add up to 180 degrees.

Vertical angles have sides that form two pairs of opposite rays.

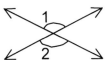

Corresponding angles are in the same corresponding position on two parallel lines cut by a transversal.

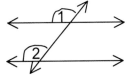

Alternate interior angles are diagonal angles on the inside of two parallel lines cut by a transversal.

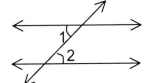

Alternate exterior angles are diagonal on the outside of two parallel lines cut by a transversal.

Perimeter, area, volume

The **perimeter** of any polygon is the sum of the lengths of the sides.

P = sum of sides

Since the opposite sides of a rectangle are congruent, the perimeter of a rectangle equals twice the sum of the length and width, or:

$P_{rect} = 2l + 2w$ or
$2(l + w)$

Similarly, since all the sides of a square have the same measure, the perimeter of a square equals four times the length of one side or

$$P_{square} = 4s$$

The **area** of a polygon is the number of square units covered by the figure.

$$A_{rect} = l \times w$$
$$A_{square} = s^2$$

<u>Example:</u>   Find the perimeter and the area of this rectangle.

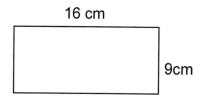

16 cm

9cm

$$P_{rect} = 2l + 2w \qquad\qquad A_{rect} = l \times w$$
$$= 2(16) + 2(9) \qquad\qquad = 16(9)$$
$$= 32 + 18 = 50 \text{ cm} \qquad\qquad = 144 \text{ cm}^2$$

<u>Example:</u>   Find the perimeter and area of this square.

3.6 in.

$$P_{square} = 4s \qquad\qquad A_{square} = s^2$$
$$= 4(3.6) \qquad\qquad = (3.6)(3.6)$$
$$= 14.4 \text{ in.} \qquad\qquad = 12.96 \text{ in}^2$$

In the following formulas, b = the base and h = the height of an altitude drawn to the base.

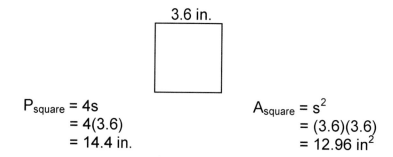

$$A_{parallelogram} = bh$$
$$A_{triangle} = \frac{1}{2}bh$$
$$A_{trapezoid} = \frac{1}{2}h(b_1 + b_2)$$

Example: Find the area of a parallelogram whose base is 6.5 cm and the height of the altitude to that base is 3.7 cm.

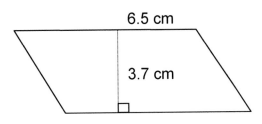

6.5 cm

3.7 cm

$$A_{parallelogram} = bh$$
$$= (3.7)(6.5)$$
$$= 24.05 \text{ cm}^2$$

Example: Find the area of this triangle.

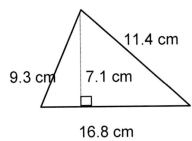

11.4 cm

9.3 cm   7.1 cm

16.8 cm

$$A_{triangle} = \frac{1}{2}bh$$
$$= 0.5\,(16.8)\,(7.1)$$
$$= 59.64 \text{ cm}^2$$

Note that the altitude is drawn to the base measuring 16.8 cm. The lengths of the other two sides are unnecessary.

Example: Find the area of a right triangle whose sides measure 10 inches, 24 inches, and 26 inches.

Since the hypotenuse of a right triangle must be the longest side, then the two perpendicular sides must measure 10 and 24 inches.

$$A_{triangle} = \frac{1}{2}bh$$
$$= \frac{1}{2}(10)\,(24)$$
$$= 120 \text{ sq. in.}$$

<u>Example:</u>   Find the area of this trapezoid.

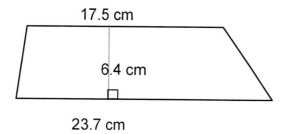

17.5 cm

6.4 cm

23.7 cm

The area of a trapezoid equals one-half the sum of the bases times the altitude.

$$A_{trapezoid} = \tfrac{1}{2}h(b_1 + b_2)$$
$$= 0.5\,(6.4)\,(17.5 + 23.7)$$
$$= 131.84 \text{ cm}^2$$

You can also compute the area remaining when sections are cut out of a given figure composed of triangles, squares, rectangles, parallelograms, trapezoids, or circles.

<u>Example:</u>   You have decided to fertilize your lawn. The shapes and dimensions of your lot, house, pool, and garden are given in the diagram below. The shaded area will not be fertilized. If each bag of fertilizer costs $7.95 and covers 4,500 square feet, find the total number of bags needed and the total cost of the fertilizer.

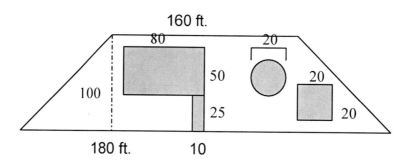

160 ft.

80   20

50   20

100

25   20

180 ft.   10

Area of Lot	Area of House	Area of Driveway
$A = \tfrac{1}{2}\,h(b_1 + b_2)$	$A = LW$	$A = LW$
$A = \tfrac{1}{2}(100)(180+160)$	$A = (80)(50)$	$A = (10)(25)$
$A = 17{,}000$ sq ft	$A = 4{,}000$ sq ft	$A = 250$ sq ft

Area of Pool

$A = \pi r^2$

$A = \pi (10)^2$

$A = 314.159$ sq. ft.

Area of Garden

$A = s^2$

$A = (20)^2$

$A = 400$ sq. ft.

Total area to fertilize = Lot area - (House + Driveway + Pool + Garden)
= 17,000 - (4,000 + 250 + 314.159 + 400)
= 12,035.841 sq ft

Number of bags needed = Total area to fertilize / 4,500 sq.ft. bag

= 12,035.841 / 4,500

= 2.67 bags

Since we cannot purchase 2.67 bags we must purchase 3 full bags.

Total cost = Number of bags x $7.95
= 3 x $7.95
= $23.85

The **lateral** area is the area of the faces excluding the bases.

The **surface area** is the total area of all the faces, including the bases.

The **volume** is the number of cubic units in a solid. This is the amount of space a figure holds.

Right prism

V = Bh (where B = area of the base of the prism and h = the height of the prism)

Rectangular right prism

S = 2(lw + hw + lh) (where l = length, w = width and h = height)
V = lwh

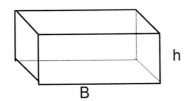

<u>Example</u>:   Find the height of a box where the volume is 120 cubic meters and the area of the base is 30 square meters.

$V = Bh$
$120 = 30h$
$h = 4$ meters

Regular pyramid

$V = \frac{1}{3}Bh$

B

Right circular cylinder

$S = 2\Pi r(r + h)$ (where r is the radius of the base)
$V = \Pi r^2 h$

Right circular cone

$V = \frac{1}{3}Bh$

Skill 8.2 Demonstrating knowledge of the relationship of units within the U.S. and metric systems

"When you can measure what you are speaking about and express it in numbers, you know something about it; but when you cannot measure it, when you cannot express it in numbers, your knowledge is of a meager and unsatisfactory kind."

—Lord Kelvin

Non-standard units of measurement are sometimes used when standard instruments might not be available. For example, students might measure the length of a room by their arm-spans. An inch originated as the length of three barley grains placed end to end. Seeds or stones might be used for measuring weight. In fact, our current "carat," used for measuring precious gems, was derived from carob seeds. In ancient times, baskets, jars, and bowls were used to measure capacity.

To estimate measurement of familiar objects, it is first necessary to determine the units to be used.

Examples:

Length
1. The coastline of Florida miles or kilometers
2. The width of a ribbon inches or millimeters
3. The thickness of a book inches or centimeters
4. The length of a football field yards or meters
5. The depth of water in a pool feet or meters

Weight or mass
1. A bag of sugar pounds or grams
2. A school bus tons or kilograms
3. A dime ounces or grams

Capacity
1. Paint to paint a bedroom gallons or liters
2. Glass of milk cups or liters
3. Bottle of soda quarts or liters
4. Medicine for child ounces or milliliters

It is necessary to be familiar with the metric and customary system in order to estimate measurements.

Some common equivalents include:

ITEM	APPROXIMATELY EQUAL TO	
	METRIC	IMPERIAL
large paper clip	1 gram	0.1 ounce
	1 quart	1 liter
average sized man	75 kilograms	170 pounds
	1 yard	1 meter
math textbook	1 kilogram	2 pounds
	1 mile	1 kilometer
	1 foot	30 centimeters
thickness of a dime	1 millimeter	0.1 inches

Estimate the measurement of the following items:

the length of an adult cow = _____ meters
the thickness of a compact disc = _____ millimeters
your height = _____ meters
length of your nose = _____ centimeters
weight of your math textbook = _____ kilograms
weight of an automobile = _____ kilograms
weight of an aspirin = _____ grams

The units of **length** in the customary system are inches, feet, yards and miles.

> 12 inches (in.) = 1 foot (ft.)
> 36 in. = 1 yard (yd.)
> 3 ft. = 1 yd.
> 5280 ft. = 1 mile (mi.)
> 1760 yd. = 1 mi.

To change from a **larger unit to a smaller unit, multiply**.
To change from a **smaller unit to a larger unit, divide**.

Example:
4 mi. = _____ yd.
Since 1760 yd. = 1 mile, multiply 4 × 1760 = 7040 yd.

Example:
21 in. = _____ ft.
21 ÷ 12 = 1.75 ft. (or 1 foot and 9 inches)

The units of **weight** are ounces, pounds, and tons.

> 16 ounces (oz.) = 1 pound (lb.)
> 2,000 lb. = 1 ton (T.)

Example:
2 T. = _____ lb
$2 \times 2,000 = 4,000$ lb.

The units of **capacity** are fluid ounces, cups, pints, quarts, and gallons.

> 8 fluid ounces (fl. oz.) = 1 cup (c.)
> 2 c. = 1 pint (pt.)
> 4 c. = 1 quart (qt.)
> 2 pt. = 1 qt.
> 4 qt. = 1 gallon (gal.)

Example:
3 gal. = _____ qt.
$3 \times 4 = 12$ qt.

Example:
1 cups = _____ oz.
$1 \times 8 = 8$ oz.

Example:
7 c. = _____ pt.
$7 \div 2 = 3.5$ pt.

Square units can be derived with knowledge of basic units of length by squaring the equivalent measurements.

> 1 square foot (sq. ft.) = 144 sq. in.
> 1 sq. yd. = 9 sq. ft.
> 1 sq. yd. = 1296 sq. in.

Example:
14 sq. yd. = _____ sq. ft.
$14 \times 9 = 126$ sq. ft.

Metric Units

The metric system is based on multiples of <u>ten</u>. Conversions are made by simply moving the decimal point to the left or right.

kilo-	1000	thousands
hecto-	100	hundreds
deca-	10	tens
unit		
deci-	.1	tenths
centi-	.01	hundredths
milli-	.001	thousandths

The basic unit for **length** is the meter.
The basic unit for **weight** or mass is the gram.
The basic unit for **volume** is the liter.

These are the most commonly used units.

1 m = 100 cm	1000 mL= 1 L	1000 mg = 1 g
1 m = 1000 mm	1 kL = 1000 L	1 kg = 1000 g
1 cm = 10 mm		
1000 m = 1 km		

The prefixes are commonly listed from left to right for ease in conversion.

k h da U d c m

<u>Example:</u>
63 km = _____ m

Since there are 3 steps from <u>Kilo</u> to <u>Unit</u>, move the decimal point 3 places to the right.

63 km = 63,000 m

<u>Example:</u>
14 mL = _____ L

Since there are 3 steps from <u>Milli</u> to <u>Unit</u>, move the decimal point 3 places to the left.

14 mL = 0.014 L

<u>Example:</u>
56.4 cm = _____ mm

56.4 cm = 564 mm

Example:
9.1 m = _____ km
    9.1 m = 0.091 km

Example:
75 kg = _____ g
    75 kg = 75,000g

The distance around a circle is the **circumference**. The ratio of the circumference to the diameter is represented by the Greek letter pi.
$$\pi \sim 3.14 \sim$$

The circumference of a circle is found by the formula $C = 2\pi r$ or $C = \pi d$, where r is the radius of the circle and d is the diameter.

The **area** of a circle is found by the formula $A = \pi r^2$.

Example: Find the circumference and area of a circle whose radius is 7 meters.

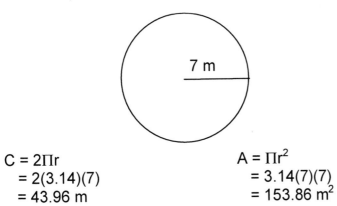

C = 2Πr $A = \Pi r^2$
  = 2(3.14)(7)   = 3.14(7)(7)
  = 43.96 m   = 153.86 m²

You can also compute the area remaining when sections are cut out of a given figure composed of triangles, squares, rectangles, parallelograms, trapezoids, or circles. The strategy for solving problems of this nature should be to identify the given shapes and choose the correct formulas. Subtract the smaller cut out shape from the larger shape.

Example: Find the area of one side of the metal in the circular flat washer shown below:

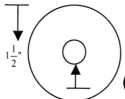

$1\frac{1}{2}"$

(Inside diameter is $3/8"$)

1. the shapes are both circles.

2. use the formula $A = \pi r^2$ for both.

Area of larger circle   Area of smaller circle

$A = \pi r^2$ $A = \pi r^2$

$A = \pi(.75^2)$ $A = \pi(.1875^2)$

$A = 1.76625\ in^2$ $A = .1104466\ in^2$

Area of metal washer = larger area - smaller area

$= 1.76625\ in^2 - .1104466\ in^2$

$= 1.6558034\ in^2$

Skill 8.3   Recognizing appropriate uses of standard measurement units, selecting appropriate measurement tools, measuring objects and events, and calculating rates and determining units.

Systems of Units

Customary or Imperial units are the everyday units used in the United States. Inches, feet, yards and miles are common units of **length.**

1 yard = 3 feet = 36 inches
1 mile = 1,760 yards

Rods, furlongs and acres (a unit of area) are less familiar units defined in terms of yards:

1 rod = 5 ½ yards
1 furlong = 220 yards
1 acre = 4,840 sq. yards = 160 sq. rods

The basic unit of **weight** is the pound (lb).

1 pound = 16 ounces (oz)
1 ounce = 16 drams
Short ton (U.S.) = 2,000 lb
Long ton (British) = 2,240 lb

The basic unit of **liquid measure** or liquid capacity is the gallon.

1 gallon = 4 quarts = 8 pints = 16 cups = 128 ounces

*The basic unit of **dry measure** or dry capacity is the bushel.*

1 bushel = 4 pecks = 32 dry quarts = 64 dry pints =

= 2,150.42 cubic inches
1 barrel = 105 dry quarts.

The **metric or SI system** is commonly used in many countries around the world for making measurements. This system is also a standard in scientific measurements. The metric system is convenient because units at different scales are related by multiples of ten (for instance, 1 meter = 10 decimeters).

The metric unit for **length** is the meter (m). The basic metric unit for **weight** or mass is the gram (g), and the basic metric unit for **volume** is the liter (L).

The following are the most commonly used units.

1 cm = 10 mm		
1 m = 1000 mm	1000 mL= 1 L	1000 mg = 1 g
1 m = 100 cm	1 kL = 1000 L	1 kg =1000 g
1000 m = 1 km		

Appropriate Units and Equivalents

Different units within the same system of measurement are selected based on the scale at which the measurement is being made. For example, the height of a person is measured in feet whereas the distances between cities are measured in miles. To estimate measurements of familiar objects, it is necessary to first determine the units to be used. Examples of particular items to be measured and appropriate units of measurement are given below.

Length
1. The coastline of Florida   miles or kilometers
2. The width of a ribbon   inches or millimeters
3. The thickness of a book   inches or centimeters
4. The length of a football field   yards or meters
5. The depth of water in a pool   feet or meters

Weight or mass
1. A bag of sugar   pounds or grams
2. A school bus   tons or kilograms
3. A dime   ounces or grams

Capacity
1. Bucket of paint for bedroom   gallons or liters
2. Glass of milk   cups or liters
3. Bottle of soda   quarts or liters
4. Medicine for child   ounces or milliliters

Selection of an appropriate tool or instrument for performing a given measurement is a crucial consideration. For instance, attempting to measure the coastline of Florida with a foot-long ruler would be a foolhardy exercise. The use of a computer program (such as a geographic information system—GIS—package) or satellite imagery (or a combination of these two) with a scale in miles would be a better choice. Thus, when choosing a method or instrument for measurement, it is necessary that the method or instrument be able to handle units that are of comparable magnitude to the object or event being measured. As a result, a stopwatch capable of measuring hundredths of a second might be appropriate for timing a runner in a 100-yard dash, but it would be entirely inadequate for determining the time it takes a beam of light to travel the same distance.

Conversions: Unit Analysis

There are many methods for converting measurements to other units within a system or between systems. One method is multiplication of the given measurement by a conversion factor. This conversion factor is the following ratio, which is always equal to unity.

$$\frac{\text{new units}}{\text{old units}} \quad \text{OR} \quad \frac{\text{what you want}}{\text{what you have}}$$

The fundamental feature of **unit analysis** (or **dimensional analysis**) is that conversion factors can be multiplied together and units cancelled in the same way as numerators and denominators of numerical fractions. The following examples help clarify this point.

Example: Convert 3 miles to yards.

Multiply the initial measurement by the conversion factor, cancel the mile units and solve:

$$\frac{3 \text{ miles}}{1} \times \frac{1,760 \text{ yards}}{1 \text{ mile}} = 5280 \text{ yards}$$

Example: It takes Cynthia 45 minutes to get ready each morning. How many hours does she spend getting ready each week?

Multiply the initial measurement by the conversion factors from minutes to hours and from days to weeks, cancel the minute and day units and solve:

$$\frac{45 \text{ min}}{\text{day}} \times \frac{1 \text{ hour}}{60 \text{ min}} \times \frac{7 \text{ days}}{\text{week}} = 5.25 \frac{\text{hours}}{\text{week}}$$

Conversion factors for different types of units are listed below:

Measurements of length (English system)

12 inches (in)	=	1 foot (ft)
3 feet (ft)	=	1 yard (yd)
1760 yards (yd)	=	1 mile (mi)

Measurements of length (metric system)

Kilometer (km)	=	1000 meters (m)
Hectometer (hm)	=	100 meters (m)
Decameter (dam)	=	10 meters (m)
Meter (m)	=	1 meter (m)
Decimeter (dm)	=	1/10 meter (m)
Centimeter (cm)	=	1/100 meter (m)
Millimeter (mm)	=	1/1000 meter (m)

Conversion of length from English to metric

1 inch	=	2.54 centimeters
1 foot	≈	30.48 centimeters
1 yard	≈	0.91 meters
1 mile	≈	1.61 kilometers

Measurements of weight (metric system)

kilogram (kg)	=	1000 grams (g)
gram (g)	=	1 gram (g)
milligram (mg)	=	1/1000 gram (g)

Conversion of weight from metric to English

28.35 grams (g)	=	1 ounce (oz)
16 ounces (oz)	=	1 pound (lb)
2000 pounds (lb)	=	1 ton (t) (short ton)
1.1 ton (t)	=	1 metric ton (t)

Conversion of weight from English to metric

1 ounce	≈	28.35 grams
1 pound	≈	0.454 kilogram
1.1 ton	=	1 metric ton

Measurement of volume (English system)

8 fluid ounces (oz)	=	1 cup (c)
2 cups (c)	=	1 pint (pt)
2 pints (pt)	=	1 quart (qt)
4 quarts (qt)	=	1 gallon (gal)

Measurement of volume (metric system)

Kiloliter (kl)	=	1000 liters (l)
Liter (l)	=	1 liter (l)
Milliliter (ml)	=	1/1000 liter (ml)

Conversion of volume from English to metric

1 teaspoon (tsp)	≈	5 milliliters
1 fluid ounce	≈	29.57 milliliters
1 cup	≈	0.24 liters
1 pint	≈	0.47 liters
1 quart	≈	0.95 liters
1 gallon	≈	3.8 liters

Note: (') represents feet and (") represents inches.

Example: Convert 8,750 meters to kilometers.

$$\frac{8,750 \text{ meters}}{1} \times \frac{1 \text{ kilometer}}{1000 \text{ meters}} = \frac{\quad}{\quad} \text{ km}$$

$$= 8.75 \text{ kilometers}$$

Example: 4 mi. = _____ yd.

1760 yd. = 1 mi.
4 mi. × 1760 yd./mi. = 7040 yd.

Square units can be derived with knowledge of basic units of length by squaring the equivalent measurements.

1 square foot (sq. ft. or ft^2) = 144 sq. in.
1 sq. yd. = 9 sq. ft.
1 sq. yd. = 1296 sq. in.

Example: 14 sq. yd. = _____ sq. ft.
            1 sq. yd. = 9 sq. ft.
            14 sq. yd. × 9 sq. ft./sq. yd. = 126 sq. ft.

Example: A car skidded 170 yards on an icy road before coming to a stop. How long is the skid distance in kilometers?

Since 1 yard ≈ 0.9 meters, multiply 170 yards by 0.9 meters/1 yard.

$$170 \text{ yd.} \times \frac{0.9 \text{ m}}{1 \text{ yd.}} = 153 \text{ m}$$

Since 1000 meters = 1 kilometer, multiply 153 meters by 1 kilometer/1000 meters.

$$153 \text{ m} \times \frac{1 \text{ km}}{1000 \text{ m}} = 0.153 \text{ km}$$

For more information on the appropriate uses of standard measurement units, **SEE** Skill 8.2

Calculating Rates

A **rate** is a change in a particular value with respect to a particular change of another value, which, in the context of real-world measurements, is often time. Speed is one particular example of a rate: the speed of an object is the change in its position divided by the corresponding change in time. Thus, a car that moves 1 mile in 1 minute has a speed (actually, an average speed) of 60 miles per hour. Other types of rates include flows of liquids (in gallons per hour, for instance), acceleration (in miles per hour squared, for instance), and slope (in vertical feet per horizontal foot, for instance).

Example: A water hose on full is able to fill a 5-gallon bucket in 20 seconds. What is the flow rate of water in the hose?

The rate of water flow in the hose is equal to 5 gallons divided by 20 seconds. We can use unit analysis to convert this to gallons per minute, which is a slightly more desirable measure.

$$\frac{5 \text{ gallons}}{20 \text{ seconds}} = 0.25 \frac{\text{gallons}}{\text{second}} \frac{60 \text{ seconds}}{1 \text{ minute}} = 15 \frac{\text{gallons}}{\text{minute}}$$

To solve word problems involving rates, first write the equation. To solve it, multiply each term by the LCD of all fractions. This will cancel out all of the denominators and give an equivalent algebraic equation that can be solved.

1. Elly Mae can feed the animals in 15 minutes. Jethro can feed them in 10 minutes. How long will it take them if they work together?

Solution: If Elly Mae can feed the animals in 15 minutes, then she could feed 1/15 of them in 1 minute, 2/15 of them in 2 minutes, $x/15$ of them in x minutes. In the same fashion, Jethro could feed $x/10$ of them in x minutes. Together they complete 1 job. The equation is:

$$\frac{x}{15} + \frac{x}{10} = 1$$

Multiply each term by the LCD of 30:

$$2x + 3x = 30$$
$$x = 6 \text{ minutes}$$

2. A salesman drove 480 miles from Pittsburgh to Hartford. The next day he returned the same distance to Pittsburgh in half an hour less time than his original trip took, because he increased his average speed by 4 mph. Find his original speed.

Since distance = rate x time   then   time = $\underline{\text{distance}}$
                                                                        rate

original time $- 1/2$ hour $=$ shorter return time

$$\frac{480}{x} - \frac{1}{2} = \frac{480}{x+4}$$

Multiplying by the LCD of $2x(x+4)$, the equation becomes:

$$480\ 2(x+4)\ -1\ x(x+4)\ = 480(2x)$$
$$960x + 3840 - x^2 - 4x = 960x$$
$$x^2 + 4x - 3840 = 0$$
$$(x+64)(x-60) = 0$$
$$x = 60 \qquad \qquad \text{60 mph is the original speed}$$
$$\text{64 mph is the faster return speed}$$

Skill 8.4   Applying knowledge of the concepts of precision, accuracy, and estimation.

Precision and Accuracy

Most numbers in mathematics are "exact" or "counted." Measurements are "approximate" and usually involve interpolation or determination of which mark on the ruler is the closest, for instance. Any measurement obtained with a measuring device is approximate; variations in measurement are defined in terms of precision and accuracy.

Precision measures the degree of variation in a particular measurement without reference to a true or real value. If a measurement is precise, it can be made repeatedly with little variation in the result. The precision of a measuring device is the smallest fractional or decimal division on the instrument. The smaller the unit or fraction of a unit on the measuring device, the more precisely it can measure.

Accuracy is a measure of how close the result of a measurement comes to the "true" value. Using the game of darts as a metaphor, the true value is the bull's eye. If three darts are tossed and each lands on the bull's eye, the dart thrower is both precise (all land near the same spot) and accurate (the darts all land on the "true" value). If the darts are all centered around the bull's eye but they land in various places, the thrower is accurate but not precise.

The greatest allowable measure of error allowed is called the **tolerance**. The least acceptable limit is called the lower limit, and the greatest acceptable limit is called the upper limit. The difference between the upper and lower limits is called the **tolerance interval**. For example, a specification for an automobile part might be 14.625 ± 0.005 mm. This means that the smallest acceptable length of the part is 14.620 mm and the largest acceptable length is 14.630 mm. The tolerance interval is 0.010 mm. One can see how it would be important for automobile parts to be within a set of limits in terms of physical dimensions. If the part is too long or too short, it will not fit properly and vibrations may occur, thereby weakening the part and eventually causing damage to other parts.

Error in measurement can also be expressed by a **percentage of error**. For example, a measurement of 12 feet can be said to be off by 2%. This means that the actual measurement could be between

12 – (2% of 12) and 12 + (2% of 12)
12 – (.02)12 and 12 + (.02)12
11.76 ft. and 12.24 feet

To determine the percent error between a measurement of a value and the actual value, use the following formula.

$$\text{Percent Error} = \frac{|\text{Measured} - \text{Actual}|}{\text{Actual}} \times 100$$

Error in measurement can also be indicated by the terms "rounded" or "to the nearest." When rounding to a given place value, it is necessary to look at the number in the next smaller place. If this number is 5 or more, the number in the place to which we are rounding is increased by one, and all numbers to the right are changed to zero. If the number is less than 5, the number in the place to which we are rounding stays the same, and all numbers to the right are changed to zero. For example, the length of a side of a square to the nearest inch may be 10 inches. This means that the actual length of the side could be between 9.5 inches and 10.4 inches (since all of these values round to 10).

Estimation

Rounding numbers is a form of estimation that is very useful in many mathematical operations. For example, when estimating the sum of two three-digit numbers, it is helpful to round the two numbers to the nearest hundred prior to addition. We can round numbers to any place value.

Rounding whole numbers

To round whole numbers, you first find the place value you want to round to (the rounding digit) and look at the digit directly to the right. If the digit is less than five, do not change the rounding digit and replace all numbers after the rounding digit with zeroes. If the digit is greater than or equal to five, increase the rounding digit by one and replace all numbers after the rounding digit with zeroes.

Example: Round 517 to the nearest ten.

1 is the rounding digit because it occupies the tens' place.

517 rounded to the nearest ten = 520; because 7 > 5 we add one to the rounding digit.

Example: Round 15,449 to the nearest hundred.

The first 4 is the rounding digit because it occupies the hundreds' place.

15,449 rounded to the nearest hundred = 15,400, because 4 < 5 we do not add to the rounding digit.

Rounding decimals

Rounding decimals is identical to rounding whole numbers except that you simply drop all the digits to the right of the rounding digit.

Example: Round 417.3621 to the nearest tenth.

3 is the rounding digit because it occupies the tenth place.

417.3621 rounded to the nearest tenth = 417.4; because 6 > 5 we add one to the rounding digit.

REGROUPING TO ESTIMATE DIFFERENCES

We can estimate the difference of two numbers by first rounding the numbers and then subtracting the rounded numbers. When subtracting two rounded numbers, one rounded up and the other rounded down, we can improve our estimate by regrouping. For example, when estimating the difference of 540 and 355, we round 540 down to 500 and 355 up to 400. Thus, our estimated difference is 500 minus 400, or 100. Note that we rounded 540 down by 40 and 355 up by 45. Thus, the total amount of rounding is 85. Rounding 85 up to 100 and adding this rounded sum to 100 (our original estimate) gives us a final estimated difference of 200. This is closer to the actual difference of 185 (540 – 355). The regrouping method of estimation only works when we round the two numbers in opposite directions.

FRONT END ESTIMATION

While we can add or subtract rounded numbers to estimate sums and differences, another method, front-end estimation, is simpler and usually delivers results that are just as accurate. Front-end estimation is an elementary form of estimation of sums and differences. To estimate a sum or difference by front-end estimation, we add or subtract only the two highest place values and filling the remaining place values with zeroes.

Example: Estimate 4987 + 3512 by front-end estimation.

The estimated sum is 8400 (4900 + 3500).

Note that we do not round the numbers, but merely drop the digits after the two highest place values. In other words, we convert 4987 to 4900, not 5000.

Example: Estimate 3894 – 617 by front-end estimation.

The estimated difference is 3200 (3800 – 600).

Note that because 617 does not have a digit in the thousands place and 3894 does, we convert 617 to 600, not 610.

Mental math and computational estimation techniques are often closely linked. Even modestly lengthy numbers can make mental calculation impossible in any reasonable amount of time. For instance, although relatively simple algorithms exist for multiplying numbers like 24 and 30, multiplication of numbers that involve many more places can be virtually impossible. Thus, good estimation skills are an integral part of much of mental math. Although estimation cannot provide exact answers generally, it can provide a way to check exact answers for reasonableness.

The most common estimation strategies taught in schools involve replacing numbers with ones that are simpler to compute with. These methods include **rounding off, front-end digit estimation** and **compensation**. Although rounding off is done to a specific place value (e.g., nearest ten or hundred), front-end estimation involves rounding off or truncating to whatever place value the first digit in a number represents. The following example uses front-end estimation.

Example: Estimate the answer:

$$\frac{58 \times 810}{1989}$$

By letting 58 become 60, 810 become 800, and 1989 become 2000, the following simplified expression can be evaluated (even mentally):

$$\frac{60 \times 800}{2000} = 24$$

Compensation involves replacing different numbers in different ways so that one change can more or less compensate for the other. For example, one might take the addition of 32 and 53 and convert this to the addition of 30 and 55, which are slightly easier to handle mentally. Here, both numbers are replaced in a way that minimizes the change; one number is increased and the other is decreased.

Another estimation strategy is to **estimate a range** for the correct answer. For example, given the addition 458 + 873, note the following inequalities:

458 + 873 > 400 + 800 = 1200
458 + 873 < 500 + 900 = 1400

Thus, one can estimate that the sum of 458 and 873 lies in the range of 1200 to 1400.

Converting to an **equivalent fraction, decimal, or percentage** can often be helpful. For example, to calculate 25% of 520, realize that 25% = 1/4 and simply divide 520 by 4 to get 130.

Clustering is a useful strategy when dealing with a set of numbers. Similar numbers can be clubbed together to simplify computation, as with the example addition below.

1210 + 655 + 1178 + 683 + 628 + 1223 + 599

Rewrite as follows:

600 + 600 + 600 + 600 + 1200 + 1200 + 1200.

Thus, an estimate of the sum is 6,000. (The exact value is 6176.)

Clubbing together **compatible numbers** is a variant of clustering. Here, instead of similar numbers, numbers that together produce easy-to-compute numbers are clubbed together. For instance, consider the following:

5 + 17 + 25 + 23 + 40 = (5+25) + (17+23) + 40

Often a problem does not require exact computation. An estimate may sometimes be all that is needed to solve a word problem as in the example below. Therefore, **assessing the needed level of precision** in a particular situation is an important skill.

Example: Janet goes into a store to purchase a CD on sale for $13.95. While shopping, she sees two pairs of shoes, prices $19.95 and $14.50. She only has $50. Can she purchase everything? (Assume there is no sales tax.)

Solve by rounding up to the nearest dollar:

$19.95→$20.00
$14.50→$15.00
$13.95→$14.00
        $49.00   Yes, she can purchase the CD and both pairs of shoes.

COMPETENCY 0009   **APPLY PRINCIPLES, CONCEPTS AND PROCEDURES RELATED TO STATISTICS AND PROBABILITY.**

Skill 9.1   **Identifying various methods (e.g., surveys, tables, graphs) of systematically collecting, organizing, and displaying data**

Suppose you want to look at the possible sequence of events for having two children in a family. Since a child will be either a boy or a girl, you would have the following tree diagram to illustrate the possible outcomes:

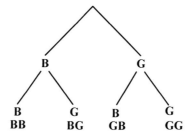

From the diagram, you see that there are 4 possible outcomes, 2 of which are the same.

SEE also Skills 1.1, 1.2 and 15.5

Skill 9.2   **Applying knowledge of statistical methods and technological tools to analyze data and describe shape, spread, and center (e.g., mean, median, mode, range)**

Mean, median and mode are three measures of central tendency. The **mean** is the average of the data items. The **median** is found by putting the data items in order from smallest to largest and selecting the item in the middle (or the average of the two items in the middle). The **mode** is the most frequently occurring item.

Range is a measure of variability. It is found by subtracting the smallest value from the largest value.

Example:
Find the mean, median, mode, and range of the test score listed below:

85   77   65
92   90   54
88   85   70
75   80   69
85   88   60
72   74   95

Mean = sum of all scores ÷ number of scores
       = 78

Median = put numbers in order from smallest to largest. Pick middle number.

54, 60, 65, 69, 70, 72, 74, 75, 77, 80, 85, 85, 85, 88, 88, 90, 92, 95
                    {both in middle}

Therefore, the median is average of two numbers in the middle, or 78.5

Mode = most frequent number
       = 85

Range = largest number minus the smallest number
       = 95 – 54
       = 41

Example: Different situations require different information. If we examine the circumstances under which an ice cream store owner may use statistics collected in the store, we find different uses for different information.

Over a 7-day period, the store owner collected data on the ice cream flavors sold. He found that the mean number of scoops sold was 174 per day. The most frequently sold flavor was vanilla. This information was useful in determining how much ice cream to order in all and in what amounts for each flavor.

In this case, the median and range had little business value for the owner.

Example: Consider the set of test scores from a math class: 0, 16, 19, 65, 65, 65, 68, 69, 70, 72, 73, 73, 75, 78, 80, 85, 88, and 92. The mean is 64.06 and the median is 71.

Since there are only three scores less than the mean out of the eighteen scores, the median (71) would be a more descriptive score.

Using Definitions in Statistical Data

An understanding of the definitions is important in determining the validity and uses of statistical data. All definitions and applications in this section apply to ungrouped data.

Data item: each piece of data is represented by the letter X.

Mean: the average of all data is represented by the symbol $\overline{X}$.

Sum of the Squares: sum of the squares of the differences between each item and the mean.
$$Sx^2 = (X - \overline{X})^2$$

Variance: the sum of the squares quantity divided by the number of items. (the lower case Greek letter sigma squared (σ^2)represents variance).
$$\frac{Sx^2}{N} = \sigma^2$$

The larger the value of the variance, the larger the spread

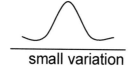

small variation   larger variation

Standard Deviation: the square root of the variance. The lower case Greek letter sigma (σ) is used to represent standard deviation.
$$\sigma = \sqrt{\sigma^2}$$

Most statistical calculators have standard deviation keys on them and should be used when asked to calculate statistical functions. It is important to become familiar with the calculator and the location of the keys needed.

Example: Given the ungrouped data below, calculate the mean, range, standard deviation, and variance.

15 22 28 25 34 38
18 25 30 33 19 23

Mean ($\overline{X}$) = 25.8333333
Range: $38 - 15 = 23$
standard deviation (σ) = 6.6936952
Variance (σ^2) = 44.805556

Skill 9.3   Making inferences based on analysis of experimental results, statistical data, and graphic representations

Combinations

Combinations are a way to demonstrate the number of ways in which elements can be arranged. Combination in probability does not involve any specific order.

For example, if you want to know how many different 12-person juries can be chosen from a pool of 20 jurors, you would use the formula:

$$_nC_r = \frac{n!}{r!(n-r)!}$$

$$\frac{20!}{12!(20-12)!} = 125,970$$

The difference between permutations and combinations is that in permutations, all the possible ways of writing an arrangement of objects are given; in a combination, a given arrangement of objects is listed only once.

Permutations

A permutation is similar to a combination, but it has an ordered arrangement.

For example, suppose 7 numbers are chosen for the lottery winning number from a possible 10 (zero to 9). The possible number of permutations would be determined as follows:

$$_nP_r = \frac{n!}{(n-r)!} = \frac{10!}{(10-7)!} = 604,800$$

Many problems involve finding both the combination and the permutation for a given set. In this way, the two concepts are inexorably linked.

<u>Example:</u>   Given the set {1, 2, 3, 4}, list the arrangements of two numbers that can be written as a combination and as a permutation.

Combination	Permutation
12, 13, 14, 23, 24, 34	12, 21, 13, 31, 14, 41, 23, 32, 24, 42, 34, 43,
six ways	twelve ways

Using the formulas given below, the same results can be found.

Permutation:

The notation $_nP_r$ is read "the number of permutations of n objects taken r at a time."

$$_nP_r = \frac{n!}{(n-r)!}$$

Substitute known values.

$$_4P_2 = \frac{4!}{(4-2)!}$$

Solve.

$$_4P_2 = 12$$

Combination:

The number of combinations when r objects are selected from n objects.

$$_nC_r = \frac{n!}{(n-r)!\,r!}$$

Substitute known values.

$$_4C_2 = \frac{4!}{(4-2)!\,2!}$$

Solve.

$$_4C_2 = 6$$

Skill 9.4   **Applying knowledge of how statistics can be used to support different points of view and identifying misuses of statistics and invalid conclusions**

Statistics are cited almost invariably, in one form or another, in studies and publications that seek to prove a point about people, animals, food, drugs, or any number of other subjects. Using summary statistics and graphs appropriately to support conclusions and predictions is a crucial skill to this end.

Summary statistics and graphs for one-variable data include the types of information (mean, median, mode, variance, etc.) and methods of display (the various types of data plots and diagrams) discussed above. Appropriate application of these statistics and methods of display requires knowledge of the particular area to which they are being applied as well as how well each aspect of the statistics represents the information. For example, consider the following frequency data distribution presented in histogram form. The frequencies (vertical axis) are shown for several discrete values (horizontal axis).

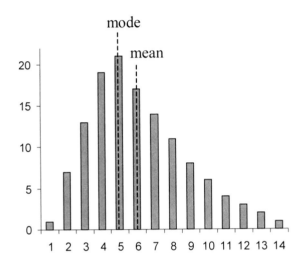

The (weighted) mean and mode of the data are labeled in the plot. Note that although the use of the mean for describing the data distribution is somewhat descriptive, it does not seem to be the best way to describe the data since it is off center. In some situations, this seemingly minor difference could drastically affect the conclusions or predictions made based on the data. Thus, means (or averages) can be deceptive or can lead to incorrect conclusions when they are used as summary statistics. If an appropriate graph or other method of displaying the data is included, however, the use of the mean as a measure of central tendency could be a little less deceptive or otherwise misleading.

As can be seen from the preceding example, then, selecting the appropriate set of numbers and visual displays for a given set of data is necessary to accurately summarize a set of data. Such accurate summary statistics are necessary to making proper predictions and to drawing warranted conclusions. The same considerations applied to measures of central tendency in the example also apply to data spread and distribution shape or skewness.

Misuse of Statistics

Statistics can be used both to inform and to mislead; thus, it is necessary to be able to discern between appropriate and inappropriate use of statistics. For instance, an improperly chosen measure of central tendency can mislead.

Consider a case where a population is divided almost exclusively into extremely poor and extremely rich. In some cases, the mean income (or other measure of wealth) might lead a reader to think that a significant number of people are in the middle class, even if no one qualifies for this categorization, simply because the average income happens to fall between rich and poor. Likewise, extremely broad distributions of particular variables can make measures of central tendency misleading as well.

In addition to the mathematical considerations associated with appropriate use of statistics, the linguistic aspect must also be considered. The numbers used in a statistical statement are interpreted in light of the language used with them. Thus, to say "Half of population X in this area contracts disease Y, therefore everyone should get tested" might not include the fact that the only ones who contract the particular disease are those who (for instance) work at a certain chemical plant—thus, only those who work at the plant would need testing for the disease. Thus, it is necessary that the use of statistics includes all relevant information.

Another common fallacy of statistics is mistaking association for causation.

Skill 9.5   Applying counting procedures to determine probabilities

Counting Procedures
So far, in all the problems we dealt with, the sample space was given or can be easily obtained. In many real life situations, the sample space and events within it are very large and difficult to find.

There are three techniques to help find the number of elements in one event or a sample space: counting principle, permutations, and combinations.

The Counting Principle: In a sequence of two distinct events in which the first one has n number of outcomes or possibilities, the second one has m number of outcomes or possibilities, the total number or possibilities of the sequence will be

$$n \cdot m$$

Example: A car dealership has three compact models and each model comes in a choice of four colors. How many compact cars are available at the dealership?

Number of available compact cars = (3)(4) = 12

Example: If a license plate consists of three digits followed by three letters, find the possible number of licenses if

a) the repetition of letters and digits are **not** allowed.
b) the repetition of letters and digits are allowed.

a) Since we have twenty-six letters and ten digits, using the counting principle, we get

possible # of licenses = (26)(25)(24)(10)(9)(8)
= 11,232,000

b) Since repetitions are allowed, we get

possible # of licenses = (26)(26)(26)(10)(10)(10)
= 17,576,000

The Addition Principle of Counting states:

If A and B are events, $n(A or B) = n(A) + n(B) - n(A \cap B)$.

Example: How many ways can you select a black card or a Jack from an ordinary deck of playing cards?

Let B denote the set of black cards and let J denote the set of Jacks. Then,

$$n(B) = 26, n(J) = 4, n(B \cap J) = 2$$
$$= 26 + 4 - 2$$
$$= 28$$

The Addition Principle of Counting for Mutually Exclusive Events states:

If A and B are mutually exclusive events, $n(A or B) = n(A) + n(B)$.

Example: A travel agency offers 40 possible trips: 14 to Asia, 16 to Europe and 10 to South America. How many trips can be taken to either Asia or Europe through this agency?

Let A denote trips to Asia and let E denote trips to Europe. Then, $A \cap E = \varnothing$ and
$n(A or E) = 14 + 16 = 30.$

Therefore, the number of trips to Asia or Europe is 30.

The Multiplication Principle of Counting for Dependent Events states:

Let A be a set of outcomes of Stage 1 and B a set of outcomes of Stage 2. The number of ways, $n(A \, and \, B)$, A and B can occur in a two-stage experiment is given by:

$$n(A \, and \, B) = n(A)n(B|A),$$

where $n(B|A)$ denotes the number of ways B can occur given that A has already occurred.

Example: How many ways from an ordinary deck of 52 cards can 2 Jacks be drawn in succession if the first card is drawn but not replaced in the deck and then the second card is drawn?

This is a two-stage experiment for which we wish to compute $n(A \, and \, B)$, where A is the set of outcomes for which a Jack is obtained on the first draw and B is the set of outcomes for which a Jack is obtained on the second draw.

If the first card drawn is a Jack, then there are only three remaining Jacks left to choose from on the second draw. Thus, drawing two cards without replacement means the events A and B are dependent.

$$n(A \, and \, B) = n(A)n(B|A) = 4 \cdot 3 = 12$$

The Multiplication Principle of Counting for Independent Events states:

Let A be a set of outcomes of Stage 1 and B a set of outcomes of Stage 2. If A and B are independent events, the number of ways, $n(A \, and \, B)$, A and B can occur in a two-stage experiment is given by:

$$n(A \, and \, B) = n(A)n(B).$$

Example: How many six-letter combinations can be formed if repetition of letters is not allowed?

A first letter *and* a second letter *and* a third letter *and* a fourth letter *and* a fifth letter *and* a sixth letter must be chosen, therefore there are six stages.

Since repetition is not allowed, there are 26 choices for the first letter, 25 for the second, 24 for the third, 23 for the fourth, 22 for the fifth and 21 for the sixth

n(six-letter combinations without repetition of letters)

$= 26 \cdot 25 \cdot 24 \cdot 23 \cdot 22 \cdot 21$
$= 165,765,600$

Permutations

In order to understand permutations, the concept of factorials must be discussed.

n factorial, written n!, is represented by $n! = n(n-1)(n-2) \ldots \ldots (2)(1)$

$$5! = (5)(4)(3)(2)(1) = 120$$
$$3! = 3(2)(1) = 6$$

By definition: $0! = 1$
$\qquad\qquad 1! = 1$

$$\frac{6!}{6!} = 1 \text{ but } \frac{6!}{2!} \neq 3!$$

$$\frac{6!}{2!} = \frac{6 \cdot 5 \cdot 4 \cdot 3 \cdot 2!}{2!} = 6 \cdot 5 \cdot 4 \cdot 3 = 360$$

The number of permutations represents the number of ways r items can be selected from n items and arranged in a specific order. It is written as $_nP_r$ and is calculated using the following relationship.

$$_nP_r = \frac{n!}{(n-r)!}$$

When calculating permutations, order counts. For example, 2, 3, 4 and 4, 3, 2 are counted as two different permutations. Calculating the number of permutations is not valid with experiments where replacement is allowed.

Example: How many different ways can a president and a vice president be selected from a math class if seven students are available?

We know we are looking for the number of permutations, since the positions of president and vice president are not equal.

$$_7P_2 = \frac{7!}{(7-2)!} = \frac{7!}{5!} = \frac{7 \cdot 6 \cdot 5!}{5!} = 7 \cdot 6 = 42$$

It is important to recognize that the number of permutations is a special case of the Counting Principle, which can also be used to solve problems dealing with the number of permutations. For instance, in this example we have seven available students to choose a president from. After a president is chosen, we have six available students to choose a vice president. Hence, using the Counting Principle, the ways a president and a vice president can be chosen = 7.6 = 42

Combinations

When dealing with the number of **combinations,** the order in which elements are selected is not important. For instance,

2, 3, 4 and 4, 2, 3 are considered the same combination.

The numbers of combinations represents the number of ways r elements are selected from n elements (in no particular order). The number of combinations is represented by $_nC_r$ and can be calculated using the following relationship.

$$_nC_r = \frac{n!}{(n-r)r!}$$

Example: In how many ways can two students be selected from a class of seven students to represent the class?

Since both representatives have the same position, the order is not important and we are dealing with the number of combinations.

$$_nC_r = \frac{7!}{(7-2)!2!} = \frac{7 \cdot 6 \cdot 5!}{5!2 \cdot 1} = 21$$

Example: In a club there are six women and four men. A committee of two women and one man is to be selected. How many different committees can be selected?

This problem has a sequence of two events. The first event involves selecting two women out of six women and the second event involves selecting one man out of four men. We use the combination relationship to find the number of ways events 1 and 2 can take place and the Counting Principle to find the number of ways the sequence can occur.

Number of possible committees = $_6C_2 \cdot {_4C_1}$

$$\frac{6!}{(6-2)!2!} x \frac{4!}{(4-1)!1!}$$
$$= \frac{6 \cdot 5 \cdot 4!}{4! \cdot 2 \cdot 1} x \frac{4 \cdot 3!}{3! \cdot 1}$$
$$= (15)x(4) = 60$$

Skill 9.6 **Applying properties of dependent and independent events to calculate probabilities**

Dependent events occur when the probability of the second event depends on the outcome of the first event. For example, consider the two events: A) it is sunny on Saturday and B) you go to the beach. If you intend to go to the beach on Saturday, rain or shine, then A and B may be independent. If however, you plan to go to the beach only if it is sunny, then A and B may be dependent. In this situation, the probability of event B will change depending on the outcome of event A.

Suppose you have a pair of dice: one red and one green. If you roll a three on the red die and then roll a four on the green die, we can see that these events do not depend on the other. The total probability of the two independent events can be found by multiplying the separate probabilities.

$$P(A \text{ and } B) = P(A) \times P(B)$$
$$= 1/6 \times 1/6$$
$$= 1/36$$

Many times, however, events are not independent. Suppose a jar contains 12 red marbles and 8 blue marbles. If you randomly pick a red marble, replace it, and then randomly pick again, the probability of picking a red marble the second time remains the same. However, if you pick a red marble, and then pick again without replacing the first red marble, the second pick becomes dependent upon the first pick.

$$P(\text{Red and Red}) \text{ with replacement} = P(\text{Red}) \times P(\text{Red})$$
$$= 12/20 \times 12/20$$
$$= 9/25$$

$$P(\text{Red and Red}) \text{ without replacement} = P(\text{Red}) \times P(\text{Red})$$
$$= 12/20 \times 11/19$$
$$= 33/95$$

Odds are defined as the ratio of the number of favorable outcomes to the number of unfavorable outcomes. The sum of the favorable outcomes and the unfavorable outcomes should always equal the total possible outcomes.

For example, given a bag of 12 red and 7 green marbles, compute the odds of randomly selecting a red marble.

$$\text{Odds of red} = \frac{12}{19} : \frac{7}{19} \text{ or } 12{:}7.$$

$$\text{Odds of not getting red} = \frac{7}{19} : \frac{12}{19} \text{ or } 7{:}12.$$

In the case of flipping a coin, it is equally likely that a head or a tail will be tossed. The odds of tossing a head are 1:1. This is called even odds.

Counting Techniques

The Addition Principle of Counting states:

If A and B are events, $n(AorB) = n(A) + n(B) - n(A \cap B)$.

Example: In how many ways can you select a black card or a Jack from an ordinary deck of playing cards?

Let B denote the set of black cards and let J denote the set of Jacks. Then, $n(B) = 26, n(J) = 4, n(B \cap J) = 2$ and
$$n(BorJ) = n(B) + n(J) - n(B \cap A)$$
$$= 26 + 4 - 2$$
$$= 28.$$

The Addition Principle of Counting for Mutually Exclusive Events states:

If A and B are mutually exclusive events, $n(AorB) = n(A) + n(B)$.

Example: A travel agency offers 40 possible trips: 14 to Asia, 16 to Europe, and 10 to South America. In how many ways can you select a trip to Asia or Europe through this agency?

Let A denote trips to Asia and let E denote trips to Europe. Then, $A \cap E = \varnothing$ and $n(AorE) = 14 + 16 = 30$.

Therefore, the number of ways you can select a trip to Asia or Europe is 30.

The Multiplication Principle of Counting for Dependent Events states:

Let A be a set of outcomes of Stage 1 and B a set of outcomes of Stage 2. Then the number of ways $\{n(AandB)\}$ that A and B can occur in a two-stage experiment is given by:
$$n(AandB) = n(A)n(B|A),$$

where $n(B|A)$ denotes the number of ways B can occur given that A has already occurred.

Example: How many ways from an ordinary deck of 52 cards can two Jacks be drawn in succession if the first card is drawn but not replaced in the deck and then the second card is drawn?

This is a two-stage experiment for which we wish to compute $n(AandB)$, where A is the set of outcomes for which a Jack is obtained on the first draw and B is the set of outcomes for which a Jack is obtained on the second draw.

If the first card drawn is a Jack, then there are only three remaining Jacks left to choose from on the second draw. Thus, drawing two cards without replacement means the events A and B are dependent.

$$n(AandB) = n(A)n(B|A) = 4 \cdot 3 = 12$$

The Multiplication Principle of Counting for Independent Events states:

Let A be a set of outcomes of Stage 1 and B a set of outcomes of Stage 2. If A and B are independent events, then the number of ways $n(AandB)$ that A and B can occur in a two-stage experiment is given by:

$$n(AandB) = n(A)n(B).$$

Example: How many six-letter code "words" can be formed if repetition of letters is not allowed?

Since these are code words, a word does not have to look like a word; for example, *abcdef* could be a code word. Since we must choose a first letter *and* a second letter *and* a third letter *and* a fourth letter *and* a fifth letter *and* a sixth letter, this experiment has six stages.

Since repetition is not allowed there are 26 choices for the first letter; 25 for the second; 24 for the third; 23 for the fourth; 22 for the fifth; and 21 for the sixth. Therefore, we have:

n(six-letter code words without repetition of letters)
$= 26 \cdot 25 \cdot 24 \cdot 23 \cdot 22 \cdot 21$
$= 165,765,600$

Skill 9.7   **Demonstrating knowledge of the use of tools (e.g., spinners, number cubes) and technology-based simulations to estimate probable outcomes**

Simulations of random events or variables can be helpful in making informal inferences about theoretical probability distributions. Although simulations can involve use of physical tools that bear some similarity to the situation of interest, they often involve computer modeling.

One of the crucial aspects of modeling probability using a computer program is the need for a random number that can be used to "randomize" the aspect of the program that corresponds to the event or variable. Although there is no function on a computer that can provide a truly random number, most programming languages have some function designed to produce a **pseudorandom number**. A pseudorandom number is not truly random, but it is sufficiently unpredictable that it can be used as a random number in many contexts.

Pseudorandom numbers can serve as the basis for simulation of rolling a die, flipping a coin, selecting an object from a collection of different objects, and a range of other situations. If, for instance, the pseudorandom number generator produces a number between zero and 1, simply divide up that range in accordance with the probabilities of each particular outcome. (For instance, assign 0 to 0.5 as heads and 0.5 to 1 as tails for the flip of a fair coin.) By performing a number of simulated trials and tallying the results, empirical probability distributions can be created.

Ideally, as the number of trials goes to infinity, the empirical probability distribution should approach the theoretical distribution. As a result, by performing a sufficiently large number of trials (this number must be at least somewhat justified for the particular situation) should allow informal inferences based on that data. Such inferences, however, must take into account the limitations of the computer, such as the inability to perform an infinite number of trials in finite time and the numerical inaccuracies that are an inherent part of computer programming.

When computers are unavailable or impractical, physical tools can instead be used to perform probability simulations. Spinners, for instance, are one possible means of simulating probabilities. An example would be simulating the roll of a fair six-sided die: if the spinner includes six (or some multiple thereof) equal areas, it can provide the same effect in terms of probability as rolling of a die. Spinning the arrow is effectively a random process (as long as there is no blatant attempt to produce certain results), so the results should be the same as the results for a die roll (each of the six areas should have a probability of 1/6 of being spun in any given spin).

The use of a spinner in place of a die (or number cube) is not necessarily practical, however, since dice are readily available and are themselves good tools for simulating probability. Likewise, coins or other flat objects can serve as probability simulation tools when events with two potential and equally probably outcomes are being studied.

DOMAIN II.   **SCIENCE**

COMPETENCY 0010   **UNDERSTAND MATTER AND ENERGY AND THEIR INTERACTION IN THE PHYSICAL SYSTEMS.**

Skill 10.1   Identifying the physical and chemical properties of matter

Everything in our world is made up of **matter**, whether it is a rock, a building, an animal, or a person. Matter is defined by its characteristics: it takes up space and it has mass.

Mass is a measure of the amount of matter in an object. Two objects of equal mass will balance each other on a simple balance scale no matter where the scale is located. For instance, two rocks with the same amount of mass that are in balance on Earth will also be in balance on the moon. They will feel heavier on the earth than on the moon because of the gravitational pull of the earth. Therefore, although the two rocks have the same mass, they will have different weight.

Weight is the measure of the earth's pull of gravity on an object. It can also be defined as the pull of gravity between other bodies. The units of weight measurement commonly used are the pound (English measure) and the kilogram (metric measure).

In addition to mass, matter also has the property of volume. **Volume** is the amount of cubic space that an object occupies. Volume and mass together give a more exact description of the object. Two objects may have the same volume, but different mass, or the same mass but different volumes. For instance, consider two cubes that are each one cubic centimeter, one made from plastic and one from lead. They have the same volume, but the lead cube has more mass. The measure that we use to describe the cubes takes into consideration both the mass and the volume. **Density** is the mass of a substance contained per unit of volume. If the density of an object is less than the density of a liquid, the object will float in the liquid. If the object is denser than the liquid, then the object will sink.

Density is stated in grams per cubic centimeter (g/cm^3), where the gram is the standard unit of mass. To find an object's density, you must measure its mass and its volume. Then divide the mass by the volume ($D = m/V$).
To discover an object's density, first use a balance to find its mass. Then calculate its volume. If the object is a regular shape, you can find the volume by multiplying the length, width, and height together. However, if it is an irregular shape, you can find the volume by seeing how much water it displaces. Measure the water in the container before and after the object is submerged. The difference will be the volume of the object.

Specific gravity is the ratio of the density of a substance to the density of water. For instance, the specific density of one liter of alcohol is calculated by comparing its mass (0.81 kg) to the mass of one liter of water (1 kg):

$$\frac{\text{mass of 1 L alcohol}}{\text{mass of 1 L water}} = \frac{0.81 \text{ kg}}{1.00 \text{ kg}} = 0.81$$

Physical properties and chemical properties of matter describe the appearance or behavior of a substance. A **physical property** can be observed without changing the identity of a substance. For instance, you can describe the color, mass, shape, and volume of a book. **Chemical properties** describe the ability of a substance to be changed into new substances. Baking powder goes through a chemical change as it changes into carbon dioxide gas during the baking process.

Matter constantly changes. A **physical change** is a change that does not produce a new substance. The freezing and melting of water is an example of physical change. A **chemical change** (or chemical reaction) is any change of a substance into one or more other substances. Burning materials turn into smoke; a seltzer tablet fizzes into gas bubbles. The **phase of matter** (solid, liquid, or gas) is identified by its shape and volume.

A **solid** has a definite shape and volume. A **liquid** has a definite volume, but no shape. A **gas** has no shape or volume because it will spread out to occupy the entire space of whatever container it is in. While **plasma** is really a type of gas, its properties are so unique that it is considered a unique phase of matter.

Plasma is a gas that has been ionized, meaning that at least one electron has been removed from some of its atoms. Plasma shares some characteristics with gas, specifically, the high kinetic energy of its molecules. Thus, plasma exists as a diffuse "cloud," though it sometimes includes tiny grains (this is termed **dusty plasma**). What most distinguishes plasma from gas is that it is electrically conductive and exhibits a strong response to electromagnetic fields. This property is a consequence of the charged particles that result from the removal of electrons from the molecules in the plasma.

Energy is the ability to cause changes in matter. Applying heat to a frozen liquid changes it from solid back to liquid. Continue heating it and it will boil and give off steam, a gas. **Evaporation** is the change in phase from liquid to gas. **Condensation** is the change in phase from gas to liquid.

Skill 10.2   Distinguishing physical and chemical changes in matter

SEE Skill 10.1

Skill 10.3   Demonstrating knowledge of how energy is transformed from one form into another and methods of energy transfer (e.g., conduction, convection, radiation)

The kinetic theory states that matter consists of molecules that possess kinetic energies in continual random motion. The state of matter (solid, liquid, or gas) depends on the speed of the molecules and the amount of kinetic energy the molecules possess. The molecules of solid matter merely vibrate, allowing strong intermolecular forces to hold the molecules in place. The molecules of liquid matter move freely and quickly throughout the body and the molecules of gaseous matter move randomly and at high speeds.

Matter changes state when energy is added or taken away. The addition of energy, usually in the form of heat, increases the speed and kinetic energy of the component molecules. Faster moving molecules more readily overcome the intermolecular attractions that maintain the form of solids and liquids. In conclusion, as the speed of molecules increases, matter changes state from solid to liquid to gas (melting and evaporation).

As matter loses heat energy to the environment, the speed of the component molecules decrease. Intermolecular forces have greater impact on slower moving molecules. Thus, as the speed of molecules decrease, matter changes from gas to liquid to solid (condensation and freezing).

Heat and temperature are different physical quantities. **Heat** is a measure of energy. **Temperature** is the measure of how hot (or cold) a body is with respect to a standard object.

Two concepts are important in the discussion of temperature changes. Objects are in thermal contact if they can affect each other's temperatures. Set a hot cup of coffee on a desk top. The two objects are in thermal contact with each other and will begin affecting each other's temperatures. The coffee will become cooler and the desktop warmer. Eventually, they will have the same temperature. When this happens, they are in **thermal equilibrium.**

We cannot rely on our sense of touch to determine temperature because the heat from a hand may be conducted more efficiently by certain objects, making them feel colder. **Thermometers** are used to measure temperature. In thermometers, a small amount of mercury in a capillary tube will expand when heated. The thermometer and the object whose temperature it is measuring are put in contact long enough for them to reach thermal equilibrium. The temperature can then be read from the thermometer scale.

Three temperature scales are used:

Celsius: The freezing point of water is set at 0 and the steam (boiling) point is 100. The interval between the two is divided into 100 equal parts called degrees Celsius.

Fahrenheit: The freezing point of water is 32 degrees and the boiling point is 212. The interval between is divided into 180 equal parts called degrees Fahrenheit.

Temperature readings can be converted from one to the other as follows.

Fahrenheit to Celsius	Celsius to Fahrenheit
$C = 5/9 \ (F - 32)$	$F = (9/5) \ C + 32$

The **Kelvin scale** has degrees the same size as the Celsius scale, but the zero point is moved to the triple point of water. Water inside a closed vessel is in thermal equilibrium in all three states (ice, water, and vapor) at 273.15 degrees Kelvin. This temperature is equivalent to .01 degrees Celsius. Because the degrees are the same in the two scales, temperature changes are the same in Celsius and Kelvin.

Temperature readings can be converted from Celsius to Kelvin:

Celsius to Kelvin	Kelvin to Celsius
$K = C + 273.15$	$C = K - 273.15$

The **heat capacity** of an object is the amount of heat energy it takes to raise the temperature of the object by one degree.

Heat capacity (C) per unit mass (m) is called **specific heat** (c):

$$c = \frac{C}{m} = \frac{Q}{m}$$

There are a number of ways that heat is measured. In each case, the measurement is dependent upon raising the temperature of a specific amount of water by a specific amount. These conversions of heat energy and work are called the **mechanical equivalent of heat**.

A **calorie** is the amount of energy that it takes to raise one gram of water one degree Celsius.

A **kilocalorie** is the amount of energy that it takes to raise one kilogram of water by one degree Celsius. Food calories are kilocalories.

In the International System of Units **(SI)**, the calorie is equal to 4.184 **joules**.

A **British thermal unit (BTU)** = 252 calories = 1.054 kJ

Heat energy that is transferred into or out of a system is **heat transfer.** The temperature change is positive for a gain in heat energy and negative when heat is removed from the object or system.

The formula for heat transfer is $Q = mc\Delta T$ where Q is the amount of heat energy transferred, m is the amount of substance (in kilograms), c is the specific heat of the substance, and ΔT is the change in temperature of the substance. It is important to assume that the objects in thermal contact are isolated and insulated from their surroundings.

If a substance in a closed container loses heat, then another substance in the container must gain heat.

A **calorimeter** uses the transfer of heat from one substance to another to determine the specific heat of the substance. When an object undergoes a change of phase it goes from one physical state (solid, liquid, or gas) to another. For instance, water can go from liquid to solid (freezing) or from liquid to gas (boiling). The heat that is required to change from one state to the other is called **latent heat.**

The **heat of fusion** is the amount of heat that it takes to change from a solid to a liquid or the amount of heat released during the change from liquid to solid.

The **heat of vaporization** is the amount of heat that it takes to change from a liquid to a gaseous state.

Heat is transferred in three ways: conduction, convection, and radiation.

Conduction occurs when heat travels through the heated solid. The transfer rate is the ratio of the amount of heat per amount of time it takes to transfer heat from area of an object to another. For example, if you place an iron pan on a flame, the handle will eventually become hot. How fast the handle gets too hot to handle is a function of the amount of heat and how long it is applied. Because the change in time is in the denominator of the function, the shorter the amount of time it takes to heat the handle, the greater the transfer rate.

Convection is heat transported by the movement of a heated substance. Warmed air rising from a heat source such as a fire or electric heater is a common example of convection. Convection ovens make use of circulating air to more efficiently cook food.

Radiation is heat transfer as the result of electromagnetic waves. The sun warms the earth by emitting radiant energy.

An example of all three methods of heat transfer occurs in a thermos bottle or Dewar flask. The bottle is constructed of double walls of Pyrex glass that have a space in between. Air is evacuated from the space between the walls and the inner wall is silvered. The lack of air between the walls lessens heat loss by convection and conduction. The heat inside is reflected by the silver, cutting down heat transfer by radiation. Hot liquids remain hotter and cold liquids remain colder for longer periods of time.

The relationship between heat, forms of energy, and work (mechanical, electrical, etc.) are the **Laws of Thermodynamics.** These laws deal strictly with systems in thermal equilibrium and not those within the process of rapid change or in a state of transition. Systems that are nearly always in a state of equilibrium are called **reversible systems.**

The first law of thermodynamics is a restatement of conservation of energy. The change in heat energy supplied to a system (Q) is equal to the sum of the change in the internal energy (U) and the change in the work done by the system against internal forces.

$$\Delta Q = \Delta U + \Delta W$$

The second law of thermodynamics is stated in two parts:

1. No machine is 100 percent efficient. It is impossible to construct a machine that only absorbs heat from a heat source and performs an equal amount of work because some heat will always be lost to the environment.

2. Heat cannot spontaneously pass from a colder to a hotter object. An ice cube sitting on a hot sidewalk will melt into a little puddle, but it will never spontaneously cool and form the same ice cube. Certain events have a preferred direction called the **arrow of time.**

Entropy is the measure of how much energy or heat is available for work. Work occurs only when heat is transferred from hot to cooler objects. Once this is done, no more work can be extracted. The energy is still being conserved, but it is not available for work as long as the objects are the same temperature. Theory has it that, eventually, all things in the universe will reach the same temperature. If this happens, energy will no longer be usable.

Skill 10.4 Recognizing properties, characteristics, and behaviors of sound, water, and light waves

Waves

A mechanical wave is a disturbance that propagates through a medium at a speed characteristic of the medium. There is a transfer of energy, but there is not a bulk transfer of matter. In the case of sound, for example, the medium is air and the disturbance is produced by perhaps a tuning fork that vibrates at a fixed rate. Each single disturbance produces a pulse.

Sound waves are produced by a vibrating body. The vibrating object moves forward and compresses the air in front of it, then reverses direction so that pressure on the air is lessened and expansion of the air molecules occurs. The vibrating air molecules move back and forth parallel to the direction of motion of the wave as they pass the energy from adjacent air molecules closer to the source to air molecules farther away from the source.

The speed of a wave is the speed the disturbance propagates through the medium. The period of a wave is the time between disturbances and the frequency is the inverse of the period. The unit of measure for frequencies is the hertz which is 1/second. The amplitude of a wave is a measure of how much the medium is being distorted. In the case of water waves, the amplitude is the height of the wave. The wavelength of a wave is the distance between the pulses or individual disturbances. The wave equation relates the frequency (f), wavelength (λ), and speed (v) of a wave: $v = \lambda f$.

Waves are also longitudinal or transverse. In transverse waves, the disturbance of the medium is perpendicular to the direction of motion of the disturbance. In longitudinal waves, the disturbance is parallel to the direction of motion. Water waves are an example of transverse waves. Sound is a longitudinal wave. A tuning fork, for example, creates alternate areas of compression of the air and rarefaction of the air.

Sound Waves

In the case of sound waves, the frequency produces the sensation of pitch when you hear it and the amplitude produces the sensation of loudness. The pitch used for tuning in Western music is 440 Hz. The intensity of a sound wave is measured in decibels.

Water Waves

Everything from earthquakes to ship wakes creates water waves; however, the most common cause is wind. As wind passes over the water's surface, friction forces it to ripple. The strength of the wind, the distance the wind blows (fetch) and the length of the gust (duration) determine how big the ripples will become. Waves are divided into several parts. The crest is the highest point on a wave, while the trough or valley between two waves is the lowest point. Wavelength is the horizontal distance, either between the crests or troughs, of two consecutive waves. Wave height is a vertical distance between a wave's crest and the next trough. The wave period can be measured by picking a stationary point and counting the seconds it takes for two consecutive crests or troughs to pass it.

If we followed a single drop of water during a passing wave, we would see it move in a vertical circle, returning to a point near its original position at the wave's end. These vertical circles are more obvious at the surface. As depth increases, their effects slowly decrease until completely disappearing about half a wavelength below the surface.

Light Waves

Visible light, radio waves, X-rays, microwaves, gamma rays, and radar consist of vibrating electric and magnetic fields. They are waves, but not mechanical waves because they travel through a vacuum. The speed of this radiation is 186,000 miles per second or 3×10^8 meters per second. Clerk Maxwell derived the speed of light in the 19th century from measurement in electricity and magnetism.

The electric and magnetic fields are perpendicular to each other and to the direction of propagation of the wave. Hence, **electromagnetic radiation** is a transverse wave. A look at a chart of electromagnetic radiation will show the different types of radiation and their wavelength and frequency. AM radio waves have a wavelength of 100 meters and a frequency of 10^6 Hz. High-energy gamma rays have a wavelength of 10^{24} Hz and a correspondingly small wavelength.

Skill 10.5 Demonstrating knowledge of basic concepts related to electricity and magnetism

Circuit breakers and fuses in a home monitor the electric current. If there is an overload, the circuit breaker will create an open circuit, stopping the flow of electricity in the fuse box, where no fire can start. Resistors are used to regulate volume on a television or radio or through a dimmer switch for lights.

Electrostatics is the study of stationary electric charges. A plastic rod that is rubbed with fur or a glass rod that is rubbed with silk will become electrically charged. The charge on the plastic rod is negative because electrons from the fur transfer to the plastic rod.

A simple device used to indicate the existence of a positive or negative charge is called an electroscope. An electroscope is made up of a metal knob with very lightweight leaves of aluminum foil attached to it. When a charged object touches the knob, the leaves push away from each other because like charges repel. It is not possible to tell whether if the charge is positive or negative. If the charged object is positive, electrons will flow from the electroscope into the charged object, making the leaves and the knob positive.

A metal rod can be given a charge by placing it in water. Water molecules are polar, that is, they have a positive side and a negative side. A metal consists of a lattice of positively charged nuclei in a sea of electrons. Water molecules will surround a metallic nuclei and cause it to go into solution, leaving behind a negative charge on the metal rod. The concentration of charge on the metal, or voltage, is determined by the properties of the metal. A battery is constructed by placing two different types of metals (terminals) in water, thereby producing a voltage difference. Voltage is measured in units called volts.

A battery produces an electric current when a wire connects the two terminals of the battery. The voltage difference will cause electrons to flow at a slow drift velocity from one terminal to the other. At the same time, metal ions will reattach to one terminal and be removed from the other until the battery goes dead. The unit of measurement for current is the ampere (amp).

Electricity can be used to change the chemical composition of a material. For instance, when electricity is passed through water, it breaks the water down into hydrogen gas and oxygen gas.

Magnets are objects with a north pole and a south pole. Like poles repel and unlike poles attract. Magnets exert a force on other magnets and on moving electric charges. A magnet creates a magnetic field is the space around it, and it is the magnetic field that exerts the force.

Magnetic fields are created by moving charges. A current flowing in a straight wire produces a circular magnetic field pointing in a direction determined by the direction of current flow. There is no north pole or south pole. However, if the wire forms a loop or circle, the magnetic field lines will enter one side of the loop and exit the other side. The side they exit is the north pole and the side the enter is the south pole. By wrapping wire around a pole, you can stack these current loops and produce a very strong magnet. Such a device is called an electromagnet.

Electrons behave like tiny magnets because they are rotating about their own axis. Electrons in an atom are also rotating around the nucleus and are creating a magnetic field in this way as well. Protons also produce a magnetic field. Most substances are not magnetized because the magnetic fields produced by electrons, atoms, and protons cancel out.

When an object is brought close to a magnet, the object will become magnetized. In other words, a north pole and south pole will be induced on the object. A few substances are diamagnetic, but all other substances are paramagnetic. With paramagnetic substances a north pole induces a south pole and the paramagnet is attracted to the magnet.

Ferromagnetism is a special case of paramagnetism. The main ferromagnetic materials are iron, nickel, and cobalt. The nuclei of these substances are connected is such a way that small magnetic domains are created where the magnetic poles of the atoms are all aligned. The north and south poles of the domains are random within the substance, but an external magnetic field will line them up and a permanent magnet can be created.

Magnetic Force occurs when magnetized items interact with other items in very specific ways. If a magnet is brought close enough to a ferromagnetic material (that is not magnetized itself) the magnet will strongly attract the ferromagnetic material regardless of orientation. Both the north and south pole of the magnet will attract the other item with equal strength. In opposition, diamagnetic materials weakly repel a magnetic field. This occurs regardless of the north/south orientation of the field. Paramagnetic materials are weakly attracted to a magnetic field. This occurs regardless of the north/south orientation of the field. Calculating the attractive or repulsive magnetic force between two magnets is, in the general case, an extremely complex operation, as it depends on the shape, magnetization, orientation, and separation of the magnets.

The electric and magnetic fields are perpendicular to each other and to the direction of propagation of the wave. Hence, electromagnetic radiation is a transverse wave. A look at a chart of electromagnetic radiation will show the different types of radiation and their wavelength and frequency. AM radio waves have a wavelength of 100 meters and a frequency of 10^6 Hz. High-energy gamma rays have a wavelength of 10^{24} Hz and a correspondingly small wavelength.

Skill 10.6   Comparing and contrasting characteristics of elements, atoms, molecules, mixtures, and compounds

An **element** is a substance that cannot be broken down into other substances. To date, scientists have identified 109 elements: 89 are found in nature and 20 are synthetic.

An **atom** is the smallest particle of an element that retains the properties of that element. All of the atoms of a particular element are the same. The atoms of each element are different from the atoms of other elements. Elements are assigned an identifying symbol of one or two letters. The symbol for oxygen is O; it stands for one atom of oxygen. However, because oxygen atoms in nature are joined together in pairs, the symbol O_2 represents oxygen.

This pair of oxygen atoms is a molecule. A **molecule** is the smallest particle of a substance that can exist independently and still have all of the properties of that substance. A molecule of most elements is made up of one atom. However, oxygen, hydrogen, nitrogen, and chlorine molecules are made of two atoms each.

A **compound** is made of two or more elements that have been chemically combined. Atoms join together when elements are chemically combined. The result is that the elements lose their individual identities; the compound that they become has different properties.

We use a formula to show the elements of a chemical compound. A **chemical formula** is a shorthand way of showing what is in a compound through symbols and subscripts. The letter symbols let us know what elements are involved and the number subscript tells how many atoms of each element are involved. No subscript is used if there is only one atom involved. For example, carbon dioxide is made up of one atom of carbon (C) and two atoms of oxygen (O_2), so the formula would be represented as CO_2.

Substances can combine without a chemical change. A **mixture** is any combination of two or more substances in which the substances keep their own properties. A fruit salad is a mixture (so is an ice cream sundae, although you might not recognize each part if it is stirred together). Colognes and perfumes are other examples. You may not readily recognize the individual elements; however, they can be separated.

Compounds and mixtures are similar in that they are made up of two or more substances. However, they have the following opposite characteristics:

Compounds:
- Made up of one kind of particle
- Formed during a chemical change
- Broken down only by chemical changes
- Properties are different from their parts
- Has a specific amount of each ingredient.

Mixtures:
- Made up of two or more particles
- Not formed by a chemical change
- Can be separated by physical changes
- Properties are the same as their parts.
- Do not have a definite amount of each ingredient.

Common compounds are **acids, bases, salts**, and **oxides**. These are classified according to their characteristics.

Atoms

The **nucleus** is the center of the atom. The positive particles inside the nucleus are called **protons.** The mass of a proton is about 2,000 times that of the mass of an electron. The number of protons in the nucleus of an atom is called the **atomic number**. All atoms of the same element have the same atomic number.

Neutrons are another type of particle in the nucleus. Neutrons and protons have about the same mass, but neutrons have no charge. Neutrons were discovered because scientists observed that not all atoms in neon gas have the same mass. They had identified isotopes. **Isotopes** of an element have the same number of protons in the nucleus, but have different masses. Neutrons explain the difference in mass.

The mass of matter is measured against a standard mass such as the gram. Scientists measure the mass of an atom by comparing it to that of a standard atom. The result is relative mass. The **relative mass** of an atom is its mass expressed in terms of the mass of the standard atom. The isotope of the element carbon is the standard atom. It has six (6) neutrons and is called carbon-12. It is assigned a mass of 12 atomic mass units (amu). Therefore, the **atomic mass unit (amu)** is the standard unit for measuring the mass of an atom. It is equal to the mass of a carbon atom.

The **mass number** of an atom is the sum of its protons and neutrons. In any element, there is a mixture of isotopes, some having slightly more or slightly fewer protons and neutrons. The **atomic mass** of an element is an average of the mass numbers of its atoms.

The following table summarizes the terms used to describe atomic nuclei:

Term	Example	Meaning	Characteristic
Atomic Number	# protons (p)	same for all atoms of a given element	Carbon (C) atomic number = 6 (6p)
Mass number	# protons + # neutrons (p + n)	changes for different isotopes of an element	C-12 (6p + 6n) C-13 (6p + 7n)
Atomic mass	average mass of the atoms of the element[BCA4]	usually not a whole number	atomic mass of carbon equals 12.011

Each atom has an equal number of electrons (negative) and protons (positive). Therefore, atoms are neutral. Electrons orbiting the nucleus occupy energy levels that are arranged in order and the electrons tend to occupy the lowest energy level available. A **stable electron arrangement** is an atom that has all of its electrons in the lowest possible energy levels.

Each energy level holds a maximum number of electrons. However, an atom with more than one level does not hold more than eight electrons in its outermost shell.

Level	Name	Max. # of Electrons
First	K shell	2
Second	L shell	8
Third	M shell	18
Fourth	N shell	32

This can help to explain why chemical reactions occur. Atoms react with each other when their outer levels are unfilled. When atoms either exchange or share electrons with each other, these energy levels become filled and the atom becomes more stable.

As an electron gains energy, it moves from one energy level to a higher energy level. The electron cannot leave one level until it has enough energy to reach the next level. **Excited electrons** are electrons that have absorbed energy and have moved farther from the nucleus.

Electrons can also lose energy. When they do, they fall to a lower level. However, they can only fall to the lowest level that has room for them. This explains why atoms do not collapse.

Skill 10.7   Recognizing that energy and matter are conserved in chemical and physical systems

The law of conservation of energy states that energy is neither created nor destroyed. Thus, energy changes form when energy transactions occur in nature. Because the total energy in the universe is constant, energy continually transitions between forms. For example, an engine burns gasoline, converting the chemical energy of the gasoline into mechanical energy; a plant converts radiant energy of the sun into chemical energy found in glucose; and a battery converts chemical energy into electrical energy.

Chemical reactions are the interactions of substances that result in chemical changes and changes in energy. Chemical reactions involve changes in electron motion as well as the breaking and forming of chemical bonds. **Reactants** are the original substances that interact to form distinct products. **Endothermic** chemical reactions consume energy while **exothermic** chemical reactions release energy with product formation. Chemical reactions occur continually in nature and are also induced by man for many purposes.

Nuclear reactions, or **atomic reactions**, are reactions that change the composition, energy, or structure of atomic nuclei. Nuclear reactions change the number of protons and neutrons in the nucleus. The two main types of nuclear reactions are **fission** (splitting of nuclei) and **fusion** (joining of nuclei). Fusion reactions are exothermic, releasing heat energy. Fission reactions are endothermic, absorbing heat energy. Fission of large nuclei (e.g., uranium) releases energy because the products of fission undergo further fusion reactions. Fission and fusion reactions can occur naturally, but are most recognized as manmade events. Particle acceleration and bombardment with neutrons are two methods of inducing nuclear reactions.

The law of conservation can also be applied to physical and biological processes. For example, when a rock is weathered, it does not just lose pieces. Instead it is broken down into its composite minerals, many of which enter the soil. Biology takes advantage of decomposers to recycle decaying material. Since energy is neither created nor destroyed, we know it must change form. An animal may die, but its body will be consumed by other animals or decay into the ecosystem. Either way, it enters another form and the matter still exists—it was not destroyed.

Dynamics is the study of the relationship between motion and the forces affecting motion. **Force** causes motion. Surfaces that touch each other have a certain resistance to motion. This resistance is **friction.**

1. The materials that make up the surfaces will determine the magnitude of the frictional force.
2. The frictional force is independent of the area of contact between the two surfaces.
3. The direction of the frictional force is opposite to the direction of motion.
4. The frictional force is proportional to the normal force between the two surfaces in contact.

Static friction describes the force of friction of two surfaces that are in contact but do not have any motion relative to each other, such as a block sitting on an inclined plane.

Kinetic friction describes the force of friction of two surfaces in contact with each other when there is relative motion between the surfaces.
When an object moves in a circular path, a force must be directed toward the center of the circle in order to keep the motion going. This constraining force is called **centripetal force.** Gravity is the centripetal force that keeps a satellite circling the earth.

In the **Nuclear Force**, the protons in the nucleus of an atom are positively charged. If protons interact, they are usually pushed apart by the electromagnetic force. However, when two or more nuclei come VERY close together, the nuclear force comes into play. The nuclear force is a hundred times stronger than the electromagnetic force, so the nuclear force may be able to "glue" the nuclei together to allow fusion to happen. The nuclear force is also known as the **strong force.** The nuclear force keeps together the most basic of elementary particles, the **quarks.** Quarks combine together to form the protons and neutrons in the atomic nucleus.

COMPETENCY 0011   UNDERSTAND THE INTERACTION OF FORCE,
MASS, AND MOTION IN PHYSICAL SYSTEMS

Skill 11.1   Applying knowledge of Newton's three laws of motion and
solving problems involving the force, mass, and motion of
objects in everyday phenomena

Electrical force is the influential power that results from electricity as an
attractive or repulsive interaction between two charged objects. The electric
force is determined using Coulomb's law. As shown below, the appropriate unit
on charge is the Coulomb (C) and the appropriate unit on distance is meters
(m). Use of these units will result in a force expressed in units of Newtons. The
demand for these units emerges from the units on Coulomb's constant.

$$F_{elect} = k \cdot Q_1 \cdot Q_2 / d^2$$

There is something of a mystery as to how objects affect each other when they
are not in mechanical contact. Newton wrestled with the concept of "action-at-a-
distance" (as Electrical Force is now classified) and eventually concluded that it
was necessary for there to be some form of ether, or intermediate medium,
which made it possible for one object to transfer force to another. We now know
that no ether exists. It is possible for objects to exert forces on one another
without any medium to transfer the force. From our fluid notion of electrical
forces, however, we still associate forces as being due to the exchange of
something between the two objects. The electrical field force acts between two
charges, in the same way that the gravitational field force acts between two
masses.

The **force of gravity** is the force at which the earth, moon, or other massively
large object attracts another object towards itself. By definition, this is the weight
of the object. All objects upon earth experience a force of gravity that is directed
"downward" towards the center of the earth. The force of gravity on earth is
always equal to the weight of the object as found by the equation:

Fgrav = m x g

where g = 9.8 m/s^2 (on Earth)
and m = mass (in kg)

Newton's Laws of Motion:

Newton's first law of motion is also called the law of inertia. It states that an
object at rest will remain at rest and an object in motion will remain in motion at
a constant velocity unless acted upon by an external force.

Newton's second law of motion states that if a net force acts on an object, it will cause the acceleration of the object. The relationship between force and motion is *force equals mass times acceleration.*   (F = ma)

Newton's third law states that for every action there is an equal and opposite reaction. Therefore, if an object exerts a force on another object, that second object exerts an equal and opposite force on the first.

Skill 11.2   Analyzing graphs that represent the motion of objects in terms of distance, time, velocity, and acceleration

Dynamics is the study of the relationship between motion and the forces affecting motion. Forces cause objects to move and can be understood as a push or a pull.

The force of gravity is the force that causes objects to fall to Earth. We can feel the force of gravity when we lift something up. The force of gravity also keeps the moon rotating around Earth and Earth rotating around the sun. The universal law of gravity states that there is a gravitational attraction between all objects on Earth determined by the equation:

$$F_{\text{gravity}} = G \frac{m_1 m_2}{d^2}$$

where G is the universal gravitational constant and d is the distance between the two masses. Mass and weight are not the same quantities. Weight refers to the force of gravity between an object and Earth.

Electrostatic forces between objects are attractive when the charges are different and repulsive when charges are the same. Charges are measured in the units coulombs and Coulomb's law states:

$$F_{\text{electric}} = k_e \frac{q_1 q_2}{d^2}$$

where k_e is Coulomb's constant. Coulomb's law is what keeps electrons rotating around the nucleus in atoms. Coulomb's law also explains ionic bonding.

Electrostatic forces can be easily observed by rubbing a glass rod with silk. Electrons on the silk transfer to the glass rod, giving the glass rod a negative charge.

Magnetic forces are observed when examining lodestones, which are pieces of an iron ore found in nature. Lodestones are magnetized, which means they have a north pole and south pole. In addition, magnets have the property of attracting iron (Fe) and a number of other ferromagnetic materials, as they are called. As with electrostatic forces, like poles repel each other and unlike poles attract each other. But unlike charges, magnetic poles always come in pairs.

Gravitational forces can be understood as objects acting at a distance. To understand electric and magnetic forces, the concept of electric and magnetic fields must be introduced. When a charge is stationary it produces an electric field in the space around it. When a charge is moving, it also produces circular magnetic fields that are perpendicular to the direction of motion. By the latter half of the nineteenth century, physicists developed a full understanding of the relationship between electric and magnetic fields and showed that light consisted of electric and magnetic fields, broken off from charges, and traveling through space.

The existence of nuclear forces is apparent from the fact that the repulsive electrostatic force between protons does not drive the protons apart. It is apparent that the neutrons in the nucleus serve as a kind of glue, because the larger the nucleus the more neutrons there are. Aluminum, for example, has one more neutron than protons, but lead has over 40 more neutrons than protons. When protons are very close to each other, there is an attractive force called the strong force. The strong force is the same when a neutron is in contact with another neutron or a proton. The lack of stability in large nuclei can be understood from the fact that all the protons in a nucleus are repelling each other, and nuclear forces only affect the adjacent proton or neutron.

Statics is the study of physical systems at rest or moving with a constant speed. This occurs when the net force acting on an object is zero. When a book is resting on a table, for example, the force of gravity is in equilibrium with the force of the table acting upward on the book. The force of the table on the book is called the normal force.

Static friction describes the force of friction of two surfaces that are in contact but do not have any motion relative to each other, such as a block sitting on an inclined plane. **Kinetic friction** describes the force of friction of two surfaces in contact with each other when there is relative motion between the surfaces. Both static and kinetic friction these rules:

1. The materials that make up the surfaces determines the magnitude of the frictional force.
2. The frictional force is independent of the area of contact between the two surfaces.
3. The direction of the frictional force is opposite to the direction of motion for kinetic friction.
4. The frictional force is proportional to the normal force between the two surfaces in contact.

Skill 11.3   Identifying the kinds of forces (e.g., frictional, gravitational) that act on objects in everyday situations

SEE Skills 10.1, 11.1, 11.2, and 12.7.

Skill 11.4   Recognizing the role that the force of gravity plays in tides and the solar system

SEE Skill 12.7

Skill 11.5   Demonstrating knowledge of the use of simple machines (i.e., lever, pulley, wedge, wheel and axle, screw) in everyday life and the mechanical advantage they provide

Six classic and simple machines evolved during the Renaissance period. These six basic machines are the lever, pulley, wedge, wheel and axle, screw and incline, and they serve as the foundation on which all complex machines are made. For example, a lawn mower is made up of wheel and axle, lever, incline plane, wedge and screw!

A wheel and axle is a lever that rotates in a circle around a center point or fulcrum. For example, a windlass device (e.g. the crank to pull a bucket of water from a well) is used to hoist heavy objects. The mechanical advantage here is that the ratio of the radius of the wheel to the radius of the axle allows the heavy lifting.

A pulley is made up of a grooved sheave (wheel). A rope runs inside the groove to change the direction of applied force or transmit rotational motion. The advantage of a pulley system is equal to the number of ropes that support the pulley. For example, if a pulley utilizes four ropes to lift 100 pounds, that means 25 pounds of effort will lift the 100 pounds. So, the mechanical advantage is 4 (the number of ropes).

An inclined plane is a flat surface with endpoints at different heights. It is easier to move an object up an inclined plane rather than a flat surface because the amount of force is reduced as the incline increases, however this is at the expense of having to move the object further as the height increases. The mechanical advantage is the ratio of the length of the sloped surface to the height it spans.

A wedge is a triangular shaped tool which is used to separate or cut objects, lift an object, or hold an object in place. A wedge works when force is applied to its blunt end and is converted to force perpendicular to its length. To determine a wedge's mechanical advantage, divide the length of slope (S) by the thickness of the blunt end.

A screw is a helical inclined plane which converts rotational force (torque) to a linear force. Screws come in many sizes and shapes to maximize their purpose, and so this impacts the mechanical advantage

The efficiency of a simple machine without friction is 100%. Friction reduces the efficiency and is defined as the work output divided by the work input. The more efficient a system is, the less energy that is lost within that system

Newton's second law defines the force as $F = ma$ and a newton is the unit of force in SI units. The unit of force in the English system is the pound, and one pound is equal to 4.4 newtons. Work is defined by the equation $W = Fs$ and a joule is the unit of work in SI units. The foot-pound is the corresponding English unit. Energy is the ability to do work and includes kinetic energy and potential energy. Power is defined by the equation $P = W/t$ and is the rate at which work is done. The unit of power is the watt in SI units and horsepower in English units. A watt is one joule per second and a horsepower is 550 foot-pounds per second. One horsepower is equal to 746 watts.

A machine is a device that makes it easier for human beings to do work. Suppose a man weighing 200 pounds wants to get to a scaffold 10 feet high. He must do 2000 foot-pounds of work. A grasshopper would do that amount of work by jumping up. But a human being uses a device called a ramp. The ramp means there is a longer distance to travel, but less force is needed.

A lever enables a human to lift very heavy objects by doing the same thing: transferring a small force exerted for big distance to a large force exerted for a small distance. In the case of rowing a boat, the opposite is desired. A big force over a short distance produces a smaller force over a greater distance. The other simple machine is the pulley. Applying the conservation of energy to simple machines when there is no friction give us:

$$F_{in} D_{in} = F_{out} D_{out}$$

The mechanical advantage is the ratio of the input force to the output force or the output distance to the input distance. This is called the ideal mechanical advantage when friction is ignored. For example, lifting a box straight up to get it on the table involves very little friction compared to sliding it up a ramp. Using the ramp involves overcoming the force of friction, so the actual mechanical advantage is less than the ideal mechanical advantage.

COMPETENCY 0012 **UNDERSTAND FUNDAMENTAL CONCEPTS AND PRINCIPLES RELATED TO EARTH AND SPACE SYSTEMS**

Skill 12.1 **Demonstrating knowledge of the processes that change the surface of the earth (e.g., soil formation, weathering, erosion, volcanism, tectonic activity) and the causes and effects of those processes**

Soil

Soils are composed of particles of sand, clay, various minerals, tiny living organisms, and humus, plus the decayed remains of plants and animals. Soils are divided into three classes according to their texture. These classes are sandy soils, clay soils, and loamy soils.

Sandy soils are gritty, and their particles do not bind together firmly. Sandy soils are porous—water passes through them rapidly. Sandy soils do not hold much water.

Clay soils are smooth and greasy; their particles bind together firmly. Clay soils are moist and usually do not allow water to pass through easily.

Loamy soils feel somewhat like velvet and their particles clump together. Loamy soils are made up of sand, clay, and silt. Loamy soils holds water but some water can pass through.

In addition to three main classes, soils are further grouped into three major types based upon their composition. These groups are pedalfers, pedocals, and laterites.

Pedalfers form in the humid, temperate climate of the eastern United States. Pedalfer soils contain large amounts of iron oxide and aluminum-rich clays, making the soil a brown to reddish brown color. This soil supports forest type vegetation.

Pedocals are found in the western United States where the climate is dry and temperate. These soils are rich in calcium carbonate. This type of soil supports grasslands and brush vegetation.

Laterites are found where the climate is wet and tropical. Large amounts of water flows through this soil. Laterites are red-orange soils rich in iron and aluminum oxides. There is little humus and this soil is not very fertile.

Types of Weathering

Erosion is the inclusion and transportation of surface materials by another moveable material—usually water, winds, or ice. The most important cause of erosion is running water. Streams, rivers, and tides are constantly at work removing weathered fragments of bedrock and carrying them away from their original location.

A stream erodes bedrock by the grinding action of the sand, pebbles, and other rock fragments. This grinding against each other is called abrasion. Streams also erode rocks by dissolving or absorbing their minerals. Limestone and marble are readily dissolved by streams.

Deposition, also known as sedimentation, is the term for the process by which material from one area is slowly deposited into another area. This is usually due to the movement of wind, water, or ice containing particles of matter. When the rate of movement slows down, particles filter out and remain behind, causing a build-up of matter. Note that this is a result of matter being eroded and removed from another site.

The breaking down of rocks at or near to the earth's surface is known as **weathering**. Weathering breaks down these rocks into smaller and smaller pieces. There are two types of weathering: physical weathering and chemical weathering.

Physical weathering is the process by which rocks are broken down into smaller fragments without undergoing any change in chemical composition. Physical weathering is mainly caused by the freezing of water, the expansion of rock, and the activities of plants and animals.

One example of physical weathering occurs through frost wedging, which is the cycle of daytime thawing and refreezing at night. This cycle causes large rock masses, especially the rocks exposed on mountain tops, to be broken into smaller pieces. Another example would be the peeling away of the outer layers from a rock, which is called exfoliation. Rounded mountain tops are called exfoliation domes; they have been formed in this way.

Chemical weathering is the breaking down of rocks through changes in their chemical composition. Water, oxygen, and carbon dioxide are the main agents of chemical weathering. When water and carbon dioxide combine chemically, they produce a weak acid that breaks down rocks. An example would be the change of feldspar in granite to clay.

Mountains

[BCA5]

Orogeny is the term given to natural mountain building. A mountain is terrain that has been raised high above the surrounding landscape by volcanic action, or some form of tectonic plate collisions. The plate collisions could either be intercontinental collisions or ocean floor collisions with a continental crust (subduction).

The physical composition of mountains includes igneous, metamorphic, and sedimentary rocks; some may have rock layers that are tilted or distorted by plate collision forces.

There are many different types of mountains. The physical attributes of a mountain range depend upon the angle at which plate movement thrusts layers of rock to the surface. Many mountains (Adirondacks, Southern Rockies) were formed along high angle faults.

Folded mountains (Alps, Himalayas) are produced by the folding of rock layers during their formation. The Himalayas are the highest mountains in the world; they contain Mount Everest, which rises almost 9 km above sea level. The Himalayas were formed when India collided with Asia. The movement that created this collision is still in process at the rate of a few centimeters per year.

Fault-block mountains (Utah, Arizona, and New Mexico) are created when plate movement produces tension forces instead of compression forces. The area under tension produces normal faults, and rock along these faults is displaced upward.

Dome mountains are formed as magma tries to push up through the crust but fails to break the surface. Dome mountains resemble a huge blister on the earth's surface.

Upwarped mountains (the Black Hills of South Dakota) are created in association with a broad arching of the crust. They can also be formed by rock thrust upward along high angle faults.

Mechanisms of Producing Mountains

Mountains are produced by different types of mountain-building processes. Most major mountain ranges are formed by the processes of **folding** and **faulting.**

In **folding**, mountains are produced by the folding of rock layers. Crustal movements may press horizontal layers of sedimentary rock together from the sides, squeezing them into wavelike folds. Up-folded sections of rock are called anticlines; down-folded sections of rock are called synclines. The Appalachian Mountains are an example of folded mountains, with long ridges and valleys in a series of anticlines, and synclines formed by folded rock layers.

Faults are fractures in the earth's crust that have been created by either tension or compression forces transmitted through the crust. These forces are produced by the movement of separate blocks of crust. Faulting are categorized on the basis of the relative movement between the blocks on both sides of the fault plane. The movement can be horizontal, vertical, or oblique.

A **dip-slip fault** occurs when the movement of the plates is vertical and opposite. The displacement is in the direction of the inclination, or dip, of the fault. Dip-slip faults are classified as normal faults when the rock above the fault plane moves down relative to the rock below.

Reverse faults are created when the rock above the fault plane moves up relative to the rock below. Reverse faults with a very low angle to the horizontal are also referred to as thrust faults.

Faults in which the dominant displacement is horizontal movement along the trend or strike (length) of the fault are called **strike-slip faults**. When a large strike-slip fault is associated with plate boundaries it is called a **transform fault**. The San Andreas Fault in California is a well-known transform fault.

Faults that have both vertical and horizontal movement are called **oblique-slip faults**.

Volcanoes

Volcanism is the term given to the movement of magma through the crust and its emergence as lava onto the earth's surface. Volcanic mountains are built up by successive deposits of volcanic materials.

An **active volcano** is one that is presently erupting or building to an eruption. A **dormant volcano** is one that is between eruptions but still shows signs of internal activity that might lead to an eruption in the future. An **extinct volcano** is said to be no longer capable of erupting. Most of the world's active volcanoes are found along the rim of the Pacific Ocean, which is also a major earthquake zone. This curving belt of active faults and volcanoes is often called the Ring of Fire. The world's best known volcanic mountains include Mount Etna in Italy and Mount Kilimanjaro in Africa. The Hawaiian Islands are actually the tops of a chain of volcanic mountains that rise from the ocean floor.

There are three types of volcanic mountains: shield volcanoes, cinder cones and composite volcanoes.

Shield Volcanoes are associated with quiet eruptions. Lava emerges from the vent or opening in the crater and flows freely out over the earth's surface until it cools and hardens into a layer of igneous rock. A repeated lava flow builds this type of volcano into the largest volcanic mountain. Mauna Loa in Hawaii is the largest shield volcano on earth.

Cinder Cone Volcanoes are associated with explosive eruptions as lava is hurled high into the air in a spray of droplets of various sizes. These droplets cool and harden into cinders and particles of ash before falling to the ground. The ash and cinder pile up around the vent to form a steep, cone-shaped hill called the cinder cone. Cinder cone volcanoes are relatively small but may form quite rapidly.

Composite Volcanoes are those built by both lava flows and layers of ash and cinders. Mount Fuji in Japan, Mount St. Helens in Washington, USA, and Mount Vesuvius in Italy are all famous composite volcanoes.

When lava cools, igneous rock is formed. This formation can occur either above ground or below ground.

Intrusive rock includes any igneous rock that was formed below the earth's surface. Batholiths are the largest structures of intrusive type rock and are composed of near granite materials; they are the core of the Sierra Nevada Mountains. **Extrusive rock** includes any igneous rock that was formed at the earth's surface.

Dikes are old lava tubes formed when magma entered a vertical fracture and hardened. Sometimes magma squeezes between two rock layers and hardens into a thin horizontal sheet called a **sill**. A **laccolith** is formed in much the same way as a sill, but the magma that creates a laccolith is very thick and does not flow easily. It pools and forces the overlying strata creating an obvious surface dome.

A **caldera** is normally formed by the collapse of the top of a volcano. This collapse can be caused by a massive explosion that destroys the cone and empties most, if not all, of the magma chamber below the volcano. The cone collapses into the empty magma chamber, forming a caldera.

An inactive volcano may have magma solidified in its pipe. This structure, called a volcanic neck, is resistant to erosion and today may be the only visible evidence of the past presence of an active volcano.

Earth's Plates

Data obtained from many sources led scientists to develop the theory of **plate tectonics**. This theory is the most current model that explains not only the movement of the continents, but also the changes in the earth's crust caused by internal forces.

Plates are rigid blocks of the earth's crust and upper mantle. These rigid solid blocks make up the lithosphere. The earth's lithosphere is broken into nine large sections and several small ones. These moving slabs are called plates. The major plates are named after the continents they are "transporting." The plates float on and move with a layer of hot, plastic-like rock in the upper mantle. Geologists believe that the heat currents circulating within the mantle cause this plastic zone of rock to slowly flow, carrying along the overlying crustal plates.

Movement of these crustal plates creates areas where the plates diverge as well as areas where the plates converge. A major area of **divergence** is located in the Mid-Atlantic. Currents of hot mantle rock rise and separate at this point of divergence, creating new oceanic crust at the rate of 2 to 10 centimeters per year. **Convergence** is when the oceanic crust collides with either another oceanic plate or a continental plate. The oceanic crust sinks, forming an enormous trench and generating volcanic activity. Convergence also includes continent to continent plate collisions. When two plates slide past one another, a transform fault is created.

These movements produce many major features of the earth's surface, such as mountain ranges, volcanoes, and earthquake zones. Most of these features are located at plate boundaries, where the plates interact by spreading apart, pressing together, or sliding past each other. These movements are very slow, averaging only a few centimeters a year.

Boundaries form between spreading plates where the crust is forced apart in a process called **rifting**. Rifting generally occurs at mid-ocean ridges. Rifting can also take place within a continent, splitting the continent into smaller landmasses that drift away from each other, thereby forming an ocean basin between them. The Red Sea is a product of rifting. As the seafloor spreading takes place, new material is added to the inner edges of the separating plates. In this way the plates grow larger, and the ocean basin widens. This is the process that broke up the super continent Pangaea and created the Atlantic Ocean.

Boundaries between plates that are colliding are zones of intense crustal activity. When a plate of ocean crust collides with a plate of continental crust, the more dense oceanic plate slides under the lighter continental plate and plunges into the mantle. This process is called **subduction**, and the site where it takes place is called a subduction zone. A subduction zone is usually seen on the sea floor as a deep depression called a trench.

The crustal movement identified by plates sliding sideways past each other produces a plate boundary characterized by major faults that are capable of unleashing powerful earthquakes. The San Andreas Fault forms such a boundary between the Pacific Plate and the North American Plate.

Skill 12.2   Recognizing the characteristics and processes of the rock cycle and physical and chemical properties of earth materials

The three major subdivisions of rocks are sedimentary, metamorphic and igneous.

Sedimentary rocks are created through a process known as lithification. It occurs when fluid sediments are transformed into solid rocks. One very common process affecting sediments is compaction, where the weights of overlying materials compress and compact the deeper sediments. The compaction process leads to cementation. Cementation is when sediments are converted to sedimentary rock.

Igneous rocks can be classified according to their texture, their composition, and the way they formed. They are made from molten rock. Molten rock is called magma. As magma cools, the elements and compounds begin to form crystals. The slower the magma cools, the larger the crystals grow. Rocks with large crystals are said to have a coarse-grained texture. Granite is an example of a coarse-grained igneous rock. Rocks that cool rapidly before any crystals can form have a glassy texture such as obsidian, also commonly known as volcanic glass.

Metamorphic rocks are formed by high temperatures and great pressures. The process by which the rocks undergo these changes is called metamorphism. The outcome of metamorphic changes include deformation by extreme heat and pressure, compaction, destruction of the original characteristics of the parent rock, bending and folding while in a plastic stage, and the emergence of completely new and different minerals due to chemical reactions with heated water and dissolved minerals.

Metamorphic rocks are classified into two groups: foliated (leaflike) rocks and unfoliated rocks. Foliated rocks consist of compressed, parallel bands of minerals, which give the rocks a striped appearance. Examples of such rocks include slate, schist, and gneiss. Unfoliated rocks are not banded and examples of such include quartzite, marble, and anthracite rocks.

Minerals are natural, non-living solids with a definite chemical composition and a crystalline structure. **Ores** are minerals or rock deposits that can be mined for a profit. **Rocks** are earth materials made of one or more minerals. A **rock facies** is a rock group that differs from comparable rocks (as in composition, age, or fossil content).

Skill 12.4 Recognizing how fossils and other evidence are used to document life and environmental changes over time

A **fossil** is the remains or trace of an ancient organism that has been preserved naturally in the earth's crust. Sedimentary rocks usually are rich sources of fossil remains. Those fossils found in layers of sediment were embedded in the slowly forming sedimentary rock strata. The oldest fossils known are the traces of 3.5 billion-year-old bacteria found in sedimentary rocks. Few fossils are found in metamorphic rock, and virtually none are found in igneous rocks. The magma is so hot that any organism trapped in the magma is destroyed.

Although the fairly well-preserved remains of a woolly mammoth embedded in ice were found in Russia in May of 2007, the best-preserved animal remains are typically discovered in natural tar pits. When an animal accidentally falls into the tar, it becomes trapped, sinking to the bottom. Preserved bones of the saber-toothed cat have been found in tar pits.

Prehistoric insects have been found trapped in ancient amber or fossil resin that was excreted by some extinct species of pine trees. Fossil molds are the hollow spaces in a rock previously occupied by bones or shells. A fossil cast is a fossil mold that fills with sediments or minerals and later hardens, forming a cast.

Fossil tracks are the imprints in hardened mud left behind by birds or animals.

Skill 12.5 Recognizing the components, structure, and interconnections among the earth's crust, atmosphere, and hydrosphere

Earth's Crust

SEE "Earth's Plates" section of 12.1.

Atmosphere

Dry air is composed of three basic components: dry gas, water vapor, and solid particles (dust from soil, etc.).

The most abundant dry gases in the atmosphere are:

(N_2)	Nitrogen	78.09 %
(O_2)	Oxygen	20.95 %
(AR)	Argon	0.93 %
(CO_2)	Carbon Dioxide	0.03 %

The atmosphere is divided into four main layers based on temperature. These layers are labeled troposphere, stratosphere, mesosphere, and thermosphere.

Troposphere – This layer is the closest to the earth's surface. All weather phenomena occur here because it is the layer with the most water vapor and dust. Air temperature decreases with increasing altitude. The average thickness of the troposphere is 7 miles (11 km).

Stratosphere – This layer contains very little water. Clouds within this layer are extremely rare. The ozone layer is located in the upper portions of the stratosphere. Air temperature is fairly constant but does increase somewhat with height due to the absorption of solar energy and ultraviolet rays from the ozone layer.

Mesosphere – Air temperature again decreases with height in this layer. It is the coldest layer, with temperatures in the range of -100^0 C at the top.

Thermosphere – This layer extends upward into space. Oxygen molecules in this layer absorb energy from the sun, causing temperatures to increase with height. The lower part of the thermosphere is called the ionosphere. Here, charged particles (ions) and free electrons can be found. When gases in the ionosphere are excited by solar radiation, the gases give off light and glow in the sky. These glowing lights are called the Aurora Borealis in the Northern Hemisphere and Aurora Australis in Southern Hemisphere. The upper portion of the thermosphere is called the exosphere. Gas molecules are very far apart in this layer. Layers of exosphere are also known as the Van Allen Belts and are held together by earth's magnetic field.

Hydrosphere

Seventy percent of the Earth's surface is covered with saltwater which is termed the hydrosphere. The mass of this saltwater is about 1.4×10^{24} grams. The ocean waters continuously circulate among different parts of the hydrosphere. There are seven major oceans: the North Atlantic Ocean, South Atlantic Ocean, North Pacific Ocean, South Pacific Ocean, Indian Ocean, Arctic Ocean, and the Antarctic Ocean.

Pure water is a combination of the elements hydrogen and oxygen. These two elements make up about 96.5% of ocean water. The remaining portion is made up of dissolved solids. The concentration of these dissolved solids determines the water's salinity.

Salinity is the number of grams of these dissolved salts in 1,000 grams of sea water. The average salinity of ocean water is about 3.5%. In other words, one kilogram of sea water contains about 35 grams of salt. Sodium Chloride or salt (NaCl) is the most abundant of the dissolved salts. The dissolved salts also include smaller quantities of magnesium chloride, magnesium and calcium sulfates, and traces of several other salt elements. Salinity varies throughout the world oceans; the total salinity of the oceans varies from place to place and also varies with depth. Salinity is low near river mouths where the ocean mixes with fresh water, and salinity is high in areas of high evaporation rates.

The temperature of the ocean water varies with different latitudes and with ocean depths. Ocean water temperature is about constant to depths of 90 meters (m). The temperature of surface water will drop rapidly from 28° C at the equator to   −2° C at the Poles. The freezing point of sea water is lower than the freezing point of pure water. Pure water freezes at 0° C. The dissolved salts in the sea water keep sea water at a freezing point of −2° C. The freezing point of sea water may vary depending on its salinity in a particular location.

The ocean can be divided into three temperature zones. The surface layer consists of relatively warm water and exhibits most of the wave action present. The area where the wind and waves churn and mix the water is called the mixed layer. This is the layer where most living creatures are found due to abundant sunlight and warmth. The second layer is called the thermocline and it becomes increasingly colder as its depth increases. This change is due to the lack of energy from sunlight. The layer below the thermocline continues to the deep dark, very cold, and semi-barren ocean floor.

Oozes is the name given to the sediment that contains at least 30% plant or animal shell fragments. Ooze contains calcium carbonate. Deposits that form directly from sea water in the place where they are found are called authigenic deposits. Maganese nodules are authigenic deposits found over large areas of the ocean floor.

Formation of Ocean Floor Features

The surface of the Earth is in constant motion. This motion is the subject of plate tectonics studies. Major plate separation lines lie along the ocean floors. As these plates separate, molten rock rises, continuously forming new ocean crust and creating new and taller mountain ridges under the ocean. The Mid-Atlantic Range, which divides the Atlantic Ocean basin into two nearly equal parts, shows evidence from mapping of these deep-ocean floor changes.

Seamounts are formed by underwater volcanoes. Seamounts and volcanic islands are found in long chains on the ocean floor. They are formed when the movement of an oceanic plate positions a plate section over a stationary hot spot located deep in the mantle. Magma rising from the hot spot punches through the plate and forms a volcano. The Hawaiian Islands are examples of volcanic island chains.

Magma that rises to produce a curving chain of volcanic islands is called an island arc. An example of an island arc is the Lesser Antilles chain in the Caribbean Sea.

Skill 12.6   Demonstrating knowledge of the water cycle and weather patterns and factors that influence weather and climate

Water Cycle

Water that falls to Earth in the form of rain and snow is called **precipitation.** Precipitation is part of a continuous process in which water at the Earth's surface evaporates, condenses into clouds, and returns to Earth. This process is termed the **water cycle**. The water located below the surface is called groundwater.

The impacts of altitude upon climatic conditions are primarily related to temperature and precipitation. As altitude increases, climatic conditions become increasingly drier and colder. Solar radiation becomes more severe as altitude increases while the effects of convection forces are minimized. Climatic changes as a function of latitude follow a similar pattern (as a reference, latitude moves either north or south from the equator). The climate becomes colder and drier as the distance from the equator increases. Proximity to land or water masses produces climatic conditions based upon the available moisture. Dry and arid climates prevail where moisture is scarce; lush tropical climates can prevail where moisture is abundant. Climate, as described above, depends upon the specific combination of conditions making up an area's environment. Man impacts all environments by producing pollutants in Earth, air, and water. It follows then, that man is a major player in world climatic conditions.

Weather and Climate

Weather is the condition of the air that affects the day-to-day atmospheric conditions. It includes factors such as temperature, air pressure, wind, and moisture or precipitation (which includes rain, snow, hail, or sleet).

Climate is the term used to describe the average weather or daily weather conditions for a specific region over a long period of time. Studying the climate of an area includes information gathered on the area's monthly and yearly temperatures as well as its monthly and yearly amounts of precipitation. In addition, one characteristic of an area's climate is the length of its growing season.

In northern and central United States, northern China, south central and southeastern Canada, and the western and southeastern parts of the former Soviet Union, there is a "climate of four seasons." This is also known as the **humid continental climate**, which includes spring, summer, fall, and winter. Cold winters, hot summers, and enough rainfall to grow a variety of crops are the major characteristics of this climate. In areas where the humid continental climate is found, there are some of the world's best farmlands as well as important activities such as trading and mining. Differences in temperatures throughout the year are typically determined by the distance a place is inland, away from the coasts.

The steppe or **prairie climate** is located in the interiors of the large continents like Asia and North America. These dry flatlands are far from ocean breezes and are called prairies (or the Great Plains in Canada and the United States and steppes in Asia). Although the summers are hot and the winters are cold, the big difference is rainfall. In the steppe climate, rainfall is light and uncertain at ten to twenty inches per year. Where rain is more plentiful, grass grows; in areas of less rainfall, the steppes or prairies gradually become deserts. These are found in the Gobi Desert of Asia, in central and western Australia, in southwestern United States, and in the smaller deserts found in Pakistan, Argentina, and Africa south of the Equator.

The two major climates found in the high latitudes are **tundra** and **taiga**. The word tundra, meaning marshy plain, is a Russian word; it aptly describes the climatic conditions in the northern areas of Russia, Europe, and Canada. Winters are extremely cold and very long. Most of the year the ground is frozen, but it becomes rather mushy during the very short summer months. Surprisingly less snow falls in the area of the tundra than in the eastern part of the United States. However, due to the harshness of the extreme cold, very few people live there and almost no crops can be raised. Despite having a small human population, many plants and animals are found there.

The **taiga** is the northern forest region located south of the tundra. The world's largest forestlands are found here, along with vast mineral wealth and fur-bearing animals. The climate is so extreme that very few people live here, as they are not able to raise crops due to the extremely short growing season. The winter temperatures are colder and the summer temperatures are hotter than those in the tundra because the taiga climate region is farther from the waters of the Arctic Ocean. The taiga is found in the northern parts of Russia, Sweden, Norway, Finland, Canada, and Alaska with most of their lands covered with marshes and swamps.

The humid **subtropical climate** is found north and south of the tropics. It is categorized by its high levels of moisture. The areas with this type of climate include the southeastern coasts of Japan, mainland China, Australia, Africa, South America, and the United States. One interesting feature of these locations is that warm ocean currents are found there. The winds that blow across these currents bring in warm moist air all year round. Long, warm summers; short, mild winters; and a long growing season allow for different crops to be grown several times a year. These conditions contribute to the productivity of this climate type, which supports more people than any of the other climates.

The **marine climate** is found in Western Europe, the British Isles, the U.S. Pacific Northwest, the western coast of Canada, southern Chile, southern New Zealand, and southeastern Australia. A common characteristic of these lands is that they are either near water or surrounded by it. The ocean winds are wet and warm, bringing a mild rainy climate to these areas. In the summer, the daily temperatures average at or below 70 degrees F. During the winter, because of the warming effect of the ocean waters, the temperatures rarely fall below freezing.

In certain areas of the earth, there exists a type of climate unique to areas with high mountains. This type of climate is called a **vertical climate** because the temperatures, crops, vegetation, and human activities change and become different as one ascends through the different levels of elevation. At the foot of the mountain, a hot and rainy climate is found with the cultivation of many lowland crops. As one climbs higher, the air becomes cooler, the climate changes sharply, and different economic activities change, such as grazing sheep and growing corn. At the top of many mountains, snow is found year round.

Skill 12.7 Demonstrating knowledge of the structure of the solar system and of the characteristics, interactions, and motions of its components

Earth is the third planet away from the sun in our solar system. Earth's numerous types of motion and states of orientation greatly affect global conditions, such as seasons, tides, and lunar phases. The earth orbits the sun within a period of 365 days. During this orbit, the average distance between the earth and the sun is 93 million miles.

The shape of the earth's orbit around the sun deviates from the shape of a circle only slightly. This deviation, known as the earth's eccentricity, has a very small effect on the earth's climate. The earth is closest to the sun at perihelion, occurring around January 2 of each year, and farthest from the sun at aphelion, occurring around July 2. Because the earth is closest to the sun in January, the northern winter is slightly warmer than the southern winter.

Seasons

The rotation axis of the earth is not perpendicular to the orbital (ecliptic) plane. The axis of the earth is tilted $23.45°$ from the perpendicular; the tilt of this axis is known as the obliquity of the ecliptic, and is mainly responsible for the four seasons of the year by influencing the intensity of solar rays received by the northern and southern hemispheres.

The four seasons—spring, summer, fall, and winter—are extended periods of characteristic average temperature, rainfall, storm frequency, and vegetation growth or dormancy. The effect of the earth's tilt on climate is best demonstrated at the solstices, the two days of the year when the sun is farthest from the earth's equatorial plane. At the **summer solstice** (June), the earth's tilt on its axis causes the northern hemisphere to the lean toward the sun, while the southern hemisphere leans away. Consequently, the northern hemisphere receives more intense rays from the sun and experiences summer during this time, while the southern hemisphere experiences winter. At the **winter solstice** (December), it is the southern hemisphere that leans toward the sun and thus experiences summer. Spring and fall are produced by varying degrees of the same leaning toward or away from the sun.

Tides

The orientation of and gravitational interaction between the earth and the moon are responsible for the ocean tides that occur on earth. The term **tide** refers to the cyclic rise and fall of large bodies of water. Gravitational attraction is defined as the force of attraction between all bodies in the universe. At the location on earth closest to the moon, the gravitational attraction of the moon draws seawater toward the moon in the form of a tidal bulge. On the opposite side of the earth, another tidal bulge forms in the direction away from the moon because at this point, the moon's gravitational pull is the weakest.

Spring tides are the especially strong tides that occur when the earth, sun, and moon are in line, allowing both the sun and the moon to exert gravitational force on the earth, thereby increasing tidal bulge height. These tides occur during the full moon and the new moon. **Neap tides** are especially weak tides occurring when the gravitational forces of the moon and the sun are perpendicular to one another. These tides occur during quarter moons.

Lunar Phases

The earth's orientation in respect to the solar system is also responsible for our perception of the phases of the moon. While the earth orbits the sun within a period of 365 days, the moon orbits the earth every twenty-seven days. As the moon circles the earth, its shape in the night sky appears to change. The changes in the appearance of the moon from earth are known as **lunar phases**.

These phases vary cyclically according to the relative positions of the moon, the earth, and the sun. At all times, half of the moon is facing the sun; thus, it is illuminated by reflecting the sun's light. As the moon orbits the earth and the earth orbits the sun, the half of the moon that faces the sun changes. However, the moon is in synchronous rotation around the earth, meaning that nearly the same side of the moon faces the earth at all times. This side is referred to as the near side of the moon. Lunar phases occur as the earth and moon orbit the sun and the fractional illumination of the moon's near side changes.

When the sun and moon are on opposite sides of the earth, observers on Earth perceive a **full moon**, meaning the moon appears circular because the entire illuminated half of the moon is visible. As the moon orbits the earth, the moon "wanes" as the amount of the illuminated half of the moon that is visible from Earth decreases. A **gibbous** moon is between a full moon and a half moon, or between a half moon and a full moon. When the sun and the moon are on the same side of Earth, the illuminated half of the moon is facing away from Earth, and the moon appears invisible. This lunar phase is known as the **new moon**. The time between each full moon is approximately 29.53 days.

A list of all lunar phases includes:

- New Moon: the moon is invisible or the first signs of a crescent appear
- Waxing Crescent: the right crescent of the moon is visible
- First Quarter: the right quarter of the moon is visible
- Waxing Gibbous: only the left crescent is not illuminated
- Full Moon: the entire illuminated half of the moon is visible
- Waning Gibbous: only the right crescent of the moon is not illuminated
- Last Quarter: the left quarter of the moon is illuminated
- Waning Crescent: only the left crescent of the moon is illuminated

Viewing the moon from the southern hemisphere causes these phases to occur in the opposite order.

Planets

There are eight established planets in our solar system: Mercury, Venus, Earth, Mars, Jupiter, Saturn, Uranus, and Neptune. Pluto was an established planet in our solar system, but as of summer 2006, its status is being reconsidered.

The planets are divided into two groups based on distance from the sun. The inner planets include Mercury, Venus, Earth, and Mars. The outer planets include Jupiter, Saturn, Uranus, and Neptune.

Mercury: the closest planet to the sun. Its surface has craters and rocks. The atmosphere is composed of hydrogen, helium, and sodium. Mercury was named after the Roman messenger god.

Venus: has a slow rotation when compared to Earth. Venus and Uranus rotate in opposite directions from the other planets. This opposite rotation is called **retrograde rotation**. The surface of Venus is not visible due to the extensive cloud cover. The atmosphere is composed mostly of carbon dioxide, while sulfuric acid droplets in the dense cloud cover give Venus a yellow appearance. Venus has a greater greenhouse effect than observed on Earth, and the dense clouds combined with carbon dioxide trap heat. Venus was named after the Roman goddess of love.

Earth: considered a water planet, with 70 percent of its surface covered by water. Gravity holds the masses of water in place. The different temperatures observed on Earth allow for the different states of water (solid, liquid, gas) to exist. The atmosphere is composed primarily of oxygen and also some nitrogen. Earth is the only planet that is known to support life.

Mars: the surface contains numerous craters, active and extinct volcanoes, ridges, and valleys with extremely deep fractures. Iron oxide found in the dusty soil makes the surface seem rust-colored and the skies seem pink in color. The atmosphere is composed of carbon dioxide, nitrogen, argon, oxygen, and water vapor. Mars has polar regions with ice caps composed of water as well as two satellites (moons). Mars was named after the Roman war god.

Jupiter: the largest planet in the solar system. Jupiter has sixteen moons. The atmosphere is composed of hydrogen, helium, methane, and ammonia. There are white-colored bands of clouds indicating rising gas and dark-colored bands of clouds indicating descending gases. The gas movement is caused by heat resulting from the energy of Jupiter's core. Jupiter has a Great Red Spot that is thought to be a hurricane-like cloud. Jupiter has a strong magnetic field.

Saturn: the second largest planet in the solar system. Saturn has rings of ice, rock, and dust particles circling it. Saturn's atmosphere is composed of hydrogen, helium, methane, and ammonia. Saturn has twenty plus satellites. Saturn was named after the Roman god of agriculture.

Uranus: the third largest planet in the solar system and has retrograde revolution. Uranus is a gaseous planet. It has ten dark rings and fifteen satellites. Its atmosphere is composed of hydrogen, helium, and methane. Uranus was named after the Greek god of the heavens.

Neptune: another gaseous planet with an atmosphere consisting of hydrogen, helium, and methane. Neptune has three rings and two satellites. Neptune was named after the Roman sea god because its atmosphere is the same color as the seas.

Pluto: once considered the smallest planet in the solar system, its status as a planet is now being reconsidered. Pluto's atmosphere probably contains methane, ammonia, and frozen water. Pluto has one satellite. Pluto revolves around the sun every 250 years. Pluto was named after the Roman god of the underworld.

The Sun and Stars

The sun is considered the nearest star to Earth that produces solar energy. By the process of nuclear fusion, hydrogen gas is converted to helium gas. Energy flows out of the core to the surface; radiation then escapes into space.

Parts of the sun include:

1) **Core**: the inner portion of the sun where fusion takes place
2) **Photosphere**: considered the surface of the sun, it also produces **sunspots** (cool, dark areas that can be seen on its surface)
3) **Chromosphere**: hydrogen gas causes this portion to be red in color (also found here are solar flares [sudden brightness of the chromosphere] and solar prominences [gases that shoot outward from the chromosphere])
4) **Corona**, the transparent area of sun visible only during a total eclipse

Solar radiation is energy traveling from the sun that radiates into space. Solar flares produce excited protons and electrons that shoot outward from the chromosphere at great speeds reaching Earth. These particles disturb radio reception and also affect the magnetic field on Earth.

A star is a ball of hot, glowing gas that is hot enough and dense enough to trigger nuclear reactions, which fuel the star. In comparing the mass, light production, and size of the sun to other stars, astronomers find that the sun is a perfectly ordinary star. It behaves exactly the way they would expect a star of its size to behave. The main difference between the sun and other stars is that the sun is much closer to Earth.

Most stars have masses similar to that of the sun. The majority of stars' masses are between 0.3 to 3.0 times the mass of the sun. Theoretical calculations indicate that in order to trigger nuclear reactions and to create its own energy—that is, to become a star—a body must have a mass greater than 7 percent of the mass of the sun. Astronomical bodies that are less massive than this become planets or objects called brown dwarfs. The largest accurately determined stellar mass is of a star called V382 Cygni; it is twenty-seven times the mass of the sun.

The range of brightness among stars is much larger than the range of mass. Astronomers measure the brightness of a star by measuring its magnitude and luminosity. **Magnitude** allows astronomers to rank how bright different stars appear to humans. Because of the way our eyes detect light, a lamp ten times more luminous than a second lamp will appear less than ten times brighter to human eyes. This discrepancy affects the magnitude scale, as does the tradition of giving brighter stars lower magnitudes. The lower a star's magnitude, the brighter it is. Stars with negative magnitudes are the brightest of all.

Magnitude is given in terms of absolute and apparent values. Absolute magnitude is a measurement of how bright a star would appear if viewed from a set distance away. Astronomers also measure a star's brightness in terms of its **luminosity**. A star's absolute luminosity, or intrinsic brightness, is the total amount of energy radiated by the star per second. Luminosity is often expressed in units of watts.

Magnitude stars are twenty-one of the brightest stars that can be seen from Earth. These are the first stars noticed at night. In the northern hemisphere, there are fifteen commonly observed first magnitude stars.

Astronomers use groups or patterns of stars called **constellations** as reference points to locate other stars in the sky. Familiar constellations include Ursa Major (also known as the big bear) and Ursa Minor (known as the little bear). Within the Ursa Major, the smaller constellation The Big Dipper is found. Within the Ursa Minor, the smaller constellation The Little Dipper is found. Different constellations appear as the earth continues its revolution around the sun with the seasonal changes.

A vast collection of stars are defined as **galaxies**. Galaxies are classified as irregular, elliptical, and spiral. An irregular galaxy has no real structured appearance; most are in their early stages of life. An elliptical galaxy consists of smooth ellipses, containing little dust and gas, but composed of millions or trillions of stars. Spiral galaxies are disk-shaped and have extending arms that rotate around its dense center. Earth's galaxy is the Milky Way. It is a spiral galaxy.

A **pulsar** is defined as a variable radio source that emits signals in very short, regular bursts; it is believed to be a rotating neutron star. A **quasar** is defined as an object that photographs like a star but has an extremely large redshift and a variable energy output; it is believed to be the active core of a very distant galaxy.

Black holes are defined as objects that have collapsed to such a degree that light can not escape from the surface; light is trapped by the intense gravitational field.

The forces of gravity acting on particles of gas and dust in a cloud in an area of space produce stars. This cloud is called a **nebula**. Particles in this cloud attract each other; as the star grows, its temperature increases. With the increased temperature, the star begins to glow. Fusion occurs in the core of the star, releasing radiant energy at the star's surface.

When hydrogen becomes exhausted in a small, or even an average star, its core will collapse and cause its temperature to rise. This released heat causes nearby gases to heat, contract, carry out fusion, and produce helium. Stars at this stage are nearing the end of their life. These stars are called **red giants** or **super giants**. A **white dwarf** is the dying core of a giant star. A **nova** is an ordinary star that experiences a sudden increase in brightness and then fades back to its original brightness. A **supernova** radiates even greater light energy. A **neutron star** is the result of mass left behind after a supernova. A **black hole** is a star with condensed matter and gravity so intense that light can not escape.

Comets, Asteroids, and Meteors

Astronomers believe that rocky fragments may have been the remains of the birth of the solar system that never formed into a planet. These **asteroids** are found in the region between Mars and Jupiter.

Comets are masses of frozen gases, cosmic dust, and small rocky particles. Astronomers think that most comets originate in a dense comet cloud beyond Pluto. A comet consists of a nucleus, a coma, and a tail. A comet's tail always points away from the sun. The most famous comet, **Halley's Comet,** is named after the person who first discovered it in 240 BCE. It returns to the skies near Earth every seventy-five to seventy-six years.

Meteoroids are composed of particles of rock and metal of various sizes. When a meteoroid travels through the earth's atmosphere, friction causes its surface to heat up and it begins to burn. The burning meteoroid falling through the earth's atmosphere is called a **meteor** (also known as a "shooting star").

Meteorites are meteors that strike the earth's surface. A physical example of a meteorite's impact on the earth's surface can be seen in Arizona; the **Barringer Crater** is a huge meteor crater. There are many other meteor craters throughout the world.

Oort Cloud and Kuiper Belt

The **Oort Cloud** is a hypothetical spherical cloud surrounding our solar system. It extends approximately three light years or 30 trillion kilometers from the sun. The cloud is believed to be made up of materials that were ejected out of the inner solar system because of interaction with Uranus and Neptune, but are gravitationally bound to the sun. It is named the Oort Cloud after Jan Oort, who suggested its existence in 1950. Comets from the Oort Cloud exhibit a wide range of sizes, inclinations, and eccentricities; they are often referred to as Long-Period Comets because they have a period of greater than 200 years.

The **Kuiper Belt** is the name given to a vast population of small bodies orbiting the sun beyond Neptune. There are more than 70,000 of these small bodies, some with diameters larger than 100 km extending outwards from the orbit of Neptune to 50AU. They exist mostly within a ring or belt surrounding the sun. It is believed that the objects in the Kuiper Belt are primitive remnants of the earliest phases of the solar system. It is also believed that the Kuiper Belt is the source of many Short-Period Comets (periods of less then 200 years). It is a reservoir for the comets in the same way that the Oort Cloud is a reservoir for Long-Period Comets.

Occasionally, the orbit of a Kuiper Belt object will be disturbed by the interactions of the giant planets in such a way as to cause the object to cross the orbit of Neptune. It will then very likely have a close encounter with Neptune, sending it out of the solar system or into an orbit crossing those of the other giant planets or even into the inner solar system. Prevailing theory states that scattered disk objects began as Kuiper Belt objects, which were scattered through gravitational interactions with the giant planets.

It seems that the Oort Cloud objects were formed closer to the sun than the Kuiper Belt objects. Small objects formed near the giant planets would have been ejected from the solar system by gravitational encounters. Those that didn't escape entirely formed the distant Oort Cloud. Small objects formed farther out had no such interactions and remained as the Kuiper Belt objects.

Origins of the Solar System and Universe

There are two main hypotheses of the origin of the solar system: 1) **the tidal hypothesis** and 2) **the condensation hypothesis**.

The tidal hypothesis proposes that the solar system began with a near collision of the sun and a large star. Some astronomers believe that as these two stars passed each other, the great gravitational pull of the large star extracted hot gases out of the sun. The mass from the hot gases started to orbit the sun, which began to cool, then condensing into the nine planets. (Few astronomers support this example.)

The condensation hypothesis proposes that the solar system began with rotating clouds of dust and gas. Condensation occurred in the center, forming the sun and the smaller parts of the cloud formed the nine planets. (This example is accepted by many astronomers.)

The two main theories to explain the origins of the universe include: 1) **the Big Bang theory** and 2) **the Steady-State theory.**

The Big Bang theory has been widely accepted by many astronomers. It states that the universe originated from a magnificent explosion spreading mass, matter, and energy into space. Galaxies formed from this material as it cooled during the next half-billion years.

The Steady-State theory is the least accepted theory. It states that the universe is continuously being renewed. Galaxies move outward and new galaxies replace the older galaxies. Astronomers have not found any evidence to prove this theory.

The future of the universe is hypothesized by the Oscillating Universe Hypothesis. It states that the universe will oscillate, or expand and contract. Galaxies will move away from one another and will in time slow down and stop. Then a gradual moving toward each other will again activate an explosion— another Big Bang.

Skill 12.8 Demonstrating knowledge of renewable and nonrenewable resources and of the effects of human activities on the environment

Natural resources are naturally occurring substances that are considered valuable in their natural form. A commodity is generally considered a natural resource when the primary activities associated with it are extraction and purification, as opposed to creation. Thus, mining, petroleum extraction, fishing, and forestry are generally considered natural resource industries while agriculture is not.

Natural resources are often classified into renewable and nonrenewable resources. Renewable resources are generally living resources (fish, coffee, and forests, for example), which can restock (renew) themselves if they are not over harvested. Renewable resources can restock themselves and be used indefinitely if they are sustained. Once renewable resources are consumed at a rate that exceeds their natural rate of replacement, the standing stock will diminish and eventually run out.

The rate of sustainable use of a renewable resource is determined by the replacement rate and amount of standing stock of that particular resource. Non-living renewable natural resources include soil, as well as water, wind, tides, and solar radiation. Nonrenewable resources are natural resources that cannot be remade or regenerated in the same proportion that they are used. Examples of nonrenewable resources are fossil fuels such as coal, petroleum, and natural gas.

Environmental policy is concerned with the sustainability of the earth, the region under the administration of the governing group or individual or a local habitat. The concern of environmental policy is the preservation of the region, habitat or ecosystem. Because humans, both individually and in community, live upon the earth, draw upon the natural resources of the earth, and affect the environment in many ways, environmental and social policy must be mutually supportive.

If modern societies have no understanding of the limitations of natural resources or how their actions affect the environment, and they act without regard for the sustainability of the earth, it will become impossible for the earth to sustain human existence. For centuries, social policies, economic policies, and political policies have ignored the impact of human existence and human civilization upon the environment. Human civilization has disrupted the ecological balance, contributed to the extinction of animal and plant species, and destroyed ecosystems through uncontrolled harvesting. In an age of global warming and unprecedented demand upon natural resources, social and environmental policies must become increasingly interdependent if the planet is to continue to support life and human civilization.

Nonrenewable resources are fragile and must be conserved for use in the future. Humankind's impact and knowledge of conservation will control our future. The following are just some of the ways in which the earth's ecology is altered by human interaction.

The human race is still growing at an exponential rate. Carrying capacity has not been met due to our ability to use technology to produce more food and housing. However, space and water cannot be manufactured; eventually, our nonrenewable resources will reach a crisis state. Our overuse affects every living thing on this planet.

COMPETENCY 0013   UNDERSTAND FUNDAMENTAL CONCEPTS AND PRINCIPLES OF LIFE SCIENCE AND LIVING SYSTEMS

Skill 13.1   Recognizing basic structures and functions of cells

The organization of living systems builds by levels from small to increasingly more large and complex. All living beings, whether a cell or an ecosystem, have the same requirements to sustain life. Life is organized from simple to complex in the following ways:

Organelles make up **cells**. Cells make up **tissues**, and tissues make up **organs**. Groups of organs make up **organ systems**. Organ systems work together to provide life for an **organism.**

Several characteristics identify living versus non-living substances.

1. **Living things are made of cells**; they grow, respond to stimuli and are capable of reproduction.

2. **Living things must adapt to environmental changes or perish**.

3. **Living things carry on metabolic processes**; they use and make energy.

All organic life has a common element: carbon. Carbon is recycled through the ecosystem through both biotic and abiotic means. It is the link between biological processes and the chemical make-up of life.

The cell is the basic unit of all living things. The two types of cells are prokaryotic and eukaryotic. **Prokaryotic** cells consist only of bacteria and blue-green algae. Bacteria were most likely the first cells; they date back in the fossil record 3.5 billion years. These cells are grouped together because of the following:

1. They have no defined nucleus or nuclear membrane. The DNA and ribosomes float freely within the cell.
2. They have a thick cell wall. This is for protection, to give shape, and to keep the cell from bursting.
3. The cell walls contain amino sugars (glycoproteins). Penicillin works by disrupting the cell wall, which is bad for the bacteria but will not harm the host.
4. Some have a capsule made of polysaccharides that make them sticky.
5. Some have pili, which is a protein strand. This also allows for attachment of the bacteria and may be used for sexual reproduction (conjugation).
6. Some have flagella for movement.

Eukaryotic cells are found in protists, fungi, plants, and animals. Some features of eukaryotic cells include the following:

1. They are usually larger than prokaryotic cells.
2. They contain many organelles, which are membrane-bound areas for specific cell functions.
3. They contain a cytoskeleton that provides a protein framework for the cell.
4. They contain cytoplasm, which supports the organelles and contains the ions and molecules necessary for cell function.

Parts of Eukaryotic Cells

1. Nucleus – the brain of the cell. The nucleus contains:

- **chromosomes**: DNA, RNA, and proteins tightly coiled to conserve space while providing a large surface area.
- **chromatin**: the loose structure of chromosomes. Chromosomes are called chromatin when the cell is not dividing.
- **nucleoli**: where ribosomes are made. These are seen as dark spots in the nucleus.
- **nuclear membrane**: contains pores that let RNA out of the nucleus. The nuclear membrane is continuous with the endoplasmic reticulum, which allows the membrane to expand or shrink if needed.

2. Ribosomes – the site of protein synthesis. Ribosomes may be free floating in the cytoplasm or attached to the endoplasmic reticulum. There may be up to a half million ribosomes in a cell, depending on how much protein is made by the cell.

3. Endoplasmic Reticulum – these are folded and provide a large surface area. They are the "roadway" of the cell and allow for transport of materials. The lumen of the endoplasmic reticulum helps to keep materials out of the cytoplasm and headed in the right direction. The endoplasmic reticulum is capable of building new membrane material. There are two types:

- **smooth endoplasmic reticulum** – contain no ribosomes on their surface.
- **rough endoplasmic reticulum** – contain ribosomes on their surface. This form of ER is abundant in cells that make many proteins, such as in the pancreas, which produces many digestive enzymes.

4. Golgi Complex or Golgi Apparatus – this structure is stacked to increase surface area. The Golgi complex functions to sort, modify, and package molecules that are made in other parts of the cell. These molecules are either sent out of the cell or to other organelles within the cell.

5. Lysosomes – found mainly in animal cells. These contain digestive enzymes that break down food, substances not needed, viruses, damaged cell components, and eventually the cell itself. It is believed that lysosomes are responsible for the aging process.

6. Mitochondria – large organelles that make ATP to supply energy to the cell. Muscle cells have many mitochondria because they use a great deal of energy. The folds inside the mitochondria are called cristae. They provide a large surface where the reactions of cellular respiration occur. Mitochondria have their own DNA and are capable of reproducing themselves if a greater demand is made for additional energy. Mitochondria are found only in animal cells.

7. Plastids – found in photosynthetic organisms only. They are similar to the mitochondria due to their double membrane structure. They also have their own DNA and can reproduce if increased capture of sunlight becomes necessary. There are several types of plastids:

- **chloroplasts**: green in color, they function in photosynthesis. They are capable of trapping sunlight.
- **chromoplasts**: make and store yellow and orange pigments. They provide color to leaves, flowers, and fruits.
- **amyloplasts**: store starch and are used as a food reserve. They are abundant in roots like potatoes.

8. Cell Wall – found in plant cells only, it is composed of cellulose and fibers. It is thick enough for support and protection, yet porous enough to allow water and dissolved substances to enter. Cell walls are cemented to each other.

9. Vacuoles – hold stored food and pigments. Vacuoles are very large in plants. This allows them to fill with water in order to provide turgor pressure. Lack of turgor pressure causes a plant to wilt.

10. Cytoskeleton – composed of protein filaments attached to the plasma membrane and organelles. They provide a framework for the cell and aid in cell movement. They constantly change shape and move about. Three types of fibers make up the cytoskeleton:

- **microtubules**: largest of the three, they are made up of cilia and flagella for locomotion. Flagella grow from a basal body. Some examples are sperm cells and tracheal cilia. Centrioles are also composed of microtubules. They form the spindle fibers that pull the cell apart into two cells during cell division. Centrioles are not found in the cells of higher plants.
- **intermediate filaments**: they are smaller than microtubules but larger than microfilaments. They help the cell to keep its shape.
- **microfilaments**: smallest of the three, they are made of actin and small amounts of myosin (as in muscle cells). They function in cell movement such as cytoplasmic streaming, endocytosis, and ameboid movement. This structure pinches the two cells apart after cell division, forming two cells.

Skill 13.2 Recognizing the characteristics, processes, and classification of living things

Carolus Linnaeus is termed the father of taxonomy. **Taxonomy** is the science of classification. Linnaeus based his system on morphology (study of structure). Later on, evolutionary relationships (phylogeny) were also used to sort and group species. The modern classification system uses binomial nomenclature. This consists of a two-word name for every species. The genus is the first part of the name and the species is the second part. Notice, in the levels explained below, that Homo sapiens is the scientific name for humans. Starting with the kingdom, the groups get smaller and more alike as one moves down the levels in the classification of humans.

Kingdom: Animalia
Phylum: Chordata
Subphylum: Vertebrata
Class: Mammalia
Order: Primate
Family: Hominidae
Genus: Homo
Species: sapiens

Species are defined by the ability to successfully reproduce with members of their own kind.

Five Kingdoms

Living organisms are divided into five major kingdoms: Monera, Protista, Fungi, Plantae, and Animalia.

Kingdom Monera – bacteria and blue-green algae; prokaryotic; have no true nucleus; unicellular.

Bacteria are classified according to their morphology (shape). **Bacilli** are rod shaped, **cocci** are round, and **spirillia** are spiral shaped. The **gram stain** is a staining procedure used to identify bacteria. Gram positive bacteria pick up the stain and turn purple. Gram negative bacteria do not pick up the stain and are pink in color.

Methods of locomotion – flagellates have a flagellum; ciliates have cilia; and ameboids move through use of pseudopodia.

Methods of reproduction – binary fission is simply dividing in half and is asexual. All new organisms are exact clones of the parent. Sexual modes provide more diversity. Bacteria can reproduce sexually through conjugation, where genetic material is exchanged.

Methods of obtaining nutrition – photosynthetic organisms or producers convert sunlight to chemical energy, while consumers or heterotrophs eat other living things. Saprophytes are consumers that live off dead or decaying material.

Kingdom Protista – eukaryotic; unicellular; some are photosynthetic; and some are consumers. Microbiologists use methods of locomotion, reproduction, and how the organism obtains its food to classify protista.

Kingdom Fungi – eukaryotic; multicellular; absorptive consumers; and contain a chitin cell wall.

Kingdom Plantae

Nonvascular Plants – small in size; they do not require vascular tissue (xylem and phloem) because individual cells are close to their environment. The nonvascular plants have no true leaves, stems, or roots.

- **Division Bryophyta** – mosses and liverworts; these plants have a dominant gametophyte generation. They possess rhizoids, which are root-like structures. Moisture in their environment is required for reproduction and absorption.

Vascular Plants – the development of vascular tissue enables these plants to grow in size. Xylem and phloem allow for the transport of water and minerals up to the top of the plant, as well as for the transport of food manufactured in the leaves to the bottom of the plant. All vascular plants have a dominant sporophyte generation.

- **Division Lycophyta** – club mosses; these plants reproduce with spores and require water for reproduction.
- **Division Sphenophyta** – horsetails; also reproduce with spores. These plants have small, needle-like leaves and rhizoids. They require moisture for reproduction.
- **Division Pterophyta** – ferns; they reproduce with spores and flagellated sperm. These plants have a true stem and need moisture for reproduction.
- **Gymnosperms** – the word means "naked seed." These were the first plants to evolve with seeds, which made them less dependent on water to assist in reproduction. Their seeds can travel by wind; pollen from the male is also easily carried by the wind. Gymnosperms have cones that protect the seeds.
- **Division Cycadophyta** – cycads; these plants look like palms with cones.
- **Divison Ghetophyta** – desert dwellers.
- **Division Coniferophyta** – pines; these plants have needles and cones.
- **Divison Ginkgophyta** – the Ginkgo is the only member of this division.

Angiosperms (Division Anthophyta) – the largest group in the plant kingdom. They are the flowering plants that produce true seeds for reproduction.

Kingdom Animalia

Annelida – the segmented worms. The Annelida have specialized tissue. The circulatory system is more advanced in these worms; it is a closed system with blood vessels. The nephridia are their excretory organs. They are hermaphrodidic, and each worm fertilizes the other upon mating. They support themselves with a hydrostatic skeleton and have circular and longitudinal muscles for movement.

Mollusca – clams, octopi, and soft-bodied animals. These animals have a muscular foot for movement. They breathe through gills, and most are able to make a shell for protection from predators. They have an open circulatory system, with sinuses bathing the body regions.

Arthropoda – insects, crustaceans, and spiders; this is the largest group of the animal kingdom. Phylum Arthropoda accounts for about 85 percent of all the animal species. Animals in the Phylum Arthropoda possess an exoskeleton made of chitin. They must molt to grow. Insects, for example, go through four stages of development. They begin as an egg, hatch into a larva, form a pupa, then emerge as an adult. Arthropods breathe through gills, trachea, or book lungs. Movement varies, with members being able to swim, fly, and crawl. There is a division of labor among the appendages (legs, antennae, etc). This is an extremely successful phylum, with members occupying diverse habitats.

Echinodermata – sea urchins and starfish; these animals have spiny skin. Their habitat is marine. They have tube feet for locomotion and feeding.

Chordata – all animals with a notocord or a backbone. The classes in this phylum include Agnatha (jawless fish), Chondrichthyes (cartilage fish), Osteichthyes (bony fish), Amphibia (frogs and toads; gills that are replaced by lungs during development), Reptilia (snakes, lizards; the first to lay eggs with a protective covering), Aves (birds; warm-blooded with wings consisting of a particular shape and composition designed for flight), and Mammalia (warm blooded animals with body hair who bear their young alive and possess mammary glands for milk production).

Skill 13.3   Demonstrating knowledge of the basic structures and functions of human body systems

Overview of Systems

The function of the **skeletal system** is support. Vertebrates have an endoskeleton, with muscles attached to bones. Skeletal proportions are controlled by area to volume relationships. Body size and shape is limited due to the forces of gravity. Surface area is increased to improve efficiency in all organ systems.

The function of the **muscular system** is movement. There are three types of muscle tissue. Skeletal muscle is voluntary. These muscles are attached to bones. Smooth muscle is involuntary. It is found in organs and enable functions such as digestion and respiration. Cardiac muscle is a specialized type of smooth muscle.

The neuron is the basic unit of the **nervous system**. It consists of an axon, which carries impulses away from the cell body, the dendrite, which carries impulses toward the cell body, and the cell body, which contains the nucleus. Synapses are spaces between neurons. Chemicals called neurotransmitters are found close to the synapse. The myelin sheath, composed of Schwann cells, covers the neurons and provides insulation.

The function of the **digestive system** is to break down food and absorb it into the blood stream where it can be delivered to all cells of the body for use in cellular respiration. As animals evolved, digestive systems changed from simple absorption to a system with a separate mouth and anus, capable of allowing the animal to become independent of a host.

The **respiratory system** functions in the gas exchange of oxygen (needed) and carbon dioxide (waste). It delivers oxygen to the bloodstream and picks up carbon dioxide for release out of the body. Simple animals diffuse gases from and to their environment. Gills allow aquatic animals to exchange gases in a fluid medium by removing dissolved oxygen from the water. Lungs maintain a fluid environment for gas exchange in terrestrial animals.

The function of the **circulatory system** is to carry oxygenated blood and nutrients to all cells of the body and return carbon dioxide waste to be expelled from the lungs. Animals evolved from an open system to a closed system with vessels leading to and from the heart.

The Human Body

The **axial skeleton** consists of the bones of the skull and vertebrae. The **appendicular skeleton** consists of the bones of the legs, arms, tail, and shoulder girdle. Bone is a connective tissue. Parts of the bone include compact bone which gives strength, spongy bone which contains red marrow to make blood cells, yellow marrow in the center of long bones to store fat cells, and the periosteum which is the protective covering on the outside of the bone. A **joint** is defined as a place where two bones meet. Joints enable movement. **Ligaments** attach bone to bone. **Tendons** attach bones to muscles.

Muscles can only contract; therefore they work in antagonistic pairs to allow back and forward movement. Muscle fibers are made of groups of myofibrils which are made of groups of sarcomeres. Actin and myosin are proteins which make up the sarcomere.

Concerning the physiology of muscle contraction, a nerve impulse strikes a muscle fiber. This causes calcium ions to flood the sarcomere. Calcium ions allow ATP to expend energy. The myosin fibers creep along the actin, causing the muscle to contract. Once the nerve impulse has passed, calcium is pumped out and the contraction ends.

Nerve action depends on depolarization and an imbalance of electrical charges across the neuron. A polarized nerve has a positive charge outside the neuron. A depolarized nerve has a negative charge outside the neuron. Neurotransmitters turn off the sodium pump which results in depolarization of the membrane. This wave of depolarization (as it moves from neuron to neuron) carries an electrical impulse. This is actually a wave of opening and closing gates that allows for the flow of ions across the synapse. Nerves have an action potential. There is a threshold of the level of chemicals that must be met or exceeded in order for muscles to respond. This is called the *all or none* response.

The **reflex arc** is the simplest nerve response. The brain is bypassed. When a stimulus (like touching a hot stove) occurs, sensors in the hand send the message directly to the spinal cord. This stimulates motor neurons that contract the muscles to move the hand.

Voluntary nerve responses involve the brain. Receptor cells send the message to sensory neurons that lead to association neurons. The message is taken to the brain. Motor neurons are stimulated and the message is transmitted to effector cells that cause the end effect.

Concerning the organization of the nervous system, the somatic nervous system is controlled consciously. It consists of the central nervous system (brain and spinal cord) and the peripheral nervous system (nerves that extend from the spinal cord to the muscles). The autonomic nervous system is unconsciously controlled by the hypothalamus of the brain. Smooth muscles, the heart and digestion are some processes controlled by the autonomic nervous system. The sympathetic nervous system works opposite from the parasympathetic nervous system. For example, if the sympathetic nervous system stimulates an action, the parasympathetic nervous system would end that action.

Neurotransmitters are chemicals released by exocytosis. Some neurotransmitters stimulate, while others inhibit, action. **Acetylcholine** is the most common neurotransmitter; it controls muscle contraction and heartbeat. The enzyme acetylcholinesterase breaks it down to end the transmission.

Epinephrine is responsible for the "fight or flight" reaction. It causes an increase in heart rate and blood flow to prepare the body for action. It is also called adrenaline. **Endorphins** and **enkephalins** are natural pain killers and are released during serious injury and childbirth.

The function of the **digestive system** is to break food down and absorb it into the blood stream where it can be delivered to all cells of the body for use in cellular respiration. The teeth and saliva begin digestion by breaking food down into smaller pieces and lubricating it so it can be swallowed. The lips, cheeks, and tongue form a bolus (ball) of food. It is carried down the pharynx by the process of peristalsis (wave like contractions) and enters the stomach through the cardiac sphincter which closes to keep food from going back up. In the stomach, pepsinogen and hydrochloric acid form pepsin, the enzyme that breaks down proteins. The food is broken down further by this chemical action and is turned into chyme. The pyloric sphincter muscle opens to allow the food to enter the small intestine. Most nutrient absorption occurs in the small intestine. Its large surface area, accomplished by its length and protrusions called villi and microvilli allow for a great absorptive surface. Upon arrival into the small intestine, chyme is neutralized to allow the enzymes found there to function. Any food left after the trip through the small intestine enters the large intestine. The large intestine functions to reabsorb water and produce vitamin K. The feces, or remaining waste, are passed out through the anus.

Although not part of the digestive tract, the **accessory organs** function in the production of necessary enzymes and bile. The pancreas makes many enzymes to break down food in the small intestine. The liver makes bile, which breaks down and emulsifies fatty acids.

In the respiratory system, air enters the mouth and nose, where it is warmed, moistened and filtered of dust and particles. Cilia in the trachea trap unwanted material in mucus, which can be expelled. The trachea splits into two bronchial tubes and the bronchial tubes divide into smaller and smaller bronchioles in the lungs. The internal surface of the lung is composed of **alveoli**, which are thin walled air sacs. These allow for a large surface area for gas exchange. The alveoli are lined with capillaries. Oxygen diffuses into the bloodstream and carbon dioxide diffuses out to be exhaled. The oxygenated blood is carried to the heart and delivered to all parts of the body.

The **thoracic cavity** holds the lungs. A muscle, the diaphragm, below the lungs, is an adaptation that makes inhalation possible. As the volume of the thoracic cavity increases, the diaphragm muscle flattens out and inhalation occurs. When the diaphragm relaxes, exhalation occurs.

Be familiar with the parts of the heart and the path blood takes from the heart to the lungs, through the body and back to the heart. Unoxygenated blood enters the heart through the inferior and superior **vena cava**. The first chamber it encounters is the right **atrium**. It goes through the tricuspid valve to the right **ventricle**, on to the pulmonary arteries, and then to the lungs where it is oxygenated. It returns to the heart through the pulmonary vein into the left atrium. It travels through the bicuspid valve to the left ventricle where it is pumped to all parts of the body through the aorta.

The **sinoatrial node** (SA node) is the pacemaker of the heart. Located on the right atrium, it is responsible for contraction of the right and left atrium. The **atrioventricular node** (AV node) is located on the left ventricle, and is responsible for contraction of the ventricles.

Blood vessels include:

- **Arteries**—Lead away from the heart. All arteries carry oxygenated blood except the pulmonary artery going to the lungs. Arteries are under high pressure.

- **Arterioles**—Arteries branch off to form these smaller passages.

- **Capillaries**—Arterioles branch off to form tiny capillaries that reach every cell. Blood moves slowest here due to the small size; only one red blood cell may pass at a time to allow for diffusion of gases into and out of cells. Nutrients are also absorbed by the cells from the capillaries.

- **Venules**—Capillaries combine to form larger venules. These vessels are now carry waste products from the cells.

- **Veins**—Venules combine to form larger veins, leading back to the heart. Veins and venules have thinner walls than arteries because they are not under as much pressure. Veins contain valves to prevent the backward flow of blood due to gravity.

Components of the blood include:

- **Plasma**—60% of the blood is plasma. It contains salts called electrolytes, nutrients, and waste. It is the liquid part of blood.
- **Erythrocytes**—Also called red blood cells; they contain hemoglobin which carries oxygen molecules.
- **Leukocytes**—Also called white blood cells. White blood cells are larger than red cells. They are phagocytic and can engulf invaders. White blood cells are not confined to the blood vessels and can enter the interstitial fluid between cells.
- **Platelets**—Assist in blood clotting. Platelets are made in the bone marrow.

In **blood clotting**, the neurotransmitter that initiates blood vessel constriction following an injury is called serotonin. A material called prothrombin is converted to thrombin with the help of thromboplastin. The thrombin is then used to convert fibrinogen to fibrin which traps red blood cells to form a scab and stop blood flow.

The **immune system** protects against disease by identifying and killing pathogens. **Nonspecific defense mechanisms** do not target specific pathogens, but are a whole body response. Nonspecific mechanisms are seen as symptoms of an infection. These mechanisms include the skin, mucous membranes, and cells of the blood (white blood cells) and lymph (macrophages). Fever is a result of an increase in white blood cells. Pyrogens are released by white blood cells, which set the body's thermostat to a higher temperature. This inhibits the growth of microorganisms. It also increases metabolism to increase phagocytosis and body repair.

Specific defense mechanisms recognize foreign material and respond by destroying the invader. These mechanisms are specific in purpose and diverse in type. They are able to recognize individual pathogens. They are able to differentiate between foreign material and body cells. Memory of the invaders provides immunity upon further exposure.

Antigens are any foreign particle that invades the body. **Antibodies** are manufactured by the body, they recognize and latch onto antigens, hopefully destroying them. **Immunity** is the body's ability to recognize and destroy an antigen before it causes harm. Active immunity develops after recovery from an infectious disease (chicken pox) or after a vaccination (mumps, measles, rubella). Passive immunity may be passed from one individual to another. It is not permanent. A good example is the immunities passed from mother to a nursing child.

The function of the **excretory system** is to rid the body of nitrogenous wastes in the form of urea. The functional unit of excretion are the nephrons, which make up the kidneys. Antidiuretic hormone (ADH), which is made in the hypothalamus and stored in the pituitary, is released when differences in osmotic balance occur. This will cause more water to be reabsorbed. As the blood becomes more dilute, ADH release ceases.

The Bowman's capsule contains the glomerulus, a tightly packed group of capillaries. The glomerulus is under high pressure. Waste and fluids leak out due to pressure. Filtration is not selective in this area. Selective secretion by active and passive transport occurs in the proximal convoluted tubule. Unwanted molecules are secreted into the filtrate. Selective secretion also occurs in the loop of Henle. Salt is actively pumped out of the tube and much water is lost due to the hyperosmosity of the inner part (medulla) of the kidney. As the fluid enters the distal convoluted tubule, more water is reabsorbed. Urine forms in the collecting duct which leads to the ureter then to the bladder where it is stored. Urine is passed from the bladder through the urethra. The amount of water reabsorbed back into the body is dependent upon how much water or fluids an individual has consumed. Urine can be very dilute or very concentrated if dehydration is present.

The function of the **endocrine system** is to manufacture proteins called hormones. Hormones are released into the bloodstream and are carried to a target tissue where they stimulate an action. Hormones may build up over time to cause their effect, as in puberty or the menstrual cycle. Hormones are specific and fit receptors on the target tissue cell surface. The receptor activates an enzyme which converts ATP to cyclic AMP. Cyclic AMP (cAMP) is a second messenger from the cell membrane to the nucleus. The genes found in the nucleus turn on or off to cause a specific response.

There are two classes of hormones. **Steroid hormones** come from cholesterol and cause sexual characteristics and mating behavior. These hormones include estrogen and progesterone in females and testosterone in males. **Peptide hormones** are made in the pituitary, adrenal glands (kidneys), and the pancreas. They include the following:

- **Follicle stimulating hormone (FSH)**—production of sperm or egg cells.
- **Luteinizing hormone (LH)**—functions in ovulation.
- **Luteotropic hormone (LTH)**—assists in production of progesterone.
- **Growth hormone (GH)**—stimulates growth.
- **Antidiuretic hormone (ADH)**—assists in retention of water.
- **Oxytocin**—stimulates labor contractions at birth and let—down of milk.
- **Melatonin**—regulates circadian rhythms and seasonal changes.
- **Epinephrine (adrenaline)**—causes fight or flight reaction of the nervous system.
- **Thyroxin**—increases metabolic rate.
- **Calcitonin**—removes calcium from the blood.
- **Insulin**—decreases glucose level in blood.
- **Glucagon**—increases glucose level in blood.

Hormones work on a feedback system. The increase or decrease in one hormone may cause the increase or decrease in another. The release of hormones causes a specific response.

Reproduction

Sexual reproduction greatly increases diversity due to the many combinations possible through meiosis and fertilization. Gametogenesis is the production of the sperm and egg cells. Spermatogenesis begins at puberty in the male. One spermatozoa produces four sperm. The sperm mature in the seminiferous tubules located in the testes. Oogenesis, the production of egg cells is usually complete by the birth of a female. Egg cells are not released until menstruation begins at puberty. Meiosis forms one ovum with all the cytoplasm and three polar bodies which are reabsorbed by the body. The ovum are stored in the ovaries and released each month from puberty to menopause.

Path of the sperm: Sperm are stored in the seminiferous tubules in the testes where they mature. Mature sperm are found in the epididymis located on top of the testes. After ejaculation, the sperm travels up the vas deferens where they mix with semen made in the prostate and seminal vesicles and travel out the urethra.

Path of the egg: Eggs are stored in the ovaries. Ovulation releases the egg into the fallopian tubes which are ciliated to move the egg along. Fertilization normally occurs in the fallopian tube. If pregnancy does not occur, the egg passes through the uterus and is expelled through the vagina during menstruation. Levels of progesterone and estrogen stimulate menstruation. In the event of pregnancy, hormonal levels are affected by the implantation of a fertilized egg, so menstruation does not occur.

If fertilization occurs, the zygote implants in about two to three days in the uterus. Implantation promotes secretion of human chorionic gonadotropin (HCG). This is what is detected in pregnancy tests. The HCG keeps the level of progesterone elevated to maintain the uterine lining in order to feed the developing embryo until the umbilical cord forms. Labor is initiated by oxytocin which causes labor contractions and dilation of the cervix. Prolactin and oxytocin cause the production of milk.

SEE also Skill 13.7

Skill 13.4   Recognizing the processes by which organisms obtain matter and energy for life processes

SEE "Digestive System" under Skill 13.3

Skill 13.5   Analyzing how organisms interact with one another and with their environment, including the effects of human activities on the environment

Animal communication is defined as any behavior by one animal that affects the behavior of another animal. Animals use body language, sound, and smell to communicate. Perhaps the most common type of animal communication is the presentation or movement of distinctive body parts. Many species of animals reveal or conceal body parts to communicate with potential mates, predators, and prey. In addition, many species of animals communicate with sound. Examples of vocal communication include the mating "songs" of birds and frogs and warning cries of monkeys. Many animals also release scented chemicals called pheromones and secrete distinctive odors from specialized glands to communicate with other animals. Pheromones are important in reproduction and mating, and glandular secretions of long-lasting smell alert animals to the presence of others.

Ecological and behavioral factors affect the interrelationships among organisms in many ways. Two important ecological factors are environmental conditions and resource availability. Important types of organismal behaviors are described as competitive, instinctive, territorial, and mating.

Competitive – In any system, organisms compete with other species for scarce resources. Organisms also compete with members of their own species for mates and territory. Many competitive behaviors involve rituals and dominance hierarchies. **Rituals** are symbolic activities that often settle disputes without undue harm. For example, dogs bare their teeth, erect their ears, and growl to intimidate competitors. A dominance hierarchy, or "pecking order," organizes groups of animals, simplifying interrelationships, conserving energy, and minimizing the potential for harm in a community.

Instinctive – Instinctive, or innate, behavior is common to all members of a given species; it is genetically preprogrammed. Environmental differences do not affect instinctive behaviors. For example, baby birds of many types and species beg for food by raising their heads and opening their beaks.

Territorial – Many animals act aggressively to protect their territory from other animals. Animals protect territories for use in feeding, mating, and rearing of young.

Mating – Mating behaviors are very important interspecies interactions. The search for a mate with which to reproduce is an instinctive behavior. Mating interrelationships often involve ritualistic and territorial behaviors that are competitive.
Environmental conditions such as climate influence organismal interrelationships by changing the dynamic of the ecosystem. Changes in climate (such as moisture levels and temperature) can alter the environment, changing the characteristics that are advantageous. For example, an increase in temperature will favor those organisms that can tolerate the temperature change. Thus, those organisms gain a competitive advantage. In addition, the availability of necessary resources influences interrelationships. For example, when necessary resources are scarce, interrelationships are more competitive than when resources are abundant.

Behavior may be innate or learned. **Innate behaviors** are defined as those that that are inborn or instinctual. An environmental stimulus (such as the length of day or temperature) results in a behavior. Hibernation among some animals is an innate behavior. **Learned behavior** is any behavior that is modified due to past experience.

Interdependence of organisms

Ecology is the study of organisms: where they live and their interactions with the environment. A **population** is a group of the same species in a specific area. A **community** is a group of populations residing in the same area. Communities that are ecologically similar in regards to temperature, rainfall, and the species that live there are called **biomes**. Specific biomes include:

- **Marine** - covers 75 percent of the earth. This biome is organized by the depth of the water. The intertidal zone is located from the tide line to the edge of the water. The littoral zone is from the water's edge to the open sea. It includes coral reef habitats and is the most densely populated area of the marine biome. The open sea zone is divided into the epipelagic zone and the pelagic zone. The epipelagic zone receives more sunlight and has a larger number of species. The ocean floor is called the benthic zone and is populated with bottom feeders.
- **Tropical Rain Forest** - temperature is constant (25 degrees C), and rainfall exceeds 200 cm per year. Located around the area of the equator, the rain forest has abundant, diverse species of plants and animals.
- **Savanna** - temperatures range from 0-25 degrees C depending on the location. Rainfall is from 90 to 150 cm per year. Plants include shrubs and grasses. The savanna is a transitional biome between the rain forest and the desert.
- **Desert** - temperatures range from 10-38 degrees C. Rainfall is under 25 cm per year. Plant species include xerophytes and succulents. Lizards, snakes, and small mammals are common animals.
- **Temperate Deciduous Forest** - temperatures range from -24 to 38 degrees C. Rainfall is between 65 to 150 cm per year. Deciduous trees are common, as are deer, bear, and squirrels.
- **Taiga** - temperatures range from -24 to 22 degrees C. Rainfall is between 35 to 40 cm per year. Taiga is located very north and very south of the equator, getting close to the poles. Plant life includes conifers and plants that can withstand harsh winters. Animals include weasels, mink, and moose.
- **Tundra** - temperatures range from -28 to 15 degrees C. Rainfall is limited, ranging from 10 to 15 cm per year. The tundra is located even further north and south than the taiga. Common plants include lichens and mosses. Animals include polar bears and musk ox.
- **Polar or Permafrost** - temperature ranges from -40 to 0 degrees C. It rarely gets above freezing. Rainfall is below 10 cm per year. Most water is bound up as ice. Life is limited.

Succession is defined as an orderly process of replacing a community that has been damaged or has begun where no life previously existed. **Primary succession** occurs after a community has been totally wiped out by a natural disaster or where life never existed before, as in a flooded area. **Secondary succession** takes place in communities that were once flourishing but were disturbed by some force, either human or natural, but not totally stripped. A **climax community** is a community that is established and flourishing.

Definitions of Feeding Relationships:

- **Parasitism** occurs when two species occupy a similar place, but the parasite benefits from the relationship while the host is harmed.
- **Commensalism** is when two species occupy a similar place, and neither species is harmed or benefits from the relationship.
- **Mutualism (symbiosis)** occurs when two species occupy a similar place and both species benefit from the relationship.
- **Competition** is when two species occupy the same habitat or eat the same food.
- **Predation** is when animals eat other animals. The animals they feed on are called the prey. Population growth depends upon competition for food, water, shelter, and space. The amount of predators determines the amount of prey, which in turn affects the number of predators.
- **Carrying capacity** is the total amount of life a habitat can support. Once the habitat runs out of food, water, shelter, or space, the carrying capacity decreases and then re-stabilizes.

Ecological Problems

Nonrenewable resources are fragile and must be conserved for use in the future. Humankind's impact and knowledge of conservation will control our future. The following are just some of the ways in which the earth's ecology is altered by human interaction.

Biological magnification - chemicals and pesticides accumulate along the food chain. Tertiary consumers have more accumulated toxins than animals at the bottom of the food chain.

Simplification of the food web - three major crops feed the world (rice, corn, and wheat). Planting these foods in abundance wipes out habitats and pushes animals residing there into other habitats, causing overpopulation or extinction.

Fuel sources - strip mining and the overuse of oil reserves have depleted these resources. At the current rate of consumption, the only way to guarantee our future fuel sources is conservation or alternate fuel sources.

Pollution - although technology gives us many advances, pollution is a side effect of production. Waste disposal and the burning of fossil fuels have polluted our land, water, and air. Global warming and acid rain are two results of the burning of hydrocarbons and sulfur.

Global warming - rainforest depletion and the use of fossil fuels and aerosols have caused an increase in carbon dioxide production. This leads to a decrease in the amount of oxygen, which is directly proportional to the amount of ozone. As the ozone layer depletes, more heat enters our atmosphere and is trapped.

This causes an overall warming effect, which may eventually melt polar ice caps and cause a rise in water levels or changes in climate that will affect weather systems world-wide.

Endangered species - construction of homes to house people has caused the destruction of habitats for other animals, leading to their extinction.

Overpopulation - the human race is still growing at an exponential rate. Carrying capacity has not been met due to our ability to use technology to produce more food and housing. However, space and water cannot be manufactured; eventually, our nonrenewable resources will reach a crisis state. Our overuse affects every living thing on this planet.

Skill 13.6 Demonstrating knowledge of characteristics of the life cycles of common plants and animals

Members of the five different kingdoms of the classification system of living organisms often differ in their basic life functions. Here we compare and analyze how members of the five kingdoms obtain nutrients, excrete waste, and reproduce.

Bacteria are prokaryotic, single-celled organisms that lack cell nuclei. The different types of bacteria obtain nutrients in a variety of ways. Most bacteria absorb nutrients from the environment through small channels in their cell walls and membranes (chemotrophs) while some perform photosynthesis (phototrophs). Chemoorganotrophs use organic compounds as energy sources while chemolithotrophs can use inorganic chemicals. Depending on the type of metabolism and energy source, bacteria release a variety of waste products (e.g., alcohols, acids, carbon dioxide) to the environment through diffusion.

All bacteria reproduce through binary fission (asexual reproduction), producing two identical cells. Bacteria reproduce very rapidly, dividing or doubling every twenty minutes in optimal conditions. Asexual reproduction does not allow for genetic variation, but bacteria achieve genetic variety by absorbing DNA from ruptured cells and conjugating or swapping chromosomal or plasmid DNA with other cells.

Animals are multicellular, eukaryotic organisms. All animals obtain nutrients by eating food (ingestion). Different types of animals derive nutrients from eating plants, other animals, or both. Animal cells perform digestion that converts food molecules, mainly carbohydrates and fats, into energy. The excretory systems of animals, like animals themselves, vary in complexity. Simple invertebrates eliminate waste through a single tube, while complex vertebrates have a specialized system of organs that process and excrete waste.

Most animals, unlike bacteria, exist in two distinct sexes. Members of the female sex give birth or lay eggs. Some less developed animals can reproduce asexually. For example, flatworms can divide in two, and some unfertilized insect eggs can develop into viable organisms. Most animals reproduce sexually through various mechanisms. For example, many aquatic animals reproduce by external fertilization of eggs, while mammals reproduce by internal fertilization. More developed animals possess specialized reproductive systems and cycles that facilitate reproduction and promote genetic variation.

Plants, like animals, are multi-cellular, eukaryotic organisms. Plants obtain nutrients from the soil through their root systems and convert sunlight into energy through photosynthesis. Many plants store waste products in vacuoles or organs (e.g., leaves, bark) that are discarded. Some plants also excrete waste through their roots.

More than half of the plant species reproduce by producing seeds from which new plants grow. Depending on the type of plant, flowers or cones produce seeds. Other plants reproduce by spores, tubers, bulbs, buds, and grafts. The flowers of flowering plants contain their reproductive organs. Pollination is the joining of male and female gametes that is often facilitated by movement of wind or animals.

Fungi are eukaryotic, mostly multi-cellular organisms. All fungi are heterotrophs, obtaining nutrients from other organisms. More specifically, most fungi obtain nutrients by digesting and absorbing nutrients from dead organisms. Fungi secrete enzymes outside of their body to digest organic material and then absorb the nutrients through their cell walls.

Most fungi can reproduce asexually and sexually. Different types of fungi reproduce asexually by mitosis, budding, sporification, or fragmentation. Sexual reproduction of fungi is different from sexual reproduction of animals. The two mating types of fungi are plus and minus, not male and female. The fusion of hyphae, the specialized reproductive structure in fungi, between plus and minus types produces and scatters diverse spores.

Protists are eukaryotic, single-celled organisms. Most protists are heterotrophic, obtaining nutrients by ingesting small molecules and cells and digesting them in vacuoles. All protists reproduce asexually by either binary or multiple fission. Like bacteria, protists achieve genetic variation by exchange of DNA through conjugation.

Skill 13.7   Recognizing the principles of the transmission of genetic information and of biological evolution

Biological evolution

Charles Darwin defined the theory of Natural Selection in the mid-1800s. Through the study of finches on the Galapagos Islands, Darwin theorized that nature selects the traits that are advantageous to the organism. Organisms that do not possess the desirable trait die, and do not pass on their genes. Those more fit to survive get the opportunity to reproduce, thus increasing that gene in the population. Darwin listed four principles to define natural selection:

1. The individuals in a certain species vary from generation to generation.
2. Some of the variations are determined by the genetic makeup of the species.
3. More individuals are produced than will survive.
4. Some genes allow for better survival of an animal.

Causes of evolution - Certain factors increase the chances of variability in a population, thus leading to evolution. Items that increase variability include mutations, sexual reproduction, immigration, and large population. Items that decrease variation include natural selection, emigration, small population, and random mating.

Sexual selection - Genes that happen to come together determine the makeup of the gene pool. Animals that use mating behaviors may be successful or unsuccessful. An animal that lacks attractive plumage or has a weak mating call will not attract the female, thereby eventually limiting that gene in the gene pool. Mechanical isolation, where sex organs do not fit the female, has an obvious disadvantage.

Reproductive System

Sexual reproduction greatly increases diversity due to the many combinations possible through meiosis and fertilization. **Gametogenesis** is the production of the sperm and egg cells. **Spermatogenesis** begins at puberty in the male. One spermatozoa produces four sperm. The sperm mature in the seminiferous tubules located in the testes. **Oogenesis**, the production of egg cells, is usually complete by the birth of a female. Egg cells are not released until menstruation begins at puberty. Meiosis forms one ovum with all the cytoplasm and three polar bodies, which are reabsorbed by the body. The ovum are stored in the ovaries and released each month from puberty to menopause.

Path of the sperm – Sperm are stored in the seminiferous tubules in the testes where they mature. Mature sperm are found in the epididymis, located on top of the testes. After ejaculation, the sperm travel up the vas deferens where they mix with semen made in the prostate and seminal vesicles; they then travel out the urethra.

Path of the egg – Eggs are stored in the ovaries. Ovulation releases the egg into the fallopian tubes, which are ciliated to move the egg along. Fertilization normally occurs in the fallopian tube. If pregnancy does not occur, the egg passes through the uterus and is expelled through the vagina during menstruation. Levels of progesterone and estrogen stimulate menstruation. In the event of pregnancy, hormonal levels are affected by the implantation of a fertilized egg, so menstruation does not occur.

Pregnancy – If fertilization occurs, the zygote implants in about two to three days in the uterus. Implantation promotes secretion of human chorionic gonadotropin (HCG). This is what is detected in pregnancy tests. The HCG keeps the level of progesterone elevated to maintain the uterine lining in order to feed the developing embryo until the umbilical cord forms. Labor is initiated by oxytocin, which causes labor contractions and dilation of the cervix. Prolactin and oxytocin cause the production of milk.

Cellular Reproduction

The purpose of cell division is to provide growth and repair in body (somatic) cells and to replenish or create sex cells for reproduction. There are two forms of cell division. **Mitosis** is the division of somatic cells and **meiosis** is the division of sex cells (eggs and sperm). The table below summarizes the major differences between the two processes.

Mitosis	Meiosis
1. Division of somatic cell	1. Division of sex cells
2. Two cells result from each division	2. Four cells or polar bodies result from each division
3. Chromosome number is identical to parent cells	3. Chromosome number is half the number of parent cells
4. For cell growth and repair	4. Recombinations provide genetic diversity

Some terms to know:

gamete - sex cell or germ cell; eggs and sperm
chromatin - loose chromosomes; this state is found when the cell is not dividing
chromosome - tightly coiled, visible chromatin; this state is found when the cell is dividing

homologues - chromosomes that contain the same information—they are of the same length and contain the same genes
diploid - two in number; diploid chromosomes are a pair of chromosomes (somatic cells)
haploid - one in number; haploid chromosomes are a half of a pair (sex cells)

Mitosis

The cell cycle is the life cycle of the cell. It is divided into two stages: **interphase** and **mitotic division** (where the cell is actively dividing). Interphase is divided into three steps:

1. G1 (growth) period, where the cell is growing and metabolizing.
2. S period (synthesis), where new DNA and enzymes are being made.
3. G2 phase (growth), where new proteins and organelles are being made to prepare for cell division.

The mitotic stage consists of the stages of mitosis and the division of the cytoplasm. The stages of mitosis and their events are as follows. Be sure to know the correct order of steps. (IPMAT)

1. Interphase - chromatin is loose, chromosomes are replicated, and cell metabolism is occurring. Interphase is technically <u>not</u> a stage of mitosis.

2. Prophase - once the cell enters prophase, it proceeds through the following steps continuously, without stopping. The chromatin condenses to become visible chromosomes. The nucleolus disappears and the nuclear membrane breaks apart. Mitotic spindles form, which will eventually pull the chromosomes apart. They are composed of microtubules. The cytoskeleton breaks down and the spindles are pushed to the poles or opposite ends of the cell by the action of centrioles.

3. Metaphase - kinetechore fibers attach to the chromosomes, which causes the chromosomes to line up in the center of the cell (think **m**iddle for **m**etaphase)

4. Anaphase - centromeres split in half and homologous chromosomes separate. The chromosomes are pulled to the poles of the cell, with identical sets at either end.

5. Telophase – there are two nuclei with a full set of DNA identical to the parent cell. The nucleoli become visible and the nuclear membrane reassembles. A cell plate is visible in plant cells, whereas a cleavage furrow is formed in animal cells. The cell is pinched into two cells. Cytokinesis, or division, of the cytoplasm and organelles occurs.

Meiosis

Meiosis contains the same five stages as mitosis, but is repeated in order to reduce the chromosome number by one half. This way, when the sperm and egg join during fertilization, the haploid number is reached. The steps of meiosis are as follows:

Meiosis I
The major function is to replicate chromosomes; cells remain diploid.

Prophase I - replicated chromosomes condense and pair with homologues. This forms a tetrad. Crossing over (the exchange of genetic material between homologues to further increase diversity) occurs during Prophase I.

Metaphase I - homologous sets attach to spindle fibers after lining up in the middle of the cell.

Anaphase I - sister chromatids remain joined and move to the poles of the cell.

Telophase I - two new cells are formed and the chromosome number is still diploid.

Meiosis II
The major function is to reduce the chromosome number in half.

Prophase II - chromosomes condense.

Metaphase II - spindle fibers form again, sister chromatids line up in center of cell, centromeres divide, and sister chromatids separate.

Anaphase II - separated chromosomes move to opposite ends of cell.

Telophase II - four haploid cells form for each original sperm germ cell. One viable egg cell gets all the genetic information and three polar bodies form with no DNA. The nuclear membrane reforms and cytokinesis occurs.

Mutations

During these very intricate steps, mistakes do happen. Inheritable changes in DNA are called **mutations**. Mutations may be errors in replication or a spontaneous rearrangement of one or more segments by factors like radioactivity, drugs, or chemicals. The amount of the change is not as critical as where the change is. Mutations may occur on somatic or sex cells. Usually the ones on sex cells are more dangerous since they contain the basis of all information for the developing offspring. Mutations are not always bad. They are the basis of evolution, and if they make a more favorable variation that enhances the organism's survival, then they are beneficial. However, mutations may also lead to abnormalities, birth defects, and even death. There are several types of mutations:

Suppose a normal sequence was as follows:

Normal -   A B C D E F

Then:

Duplication - one gene is repeated   A B C C D E F

Inversion - a segment of the sequence is flipped around   A E D C B F

Deletion - a gene is left out   A B C E F

Insertion or Translocation - a segment from another   A B C R S D E F
place on the DNA is inserted in the wrong place

Breakage - a piece is lost   A B C (DEF is lost)

Nondisjunction occurs during meiosis when chromosomes fail to separate properly. One sex cell may get both genes and another may get none. Depending on the chromosomes involved, this may or may not be serious. Offspring end up with either an extra chromosome or are missing one. An example of nondisjunction is Down syndrome, where three of chromosome #21 are present.

Genetics

Gregor Mendel is recognized as the father of genetics. His work in the late 1800s is the basis of our knowledge of genetics. Although unaware of the presence of DNA or genes, Mendel realized there were factors (now known as **genes**) that were transferred from parents to their offspring. Mendel worked with pea plants; he fertilized the plants himself, keeping track of subsequent generations. His findings led to the Mendelian laws of genetics. Mendel found that two "factors" governed each trait, one from each parent. Traits or characteristics came in several forms, known as **alleles**. For example, the trait of flower color had white alleles and purple alleles.

Mendel formed three laws:

Law of dominance - In a pair of alleles, one trait may cover up the allele of the other trait. Example: brown eyes are dominant to blue eyes.

Law of segregation - Only one of the two possible alleles from each parent is passed on to the offspring. (During meiosis, the haploid number insures that half the sex cells get one allele and half get the other.)

Law of independent assortment - Alleles sort independently of each other. (Many combinations are possible, depending on which sperm ends up with which egg. Compare this to the many combinations of hands possible when dealing a deck of cards.)

Punnet squares are used to show the possible ways that genes combine and indicate probability of the occurrence of a certain genotype or phenotype. One parent's genes are put at the top of the box and the other parent at the side of the box. Genes combine on the square just like numbers that are added in addition tables we learned in elementary school. Below is an example of a **monohybrid cross**, which is a cross using only one trait—in this case, a trait labeled "g."

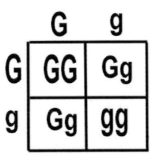

In a **dihybrid cross**, sixteen gene combinations are possible, as each cross has two traits.

Some definitions to know:

Dominant - the stronger of two traits. If a dominant gene is present, it will be expressed. It is shown by a capital letter.

Recessive - the weaker of two traits. In order for the recessive gene to be expressed, there must be two recessive genes present. It is shown by a lower case letter.

Homozygous - (purebred) having two of the same genes present; an organism may be homozygous dominant with two dominant genes or homozygous recessive with two recessive genes.

Heterozygous - (hybrid) having one dominant gene and one recessive gene. Due to the Law of Dominance, the dominant gene will be expressed.

Genotype - the genes the organism has. Genes are represented with letters. AA, Bb, and tt are examples of genotypes.

Phenotype - how the trait is expressed in an organism. Blue eyes, brown hair, and red flowers are examples of phenotypes.

Incomplete dominance - neither gene masks the other; a new phenotype is formed. For example, red flowers and white flowers may have equal strength. A heterozygote (Rr) would have pink flowers. If a problem occurs with a third phenotype, incomplete dominance is occurring.

Codominance - genes may form new phenotypes. The ABO blood grouping is an example of codominance. A and B are of equal strength and O is recessive. Therefore, type A blood may have the genotypes of AA or AO, type B blood may have the genotypes of BB or BO, type AB blood has the genotype A and B, and type O blood has two recessive O genes.

Linkage - genes that are found on the same chromosome usually appear together unless crossing over has occurred in meiosis (for example blue eyes and blonde hair commonly occur together).

Lethal alleles - these are usually recessive due to the early death of the offspring. If a 2:1 ratio of alleles is found in offspring, a lethal gene combination may be the reason. Some examples of lethal alleles include sickle cell anemia, Tay-sachs disease, and cystic fibrosis. In most cases, the coding for an important protein is affected.

Inborn errors of metabolism - these occur when the protein affected is an enzyme. Examples include PKU (phenylketonuria) and albinism.

Polygenic characters - many alleles code for a phenotype. There may be as many as twenty genes that code for skin color. This is why there is such a variety of skin tones. Another example is height. A couple of medium height may have very tall offspring.

Sex linked traits - the Y chromosome found only in males (XY) carries very little genetic information, whereas the X chromosome found in females (XX) carries very important information. Since men have no second X chromosome to cover up a recessive gene, the recessive trait is expressed more often in men. Women need the recessive gene on both X chromosomes to show the trait. Examples of sex linked traits include hemophilia and color-blindness.

Sex influenced traits - traits are influenced by the sex hormones. Male pattern baldness is an example of a sex influenced trait. Testosterone influences the expression of the gene. Most men lose their hair due to this trait.

COMPETENCY 0014   UNDERSTAND THE NATURE, SKILLS, AND PROCESSES OF SCIENTIFIC INQUIRY.

Skill 14.1   Recognizing the nature of scientific inquiry, including how scientific theories explain facts using inferential logic and the role of curiosity, honesty, skepticism, observation, and openness in the scientific process

Science may be defined as a body of knowledge that is systematically derived from study, observations, and experimentation. Its goal is to identify and establish principles and theories that may be applied to solve problems. Pseudoscience, on the other hand, is a belief that is not warranted. There is no scientific methodology or application. Some of the more classic examples of pseudoscience include witchcraft, alien encounters, or any topics that are explained by hearsay.

Scientific inquiry starts with observation. Observation is a very important skill by itself, as it leads to experimentation and communicating the experimental findings to the public. After observing, a question is formed, which starts with "why" or "how." To answer these questions, experimentation is necessary. Between observation and experimentation there are three more important steps. These are gathering information (or researching about the problem), forming a hypothesis, and designing the experiment.

Designing an experiment is very important since it involves identifying control, constants, independent variables, and dependent variables. A **control** is something we compare our results with at the end of the experiment. It is like a reference. **Constants** are the factors that are kept the same in an experiment to get reliable results. **Independent variables** are factors we change in an experiment. **Dependent variables** are the changes that arise from the experiment. It is very important to bear in mind that there should be more constants than variables to obtain reproducible results in an experiment.

After the experiment is done, it is repeated and results are graphically presented. The results are then analyzed and conclusions drawn. After the conclusion is drawn, the final step is communication. It is the responsibility of scientists to share the knowledge they obtain through their research. In this age, much emphasis is put on the way and the method of communication. The conclusions must be communicated by clearly describing the information using accurate data and visual presentations like graphs (bar/line/pie), tables/charts, diagrams, artwork, and other appropriate media. Modern technology should be used whenever it is necessary. The method of communication must be suitable to the audience.

Written communication is as important as oral communication. This is essential for submitting research papers to scientific journals, newspapers, and other magazines.

Whenever scientists begin an experiment or project, they must decide what pieces of data they are going to collect. This data could be qualitative or quantitative. Scientists use a variety of methods to gather and analyze this data. Some possibilities include storing the data in a table or analyzing the data using a graph. Scientists also make notes of their observations (what they see, hear, smell, etc.), throughout the experiment. Scientists are then able to use the data and observations to make inferences and draw conclusions about a question or problem.

Several steps should be followed in the interpretation and evaluation of data.

First the scientist should **apply critical analysis and thinking strategies** asking questions about the accuracy of the data and the procedures of the experiment and procurement of the data.

Second is to **determine the important of information and its relevance to the essential question**. Any experiment may produce a plethora of data, not all of which is necessary to consider when analyzing the hypothesis. The useful information must then be **separated into component parts**.

At this point, the scientist may then **make inferences, identify trends, and interpret data**. The final step is to determine the most appropriate method of communicating these inferences and conclusions to the intended audience.

The scientific attitude is to be curious, open to new ideas, and skeptical. In science, there is always new research, new discoveries, and new theories proposed. Sometimes, old theories are disproved. To view these changes rationally, one must have openness, curiosity, and skepticism. (Skepticism is a Greek word, meaning a method of obtaining knowledge through systematic doubt and continual testing. A scientific skeptic is one who refuses to accept certain types of claims without subjecting them to a systematic investigation.)

The students may not have these attitudes inherently, but it is the responsibility of the teacher to encourage, nurture, and practice these attitudes so that students will have a good role model.

SEE also Skill 14.3

Skill 14.2 **Identifying controlled, manipulated (i.e., independent), and responding (i.e., dependent) variables in scientific investigations**

SEE Skill 14.1

Skill 14.3 **Demonstrating knowledge of the skills and processes of scientific inquiry, including planning scientific investigations, collecting and presenting data in different contexts, and drawing conclusions from data and evidence**

A **scientific theory** is an explanation of a set of related observations based on a proven hypothesis. A **scientific law** usually lasts longer than a scientific theory and has more experimental data to support it.

Simple Investigations

The scientific method is the basic process behind science. It involves several steps, beginning with hypothesis formulation and working through to the conclusion.

Posing a question: Although many discoveries happen by chance, the standard thought process of a scientist begins with forming a question to research. The more limited the question, the easier it is to set up an experiment to answer it.

Form a hypothesis: Once the question is formulated, researchers should take an educated guess about the answer to the problem or question. This "best guess" is the hypothesis.

Do the test: To make a test fair, data from an experiment must have a variable or any condition that can be changed, such as temperature or mass. A good test will try to manipulate as few variables as possible to see which variable is responsible for the result. This requires a second example of a control. A control is an extra setup in which all the conditions are the same except for the variable being tested.

Observe and record the data: Reporting the data should include the specifics of how measurements were calculated. For example, a graduated cylinder needs to be read with proper procedures. As beginning students, technique must be part of the instructional process so as to give validity to the data.

Drawing a conclusion: After recording data, compare your data with that of other groups. A conclusion is the judgment derived from the data results.

Graphing data: Graphing utilizes numbers to demonstrate patterns. The patterns offer a visual representation, making it easier to draw conclusions.

Apply knowledge of designing and performing investigations: Normally, knowledge is integrated in the form of a lab report. A report has many sections. It should include a specific **title** that tells exactly what is being studied. The **abstract** is a summary of the report written at the beginning of the paper. The **purpose** should always be defined to state the problem. The purpose should include the **hypothesis** (educated guess) of what is expected from the outcome of the experiment. The entire experiment should relate to this problem.

It is important to describe exactly what was done to prove or disprove a hypothesis. A **control** is necessary to prove that the results occurred from the changed conditions and would not have happened normally. Only one variable should be manipulated at a time. **Observations** and **results** of the experiment, including all results from data, should be recorded. Drawings, graphs, and illustrations should be included to support information. Observations are objective, whereas analysis and interpretation are subjective. A **conclusion** should explain why the results of the experiment either proved or disproved the hypothesis.

Skill 14.4 Recognizing appropriate procedures for making scientific investigations reliable and valid

Designing an experiment is very important since it involves identifying the control, constants, independent variables and dependent variables. A control/standard is something we compare our results with at the end of the experiment. It is like a reference. Constants are the factors we have to keep constant in an experiment to get reliable results. Independent variables are factors we change in an experiment. It is very important to bear in mind that there should be more constants than variables to obtain reproducible results in an experiment.

Skill 14.5 Recognizing potential safety hazards, sources of information, and appropriate protocols for maintaining safety and responding to emergencies in laboratory situations

Management of Laboratory Equipment

Hot plates should be used whenever possible to avoid the risk of burns or fire. If **Bunsen burners** are used, the following precautions should be followed:

1. Know the location of fire extinguishers and safety blankets and train students in their use. Long hair and long sleeves should be secured and out of the way.
2. Turn the gas all the way on and make a spark with the striker. The   preferred method to light burners is to use strikers rather than matches.
3. Adjust the air valve at the bottom of the Bunsen burner until the flame shows an inner cone.
4. Adjust the flow of gas to the desired flame height by using the adjustment valve.

5. Do not touch the barrel of the burner (it is hot).

All science labs should contain the following items of safety equipment. The following are requirements by law.

- Fire blanket which is visible and accessible
- Ground-fault circuit Interrupters (GFCI) within two feet of water supplies
- Emergency shower capable of providing a continuous flow of water
- Signs designating room exits
- Emergency eye wash station which can be activated by the foot or forearm
- Eye protection for every student and a means of sanitizing equipment
- Emergency exhaust fans providing ventilation to the outside of the building
- Master cut-off switches for gas, electric, and compressed air. Switches must have permanently attached handles. Cut-off switches must be clearly labeled.
- An ABC fire extinguisher
- Storage cabinets for flammable materials

Also recommended, but not required by law:

- Chemical spill control kit
- Fume hood with a motor which is spark proof
- Protective laboratory aprons made of flame retardant material
- Signs which will alert people to potential hazardous conditions
- Containers for broken glassware, flammables, corrosives, and waste.
- Containers should be labeled.

It is the responsibility of teachers to provide a safe environment for their students. Proper supervision greatly reduces the risk of injury and a teacher should never leave a class for any reason without providing alternate supervision. After an accident, two factors are considered; foreseeability and negligence.

Foreseeability is the anticipation that an event may occur under certain circumstances. **Negligence** is the failure to exercise ordinary or reasonable care. Safety procedures should be a part of the science curriculum and a well managed classroom is important to avoid potential lawsuits

The **right-to-know statutes** cover science teachers who work with potentially hazardous chemicals. Briefly, the law states that employees must be informed of potentially toxic chemicals. An inventory must be made available if requested. The inventory must contain information about the hazards and properties of the chemicals. Training must be provided in the safe handling and interpretation of the material safety data sheet (MSDA).

The following chemicals are potential carcinogens and are not allowed in school facilities:

acrylonitrile, arsenic compounds, asbestos, benzidine, benzene,   cadmium compounds, chloroform, chromium compounds, ethylene oxide, ortho-toluidine, Nickel powder, Mercury.

All laboratory solutions should be prepared as directed in the lab manual. Care should be taken to avoid contamination. All glassware should be rinsed thoroughly with distilled water before using, and cleaned well after use. Safety goggles should be worn while working with glassware in case of an accident. All solutions should be made with distilled water as tap water contains dissolved particles which may affect the results of an experiment. Chemical storage should be located in a secured, dry area. Chemicals should be stored in accordance with reactability. Acids are to be locked in a separate area. Used solutions should be disposed of according to local disposal procedures. Any questions regarding safe disposal or chemical safety may be directed to the local fire department.

Safety in the science classroom and laboratory is of paramount importance to the science educator. The following is a general summary of the types of safety equipment that should be made available within a given school system as well as general locations where the protective equipment or devices should be maintained and used. Please note that this is only a partial list and that your school system should be reviewed for unique hazards and site-specific hazards at each facility.

The key to maintaining a safe learning environment is through proactive training and regular in-service updates for all staff and students who utilize the science laboratory. Proactive training should include how to **identify potential hazards**, **evaluate potential hazards**, and **how to prevent or respond to hazards**. The following types of training should be considered:

- Right to Know (OSHA training on the importance and benefits of properly recognizing and safely working with hazardous materials) along with some basic chemical hygiene as well as how to read and understand a material safety data sheet,
- instruction in how to use a fire extinguisher,
  instruction in how to use a chemical fume hood,
  general guidance in when and how to use personal protective equipment (e.g. safety glasses or gloves),
- instruction in how to monitor activities for potential impacts on indoor air quality.

It is also important for the instructor to utilize **Material Data Safety Sheets**. Maintain a copy of the material safety data sheet for every item in your chemical inventory. This information will assist you in determining how to store and handle your materials by outlining the health and safety hazards posed by the substance. In most cases the manufacturer will provide recommendations with regard to protective equipment, ventilation and storage practices. This information should be your first guide when considering the use of a new material.

Frequent monitoring and in-service training on all equipment, materials, and procedures will help to ensure a safe and orderly laboratory environment. It will also provide everyone who uses the laboratory the safety fundamentals necessary to discern a safety hazard and to respond appropriately.

Maintain safe practices and procedures in all areas related to science instruction

In addition to requirements set forth by your place of employment, the NABT (National Association of Biology Teachers) and ISEF (International Science Education Foundation) have been instrumental in setting parameters for the science classroom. All science labs should contain the following items of **safety equipment**. Those marked with an asterisk are requirements by state laws.

* fire blanket which is visible and accessible
* Ground Fault Circuit Interrupters (GCFI) within two feet of water supplies
* signs designating room exits
* emergency shower providing a continuous flow of water
* emergency eye wash station which can be activated by the foot or forearm
* eye protection for every student and a means of sanitizing equipment
* emergency exhaust fans providing ventilation to the outside of the building
* master cut-off switches for gas, electric and compressed air. Switches must have permanently attached handles. Cut-off switches must be clearly labeled.
* an ABC fire extinguisher
* storage cabinets for flammable materials

1. chemical spill control kit
2. fume hood with a motor which is spark proof
3. protective laboratory aprons made of flame retardant material
4. signs which will alert potential hazardous conditions
5. containers for broken glassware, flammables, corrosives, and waste
6. containers should be labeled.

Students should wear safety goggles when performing dissections, heating, or while using acids and bases. Hair should always be tied back and objects should never be placed in the mouth. Food should not be consumed while in the laboratory. Hands should always be washed before and after laboratory experiments. In case of an accident, eye washes and showers should be used for eye contamination or a chemical spill that covers the student's body. Small chemical spills should only be contained and cleaned by the teacher. Kitty litter or a chemical spill kit should be used to clean spill. For large spills, the school administration and the local fire department should be notified. Biological spills should also be handled only by the teacher. Contamination with biological waste can be cleaned by using bleach when appropriate.

Accidents and injuries should always be reported to the school administration and local health facilities. The severity of the accident or injury will determine the course of action to pursue.

It is the responsibility of the teacher to provide a safe environment for their students. Proper supervision greatly reduces the risk of injury and a teacher should never leave a class for any reason without providing alternate supervision. After an accident, two factors are considered; **foreseeability** and **negligence**. Foreseeability is the anticipation that an event may occur under certain circumstances. Negligence is the failure to exercise ordinary or reasonable care. Safety procedures should be a part of the science curriculum and a well managed classroom is important to avoid potential lawsuits.

Apply first response procedures, including first aid, for responding to accidents

All students and staff should be trained in first aid in the science classroom and laboratory. Please remember to always report all accidents, however minor, to the lab instructor immediately. In most situations 911 should immediately be called. Please refer to your school's specific safety plan for accidents in the classroom and laboratory. The classroom/laboratory should have a complete first-aid kit with supplies that are up-to-date and checked frequently for expiration.

Know the location and use of fire extinguishers, eye-wash stations, and safety showers in the lab.

Do not attempt to smother a fire in a beaker or flask with a fire extinguisher. The force of the stream of material from it will turn over the vessel and result in a bigger fire. Just place a watch glass or a wet towel over the container to cut off the supply of oxygen.

If your clothing is on fire, **do not run** because this only increases the burning. It is normally best to fall on the floor and roll over to smother the fire. If a student, whose clothing is on fire panics and begins to run, attempt to get the student on the floor and roll over to smother the flame. If necessary, use the fire blanket or safety shower in the lab to smother the fire.

Students with long hair should put their hair in a bun or a pony-tail to avoid their hair catching fire.

Below are common accidents that everyone who uses the laboratory should be trained in how to respond.

Burns (Chemical or Fire) – Use deluge shower for 15 minutes.

Burns (Clothing on fire) – Use safety shower immediately. Keep victim immersed 15 minutes to wash away both heat and chemicals. All burns should be examined by medical personnel.

Chemical spills – Chemical spills on hands or arms should be washed immediately with soap and water. Washing hands should become an instinctive response to any chemical spilled on hands. Spills that cover clothing and other parts of the body should be drenched under the safety shower. If strong acids or bases are spilled on clothing, the clothing should be removed. If a large area is affected, remove clothing and immerse victim in the safety shower. If a small area is affected, remove article of clothing and use deluge shower for 15 minutes.

Eyes (chemical contamination) – Hold the eye wide open and flush with water from the eye wash for about 15 minutes. Seek medical attention.

Ingestion of chemicals or poisoning – See antidote chart on wall of lab for general first-aid directions. The victim should drink large amounts of water. All chemical poisonings should receive medical attention.

Skill 14.6	Demonstrating knowledge of appropriate tools, equipment, and procedures to collect, record, measure, and represent data in scientific investigations

Common Measurements in a Laboratory

Graduated cylinders and beakers are used for measuring the volume of liquids. There are many sizes and shapes. The surface of the liquid will be curved and this curve is called the meniscus. For water, the meniscus is concaved and for mercury the meniscus is convex. Measurements are made by holding the graduated cylinder at eye-level and reading it from the top or the bottom of the meniscus.

Masses are measured with a triple-beam balance or electronic balance. Temperatures are measured with thermometers, time is measured with a stopwatch, and length is measured with a meter stick. A multimeter is used to measure electric currents and voltages.

Organizing Data

Data from research or experiments is usually obtained in a way that is unrelated to the hypothesis or problem that is being investigated. This is called raw data. The raw data should be organized on a data table with column headings in a way that promotes the purpose of the investigation. There may be more than one column heading depending on the investigation. Also, categories for the data may be selected and the data is put under the defined categories. The data can also be presented in various kinds of graphs: line graphs, bar graphs, pie graphs, etc.

Sampling

In cases where the number of events or individuals is too large to collect data on each one, scientists collect information from only a small percentage. This is known as **sampling** or **surveying**. If sampling is done correctly, it should give the investigator nearly the same information he would have obtained by testing the entire population. The survey must be carefully designed, considering both the sampling technique and the size of the sample.

Bias occurs in a sample when some members or opinions of a population are less likely to be included than others. The method a survey is taken can contribute to bias in a survey.

There are a variety of sampling techniques: random, systematic, stratified, cluster, and quota are just a few. A truly **random** sample must choose events or individuals without regard to time, place, or result. Random samples are least likely to be biased because they are most likely to represent the population from which they are taken. **Stratified, quota,** and **cluster** sampling all involve the definition of sub-populations. Those subpopulations are then sampled randomly in an attempt to represent many segments of a data population evenly. While random sampling is typically viewed as the "gold standard", sometimes compromises must be made to save time, money, or effort. For instance, when conducting a phone survey, calls are typically only made in a certain geographical area and at a certain time of day. This is an example of cluster sampling. There are three stages to cluster or area sampling: the target population is divided into many regional clusters (groups); a few clusters are randomly selected for study; a few subjects are randomly chosen from within a cluster

Systematic sampling involves the collection of a sample at defined intervals (for instance, every 10th part to come off a manufacturing line).

Convenience sampling is the method of choosing items arbitrarily and in an unstructured manner from the frame. Convenience samples are most likely to be biased because they are likely to exclude some members of a population.

Another important consideration in sampling is sample size. Again, a large sample will yield the most accurate information but other factors often limit sample size. Statistical methods may be used to determine how large a sample is necessary to give an investigator a specified level of certainty (95% is a typical confidence interval).

Conversely, if a scientist has a sample of certain size, those same statistical methods can be used to determine how confident the scientist can be that the sample accurately reflects the whole population. The smaller the sample size, the more likely the sample is biased.

Example: Brittany called 500 different phone numbers from the phone book to ask people which candidate they were voting for. Which type of sample did Brittany use? Is the sample biased?

Brittany used a random sample. The sample is not biased because it is random and the sample size is appropriate.

Example: Jacob surveyed the girls' softball team on their favorite foods. Which type of sample did he use? Is the sample biased?

Jacob used a convenience sample. The sample is biased because it only sampled a small population of girls.

COMPETENCY 0015   UNDERSTAND PROBLEM-SOLVING STRATEGIES
AND MATHEMATICAL THINKING USED IN
SCIENTIFIC INVESTIGATIONS

Skill 15.1   Recognizing appropriate use of charts, tables, and graphs for
data display and analysis in different contexts

Scientists can organize the raw data obtained from an investigation by
constructing elaborate tables, charts, and graphs.

In a typical investigation, there will be a dependent variable and an independent
variable. The dependent variable is the observed or measured variable. The
independent variable is the one manipulated or selected by the investigator. For
example, the population of a species in a particular area might be the dependent
variable with time as the independent variable, or the population of a species
may be the dependent variable and the location of the species the manipulated
variable.

The horizontal axis is generally chosen to represent the independent variable in
order to conform to the mathematical definition of a function, which distinguishes
between the domain and the range. The axes are marked off with equal line
segments and a scale is decided upon (e.g., 1 segment = 3 seconds). The axes
are labeled and the data points are placed on the graph as dots or x-marks.

If the data points (dots) are scattered on the graph paper, no line graph can be
drawn. If there is a discernable relationship between the points, a straight line,
parabola, exponential curve, or any continuous line can be drawn that best fits
the data. In a double-line graph, the same grid is used for two separate sets of
data. All graphs should be given a descriptive title.

A bar graph is convenient if the independent variables are discrete. For example,
the populations of four different cities can be represented with a bar graph. In a
circle graph, the dependent variables are percentages of a total and the
independent variables are labeled around the rim of the circle.

Skill 15.2 Applying basic mathematical procedures (e.g., averaging, estimating, using ratios and proportions) to interpret scientific data

Averaging

In performing measurements and making observations, investigators frequently repeat the measurement or perform the same measurement on identical samples, for example *n* times. The value reported for the measurement is the mean of all the measurements:

$$\bar{x} = \frac{x_i}{n}$$

Random errors are the deviations of the individual measurements from the average. The standard deviation is also called the root mean square deviation and is defined as follows:

$$s = \sqrt{\frac{(x_i - \bar{x})^2}{n-1}}$$

Since the errors in a repeated measurement are random, statistical analysis can show that there is a 95% probability that any measurement will be within 2 standard deviations of the mean value. If you are comparing $\bar{x}$ with another measurement, or standard value, you will want to know how many standard deviations they are separated by, as well as the percentage difference.

Ratios and Proportions

A quantity is a certain amount of something so it involves a pure number and a unit. Five apples is a quantity and five by itself is a pure number. Measurements are also quantities, for example, 5 miles and 20 kg are quantities. You can multiply and divide units like algebraic symbols. For example, the area of a square with a side of 2 meters is

$$2 \text{ meters} \times 2 \text{ meters} = 4 \text{ meters}^2$$

When you express one quantity in terms of another it is called a *ratio, proportion,* or *rate*. For example, 5 apples per 3 dollars can be expressed as a fraction or a proportion:

$$\frac{5 \text{ apples}}{3 \text{ dollars}}, \frac{3 \text{ dollars}}{5 \text{ apples}}, \text{ or 3 dollars:5 apples}$$

One can also write: 3 dollars = 5 apples. A unitary rate is has as a quantity 1 unit in the denominator. For example, 55 miles per hour means 55 miles ÷ 1 hour or 55 mile/hour. Rates are used to solve many problems in physics and chemistry. Problem: How many 2 oz. bottles of rum can be made 3.6 gallons of rum?

Solution:

$$3.6 \text{ gal} \times \frac{4 \text{ qts.}}{\text{gal}} \times \frac{2 \text{ pts.}}{\text{qt.}} \times \frac{2 \text{ cups}}{\text{pt.}} \times \frac{8 \text{ oz.}}{\text{cup}} \times \frac{1 \text{ bottle}}{2 \text{ oz.}} = 57.6 \text{ bottles}$$

Skill 15.3   Recognizing the appropriate use of fractions, percents, and decimals to represent data

Pie charts, also called circle graphs, and bar graphs are used to display the results of investigations where the independent (manipulated) variable is a set of objects rather than numbers. They are also used when it is desirable to compare the information. The raw data on the populations of the biggest cities in the United States in millions is (NYC, 8), (Houston, 2), (Chicago, 3), and (LA, 4). A bar graph would enable one to see NYC was twice as populous as LA.

For a circle graph, the total population (17 million) is calculated and the relative populations are displayed:

Decimals

When recording a measurement, the last digit in the measurement is uncertain because the investigator is expected to make an estimate. Using a typical meter stick, the length of an object is 23.4 mm not 23.40 mm. The latter number has four significant digits and indicates a more precise measurement than was actually performed. Converting to meters, the measurement becomes 0.0234 m. There has been no change in the precision, so there is no change in the number of significant digits. The rule is that 0s do not count toward the number of significant digits when they occur before (to the left of) the observed numbers. For example, 0.0203 m has three significant figures. Only the first two 0s don't count. For large numbers, the practice is to use scientific notation. For example, 2.34×10^3 km has three significant figures and 2.340×10^3 has four significant figures.

Skill 15.4 **Recognizing how physical models (e.g., relating electric current to flowing water, using a globe and lamp to demonstrate changing seasons) and computer simulations (e.g., weather forecasting, earthquake analysis) are used to explain systems and processes**

Much progress in science is due to the construction and use of models and modeling. A simple kind of model scales up or down the target. Examples are wooden cars, models of bridges, globes to represent Earth, models of molecules, etc. The discovery of the double-helix shape of DNA was the discovery of the correct model of DNA.

Another kind of modeling involves the simplification of reality. In studying gravity, for example, we assume the Earth is an infinitesimally small point located 4,000 miles away from Earth's surface. In kinematics, we assume there is no friction and that all objects fall down at 9.8 m/s^2. In fact, Newton's laws only apply to point masses. There are separate equations for describing the rotation of three-dimensional objects. These equations are derived from Newton's laws. This is done by assuming the objects are made up of point masses connected by massless rods. Newton's equations themselves can be considered models because they explain a wide variety of phenomena.

There are also models by analogy. For example, the gas laws can be derived by assuming atoms behave like billiard balls. Carnot's heat engine is an imaginary engine that does work by taking heat from a reservoir. It is used to prove that machines cannot be 100% efficient. Water flowing in a system of pipes is analogous to an electric current flowing in a circuit.

In using models it is important to understand their shortcomings. Newton's laws for example, only apply for speeds small compared to the speed of light. The drift velocity of electrons in a wire is only about one meter per hour, much less than the speed of water flowing in a pipe. But a battery increases the electrical potential energy of an electron, just as a water pump can increases the gravitational potential energy of water. Also, the amount of water flowing is conserved, just as charge is conserved in an electric circuit.

Another type of modeling takes place when we construct best-fit continuous lines from a grid filled with data points. Some models can be considered fictions. For example, in the plum pudding model of the atom electrons were assumed to be placed is some kind of soup of positive charge. The Bohr model of the atom is fictitious because it assumes the electrons are particles without wavelike properties.

Computer simulations have become important in science in recent years. In connection with global warming, for example, computers are used to predict future temperatures on Earth. These calculations are called computer simulations and are based on climate models. A climate model makes various assumptions about the atmosphere, oceans, land, energy from the Sun, etc.

Skill 15.5   Demonstrating knowledge of the appropriate metric units and levels of precision used in scientific investigations

The International System of Units defines seven base units: meter (m), kilogram (kg), second (s), ampere (A), kelvin, candela (cd), and mole (mol). The kilogram is the only unit defined with an artifact. It is the mass of a platinum-iridium cylinder kept in air under three bell jars at the headquarters of the International Bureau of Weights and Measures in France. The United States, Myanmar, and Liberia don't use the metric system, but an inch is defined to be exactly 2.54 centimeters (cm).

The unit for measuring force is the newton (N) which is defined as follows: $N = m/s^2$. The ampere is the amount of current in two parallel wires, one meter apart, that produces a force of 2×10^{-7} N per meter of wire. The unit of charge is the coulomb ($C = A \times s$). The unit of energy is the joule ($J = m \times N$), the unit of power is the watt ($W = J/s$), and the unit for pressure is the pascal ($Pa = N/m^2$). The units for measuring resistance (ohms) and electrical potential (volts) have similar definitions in terms of the base units.

A kelvin is defined so that the temperature of water at its triple point is 273.16 K. A mole is the number of atoms in 0.012 kilograms of the isotope of carbon with six neutrons. A candela is used only when measuring the perceived brightness of visible light. It has an operational definition using the intensity of green light. A meter is defined so that light travels 299, 792, 458 meters in one second. A second is defined from the frequency of the microwaves absorbed by the valence electron in cesium-133: 1/(9,192,631,770 Hz) = 1.

There is anecdotal evidence concerning the reason the United States stays with English units, except in medicine and science. Some say that it is easier to remember an integer plus a fraction than a decimal. That the metric system is based on the number 10 is one of its benefits. The prefixes that multiply by 10 are *deca-, hecto-, kilo-, mega-, giga-, tera-, peta-, exa-, zetta-,* and *yotta-. Yotta-* means multiplying by 10^{24}. The prefixes that divide by 10 are *deci-, centi-, milli-, micro-, nano-, pico-, femto-, atto-, zepto-,* and *yocto-.*

In the definition of the second there are 10 significant digits, so there is at least an uncertainty of ±0.0000000001 second in any measurement of time. In a typical laboratory, the uncertainties are much greater. A typical triple-beam balance has an uncertainty of ±0.01 g. A thermometer graduated to 1 °C has an uncertainty of ±0.2 °C. A 10-mL graduated cylinder has an uncertainty of ±0.1 mL. Hence, using significant figures to express uncertainty is not as clear as giving the ± range.

Significant Digits, Precision, and Accuracy

In recording measurements, the precision of the measurement should be indicated with the use of significant digits. Precision should not be confused with accuracy. The accuracy of a measurement is a comparison of the measurement with some standard. One might, for example, compare an experimental measurement with a predicted or theoretical value. Precision refers to the measurement process itself.

As an example of precision and significant digits, consider measuring the length of an object with a meter stick. Suppose the investigator observes that the length is between 23 mm and 24 mm. The observer is expected to make an estimate about the length of the object by imagining additional graduation marks and estimating the length as 23.4, 23.9, etc. The precision of the measurement or degree of uncertainty is at least ±0.1 mm and the number of significant digits in the measurement is 3. There are rules for multiplying and adding significant digits. The final answer should have no more significant digits than the measurement with the least number of significant digits.

Generally speaking, when making measurements an investigator repeats the measurement or does the same measurement on duplicate samples. The precision of the measurement is the spread of the measurements around the average value.

COMPETENCY 0016   **UNDERSTAND THE HISTORICAL DEVELOPMENT OF SCIENCE AND THE INTERCONNECTIONS AMONG SCIENCE, TECHNOLOGY, AND SOCIETY**

Skill 16.1   Recognizing the contributions of individuals from diverse cultures to the development of science and technology

Most scientists support the view that modern human beings evolved in Africa 150, 000 years ago and then migrated to other parts of the planet. Modern humans replaced existing hominid species, such as the Neanderthals. The other hominids are also assumed to have an African origin. Many scientists reject the idea human beings can be classified according to race, even though skin color and other traits causes people to identify themselves as belonging to a particular race.

Science began with the agricultural revolution 10,000 years ago because there was apparently a body of knowledge than enabled humans to increase production. Pythagoras' theorem (circa 490 BC) was actually recorded on Mesopotamian cuneiform tablets in 1800 BC. Ancient Greeks discovered the principle behind buoyancy and the approximate radius of Earth. Indians made considerable discoveries in mathematics and astronomy from the 5th to 15th centuries AD. During this period, there were many pure and applied scientific discoveries in China: compasses, movable-type printing, atlases of stars, cast iron, the iron plough, the wheelbarrow, the suspension bridge, solid fuel rocket, and many more.

The scientific method began with Muslim scientists in the Middle Ages, not only because of their achievements in optics, mathematics, chemistry, and astronomy, but because philosophers of the Arab Empire explicitly advocated the need for experiments, observations, and measurements.

The rise of science in the West began with the rise of universities in the 12 century. Roger Bacon (1224–1294) is considered one of the early advocates of the scientific method. In the 14th century, there was scientific progress in kinematics, but the Scientific Revolution began in the 16th century with the heliocentric theory of Nicolaus Copernicus. In 1605, Johannes Kepler discovered that planets orbit the sun in elliptical, not circular paths. In 1677, Isaac Newton derived Kepler's laws from the second law of motion.

In the 19th century, science became a profession and an institution in Western nation-states. The economic progress was due in part to the technological advances made possible by science and scientific progress was made possible by the economic progress. The rise in science in the West was caused the cultural and institutional circumstances that existed in Western countries. The increase in the number of women scientists and other minority groups in recent years was caused by the changing values of individuals and changes in institutional structures.

Skill 16.2   Analyzing how science and technology have affected individuals, cultures, and societies throughout history

The history of biology follows man's understanding of the living world from the earliest recorded history to modern times. Though the concept of biology as a field of science arose only in the nineteenth century, its origins can be traced back to the ancient Greeks (Galen and Aristotle). During the Renaissance and Age of Discovery, renewed interest in the rapidly increasing number of known organisms generated much interest in biology.

Andreas Vesalius (1514-1564) was a Belgian anatomist and physician whose dissections of the human body and written findings helped to correct the misconceptions of science. The books Vesalius wrote on anatomy were the most accurate and comprehensive anatomical texts of time.

Anton van Leeuwenhoek is known as the father of microscopy. In the 1650s, Leeuwenhoek began making tiny lenses that gave magnifications up to 300x. He was the first to see and describe bacteria, yeast plants, and the microscopic life found in water. Over the years, light microscopes have advanced to produce greater clarity and magnification. The scanning electron microscope (SEM) was developed in the 1950s. Instead of light, a beam of electrons passes through the specimen. Scanning electron microscopes have a resolution about one thousand times greater than light microscopes. The disadvantage of the SEM is that the chemical and physical methods used to prepare the sample result in the death of the specimen.

Carl Von Linnaeus (1707-1778), a Swedish botanist, physician, and zoologist, is well-known for his contributions in ecology and taxonomy. Linnaeus is famous for his binomial system of nomenclature in which each living organism has two names: a genus and a species name. He is considered the father of modern ecology and taxonomy.

In the late 1800s, Louis Pasteur discovered the role of microorganisms in the cause of disease; he also discovered pasteurization and the rabies vaccine. Robert Koch took his observations one step further by postulating that specific diseases were caused by specific pathogens. **Koch's postulates** are still used as guidelines in the field of microbiology. They state that the same pathogen must be found in every diseased person, the pathogen must be isolated and grown in culture, the disease must be induced in experimental animals from the culture, and the same pathogen must be isolated from the experimental animal. In the eighteenth century, many fields of science like botany, zoology, and geology began to evolve as scientific disciplines in the modern sense.

In the twentieth century, the rediscovery of Mendel's work led to the rapid development of genetics by Thomas Hunt Morgan and his students.

DNA structure was another key event in biological study. In the 1950s, James Watson and Francis Crick discovered the structure of a DNA molecule as that of a double helix. This structure made it possible to explain DNA's ability to replicate and to control the synthesis of proteins.

Following the cracking of the genetic code, biology has largely split between organismal biology (consisting of ecology, ethology, systematics, paleontology, evolutionary biology, developmental biology, and other disciplines that deal with whole organisms or group of organisms) and the disciplines related to molecular biology (which include cell biology, biophysics, biochemistry, neuroscience, and immunology).

The use of animals in biological research has expedited many scientific discoveries. Animal research has allowed scientists to learn more about animal biological systems, including the circulatory and reproductive systems. One significant use of animals is for the testing of drugs, vaccines, and other products (such as perfumes and shampoos) before use or consumption by humans. There are both significant pros and cons of animal research. The debate about the ethical treatment of animals has been ongoing since the introduction of animals to research. Many people believe the use of animals in research is cruel and unnecessary. Animal use is federally and locally regulated. The purpose of the Institutional Animal Care and Use Committee (IACUC) is to oversee and evaluate all aspects of an institution's animal care and use program.

Society, as a whole, influences biological research. For example, the pressure from the majority of society has led to bans and restrictions on human cloning research. Human cloning has been restricted in the United States and many other countries. The U.S. legislature has banned the use of federal funds for the development of human cloning techniques. Some individual states have banned human cloning regardless of where the funds originate.

The demand for genetically modified crops by society and industry has steadily increased over the years. Genetic engineering in the agricultural field has led to improved crops for human use and consumption. Crops are genetically modified for increased growth and insect resistance because of the demand for larger and greater quantities of produce.

With advances in biotechnology come those in society who oppose it. Ethical questions come into play when discussing animal and human research. Does it need to be done? What are the effects on humans and animals? There are no right or wrong answers to these questions. There are governmental agencies in place to regulate the use of humans and animals for research.

Skill 16.3   Demonstrating knowledge of how science and technology are used to develop solutions to economic, societal, and environmental problems

Math, science, and technology have common themes in how they are applied and understood. All three use models, diagrams, and graphs to simplify a concept for analysis and interpretation. Patterns observed in these systems lead to predictions based on these observations. Another common theme among these three systems is equilibrium. **Equilibrium** is a state in which forces are balanced, resulting in stability. **Static equilibrium** is stability due to a lack of changes and **dynamic equilibrium** is stability due to a balance between opposite forces.

The fundamental relationship between the natural and social sciences is the use of the scientific method and the rigorous standards of proof that both disciplines require. This emphasis on organization and evidence separates the sciences from the arts and humanities. Natural science, particularly biology, is closely related to social science, the study of human behavior. Biological and environmental factors often dictate human behavior; an accurate assessment of behavior requires a sound understanding of biological factors.

[BCA6]Science changes over time and is limited by the available technology. An example of this is the relationship of the discovery of the cell and the invention of the microscope. As our technology improves, more hypotheses will become theories and possibly laws.

However, science is also limited by the data that is able to be collected. Data may be interpreted differently on different occasions. Science limitations cause explanations to be changeable as new technologies emerge. New technologies gather previously unavailable data and enable us to build upon current theories with new information.

The combination of science, mathematics, and technology forms the scientific endeavor and makes science a success. It is impossible to study science on its own without the support of other disciplines like mathematics, technology, geology, physics, and other disciplines.

Science is tentative. By definition it is searching for information by making educated guesses. It must be replicable. Another scientist must be able to achieve the same results under the same conditions at a later time. The term **empirical** means a phenomenon must be assessed through tests and observations. Science changes over time. Science is limited by the available technology. An example of this would be the relationship of the discovery of the cell and the invention of the microscope. As our technology improves, more hypotheses will become theories and possibly laws.

Science is also limited by the data that is able to be collected. Data may be interpreted differently on different occasions. Science limitations cause explanations to be changeable as new technologies emerge. New technologies gather previously unavailable data and enable us to build upon current theories with new information.

Skill 16.4 Recognizing the integration and interdependence of science, technology, society, the workplace, and the environment

Society is not the same as it used to be even twenty-five years ago. The use of technology has changed our patterns of lifestyle, our behavior, our ethical and moral thinking, our economy, and our career opportunities.

Science is an interesting, innovative, and thoroughly enjoyable subject. Science careers are challenging and stimulating, and the possibilities for scientific careers are endless.

Why do people choose careers in science? This is a very important question. The reasons are manifold and may include:

- A passion for science
- A desire to experiment and gain knowledge
- A desire to contribute to society's betterment
- An inquiring mind
- Wanting to work in a team

There are a number of opportunities in science. For the sake of ease and convenience, they are grouped under various categories:

1. Biological sciences: The study of living organisms and their life cycles, medicinal properties, and the like.
* Botanist
* Microbiologist

2. Physical Science: The study of matter and energy.
* Analytical Chemist
* Biochemist
* Chemist
* Physicist[BCA7]

3. Earth Science: Studying the earth, its changes over the years, and natural disasters such as earthquakes and hurricanes.
* Geologist
* Meteorologist
* Oceanographer
* Seismologist
* Volcanologist

4. Space science: Studying space, the universe, and planets.
* Astrophysicist
* Space scientist

5. Forensic science: Solving crimes using various techniques.
* Forensic Pathologist

6. Medical science: Science with practical applications to the care and cure of diseases.
* Biomedical scientist
* Clinical scientist

7. Agricultural science: Using science to grow and improve upon crops.
* Agriculturist
* Agricultural Service Industry
* Agronomist
* Veterinary science

DOMAIN III.   HEALTH/FITNESS

COMPETENCY 0017   UNDERSTAND TYPICAL FACTORS, PRINCIPLES, AND PRACTICES RELATED TO THE DEVELOPMENT OF PERSONAL HEALTH AND SAFETY.

Skill 17.1   **Recognizing patterns and stages of child growth and development and factors that affect growth and development, including the ways in which health and fitness choices and habits affect quality of life, health, and life span**

The teacher of students in early childhood should have a broad knowledge and understanding of the phases of development which typically occur during this stage of life. And the teacher must be aware of how receptive children are to specific methods of instruction and learning during each period of development. A significant premise in the study of child development holds that all domains of development (physical, social, and academic) are integrated. Development in each dimension is influenced by the others. Equally important to the teacher's understanding of the process is the knowledge that developmental advances within the domains occur neither simultaneously nor parallel to one another, necessarily.

STAGES OF MOTOR LEARNING

Stage 1 – Children progress from simple reflexes to basic movements such as sitting, crawling, creeping, standing, and walking.

Stage 2 – Children learn more complex motor patterns including running, climbing, jumping, balancing, catching, and throwing.

Stage 3 – During late childhood, children learn more specific movement skills. In addition, the basic motor patterns learned in stage 2 become more fluid and automatic.

Stage 4 – During adolescence, children continue to develop general and specific motor skills and master specialized movements. At this point, factors including practice, motivation, and talent begin to affect the level of further development.

SEQUENTIAL DEVELOPMENT FOR LOCOMOTOR SKILLS ACQUISITION

Sequential Development = crawl, creep, walk, run, jump, hop, gallop, slide, leap, skip, step-hop.

SEQUENTIAL DEVELOPMENT FOR NONLOCOMOTOR SKILL ACQUISITION

Sequential Development = stretch, bend, sit, shake, turn, rock and sway, swing, twist, dodge, and fall.

SEQUENTIAL DEVELOPMENT FOR MANIPULATIVE SKILL ACQUISITION

Sequential Development = striking, throwing, kicking, ball rolling, volleying, bouncing, catching, and trapping.

Physical development – Small children (ages 3-5) have a propensity for engaging in periods of a great deal of physical activity, punctuated by a need for a lot of rest. Children at this stage lack fine motor skills and cannot focus on small objects for very long. Their bones are still developing. At this age, girls tend to be better coordinated, and boys tend to be stronger.

The lag in fine motor skills continues during the early elementary school years (ages 6-8).

Pre-adolescent children (ages 9-11) become stronger, leaner, and taller. Their motor skills improve, and they are able to sit still and focus for longer periods of time. Growth during this period is constant. This is also the time when gender physical predispositions will begin to manifest. Pre-adolescents are at risk of obesity without proper nutritional and adequate activity.

Young adolescents (ages 12-14) experience drastic physical growth (girls earlier than boys do), and are highly preoccupied with their physical appearance.

As children proceed to the later stages of adolescence (ages 15-17), girls will reach their full height, while boys will still have some growth remaining. The increase in hormone levels will cause acne, which coincides with a slight decrease of preoccupation with physical appearance. At this age, children may begin to initiate sexual activity (boys generally more motivated by hormones, and girls more by peer pressure). There is a risk of teen pregnancy and sexually transmitted diseases.

Cognitive development – Language development is the most important aspect of cognitive development in small children (ages 3-5). Allowing successes, rewarding mature behavior, and allowing the child to explore can improve confidence and self-esteem at this age.

Early elementary school children (Ages 6-8) are eager to learn and love to talk. Children at this age have a very literal understanding of rules and verbal instructions and must develop strong listening skills.

Pre-adolescent children (ages 9-11) display increased logical thought, but their knowledge or beliefs may be unusual or surprising. Differences in cognitive styles develop at this age (e.g. field dependant or independent preferences).

In early adolescence (ages 12-14), boys tend to score higher on mechanical/spatial reasoning, and girls on spelling, language, and clerical tasks. Boys are better with mental imagery, and girls have better access and retrieval of information from memory. Self-efficacy (the ability to self-evaluate) becomes very important at this stage.

In later adolescence (ages 15-17), children are capable of formal thought, but don't always apply it. Conflicts between teens' and parents' opinions and worldviews will arise. Children at this age may become interested in advanced political thinking.

Social development – Small children (ages 3-5) are socially flexible. Different children will prefer solitary play, parallel play, or cooperative play. Frequent minor quarrels will occur between children, and boys will tend to be more aggressive (children at these ages are already aware of gender roles).

Early elementary school children (ages 6-8) are increasingly selective of friends (usually of the same sex). Children at this age enjoy playing games, but are excessively preoccupied by the rules. Verbal aggression becomes more common than physical aggression, and adults should encourage children of this age to solve their own conflicts.

Pre-adolescent children (ages 9-11) place great importance on the (perceived) opinions of their peers and of their social stature, and will go to great lengths to 'fit in'. Friendships at this age are very selective, and usually of the same sex.

Young adolescents (ages 12-14) develop greater understanding of the emotions of others, which results in increased emotional sensitivity and impacts peer relationships. Children at this age develop an increased need to perform.

In the later stages of adolescence (ages 15-17), peers are still the primary influence on day-to-day decisions, but parents will have increasing influence on long-term goals. Girls' friendships tend to be close and intimate, whereas boys' friendships are based on competition and similar interests. Many children this age will work part-time, and educators should be alert to signs of potential school dropouts.

Emotional development – Small children (ages 3-5) express emotion freely and have a limited ability to learn how emotions influence behavior. Jealousy at this age is common.

Early elementary school children (ages 6-8) have easily bruised feelings and are just beginning to recognize the feelings of others. Children this age will want to please teachers and other adults.

Pre-adolescent children (ages 9-11) develop a global and stable self-image (self-concept and self-esteem). Comparisons to their peers and the opinions of their peers are important. An unstable home environment at this age contributes to an increased risk of delinquency.

Young adolescence (ages 12-14) can be a stormy and stressful time for children, but, in reality, this is only the case for roughly 20% of teens. Boys will have trouble controlling their anger and will display impulsive behavior. Girls may suffer depression. Young adolescents are very egocentric and concerned with appearance, and will feel very strongly that "adults don't understand."

In later stages of adolescence (ages 15-17), educators should be alert to signs of surfacing mental healthy problems (e.g. eating disorders, substance abuse, schizophrenia, depression, and suicide).

Piaget's Stages of Cognitive Development

According to Swiss philosopher and natural scientist Jean Piaget, human cognitive development can be broken down into four separate levels. These levels are usually called Piaget's *Four Levels of Cognitive Development* or *Piaget's Stages*. They include infancy, preschool, childhood, and adolescence. Progressing through each level a human develops more sophisticated stages of mental representation. Physical activity is also important during each stage as it creates a channel for new information and development.

The first stage is the Sensorimotor Stage which covers birth to 24 months. This level is where spatial abilities are developed including reflexes, development of coordination, and development of habits. An infant also acts in a manner similar to a scientist, making observations and conducting "experiments." As the Sensorimotor Stage ends a child is able to go beyond trial-and-error and use skills to achieve a goal.

The second stage, the Preoperational Stage, includes the time between ages 2 and 7. In this stage, a child lacks the necessary mental skills to problem solve beyond the superficial level. A child is able to identify an object by a single feature, but cannot sort through objects based on differing features. The period is crucial for language development as objects and actions begin to be associated with words. The child still is unable to use logical reason and is egocentric; they don't realize other people don't experience the world in the same fashion they do. As a child reaches the end of the Preoperational Stage their problem solving skills improve significantly, but they are unaware of how they came to their conclusions.

The Concrete Operational Stage, from ages 7 and 11, is the third stage. At this point a child is able use logic to solve problems. This is marked by a variety of abilities including seriation, transitivity, classification, decentering, reversibility, and conservation. Seriation is the ability to sort objects by characteristics. Transitivity is the ability to understand relationships based on order. Classification is the ability to name an object by a specific characteristic. Decentering allows a child to take into account multiple aspects of a problem to solve it. Reversability is the changing of an object, then returning it to its original form. In this context, conservation refers to the knowledge that an item's value may not be related to its appearance. As the Concrete Operational Stage ends a child is able to look at the world from another person's point of view, this is often called the elimination of egocentrism.

The final stage covers ages 11 through adulthood and is referred to as the Formal Operational Stage. This stage builds upon the previous three and is characterized by the ability to think and reason logically, draw conclusions from multiple sources, make value judgments on sources, and think deeply about hypothetical situations.

Eric Erickson

Eric Erikson articulated a theory that humans go through eights stages of development as they go from infancy to adulthood. Here are the stages that pertain to early childhood programs:

- **Infancy to 12 months**
  During this phase the young child develops the ideas of trust and mistrust. This is evident when the child can't lose sight of the mother or cries when strangers get too close. One has to slowly approach a baby of this age in order to let the child learn whether or not the person is to be trusted.
- **Young Childhood - Ages 1 to 3**
  During this stage, the child develops feelings of shame and doubt along with learning about autonomy. The child wants to be independent and if denied, this could translate into temper tantrums as he tests the adults in charge. Play of all kinds is very important as the child learns the language and self-control.
- **Early Childhood – Ages 3 – 5**
  Here the child learns how to initiate tasks and carry them out. However, the child also learns the quality of guilt in this stage when tasks are not completed. He/She learns how to dream about goals associated with adult life. During this stage the child will begin playing with other children and become aware of the differences between the sexes. There is also some moral development taking place as well.
- **Middle Childhood – Ages 6 – 10**
  The child begins to take pride in work and has a sense of achievement. Friendships develop during this stage as well as learning skills. The child also learns how to act as part of a team.

Skill 17.2   Demonstrating knowledge of nutritional principles and the influence of nutritional practices on health and development

The components of nutrition are **carbohydrates, proteins, fats, vitamins, minerals, and water.**

Carbohydrates – the main source of energy (glucose) in the human diet. The two types of carbohydrates are simple and complex. Complex carbohydrates have greater nutritional value because they take longer to digest, contain dietary fiber, and do not excessively elevate blood sugar levels. Common sources of carbohydrates are fruits, vegetables, grains, dairy products, and legumes.

Proteins – are necessary for growth, development, and cellular function. The body breaks down consumed protein into component amino acids for future use. Major sources of protein are meat, poultry, fish, legumes, eggs, dairy products, grains, and legumes.

Fats – a concentrated energy source and important component of the human body. The different types of fats are saturated, monounsaturated, and polyunsaturated. Polyunsaturated fats are the healthiest because they may lower cholesterol levels, while saturated fats increase cholesterol levels. Common sources of saturated fats include dairy products, meat, coconut oil, and palm oil. Common sources of unsaturated fats include nuts, most vegetable oils, and fish.

Vitamins and minerals – organic substances that the body requires in small quantities for proper functioning. People acquire vitamins and minerals in their diets and in supplements. Important vitamins include A, B, C, D, E, and K. Important minerals include calcium, phosphorus, magnesium, potassium, sodium, chlorine, and sulfur.

Water – makes up 55 – 75% of the human body. Essential for most bodily functions. Attained through foods and liquids.

Determine the adequacy of diets in meeting the nutritional needs of students

Nutritional requirements *vary from person-to-person.* General guidelines for meeting adequate nutritional needs are: *no more than 30% total caloric intake from fats* (preferably 10% from saturated fats, 10% from monounsaturated fats, 10% from polyunsaturated fats), *no more than 15% total caloric intake from protein* (complete), *and* <u>at least</u> *55% of caloric intake from carbohydrates* (mainly complex carbohydrates).

Exercise and diet help maintain proper body weight by equalizing caloric intake and caloric output.

SEE also Skill 17.3

Skill 17.3   Identifying principles, practices, and skills for maintaining personal health and safety and for reducing health risks (e.g., using health-care products safely, recognizing risky situations, demonstrating injury-prevention techniques)

Exercise and diet maintain proper body weight by equalizing caloric intake to caloric output.

Nutrition and exercise are closely related concepts important to student health. An important responsibility of physical education instructors is to teach students about proper nutrition and exercise and how they relate to each other. The two key components of a healthy lifestyle are consumption of a balanced diet and regular physical activity. Nutrition can affect physical performance. Proper nutrition produces high energy levels and allows for peak performance. Inadequate or improper nutrition can impair physical performance and lead to short-term and long-term health problems (e.g. depressed immune system and heart disease, respectively). Regular exercise improves overall health. Benefits of regular exercise include a stronger immune system, stronger muscles, bones, and joints, reduced risk of premature death, reduced risk of heart disease, improved psychological well-being, and weight management.

The health risk factors improved by physical activity include cholesterol levels, blood pressure, stress related disorders, heart diseases, weight and obesity disorders, early death, certain types of cancer, musculoskeletal problems, mental health, and susceptibility to infectious diseases.

Physiological benefits of physical activity include:
- improved cardio-respiratory fitness
- improved muscle strength
- improved muscle endurance
- improved flexibility
- more lean muscle mass and less body fat
- quicker rate of recovery
- improved ability of the body to utilize oxygen
- lower resting heart rate
- increased cardiac output
- improved venous return and peripheral circulation
- reduced risk of musculoskeletal injuries
- lower cholesterol levels
- increased bone mass
- cardiac hypertrophy and size and strength of blood vessels
- increased number of red cells
- improved blood-sugar regulation
- improved efficiency of thyroid gland
- improved energy regulation
- increased life expectancy

Diet

In order to maintain a healthy lifestyle, a balanced diet is crucial. Pieces of a balanced diet include food choice, portion size, and caloric intake. In terms of caloric intake, an ideal diet would be 40 percent carbohydrates, 30 percent healthy fats, and 30 percent protein. While fat is an important part of a balanced diet, foods that contain large amounts of unsaturated fats, such as fried foods, are generally only acceptable in moderation. In order to control total calories eaten, portion control is important and yet most restaurants have increased portion size over the last 20 years. Limiting the size of meals will do a great job of limiting your overall caloric intake.

Exercise

A significant component of a healthy lifestyle is an exercise program that fits with your fitness level. According to the Centers for Disease Control and Prevention, adults need at least 150 minutes of moderate-intensity aerobic activity, such as brisk walking, every week and two or more days each week of muscle-strengthening activity. If the activity is more vigorous, the CDC recommends less time each week. They also recommend that children get at least one-hour a day of aerobic activity.

Stress Management

In order to deal with the stresses in your day-to-day life it is necessary to identify your stressors. Once you identify your stressors you need to develop a plan to deal with the stressors. The goal is not to necessarily remove the stressors from your life, but to create a plan to deal with them. Most stress management strategies include some type of physical activity or quiet time when you can relax.

Be Active

Physical activity doesn't necessarily need to be scheduled. Think about times throughout your day where you can become more active. Parking farther away and walking into a store, taking the stairs instead of elevator, and walking around during breaks are common strategies. Small changes can add up over time.

Have Regular Medical Checkups

Self-care is an important part of health. Regularly seeing a physician for check-ups allows you to catch problems before they get too big. Proper dental care and preventative maintenance can pay big dividends down the road. Everyone has individual needs and it is best to consult with your primary physician on your medical checkup needs.

Prevention

Proper **hydration** is an ongoing process, not something that occurs only during training. While many experts differ on exactly how much water should be consumed each day, what is important is making sure the body has enough water to function normally. A dehydrated body has a decreased ability to cool itself which increases the risk of heat exhaustion and heat stroke. Even minor dehydration can result in cramps and decreased energy.

Stretching is an important part of overall health and if done properly can improve athletic performance. Static stretching has long been the standard for athletes, but recent research indicates static stretching prior to an activity may even be detrimental to performance. During a static stretch a person slowly makes a move and then holds that movement for an extended period of time. Today many athletes focus on dynamic stretching which are activity-specific movements used to prime the body for activity.

Overtraining often leads to injury. When a person overuses their body, form is often the first thing to go. Once form is lost, the risk of injury increases dramatically. A body that is fatigued is also at direct risk of injury, muscles pushed to their limit will not always respond. When training, rest and recovery can be just as important as a workout.

Skill 17.4 **Applying knowledge of how to use social skills to respond to peer pressure, to express opinions and resolve conflicts constructively, and to maintain safe and respectful relationships**

For most people, the development of social roles and appropriate social behaviors occurs during childhood. Physical play between parents and children, as well as between siblings and peers, serves as a strong regulator in the developmental process. Chasing games, roughhousing, wrestling, or practicing sport skills such as jumping, throwing, catching, and striking, are some examples of childhood play. These activities may be competitive or non-competitive and are important for promoting social and moral development of both boys and girls. Unfortunately, fathers will often engage in this sort of activity more with their sons than their daughters. Regardless of the sex of the child, both boys and girls enjoy these types of activities.

Physical play during infancy and early childhood is central to the development of social and emotional competence. Research shows that children who engage in play that is more physical with their parents, particularly with parents who are sensitive and responsive to the child, exhibited greater enjoyment during the play sessions and were more popular with their peers. Likewise, these early interactions with parents, siblings, and peers are important in helping children become more aware of their emotions and to learn to monitor and regulate their own emotional responses. Children learn quickly through watching the responses of their parents which behaviors make their parents smile and laugh and which behaviors cause their parents to frown and disengage from the activity.

If children want the fun to continue, they engage in the behaviors that please others. As children near adolescence, they learn through rough-and-tumble play that there are limits to how far they can go before hurting someone (physically or emotionally), which results in termination of the activity or later rejection of the child by peers. These early interactions with parents and siblings are important in helping children learn appropriate behavior in the social situations of sport and physical activity.

Children learn to assess their social competence (i.e., ability to get along with and acceptance by peers, family members, teachers and coaches) in sport through the feedback received from parents and coaches. Initially, authority figures teach children, "You can't do that because I said so." As children approach school age, parents begin the process of explaining why a behavior is right or wrong because children continuously ask, "why?"

Similarly, when children engage in sports, they learn about taking turns with their teammates, sharing playing time, and valuing rules. They understand that rules are important for everyone and without these regulations, the game would become unfair. The learning of social competence is continuous as we expand our social arena and learn about different cultures. A constant in the learning process is the role of feedback as we assess the responses of others to our behaviors and comments.

In addition to the development of social competence, sport participation can help youth develop other forms of self-competence. Most important among these self-competencies is self-esteem. Self-esteem is how we judge our worth and indicates the extent to which an individual believes he is capable, significant, successful and worthy. Educators have suggested that one of the biggest barriers to success in the classroom today is low self-esteem.

Children develop self-esteem by evaluating abilities and by evaluating the responses of others. Children actively observe parents' and coaches' responses to their performances, looking for signs of approval or disapproval of their behavior. Children often interpret feedback and criticism as either a negative or a positive response to the behavior. In sports, research shows that the coach is a critical source of information that influences the self-esteem of children.

Little League baseball players whose coaches use a "positive approach" to coaching (e.g. more frequent encouragement, positive reinforcement for effort and corrective, instructional feedback), had significantly higher self-esteem ratings over the course of a season than children whose coaches used these techniques less frequently. The most compelling evidence supporting the importance of coaches' feedback was found for those children who started the season with the lowest self-esteem ratings and increased considerably their self-assessment and self-worth. In addition to evaluating themselves more positively, low self-esteem children evaluated their coaches more positively than did children with higher self-esteem who played for coaches who used the "positive approach." Moreover, studies show that 95 percent of children who played for coaches trained to use the positive approach signed up to play baseball the next year, compared with 75 percent of the youth who played for untrained adult coaches.

We cannot overlook the importance of enhanced self-esteem on future participation. A major part of the development of high self-esteem is the pride and joy that children experience as their physical skills improve. Children will feel good about themselves as long as their skills are improving. If children feel that their performance during a game or practice is not as good as that of others, or as good as they think mom and dad would want, they often experience shame and disappointment.

Some children will view mistakes made during a game as a failure and will look for ways to avoid participating in the task if they receive no encouragement to continue. At this point, it is critical that adults (e.g., parents and coaches) intervene to help children to interpret the mistake or "failure." We must teach children that a mistake is not synonymous with failure. Rather, a mistake shows us that we need a new strategy, more practice, and/or greater effort to succeed at the task.

Physical education activities can promote positive social behaviors and traits in a number of different ways. Instructors can foster improved relations with adults and peers by making students active partners in the learning process and delegating responsibilities within the class environment to students. Giving students leadership positions (e.g. team captain) can give them a heightened understanding of the responsibilities and challenges facing educators.

Team-based physical activities like team sports promote collaboration and cooperation. In such activities, students learn to work together, both pooling their talents and minimizing the weaknesses of different team members, in order to achieve a common goal. The experience of functioning as a team can be very productive for development of loyalty between children, and seeing their peers in stressful situations that they can relate to can promote a more compassionate and considerate attitude among students. Similarly, the need to maximize the strengths of each student on a team (who can complement each other and compensate for weaknesses) is a powerful lesson about valuing and respecting diversity and individual differences. Varying students between leading and following positions in a team hierarchy are good ways to help students gain a comfort level being both followers and leaders.

Fairness is another trait that physical activities, especially rules-based sports, can foster and strengthen. Children are by nature very rules-oriented, and have a keen sense of what they believe is and isn't fair. Fair play, teamwork, and sportsmanship are all values that stem from proper practice of the spirit of physical education classes. Of course, a pleasurable physical education experience goes a long way towards promoting an understanding of the innate value of physical activity throughout the life cycle.

Finally, communication is another skill that improves enormously through participation in sports and games. Students will come to understand that skillful communication can contribute to a better all-around outcome, whether it be winning the game or successfully completing a team project. They will see that effective communication helps to develop and maintain healthy personal relationships, organize and convey information, and reduce or avoid conflict.

Skill 17.5 **Identifying types and effects of stress, factors that affect family life and mental and emotional health, and strategies for managing stress and for maintaining healthy family relationships and positive mental, emotional, physical, and sexual health**

Helping students to develop healthy self-images and self-worth are integral to the learning and development experiences. Learning for students who are experiencing negative self-image and peer isolation is not necessarily the top priority, when students are feeling bullied or negated in the school community. When a student is attending school from a homeless shelter or is lost in the middle of a parent's divorce or feeling a need to conform to fit into a certain student group, the student is being compromised and may be unable to effectively navigate the educational process or engage in the required academic expectations towards graduation or promotion to the next grade level or subject core level.

Most schools will offer health classes that address teen issues around sexuality, self-image, peer pressure, nutrition, wellness, gang activity, drug engagement and a variety of other relevant teen experiences. Students are required to take a health class as a core class requirement and graduation requirement, so the incentive from the district and school's standpoint is that students are exposed to issues that directly affect them. The fact that one health class is not enough to effectively appreciate the multiplicity of issues that could create a psychological or physiological trauma for a teenager is lost in today's era of school budgets and financial issues that provide the minimum educational experience for students, but loses the student in the process.

Some schools have contracted with outside agencies to develop collaborative partnerships to bring in after school tutorial classes; gender and cultural specific groupings where students can deal authentically with integration of cultural and ethic experiences and lifestyles. Drug intervention programs and speakers on gang issues have created dynamic opportunities for school communities to bring the "undiscussable" issues to the forefront and alleviate fears that are rampant in schools that are afraid to say "No to Drugs and Gangs." Both students and teachers must be taught about the world of teenagers and understand the social, psychological and learning implications that underscore the process of academic acquisition for societies most vulnerable citizens.

Unfortunately, many students come from past or previous exposure to dangerous situations Child abuse may perpetuate itself in a phenomenon known as chronic shock. The system becomes geared up to handle the extra flow of hormones and electrical impulses accompanying the "fight or flight" syndrome each time the abuse happens, creating a shift in the biology of the brain and allied systems. Essentially, the victim becomes allergic (hypersensitized) to stress of the kind that prevailed during the period of abuse. Recent research indicates such a shift is reflected in brain chemistry and structural changes and may last a lifetime.

The neglected child may appear malnourished, may gorge at lunch, yet still be thin and underweight. Quiet and shy, he's typically shabby looking, and doesn't seem to care about his appearance. Poor nutrition at home may result in him having more than his share of colds and it is of utmost importance to guarantee that his immunizations are current, as they probably have been overlooked. He is not usually a very social child, may isolate, and not respond to invitations to join in. Many children display this trait, but a persistence in social anxiety with a sad effect will indicate that something is happening at home to be concerned about.

Stress

There is an important relationship to consider between physical activity and the development of personal identity and emotional and mental well-being, most notably the impact of positive body image and self-concept. Instructors can help children develop positive body image and self-concept by creating opportunities for the children to experience successes in physical activities and to develop a comfort level with their bodies. This is an important contributor to their personal and physical confidence. The following are lists of the emotional, behavioral, and physical signs of stress:

Emotional signs of stress include: depression, lethargy, aggressiveness, irritability, anxiety, edginess, fearfulness, impulsiveness, chronic fatigue hyper excitability, inability to concentrate, frequent feelings of boredom, feeling overwhelmed, apathy, impatience, pessimism, sarcasm, humorlessness, confusion, helplessness, melancholy, alienation, isolation, numbness, purposelessness, isolation, numbness, self-consciousness; inability to maintain an intimate relationship.

Behavioral signs of stress include: elevated use of substances (alcohol, drugs; tobacco), crying, yelling, insomnia or excessive sleep, excessive TV watching, school/job burnout, panic attacks, poor problems solving capability, avoidance of people, aberrant behavior, procrastination, accident proneness, restlessness, loss of memory, indecisiveness, aggressiveness, inflexibility, phobic responses, tardiness, disorganization; sexual problems.

Physical signs of stress: pounding heart, stuttering, trembling/nervous tics, excessive perspiration, teeth grinding, gastrointestinal problems (constipation, indigestion, diarrhea, queasy stomach), dry mouth, aching lower back, migraine/tension headaches, stiff neck, asthma attacks, allergy attacks, skin problems, frequent colds or low grade fevers, muscle tension, hyperventilation, high blood pressure, amenorrhea, nightmares; cold intolerance.

Positive coping strategies to cope with stress include using one's social support system, spiritual support, managing time, initiating direct action, re-examining priorities, active thinking, acceptance, meditation, imagery, biofeedback, progressive relaxation, deep breathing, massage, sauna, Jacuzzi, humor, recreation and diversions, and exercise.

Negative coping strategies to cope with stress include: using alcohol or other mind altering substances, smoking, excessive caffeine intake, poor eating habits, negative "self-talk;" expressing feelings of distress, anger, and other feelings in a destructive manner.

Sexual Health

There are many possible consequences for students who become sexually active. Possible consequences include HIV infection, infection with other sexually transmitted diseases, unintended pregnancies, and emotional difficulties.

The human immunodeficiency virus (HIV) is the virus that causes AIDS. Currently, there is no cure for AIDS. Many young adults currently infected with HIV acquired the infection during sexual activity in their adolescent years. In addition to HIV, there are also numerous other sexually transmitted diseases. Sexually transmitted diseases frequently reported in adolescents include gonorrhea, syphilis, pelvic inflammatory disease, bacterial vaginosis, genital herpes, chlamydia, genital warts, and human papillomavirus (HPV). Some of these diseases can result in infertility, and HPV can result in a deadly form of cervical cancer. Some of these diseases, such as genital herpes, are chronic. Additionally, condom use cannot prevent HPV and genital herpes.

Sexually transmitted disease infection can occur without having sexual intercourse. Oral or anal sex can cause infection with a sexually transmitted disease as easily as sexual intercourse. The only guaranteed method to prevent these diseases is abstinence.

In addition to possible infection with a sexually transmitted disease, adolescents that choose to become sexually active may also face the consequences of an unplanned pregnancy. Rates of child abuse and neglect are much higher in adolescent parents. Babies born to teenage parents are also more likely have a lower birth weight, which can affect the babies' overall wellbeing. The suicide rate among teen mothers is significantly higher than other teens.

There is no doubt that teachers must encourage students to choose abstinence and responsible sexual behavior. Abstinence is choosing not to engage in sexual activity. Choosing abstinence is often a difficult decision for a teenager. In order to stand firm against the pressures to become sexually active, adolescents can become involved in activities in their school and community, work to develop strong family relationships, socialize with other teens that have chosen abstinence, avoid situations that increase sexual feelings and temptation, avoid using alcohol and other drugs, and select wholesome entertainment.

Skill 17.6 Recognizing the physical, emotional, and legal consequences of using alcohol, tobacco, and other drugs, and identifying techniques and strategies for resisting pressures and unhealthy messages related to drug use

Drugs

Drugs produce a variety of effects on the body, abuse of drugs can produce many negative affects, including distortion of memory, perceptions, and sensation. Amphetamines and cocaine give users an inflated sense of performance. Drugs such as ecstasy in some cases have caused brain damage and death. Mixing prescription drugs has also been shown to be dangerous and a rising concern as young people often have access to prescription drugs in their homes. Over the counter drugs, such as Robitussin, can easily be acquired and when taken in large doses can be very harmful. Many students have access to ADHD medication, either legally or illegally, and abuse of these prescription drugs is on the rise. While illegal drugs have stiff legal consequences, the physical and emotional toll these drugs can take on an abuser and their family is often worse.

Substance abuse can lead to adverse behaviors and increased risk of injury and disease. Any substance affecting the normal functions of the body, illegal or not, is potentially dangerous and students and athletes should avoid them completely. Factors contributing to substance abuse include peer pressure, parental substance abuse, physical or psychological abuse, mental illness, and physical disability. Education, vigilance, and parental oversight are the best strategies for the prevention of substance abuse.

Anabolic steroids – The alleged benefit is an increase in muscle mass and strength. However, this substance is illegal and produces harmful side effects. Premature closure of growth plates in bones can occur if abused by a teenager, limiting adult height. Other effects include bloody cysts in the liver, increased risk of cardiovascular disease, increased blood pressure, and dysfunction of the reproductive system.

Alcohol – This is a legal substance for adults but is very commonly abused. Moderate to excessive consumption can lead to an increased risk of cardiovascular disease, nutritional deficiencies, and dehydration. Alcohol also causes ill effects on various aspects of performance such as reaction time, coordination, accuracy, balance, and strength.

Nicotine – Another legal but often abused substance that can increase the risk of cardiovascular disease, pulmonary disease, and cancers of the mouth. Nicotine consumption through smoking severely hinders athletic performance by compromising lung function. Smoking especially affects performance in endurance activities.

Marijuana – This is the most commonly abused illegal substance. Adverse effects include a loss of focus and motivation, decreased coordination, and lack of concentration.

Cocaine – Another illegal and somewhat commonly abused substance. Effects include increased alertness and excitability. This drug can give the user a sense of over confidence and invincibility, leading to a false sense of one's ability to perform certain activities. A high heart rate is associated with the use of cocaine, leading to an increased risk of heart attack, stroke, potentially deadly arrhythmias, and seizures.

Alcohol

A variety of sources, including the CDC, estimate that nearly 100,000 deaths each year in the United States are connected to excessive alcohol consumption. These deaths come in the form of cirrhosis of the liver, cancer, and car accidents. Not only does alcohol abuse lead to many deaths, it also greatly decreases the lifespan for those who abuse it. Even in modest quantities alcohol can impair judgment and coordination. In addition to the short-term effects of intoxication, long-term effects of alcohol abuse are significant. Alcohol abusers suffer damage to vital organs, increased risk of several types of cancer, malnutrition, high blood pressure, and a weakened immune system. Mothers who drink during pregnancy greatly increase the risk of birth defects for infants. In addition to the physical consequences of alcohol, the emotional consequences are severe; many alcohol abusers have trouble maintaining work and personal relationships. They are also prone to erratic and unreliable behavior.

Tobacco

In the United States tobacco is most often consumed by smoking. Smoking tobacco increases the risk of cancer, heart disease, and stroke. It has also been shown to cause respiratory problems. Smoking causes harm to vital organs, according to the United States Department of Health and Human Services, 440,000 deaths each year in the country can be linked to cigarette smoking which makes it the leading preventable cause of death in the country. The overall leading cause of death in the United States is heart disease and smoking is shown to contribute to heart disease. Today smoking has been banned from nearly all public places and smokers have been stigmatized by society.

How to Say No

Open, honest communication between parents and teens has been shown to be among the most effective ways of preventing drug use. A teen with a strong sense of self and a desire to avoid drugs will be able to say no when presented the opportunity. Educating a teen about the true effects of drug use can be a powerful deterrent. Social messages involving drug use are generally mixed, for every "loser druggie" portrayed in media, there is a glamorized version as well. While all drugs can be abused, the abuse of those drugs is treated differently by society. Those who abuse tobacco are not cast in the same light as those who abuse methamphetamine. Involvement in activities where drug use is prohibited can send a strong social message to a teen to avoid drug use.

Skill 17.7   Demonstrating knowledge of practices and skills that prevent and reduce the risk of contracting and transmitting communicable diseases and that help prevent and control noncommunicable diseases

When children and teachers spend a great portion of the day in close contact with each other there is bound to be occasions when diseases are communicated from one to the other. Some of the communicable diseases common among children are:

- chicken pox
- measles
- pink eye
- Fifth disease
- Common cold

Teachers may be immune to chicken pox and measles, but have and will come down with the others.

By teaching good health practices to children and encouraging them to use them on a daily basis, the possibility of contracting and transmitting communicable diseases can be prevented and reduced. Health classes should consist of lessons on the importance of hand washing after using the washroom and when hands become dirty after different activities both inside and outside the classroom.

Children have a habit of sharing drinks with one another, drinking from the same straw or container. This is one of the ways in which communicable diseases are spread from one person to another and the reasons for not engaging in this practice should be fully explained in class. Another habit that children have is that they put pens, pencils and markers in their mouths and then share them with their friends and in so doing spread their germs.

The importance of covering one's mouth when coughing or sneezing is very important to prevent the spread of disease. Tissues should be readily available in the classroom for children to use when they are needed.

Many schools have a policy in place in which children who do have a communicable disease should remain out of school until the contagious period has passed. However, many diseases are contagious in the incubation period before it is even known that a child has the disease.

Non-communicable diseases include such conditions as asthma, allergies and diabetes. When a student has been diagnosed with one of these conditions, there must be written instructions concerning what the teacher's duty should be in the control of the disease. Most schools have policies in place regarding the distribution of medication, such as keeping the medication in a locked file in the office and having to visit the office at a specific time during the day to receive the medication.

COMPETENCY 0018 DEMONSTRATE KNOWLEDGE OF BASIC MOVEMENT CONCEPTS, MOTOR SKILLS, RHYTHMIC ACTIVITIES, FITNESS ACTIVITIES, GAMES, AND SPORTS.

Skill 18.1 Demonstrating knowledge of movement concepts related to body awareness, spatial awareness, and direction, and of the ways in which children grow and develop kinesthetically

Concept of Body Awareness Applied to Physical Education Activities

Body awareness is a person's understanding of his or her own body parts and their capability of movement.

Instructors can assess body awareness by playing and watching a game of "Simon Says" and asking the students to touch different body parts. You can also instruct students to make their bodies into various shapes, from straight to round to twisted, and varying sizes, to fit into different sized spaces.

In addition, you can instruct children to touch one part of their body to another and to use various body parts to stamp their feet, twist their neck, clap their hands, nod their heads, wiggle their noses, snap their fingers, open their mouths, shrug their shoulders, bend their knees, close their eyes, bend their elbows, or wiggle their toes.

Concept of Spatial Awareness Applied to Physical Education Activities

Spatial awareness is the ability to make decisions about an object's positional changes in space (i.e. awareness of three-dimensional space position changes). Developing spatial awareness requires two sequential phases: 1) identifying the location of objects in relation to one's own body in space, and 2) locating more than one object in relation to each object and independent of one's own body. Plan activities using different size balls, boxes, or hoops and have children move towards and away; under and over; in front of and behind; and inside, outside, and beside the objects.

Concepts of Space, Direction, and Speed Related to Movement of Concepts

Research shows that the concepts of space, direction, and speed are interrelated with movement concepts. Such concepts and their understanding are extremely important for students, as they need to relate movement skills to direction in order to move with confidence and avoid collisions.

A student or player in motion must take the elements of space, direction, speed, and vision into consideration in order to perform and understand a sport. A player must decide how to handle their space as well as numerous other factors that arise on the field.

For a player, the concepts are all interlinked. He has to understand how to maintain or change pathways with speed. This ability allows him to change motion and perform well in space (or the area that the players occupy on the field).

Skill 18.2 **Recognizing types and elements of basic motor skills (e.g., locomotor, nonlocomotor, manipulative) and techniques, cues, and prompts for developing fundamental and specialized motor skills (e.g., run, throw, kick)**

In order for a child to write correctly, they must first develop their fine motor skills. Before being required to manipulate a pencil, children should have dexterity and strength in their fingers, which helps them to gain more control of small muscles.

These hands-on activities are excellent activities for practicing fine motor skills:

Tearing
- Tear newspaper into strips and then crumple them into balls. Use the balls to stuff a Halloween pumpkin or other art creation.

Cutting
- Cut pictures from magazines
- Cut a fringe on the edge of a piece of construction paper

Puzzles
- Have children put together a puzzle with large puzzles pieces. This will help to develop proper eye-hand coordination

Clay
- Manipulating play dough into balls strengthens a child's grasp. Let the children explain to what they created from their play dough objects

Finger Painting
- Many times when a child has not developed fine motor skills yet, it helps to trace the pattern with his finger before he tries it with a pencil. Have the child trace a pattern in sand, cornmeal, finger paint, etc.

Drawing
- Draw at an easel with a large crayon. Encourage children to practice their name or letters of the alphabet

The above activities will build strength in their fingers and hands, which will aid in the development of a child's writing skills.

The most important factors of learning to write are the grip on the writing instrument, the position of the arm and wrist, and the position of the writing paper.

Gross Motor Development

Gross motor skills refer to the movements of the large muscles of the body. The development of these skills is important for children to move about freely, such as in jumping, running, climbing stairs, etc. It is necessary to build activities for this development into the curriculum of early childhood classes. However, some of these should be developed by the time children reach school age. They include:

- Running
- Walking in a straight line
- Jumping up and down and over obstacles
- Hopping on one foot
- Walking down stairs using one foot after the other
- Marching
- Standing on one foot for at least 10 seconds
- Walking backwards
- Throwing a ball
- Sliding

Play as part of the classroom routine is essential in the development of gross motor skills. The toys used should be age appropriate and there should be an open space in the classroom. Outside activities as well as those in the school gymnasium help to develop the skills the children need.

Locomotor Skills

Locomotor skills move an individual from one point to another.
1. **Walking** - with one foot contacting the surface at all times, walking shifts one's weight from one foot to the other while legs swing alternately in front of the body.
2. **Running** - an extension of walking that has a phase where the body is propelled with no base of support (speed is faster, stride is longer, and arms add power).
3. **Jumping** - projectile movements that momentarily suspend the body in midair.
4. **Vaulting** - coordinated movements that allow one to spring over an obstacle.
5. **Leaping** - similar to running, but leaping has greater height, flight, and distance.

6. **Hopping** - using the same foot to take off from a surface and land.
7. **Galloping** - forward or backward advanced elongation of walking combined and coordinated with a leap.
8. **Sliding** - sideward stepping pattern that is uneven, long, or short.
9. **Body Rolling** - moving across a surface by rocking back and forth, by turning over and over, or by shaping the body into a revolving mass.
10. **Climbing** - ascending or descending using the hands and feet with the upper body exerting the most control.

Nonlocomotor Skills

Nonlocomotor skills are stability skills where the movement requires little or no movement of one's base of support and does not result in change of position.

1. **Bending** - movement around a joint where two body parts meet.
2. **Dodging** - sharp change of direction from original line of movement such as away from a person or object.
3. **Stretching** - extending/hyper-extending joints to make body parts as straight or as long as possible.
4. **Twisting** - rotating body/body parts around an axis with a stationary base.
5. **Turning** - circular moving the body through space releasing the base of support.
6. **Swinging** - circular/pendular movements of the body/body parts below an axis.
7. **Swaying** - same as swinging but movement is above an axis.
8. **Pushing** - applying force against an object or person to move it away from one's body or to move one's body away from the object or person.
9. **Pulling** - executing force to cause objects/people to move toward one's body.

Mnaipulative Skills

Manipulative skills use body parts to propel or receive an object, controlling objects primarily with the hands and feet. Two types of manipulative skills are receptive (catch + trap) and propulsive (throw, strike, kick).

1. **Bouncing/Dribbling** - projecting a ball downwards.
2. **Catching** - stopping momentum of an object (for control) using the hands.
3. **Kicking** - striking an object with the foot.
4. **Rolling** - initiating force to an object to instill contact with a surface.
5. **Striking** - giving impetus to an object with the use of the hands or an object.
6. **Throwing** - using one or both arms to project an object into midair away from the body.
7. **Trapping** - without the use of the hands, receiving and controlling a ball

KNOWLEDGE OF ACTIVITIES FOR BODY MANAGEMENT SKILL DEVELOPMENT

Sequential development and activities for locomotor skills acquisition:
Sequential Development = crawl, creep, walk, run, jump, hop, gallop, slide, leap, skip, step-hop.

- **Activities to develop walking skills** include walking slower and faster in place; walking forward, backward, and sideways with slower and faster paces in straight, curving, and zigzag pathways with various lengths of steps; pausing between steps; and changing the height of the body.
- **Activities to develop running skills** include having students pretend they are playing basketball, trying to score a touchdown, trying to catch a bus, finishing a lengthy race, or running on a hot surface.
- **Activities to develop jumping skills** include alternating jumping with feet together and feet apart, taking off and landing on the balls of the feet, clicking the heels together while airborne, and landing with a foot forward and a foot backward.
- **Activities to develop galloping skills** include having students play a game of Fox and Hound, with the lead foot representing the fox and the back foot the hound trying to catch the fox (alternate the lead foot).
- **Activities to develop sliding skills** include having students hold hands in a circle and sliding in one direction, then sliding in the other direction.
- **Activities to develop hopping skills** include having students hop all the way around a hoop and hopping in and out of a hoop reversing direction. Students can also place ropes in straight lines and hop side-to-side over the rope from one end to the other and change (reverse) the direction.
- **Activities to develop skipping skills** include having students combine walking and hopping activities leading up to skipping.
- **Activities to develop step-hopping skills** include having students practice stepping and hopping activities while clapping hands to an uneven beat.

Sequential development and activities for nonlocomotor skill acquisition:
Sequential Development = stretch, bend, sit, shake, turn, rock and sway, swing, twist, dodge, and fall.

- **Activities to develop stretching** include lying on the back and stomach and stretching as far as possible; stretching as though one is reaching for a star, picking fruit off a tree, climbing a ladder, shooting a basketball, or placing an item on a high self; waking and yawning.
- **Activities to develop bending** include touching knees and toes then straightening the entire body and straightening the body halfway; bending as though picking up a coin, tying shoes, picking flowers/vegetables, and petting animals of different sizes.
- **Activities to develop sitting** include practicing sitting from standing, kneeling, and lying positions without the use of hands.
- **Activities to develop falling skills** include first collapsing in one's own space and then pretending to fall like bowling pins, raindrops, snowflakes, a rag doll, or Humpty Dumpty.

Sequential development and activities for manipulative skill development:
Sequential Development = striking, throwing, kicking, ball rolling, volleying, bouncing, catching, and trapping.

- **Activities to develop striking** begin with the striking of stationary objects by a participant in a stationary position. Next, the person remains still while trying to strike a moving object. Then, both the object and the participant are in motion as the participant attempts to strike the moving object.
- **Activities to develop throwing** include throwing yarn/foam balls against a wall, then at a big target, and finally at targets decreasing in size.
- **Activities to develop kicking** include alternating feet to kick balloons/beach balls, then kicking them under and over ropes. Change the type of ball as proficiency develops.
- **Activities to develop ball rolling** include rolling different size balls to a wall, then to targets decreasing in size.
- **Activities to develop volleying** include using a large balloon and, first, hitting it with both hands, then one hand (alternating hands), and then using different parts of the body. Change the object as students progress (balloon, to beach ball, to foam ball, etc.)
- **Activities to develop bouncing** include starting with large balls and, first, using both hands to bounce and then using one hand (alternate hands).
- **Activities to develop catching** include using various objects (balloons, beanbags, balls, etc.) to catch and, first, catching the object the participant has thrown him/herself, then catching objects someone else threw, and finally increasing the distance between the catcher and the thrower.
- **Activities to develop trapping** include trapping slow and fast rolling balls; trapping balls (or other objects such as beanbags) that are lightly thrown at waist, chest, and stomach levels; trapping different size balls.

Skill 18.3 **Demonstrating knowledge of appropriate strategies, activities, games, and sports for various purposes and for various developmental, age, and ability levels**

The activities, games and sports in a Physical Education program vary according to the developmental and chronological age of the students and their ability levels. In addition, one of the main skills involved in teaching Physical Education at the elementary and middle school level is to instill a sense of fair play in the students along with helping them keep active to develop a healthy lifestyle.

Even further, all the activities used in the program it is important for teachers to be mindful of any special needs children in the class. They may or may not be able to do the same types of activities as the rest of the students so accommodations must be included in the program to teach them how they can be healthy and active as well as develop a repertoire of physical skills.

Therefore, different strategies and activities must be used with different grade levels. The curriculum is spiral in nature so that children learn very basic skills in the primary grades and then expand on these skills to incorporate other and more complex skills in the higher grades.

Most physical education programs encompass varying levels of instruction in the areas of health, individual sports and skills, and team sports, skills, and activities. For health components, **SEE** Skill 18.5. At all ages, students should be taught to warm up before beginning exercises and to cool down afterwards. In developing activities to help strengthen students' non-locomotor skills, young children can begin by imitating the actions of animals, such as the swaying trunk of an elephant.

At the upper elementary and middle school levels, students will demonstrate rules, skills, and terminology associated with individual physical activities. These activities include dance, rhythm, track & field, wrestling, tennis and more. It is within individual activities such as these where locomotor skills are important in the Physical Education curriculum. Strategies that practice flexibility, agility and basic physical skill drills are important. For example, obstacle courses are effective at all age levels but must include objects which the students are able to jump or climb over with ease. These can be taller for older students. Another example includes kicking a ball and throwing a ball and catching it are important skills for students. These activities usually start off with each student with a soccer ball that they learn to control with their feet and keep inside a designated space.

As students progress in development with flexibility and locomotor skills, competitive activities can be included. Usually around grade 3 or 4, students begin with organized team or group activities.

Some games and activities to use at this level include:

- Stop and start games (in which students learn how to follow directions and follow a designed path)
- Tag and dodge ball games (where there is a safe personal space for the students and at the same time they learn how to avoid others so as to be safe)
- Flag football
- Basketball
- Volleyball
- Soccer
- Ultimate Frisbee
- Floor hockey
- Other large group games

With these games, the rules, skills and terms associated with the game are covered, as well as elements of group activities including sportsmanship, healthy competition, social skills, and the emphasis on fun, physical activity.

Skill 18.4 Recognizing appropriate principles, techniques, cues, prompts, and feedback for promoting skill development and safe participation in rhythmic activities, games, and sports

Safety

The practice of progressive resistance has become ingrained in the physical development and training programs of individuals, be it children or adults. Progressive resistance, like all other forms of exercises, should always be performed while following certain principles and safety practices. A considerable amount of controversy and debate exists as to the proper procedures for developing fitness.

As a safety precaution, a health or medical questionnaire should be formulated and completed. This can serve as a screening before enrolling a student into a progressive resistance program. While training, too much weight should not be undertaken by a novice.

Other principles and guidelines which should be followed include:
- A warm-up prior to performing resistance exercises
- A gradual increase in the number of repetitions for the exercise
- Exercising at least two days and resting for a while in order to achieve proper muscle development
- Performing exercises in a controlled manner
- Performing each exercise through a functional range of motion
- Working in conjunction with instructors who provide adequate feedback and guidance

Apart from the aforementioned principles, there are other basic principles of progressive resistance training which include careful monitoring of types of lifts, intensity, volume, and variety of lifts, and taking adequate rest for recovery.

The equipment used for progressive resistance training or exercise includes fit strips, dumbbells or barbells, and other equipment used to develop resistance and endurance.

Object control skills help kids to remain fit and agile. These skills also help students to become better performers. Physical educators will often combine a number of object control skills to enhance a child's reflexes.

Catch and throw is an ideal example of integrating such skills. This type of skill requires a high level of concentration and nimbleness. A combination of object control skills is always at the heart of any physical activity.

Object control skills make all the difference when it comes to imparting a comprehensive physical training program. An ideal combination of these skills keeps students healthy.

Object control skills (e.g., run and catch, pivot and throw)

Whether it's locomotor, nonlocomotor or object control skills, physical educators plan innovative strategies to help students pick up the nuances of such skills quickly. Physical education teachers should also present these skills in an entertaining manner for students.

If a teacher starts a training schedule with simple activities, they are more likely to keep the students interested. Once the interest is developed, teachers should introduce complex activities such as running and catching, pivoting and throwing, running and jumping, etc.

The above strategy is the most acclaimed for combining locomotor, nonlocomotor, and object control skills. The moment students start taking interest in what they have been asked to do, the job becomes easier for the teachers as well as the students.

Rhythmic Awareness

Instilling rhythmic awareness among students is another vital aspect of fitness that physical educators must not overlook. One of the basic elements of rhythm is to understand the fundamental movement models. Students should be trained in responding to different verbal commands.

Instructors also have a big role to play. They have to demonstrate how to use suitable terms related to rhythm, movement and position. For the students, they will have to carry out locomotor movements rhythmically as well such movements as 45 degree turns, etc. At the next level, teachers should encourage students to integrate movement patterns with music (i.e., dance aerobics).

Techniques for assessing rhythmic skills

There are some proven techniques with which one can assess rhythmic skills. Students are often asked to demonstrate a known vocabulary of basic movement concepts. Physical education teachers should make sure whether the students are responding the verbal commands or not. This particular exercise gives the teachers a proper idea on their students' performances.

Sometimes, the students have to perform locomotor movements at different levels while going in different directions. This will give the physical educator teacher a better understanding of a student's proficiency. Performing dance routines are another parameter for assessing rhythmic skills.

SEE also Skill 18.2

Skill 18.5   Demonstrating knowledge of physical fitness principles and activities for developing healthy levels of cardio respiratory fitness, muscular strength and endurance, flexibility, and body composition

Muscular Strength

Level techniques to promote fundamental movement involve a sequential learning of movement. Beginning with running, hopping, jumping, skipping, catching, throwing, kicking, rolling, balancing, twisting and turning. Through a wide range of activities involving these fundamental levels, students begin to progressively gain control of their movements and can begin to learn to combine them or to build upon them to learn new levels of movements.

The following displays fitness principle and example applications pertaining to overload, progression, and specificity to muscular strength and endurance development program design.

Overloading for muscle strength:
- **Frequency** = every other day
- **Intensity** = 60% to 90% of assessed muscle strength
- **Time** = 3 sets of 3 - 8 reps (high resistance with a low number of repetitions)

Progression for muscle strength:
- begin 3 days/week and work up to every other day
- begin near 60% of determined muscle strength and work up to no more than 90% of muscle strength
- begin with 1 set with 3 reps and work up to 3 sets with 8 reps

Specificity for muscle strength:
to increase muscle strength for a specific part(s) of the body, we must target that/those part(s) of the body

Muscle Endurance

Overloading for muscle endurance:
- **Frequency** = every other day
- **Intensity** = 30% to 60% of assessed muscle strength
- **Time** = 3 sets of 12 - 20 reps (low resistance with a high number of repetitions)

Progression for muscle endurance:
- begin 3 days/week and work up to every other day
- begin at 20% to 30% of muscle strength and work up to no more than 60% of muscle strength
- begin with 1 set with 12 reps and work up to 3 sets with 20 reps

Specificity for muscle endurance: same as muscle strength

Flexibility

Flexibility is the range of motion around a joint or muscle. Flexibility has two major components: static and dynamic. Static flexibility is the range of motion without a consideration for speed of movement. Dynamic flexibility is the process of using a desired range of motion at a desired velocity. Flexibility exercises are useful for most athletes.

Good flexibility can help prevent injuries during all stages of life and can keep an athlete safe. To improve flexibility, you can lengthen muscles through activities such as swimming, a basic stretching program, or Pilates. These activities improve your muscles' range of motion, since muscles are the main target of flexibility training. Muscles are the most elastic component of joints while ligaments and tendons are less elastic and resist elongation. Overstretching tendons and ligaments can weaken joint stability and lead to injury.

Coaches, teachers, athletes and sports medicine personnel use stretching methods as part of their training routine for athletes. Flexibility exercises help the body to relax and help muscles warm-up for more intense fitness activities.

Components of Flexibility

Muscles – Muscle is the body's contractile tissue. Its function is to produce force and cause motion (movement within the internal organs and, especially for our purposes, locomotion). Muscles are generally split into Type I (slow twitch) and Type II (fast twitch). Type I muscles carry more oxygen and sustains aerobic activity, whereas, Type II muscles carry less oxygen and powers anaerobic activity. Muscles that are too short can limit flexibility. Individuals who fail to stretch after resistance training can cause the muscles to shorten. The stretch reflex, whereby the opposing muscle will contract in order to prevent over-expansion, can also curtail flexibility (this contraction is generally premature, and part of flexibility training is to re-train the opposing muscle not to contract as quickly).

Joints – Joints allow bones to connect. Their construction allows movement and provides functional mechanical support. Joints are classified as fibrous (connected by collagen), cartilaginous (connected by cartilage), or synovial (capped by cartilage, supported by ligaments, enveloped by the synovial membrane, and filled with synovial fluid). Joint flexibility is limited of range of motion that is imposed by the joint's physical structure orby the lack of flexibility of the muscles, ligaments and tendons.

Ligaments – A ligament is a short band of tough fibrous connective tissue composed mainly of long, stringy collagen fibers. They connect bones to other bones to form a joint. Ligaments can limit the mobility of a joint or prevent certain movements altogether. Ligaments are slightly elastic and under tension they will gradually lengthen. Ligaments that are too short may curtail flexibility by limiting a joint's range of motion.

Tendons – A tendon (or sinew) is a tough band of fibrous connective tissue (similar in structure to ligaments) that connects muscle to bone or muscle to muscle. Tendons are composed mainly of water, type-I collagen, and cells called tenocytes. Most of the strength of tendons stems from the parallel, hierarchical arrangement of densely packed collagen fibrils, which have great strength, little extensibility, and no ability to contract

Cardiovascular Fitness

The term aerobic refers to conditioning or exercise that requires the use of oxygen to derive energy. Aerobic conditioning is essential for fat loss, energy production, and effective functioning of the cardiovascular system. Aerobic exercise is difficult to perform for many people and participants must follow certain principles and activities in order to develop aerobic endurance.

Slow twitch muscle tissue, fueled by oxygen, power aerobic activities. For the body to sustain aerobic activity for an extended period of time, the heart must pump oxygen-rich blood to the muscles of the body. When the heart tires due to insufficient cardio respiratory fitness, the quantities of oxygen delivered to the muscles decreases to levels that cannot sustain the activity.

Other physiological processes involved in aerobic endurance include the respiratory system (which must take sufficient air into the body and efficiently supply oxygen to the blood), the blood itself (which must efficiently carry oxygen), the circulatory system (that takes blood to the muscles and then returns it to the heart), and the muscles themselves (which must efficiently extract oxygen from the blood).

Tips that aid in developing and building aerobic endurance include working out for extended periods at the target heart rate, slowly increasing aerobic exercises, exercising for three or four times per week, and taking adequate rest to help the body recover. Exercising in the target heart rate zone for 30-45 minute periods is the most important principle in the development of aerobic endurance. Sub maximal intensity activities, such as walking and slow jogging, are effective aerobic activities that improve aerobic endurance without unnecessary strain on the body.

We can measure cardio respiratory fitness in a number of ways. The simplest way is for the students to check their resting heart rate. To do this, the students should:

- Find their pulse in any point of the body where an artery is close to the surface (e.g., wrist [radial artery], neck [carotid artery], or the elbow [brachial artery]).
- Count the number of beats felt within one minute.

We usually express resting heart rate in "beats per minute" (bpm). For males, the norm is about 70 bpm. For women, the norm is about 75 bpm. This rate varies between people and the reference range is normally between 60 bpm and 100 bpm. It is important to note that resting heart rates can be significantly lower in athletes, and significantly higher in the obese.

Another way to measure cardio respiratory fitness is by having students determine their Target Heart Rate (THR). THR is determined by the following formula: 220-age multiplied by .60 to .80. (.60= 60% of the Maximum Heart Rate and .80= 80% of the Maximum Heart Rate).The Target Heart Rate, or Training Heart Rate, is a desired heart rate range that is reached during aerobic exercise. This range allows a student's heart and lungs to receive the most benefit from a workout.

SEE **also Skills 13.3, 17.2 and 17.3**

Skill 18.6 **Recognizing the health-related benefits of movement and fitness activities and the role of physical activities in promoting social skills such as cooperation, support, respect, inclusion, and understanding and appreciation of similarities and differences**

Physical education instructors instill in their students a respect for and appreciation of the aesthetic and creative aspects of skilled performances. Dance, gymnastics, and figure skating are examples of performance activities that have an obvious creative and expressive element. In addition, all sports require creativity and have aesthetic elements.

For example, the ball control of an expert soccer player, the touch, control, and power of a professional tennis player, and the elegance and grace of a basketball player soaring for a slam-dunk are all aesthetically pleasing and awe inspiring to the trained eye. To truly appreciate the complexity and difficulty of skilled performances, one must have sufficient knowledge and understanding of the activity. Thus, the role of physical education is to introduce students to various physical activities so they can understand the aesthetic elements.

Physical fitness activities incorporate group processes, group dynamics, and a wide range of cooperation and competition. Additionally, mutual respect, safe cooperative participation, analytical skills, problem solving skills, teamwork and leadership skills are important during competitive or cooperative team sports, individual competitive sports and cooperative team activities.

Teamwork activities create an opportunity for students who do not normally interact or get along. Also, through teamwork, students begin to understand the value of diversity and the different skills an array of people can bring to a team. It also creates opportunities for students to develop reliance on each other and practice interdependence. Cooperation and competition can also offer opportunities for children to practice group work. These situations provide good opportunities to practice analytical thinking and problem solving in a practical setting.

Physical education in the affective domain contributes to self-actualization, self-esteem, and a healthy response to physical activity; contributes to an appreciation of beauty; contributes to directing one's life toward worthy goals; emphasizes humanism; affords individuals the chance to enjoy rich social experiences through play; assists cooperative play with others; teaches courtesy, fair play, and good sportsmanship; contributes to humanitarianism.

Social skills and values gained from participation in physical activities

- The ability to make adjustments to both self and others by an integration of the individual to society and the environment.
- The ability to make judgments in a group situation.
- Learning to communicate with others and cooperate.
- The development of the social phases of personality, attitudes, and values in order to become a functioning member of society such as being considerate.
- The development of a sense of belonging and acceptance by society.
- The development of positive personality traits.
- Learning for constructive use of leisure time.
- A development of attitude that reflects good moral character.
- Respect of school rules and property.

DOMAIN IV.   **ENGLISH LANGUAGE ARTS**

COMPETENCY 0019   UNDERSTAND THE NATURE OF FIRST- AND SECOND-LANGUAGE ACQUISITION AND DEVELOPMENT.

Skill 19.1   Demonstrating knowledge of the grammar of Standard American English, including semantics, syntax, morphology, and phonology

Semantics refers to the meaning expressed when words are arranged in a specific way. This is where connotation and denotation of words eventually will have a role with readers.

Syntax refers to the rules or patterned relationships that correctly create phrases and sentences from words. When readers develop an understanding of syntax, they begin to understand the structure of how sentences are built, and eventually the beginning of grammar.

Example: "I am going to the movies"
This statement is syntactically and grammatically correct.

Example: "They am going to the movies."
This statement is syntactically correct since all the words are in their correct place, but it is grammatically incorrect with the use of the word "They" rather than "I."

All of these skill sets are important to eventually developing effective word recognition skills, which help emerging readers develop fluency.

Morphology

Morphology is a branch of linguistics that uses applied rules of these word formation processes. The word formation processes are built on specific patterns (or regularities) in the way words are formed from smaller units, and they determine how those smaller units interact in speech. At the simplest level, they connect such words as "dog," "dogs," "dog-lover," and dog-catcher" according to relationships of spelling, meaning, use, and variation.

Unless rules are applied, ambiguity develops in defining a word. For example, "dog" and "dogs" are—in a sense—the same word. They are both nouns that refer to the same kind of animal, differing only in number. However, by application, they are different words. They are not interchangeable in a sentence without altering other words to support the change.

For example:

That dog is one of the best hunters in this area
      but
Those dogs are some of the best hunters in this area.

In the sense that "dog" and "dogs" are the same "word," the morphological term is a **lexeme**. In the second sense, when the two are different "words," the descriptive term is **word-form**. Thus, "dog" and "dogs" are different forms of the same lexeme. Dog, dog-catcher and dog-lover, on the other hand, are different lexemes; they refer to three different kinds of entities and are considered word-forms.

It is possible to distinguish two kinds of morphological rules. Some morphological rules relate different forms of the same lexeme, while other rules relate two different lexemes. Rules of the first kind are called **inflectional rules**, while those of the second kind are called **word-formation**. The English plural, as illustrated by "dog" and "dogs," is an inflectional rule; compounds like "dog-catcher" or "dog-lover" provide examples of a word-formation rule.

Furthermore, there are two distinctive types of word-formation: compounding and derivation. **Compounding** is the process of word-formation that involves combining complete word-forms into a single compound form. For example, dog-catcher is a compound because both dog and catcher were complete word-forms in their own right before the compounding process was applied. **Derivation** involves affixing bound (non-independent) forms to existing lexemes, whereby the addition of the affix derives a new lexeme. For example, the word "independent" is derived from the word "dependent" by prefixing it with the derivational prefix "in-," while "dependent" itself is derived from the verb "depend."

A **paradigm** is the complete set of related word-forms associated with a given lexeme. The conjugations of verbs and the declensions of nouns are examples of paradigms. Accordingly, the word-forms of a lexeme may be arranged conveniently into tables by classifying them according to shared inflectional categories such as tense, aspect, mood, number, gender, or case. For example, the personal pronouns in English can be organized into tables, using the categories of person, number, gender, and case.

An important difference between inflection and word-formation is that inflected word-forms of lexemes are organized into paradigms, which are defined by the requirements of syntactic rules, whereas the rules of word-formation are not restricted by any corresponding requirements of syntax. Inflection is therefore relevant to syntax, while word-formation is not. The part of morphology that covers the relationship between syntax and morphology is called **morphosyntax**; it concerns itself with inflection and paradigms, but not with word-formation or compounding.

Thus far, we have used morphological rules as analogies between word-forms: "dog" is to "dogs" as "cat" is to "cats" or as "dish" is to "dishes." In this instance, the analogy applies both to the form of the words and to their meanings: in each pair, the first word means "one of," while the second word means "two or more of." In these examples, the difference is always in having the plural form "-s" affixed to the second word, providing the distinction between singular and plural entities. In English, this one-to-one correspondence between meaning and form does not apply to every case. There are instances of word form pairs like ox/oxen, goose/geese, and sheep/sheep, where the difference between the singular and the plural is provided in a way that departs from the regular pattern. These cases, where the same distinction is affected by alternative changes to the form of a word, are called **allomorphy**.

Phonics

As opposed to phonemic awareness (SEE Skill 20.2), the study of phonics must be done with the eyes open. It's the connection between the sounds and letters on a page. In other words, students learning phonics might see the word "bad" and sound each letter out slowly until they recognize that they just said the word.

Phonological awareness means the ability of the reader to recognize the sound of spoken language. This recognition includes how these sounds can be blended together, segmented (divided up), and manipulated (switched around). This awareness then leads to phonics, a method for teaching children to read. It helps them "sound out words."

Development of phonological skills may begin during pre-K years. Indeed by the age of 5, a child who has been exposed to rhyme can recognize a rhyme. Such a child can demonstrate phonological awareness by filling in the missing rhyming word in a familiar rhyme or rhymed picture book.

You teach children phonological awareness when you teach them the sounds made by the letters, the sounds made by various combinations of letters and to recognize individual sounds in words.

Phonological awareness skills include:

1. Rhyming and syllabification
2. Blending sounds into words—such as pic-tur-bo-k
3. Identifying the beginning or starting sounds of words and the ending or closing sounds of words
4. Breaking words down into sounds-also called "segmenting" words
5. Recognizing other smaller words in the big word, by removing starting sounds, "hear" to ear

Skill 19.2   Recognizing the interrelationship between first- and second-language acquisition and literacy

Theories of Language Development

Learning Approach

Early theories of language development were formulated from learning theory research. The assumption was that language development evolved from learning the rules of language structures and applying them through imitation and reinforcement. This approach also assumed that linguistic, cognitive, and social developments were independent of each other. Thus, children were expected to learn language from patterning after adults who spoke and wrote Standard English. No allowance was made for communication through child jargon, idiomatic expressions, or grammatical and mechanical errors resulting from too strict adherence to the rules of inflection (*childs* instead of *children*) or conjugation (*runned* instead of *ran*). No association was made between physical and operational development and language mastery.

Linguistic Approach

Studies spearheaded by Noam Chomsky in the 1950s formulated the theory that language ability is innate and develops through natural human maturation as environmental stimuli trigger the acquisition of syntactical structures appropriate to each exposure level. The assumption of a hierarchy of syntax downplayed the significance of semantics. Because of the complexity of syntax and the relative speed with which children acquire language, linguists attributed language development to biological rather than cognitive or social influences.

Cognitive Approach

Researchers in the 1970s proposed that language knowledge derives from both syntactic and semantic structures. Drawing on the studies of Piaget and other cognitive learning theorists, supporters of the cognitive approach maintained that children acquire knowledge of linguistic structures after they have acquired the cognitive structures necessary to process language. For example, joining words for specific meaning necessitates sensory motor intelligence. The child must be able to coordinate movement and recognize objects before he or she can identify words to name the objects or word groups to describe the actions of these objects. Children must have developed the mental abilities for organizing concepts as well as performing concrete operations, predicting outcomes, and theorizing before they can assimilate and verbalize complex sentence structures, choose vocabulary for particular nuances of meaning, and examine semantic structures for tone and manipulative effect.

Sociocognitive Approach

Other theorists in the 1970s proposed that language development results from sociolinguistic competence. This theory finds that the different aspects of linguistic, cognitive, and social knowledge are interactive elements of total human development. Emphasis on verbal communication as the medium for language expression resulted in the inclusion of speech activities in most language arts curricula.

Unlike previous approaches, the sociocognitive allows that determining the appropriateness of language in given situations for specific listeners is as important as understanding semantic and syntactic structures. By engaging in conversation, children at all stages of development have opportunities to test their language skills, receive feedback, and make modifications. As a social activity, conversation is as structured by social order as grammar is structured by the rules of syntax. Conversation satisfies the learner's need to be heard, to be understood, and to influence others. Thus, his or her choices of vocabulary, tone, and content are dictated by the ability to assess the linguistic knowledge of his or her listeners. The learner is constantly applying cognitive skills in using language as a form of social interaction. Although the capacity to acquire language is inborn, a child would not pass beyond grunts and gestures without an environment in which to practice language.

Of course, the varying degrees of environmental stimuli to which children are exposed at all age levels create a slower or faster development of language. Some children are prepared to articulate concepts and recognize symbolism by the time they enter fifth grade, either because they have been exposed to challenging reading and conversations with well-spoken adults at home, or in their social groups. Others are still trying to master the sight recognition skills and are not yet ready to combine words in complex patterns.

Second Language Learners

Students who are raised in homes where English is not the first language and/or where standard English is not spoken, may have difficulty with hearing the difference between similar sounding words like "send" and "sent." Any student who is not in an environment where English phonology operates, may have difficulty perceiving and demonstrating the differences between English language phonemes. If students can not hear the difference between words that "sound the same" like "grow" and "glow," they will be confused when these words appear in a print context. This confusion will of course, sadly, impact their comprehension.

Considerations for teaching to English Language Learners include recognition by the teacher that what works for the English language speaking student from an English language speaking family, does not necessarily work in other languages.

Research recommends that ELL students learn to read initially in their first language. It has been found that a priority for ELL should be learning to speak English before being taught to read English. Research supports oral language development, since it lays the foundation for phonological awareness.

Skill 19.3 Identifying examples of diversity in language use (e.g., grammar, patterns, dialects)

Cultural differences play a large role in the diversity of language. Depending on the home country of the student or parents as well as different regions within the US, students can use different forms of grammar and dialects in the classroom. Since they learn the language from the parents, they do adopt the parent's manner of speaking.

One can usually tell what part of the country students are from by the accent they have. There may be idioms and expressions native to a specific region that are unknown to others, and this may make it difficult to understand what a student is saying.

Young children often do not use the proper grammar when speaking and may use other forms of the past tense, for example, saying "breaked" instead of "broke". Grammar also poses a problem for students whose first language is not English and may make many mistakes in speaking and writing.

Students must be able to understand the information presented to them in class and where possible extra help should be provided in the student's own language. Problems with grammar and patterns of language naturally lead teachers to correct the student's mistakes, but this should be done in such a way as not to embarrass the student.

Teachers must also respect the student's home environment. While certain types of speech may be acceptable at home and not acceptable in school, teachers should take care to point this out to the student. At no time, should the teacher may any disparaging comments about the dialect or grammar usage so that it would appear to reflect negatively on the home environment.

Skill 19.4   Recognizing ways in which linguistic and rhetorical patterns affect written and oral expression

Skill 19.5   Identifying skills that promote respectful communication and factors that affect intercultural communication

Due to the fact that teachers are dealing with students from almost every culture of the world in their classrooms, intercultural communication is more important today than it has been in the past. There are two aspects to this process – intercultural sensitivity and intercultural communication awareness. Sensitivity is refers to the way in which individuals can manage their emotions when dealing with those from another culture and awareness refers to being aware of the way in which you communicate them.

Even though it may be difficult to communicate with parents and students who are just learning English, teachers must show respect in that they do all that they can to make sure they understand the parents' wishes. Having translators at the school, for example, will show the parents and students that they respect their native language and are doing everything possible to help them.

Since many cultures of the world do not follow the same traditions, it is important to respect the traditions and allow the students time off from school when needed. Prayer centers have been established in some high schools for Muslim students so that they can attend to the aspects of their religion on a daily basis. This also applies to being respectful for the dress of those from other cultures.

When students from other cultures see that the school does respect their heritage, they will also reciprocate and communicate better on their own.

Social Influences

Social influences that impact language are mostly those imposed by family, peer groups, and mass media. For the most part, the economic and educational levels of families determine the properness of language use. Exposure to adults who encourage and assist children to speak well enhances readiness for other areas of learning; it also contributes to a child's ability to communicate his or her needs.

Historically, children learned language, speech patterns, and grammar from members of the extended family just as they learned the rules of conduct within their family unit and community. In modern times, the mother in a nuclear family became the dominant force in influencing the child's development. With increasing social changes, many children are not receiving the proper guidance in all areas of development, especially language.

Those who are fortunate to be in educational daycare programs like Head Start or in certified preschools develop better language skills than those whose care is entrusted to untrained care providers. Once a child enters elementary school, he or she is also greatly influenced by peer language. This peer influence becomes significant in adolescence, as the use of teen jargon gives teenagers a sense of identity within the chosen group(s) and independence from the influence of adults. In some lower socio-economic groups, children use Standard English in school and street language outside the school. Some children of immigrant families become bilingual by necessity if no English is spoken in the home.

Research has shown a strong correlation between socio-economic characteristics and all areas of intellectual development. Traditional paper measurement instruments rely on verbal ability to establish intelligence. Research findings and test scores reflect that children, reared in nuclear families who provide cultural experiences and individual attention, become more language proficient than those who are denied that security and stimulation.

Personal Influences

The rates of physical development and identifiable language disabilities also influence language development. Nutritional deficiencies, poor eyesight, and conditions such as stuttering or dyslexia can inhibit a child's ability to master language. Unless diagnosed early, these conditions can hamper communication into adulthood. These conditions also stymie the development of self-confidence and, therefore, the willingness to learn or to overcome the handicap. Children should receive proper diagnosis and positive corrective instruction.

In adolescence, children's choice of role models and their decisions about the future determine the growth of identity. Rapid physical and emotional changes and the stress of coping with the pressure of sexual awareness make concentration on any educational pursuits difficult. The easier the transition from childhood to adulthood, the better the competence will be in all learning areas.

Middle school and junior high school teachers are confronted by a student body ranging from fifth graders, who are still childish, to eighth or ninth graders who, if not in fact at least in their minds, are young adults. Teachers must approach language instruction as a social development tool with more emphasis on vocabulary acquisition, reading improvement, and speaking/writing skills.

COMPETENCY 0020   UNDERSTAND THE DEVELOPMENTAL PROCESSES OF READING AND READING COMPREHENSION.

Skill 20.1   Recognizing concepts of print (e.g., holding a book, directionality, tracking of print)

Since there are children who do come to school with little or no experience with books, the teacher does need to incorporate book handling skills into the lessons. This includes such strategies as:

- Practicing how to handle a book: How to turn pages, to find the top and bottom of pages, and how to tell the difference between the front and back covers.
- Book organization: Students demonstrate an understanding of the organization of books by being able to identify the title, cover, author, left to right progression, top to bottom order, and one to one correspondence. Students may learn these skills individually as they become more familiar with books.

Directionality of Print

Since the English language is written in a left-to-right format, it is essential that this format be taught to students from the very beginning. If the format is not learned, the child will not understand how to interpret a page of print. Imagine students with advanced skills in phonemic awareness and phonics, but still unable to read a text because they did not understand left-to-right progression.

Another concept of print that would directly impact students' ability to progress is the idea of a return sweep. Children could begin to read and come to the end of the first line; and, without efficiently knowing to return back to the left and begin again, they would become confused by the words on the page.

In order to become proficient readers, young students need to develop a complete understanding that all print is read from left to right and top to bottom. Modeling is one of the most important strategies a teacher can use to develop this understanding in children. The use of big books, poems, and charts are strategies teachers can use in both large and small group instruction. Simple questions can engage the students to pay closer attention to these skills (i.e. "We are going to read this passage, where should I put my pointer to start reading?").

Techniques for Promoting the Ability to Track Print in Connected Texts

Model directionality and one-to-one word matching by pointing to words while using a big book, pocket chart, or poem written out on a chart. As you repeatedly lead the children in this reading, they can follow along and eventually track the print and make one to one matches on the connected text independently. They can also practice by using a pointer (all children love to use the pointer because then pleasure becomes associated with the reading) or their fingers to follow the words. Children happily volunteer to be the point person.

Understanding that print carries meaning

This understanding is demonstrated every day in the elementary classroom as the teacher holds up a selected book to read it aloud to the class. The teachers explicitly and deliberately think aloud about how to hold the book, how to focus the class on looking at its cover, where to start reading, and in what direction to begin.

Even in writing the morning message on the board, the teacher targets the children on the placement of the message and its proper place at the top of the board to be followed by additional activities and a schedule for the rest of the day.

When the teacher challenges children to make letter posters of a single letter and the items in the classroom, their home, or their knowledge base which start with that letter, the children are making concrete the understanding that print carries meaning.

During the preschool years, children acquire cognitive skills in oral language that they apply later on to reading comprehension. Reading aloud to young children is one of the most important things that an adult can do because they are teaching children how to monitor, question, predict, and confirm what they hear in stories. Reid (1988) described three metalinguistic abilities that young children acquire through early involvement in reading activities:

1. *Word consciousness.* Children who have access to books can first understand the story through the pictures. Gradually, they begin to realize the connection between the spoken words and the printed words. The beginning of letter and word discrimination begins in the early years.

2. *Language and conventions of print.* During this early stage, children learn the way to hold a book, where to begin to read, left to right tracking, and how to continue from one line to another.

3. *Functions of print.* Children discover that print can be used for a variety of purposes and functions, including entertainment and information.

The typical variation in literacy backgrounds that children bring to reading can make teaching more difficult. Oftentimes, a teacher has to choose between focusing on the learning needs of a few students at the expense of the group, or focusing on the group at the risk of leaving some students behind academically. This situation is particularly critical for diverse learners who have gaps in their literacy knowledge.

Areas of Emerging Evidence

Experiences with print (through reading and writing) help preschool children to develop an understanding of the conventions, purpose, and functions of print. Children learn about print from a variety of sources, and in the process, they come to realize that print carries a story. They also learn how text is structured visually (e.g., in English, the text begins at the top of the page, moves from left to right, and carries over to the next page when it is turned). While knowledge about the conventions of print enables children to understand the physical structure of language, the conceptual knowledge that printed words convey a message also helps children to bridge the gap between oral and written language.

Phonological awareness and letter recognition contribute to initial reading acquisition by helping children to develop efficient word recognition strategies (e.g., detecting pronunciations and storing associations in memory). Phonological awareness and knowledge of print-speech relations play an important role in facilitating reading acquisition. Therefore, phonological awareness instruction should be an integral component of early reading programs. Within the emergent literacy research, viewpoints diverge on whether acquisition of phonological awareness and letter recognition are preconditions of literacy acquisition or whether they develop interdependently with literacy activities such as story reading and writing.

Storybook reading affects children's knowledge about, strategies for, and attitudes towards reading. Of all the strategies intended to promote growth in literacy acquisition, none is as commonly practiced, nor as strongly supported across the emergent literacy literature, as storybook reading. Children in different social and cultural groups have differing degrees of access to storybook reading. For example, it is not unusual for a teacher to have students who have experienced thousands of hours of story reading time along with other students who have had little or no such exposure.

Emergent Literacy is the concept that young children are emerging into reading and writing with no real ending or beginning point. This stage of reading is when the reader understands that print contains a consistent message. The approach for many emergent readers focuses on the idea that children develop their ability to construct meaning by sharing books they care about with responsive peers and adults. Some characteristics of emerging readers include 1) the emergent reader can attend to left to right directionality and features of print., 2) an emergent reader can identify some initial sounds and ending sounds in words, 3) the reader can recognize some high frequency words, names, and simple words in context, and 4) pictures can be used to predict meaning.

As young student enter and work through this stage of literacy, some common difficulties may be noticed by the teacher. Some of these common problems include

- Difficulty maintaining concentration
- Finding the appropriate text level
- Frustration with not being able to understand the text
- Limited vocabulary hindering comprehension

Skill 20.2 Demonstrating knowledge of phonemic awareness and its importance to reading development

Phonemic awareness is the acknowledgement of sounds and word, for example, a child's realization that some words rhyme. Onset and rhyme, for example, are skills that might help students learn that the sound of the first letter "b" in the word "bad" can be changed with the sound "d" to make it "dad." The key in phonemic awareness is that when you teach it to children, it can be taught with the students' eyes closed. In other words, it's all about sounds, not about ascribing written letters to sounds.

To be phonemically aware, means that the reader and listener can recognize and manipulate specific sounds in spoken words. Phonemic awareness deals with sounds in words that are spoken. The majority of phonemic awareness tasks, activities, and exercises are ORAL.

Since the ability to distinguish between individual sounds, or phonemes, within words is a prerequisite to association of sounds with letters and manipulating sounds to blend words—a fancy way of saying "reading," the teaching of phonemic awareness is crucial to emergent literacy (early childhood K-2 reading instruction). Children need a strong background in phonemic awareness in order for phonics instruction (sound –spelling relationship-printed materials) to be effective.

SEE also the discussion on morphology, semantics, syntax, pragmatics and phonics in Skill 19.1

Skill 20.3   Demonstrating knowledge of the basic principles of phonics

As opposed to phonemic awareness, the study of phonics must be done with the eyes open. It is the connection between the sounds and letters on a page. In other words, students learning phonics might see the word "bad" and sound each letter out slowly until they recognize that they just said the word.

Phonological awareness means the ability of the reader to recognize the sounds of spoken language. This recognition includes how these sounds can be blended together, segmented (divided up), and manipulated (switched around). This type of awareness then leads to phonics, which is a method for teaching children to read. It helps them to "sound out words."

Development of phonological skills may begin during the pre-K years. Indeed, by the age of five, a child who has been exposed to rhyme can typically recognize another rhyme. Such a child can demonstrate phonological awareness by filling in the missing rhyming word in a familiar rhyme or rhymed picture book. It isn't unheard of for children to surprise their parents by filling in missing rhymes in a familiar nursery rhyme book at the age of four or even earlier.

Children are taught phonological awareness when they are taught the sounds made by the letters, the sounds made by various combinations of letters, and the ability to recognize individual sounds in words.

Phonological awareness skills include:

1. Rhyming and syllabification
2. Blending sounds into words (such as pic-tur-bo-k)
3. Identifying the beginning or starting sounds of words and the ending or closing sounds of words
4. Breaking words down into sounds (also called "segmenting" words)
5. Recognizing small words contained in bigger words by removing starting sounds (hear to ear)

Skill 20.4   Identifying strategies for monitoring and facilitating comprehension before, during, and after reading

Before Reading

Making Predictions
One theory or approach to the teaching of reading that gained currency in the late 1960s and the early 70s was the importance of asking inferential and critical thinking questions of the reader meant to challenge and engage the children in the text. This approach to reading went beyond the literal level of what was stated in the text to an inferential level of using text clues to make predictions and to a critical level of involving the child in evaluating the text.

While asking engaging and thought-provoking questions is still viewed as part of the teaching of reading, it is only viewed currently as a component of the teaching of reading.

Prior knowledge can be defined as all of an individual's prior experiences, education, and development that precede his or her entrance into a specific learning situation or his or her attempts to comprehend a specific text. Sometimes, prior knowledge can be erroneous or incomplete. Obviously, if there are misconceptions in a child's prior knowledge, these must be corrected so that the child's overall comprehension skills can continue to progress. Even kindergarteners display prior knowledge, which typically includes their accumulated positive and negative experiences both in and out of school. Prior knowledge activities and opportunities might range from traveling with family, watching television, visiting museums, and visiting libraries to staying in hospitals, visiting prisons, and surviving poverty.

Whatever prior knowledge the child brings to the school setting, the independent reading and writing the child does in school will immeasurably expand his or her prior knowledge. This will further broaden his or her reading comprehension capabilities.

Literary response skills are dependent on prior knowledge, schemata, and background. **Schemata** (the plural of schema) are those structures that represent generic concepts stored in our memories. Effective comprehenders of text, whether they are adults or children, use both their schemata and prior knowledge *plus* the ideas from the printed text for reading comprehension, and graphic organizers help organize this information.

During Reading

Graphic Organizers
Graphic organizers solidify, in a chart format, a visual relationship among various reading and writing ideas. The content of a graphic organizer may include sequence, timelines, character traits, fact and opinion, main idea and details, and differences and likenesses (generally done using a Venn diagram of interlocking circles, a KWL Chart, etc). These charts and formats are essential for providing scaffolding for instruction through activating pertinent prior knowledge.

KWL charts are exceptionally useful for reading comprehension, as they outline what children <u>K</u>NOW, what they <u>W</u>ANT to know, and what they've <u>L</u>EARNED after reading. Students are asked to activate prior knowledge about a topic and further develop their knowledge about a topic using this organizer. Teachers often opt to display and maintain KWL charts throughout a text to continually record pertinent information about students' reading.

What do I KNOW?	What do I WANT to know?	What did I LEARN?

When the teacher first introduces the KWL strategy, the children should be allowed sufficient time to brainstorm what they all actually know about the topic. The children should have a three-columned KWL worksheet template for their journals, and there should be a chart to record the responses from class or group discussion. The children can write under each column in their own journal; they should also help the teacher with notations on the chart. This strategy involves the children in actually gaining experience in note taking and in having a concrete record of new data and information gleaned from the passage.

Depending on the grade level of the participating children, the teacher may also want to channel them into considering categories of information they hope to find out from the expository passage. For instance, they may be reading a book on animals to find out more about the animals' habitats during the winter or about the animals' mating habits.

When children are working on the middle (the *what I want to know* section of their KWL strategy sheet), the teacher may want to give them a chance to share what they would like to learn further about the topic and help them to express it in question format.

KWL can even be introduced as early as second grade with extensive teacher discussion support. It not only serves to support the child's comprehension of a particular expository text, but it also models for children a format for note taking. Additionally, when the teacher wants to introduce report writing, the KWL format provides excellent outlines and question introductions for at least three paragraphs of a report.

Cooper (2004) recommends this strategy for use with thematic units and with reading chapters in required science, social studies, or health text books. In addition to its usefulness with thematic unit study, KWL is wonderful for providing the teacher with a concrete format to assess how well children have absorbed pertinent new knowledge within the passage (by looking at the third L section). Ultimately it is hoped that students will learn to use this strategy, not only under explicit teacher direction with templates of KWL sheets, but also on their own by informally writing questions they want to find out about in their journals and then going back to their own questions and answering them after the reading.

Note Taking

Older children take notes in their reading journals, while younger children and those more in need of explicit teacher support contribute their ideas and responses as part of the discussion in class. Their responses can be recorded on an experiential chart.

After Reading

Connecting Texts

The concept of readiness is generally regarded as a developmentally-based phenomenon. Various abilities, whether cognitive, affective, or psychomotor, are perceived to be dependent upon the mastery or development of certain prerequisite skills or abilities. Readiness, then, implies that the necessary prior knowledge, experience, and readiness prerequisites should be present before the child engages in the new task.

Readiness for subject area learning is dependent not only on prior knowledge, but also on affective factors such as interest, motivation, and attitude. These factors are often more influential on student learning than the pre-existing cognitive base.

When texts relate to a student's life, to other reading materials, or to additional areas of study, they become more meaningful and relevant to students' learning. Students enjoy seeing reading material that they can connect to on a deeper level.

Discussing the Text

Discussion is an activity in which the children concentrate on a particular text. Among the prompts, the teacher-coach might suggest that the children focus on words of interest they encountered in the text. These can also be words that they heard if the text was read aloud. Children can be asked to share something funny or upsetting or unusual about the words they have read. Through this focus on children's responses to words as the center of the discussion circle, peers become more interested in word study.

Furthermore, in the current teaching of literacy, it is not uncommon for reading and writing, and thinking, listening, viewing, and discussing to be developed and nurtured simultaneously and interactively.

Skill 20.5   Recognizing the components of reading fluency, factors that affect fluency, and the relationship between fluency and reading comprehension

Foundations of literacy and reading instruction

When students practice fluency, they practice reading connected pieces of text. In other words, instead of looking at a word as just a word, they might read a sentence straight through. The point of this is that in order for the student to comprehend what he or she is reading, it is necessary to be able to "fluently" piece words in a sentence together. If a student is NOT fluent in reading, he or she sounds each letter or word out slowly and pays more attention to the phonics of each word. A fluent reader is more likely to read a sentence out loud using appropriate intonations.

The best way to test for fluency is to have a student read something out loud, preferably a few sentences in a row. Most students just learning to read are probably not fluent right away; with practice, they will increase their fluency. Even though fluency is not the same as comprehension, it is said that fluency is a good predictor of comprehension. Think about it: if a student is focusing too much on sounding out each word, he or she is not going to be paying attention to the meaning.

When students practice fluency, they practice reading connected pieces of text. In other words, instead of looking at a word as just a word, they might read a sentence straight through. The point of this is that in order for the student to comprehend what she is reading, she would need to be able to "fluently" piece words in a sentence together quickly. If a student is NOT fluent in reading, he or she would sound each letter or word out slowly and pay more attention to the phonics of each word. A fluent reader, on the other hand, might read a sentence out loud using appropriate intonations. The best way to test for fluency, in fact, is to have a student read something out loud, preferably a few sentences in a row— or more. Sure, most students just learning to read will probably not be very fluent right away; but with practice, they will increase their fluency. Even though fluency is not the same as comprehension, it is said that fluency is a good predictor of comprehension. Think about it: If you're focusing too much on sounding out each word, you're not going to be paying attention to the meaning.

Accuracy

One way to evaluate reading fluency is to look at student accuracy, and one way to do this is to record running records of students during oral reading. Calculating the reading level lets you know if the book is at the level from which the child can read it independently or comfortably with guidance or if the book is at a level where reading it frustrates the child.

As part of the informal assessment of primary grade reading, it is important to record the child's word insertions, omissions, requests for help, and attempts to get the word. In informal assessment the rate of accuracy can be estimated from the ratio of errors to total words read.

Results of Running Record Informal Assessment can be used for teaching based on Text Accuracy. If a child reads from 95%-100% correct, the child is ready for independent reading. If the child reads from 92% to 97% right, the child is ready for guided reading. Below 92% the child needs a read-aloud or shared reading activity.

Automacity

Fluency in reading is dependent on automatic word identification, which assists the student in achieving comprehension of the material. Even slight difficulties in word identification can significantly increase the time it takes a student to read material, may require rereading parts or passages of the material and reduces the level of comprehension expected. If the student experiences reading as a constant struggle or an arduous chore then he or she will avoid reading whenever possible and consider it a negative experience when necessary. Obviously, the ability to read for comprehension, and learning in general, will suffer if all aspects of reading fluency are not presented to the student as acquirable skills which will be readily accomplished with the appropriate effort.

Automatic reading involves the development of strong orthographic representations, which allows fast and accurate identification of whole words made up of specific letter patterns. Most young students move easily from the use of alphabetic strategies to the use of orthographic representations which can be accessed automatically. Initially word identification is based on the application of phonic word-accessibility strategies (letter-sound associations). These strategies are in turn based on the development of phonemic awareness, which is necessary to learn how to relate speech to print.

One of the most useful devices for developing automaticity in young students is through the visual pattern provided in the six syllable types.

EXAMPLES OF THE SIX SYLLABLE TYPES

1. **NOT** (CLOSED)
    Closed in by a consonant—vowel makes its **short** sound
2. **NO** (OPEN)
    Ends in a vowel—vowel makes its **long** sound
3. **NOTE** (SILENT "E")
    Ends in vowel consonant "e"--vowel makes its **long** sound
4. **NAIL** (VOWEL COMBINATION)
    Two vowels together make the sound
5. **BIRD** ("R" CONTROLLED)
    Contains a vowel plus 4—vowel sound is changed
6. **TABLE** (CONSONANT "L"-"E")
    Applied at the end of a word

These orthographic (letter) patterns signal vowel pronunciation to the reader. Students must become able to apply their knowledge of these patterns to recognize the syllable types and to see these patterns automatically and ultimately, to read words as wholes. The move from decoding letter symbols to identify recognizable terms, to automatic word recognition is a substantial move toward fluency. A significant aid for helping students move through this phase was developed by Anna Gillingham when she incorporated the Phonetic Word Cards activity into the Orton-Gillingham lesson plan (Gillingham and Stillman, 1997). This activity involves having the students practice reading words (and some non words) on cards as wholes, beginning with simple syllables and moving systematically through the syllable types to complex syllables and two-syllable words. The words are divided into groups that correspond to the specific sequence of skills being taught.

The student's development of the elements necessary to automaticity continually moves through stages. Another important stage involves the automatic recognition of single graphemes as a critical first step to the development of the letter patterns that make up words or word parts. English orthography is made up of four basic word types:

1. Regular, for reading and spelling (e.g., <u>cat, print</u>
2. Regular, for reading but not for spelling (e.g. <u>float, brain</u> - could be spelled "flote" or "brane," respectively)
3. Rule based (e.g., <u>canning</u> - doubling rule, <u>faking</u> - drop e rule)
4. Irregular (e.g., <u>beauty</u>).

Students must be taught to recognize all four types of words automatically in order to be effective readers. Repeated practice in pattern recognition is often necessary. Practice techniques for student development can include speed drills in which they read lists of isolated words with contrasting vowel sounds that are signaled by the syllable type. For example, several closed syllable and vowel-consonant-"e" words containing the vowel *a* are arranged randomly on pages containing about 12 lines and read for one minute. Individual goals are established and charts are kept of the number of words read correctly in successive sessions. The same word lists are repeated in sessions until the goal has been achieved for several succeeding sessions. When selecting words for these lists, the use of high-frequency words within a syllable category increases the likelihood of generalization to text reading.

True automaticity should be linked with prosody and anticipation to acquire full fluency. Such things as which syllable is accented and how word structure can be predictive are necessary to true automaticity and essential to complete fluency.

A student whose reading rate is slow, or halting and inconsistent, is exhibiting a lack of reading fluency. According to an article by Mastropieri, Leinart, & Scruggs (1999), some students have developed accurate word pronunciation skills but read at a slow rate. They have not moved to the phase where decoding is automatic, and their limited fluency may affect performance in the following ways:

1. They read less text than peers and have less time to remember, review, or comprehend the text
2. They expend more cognitive energy than peers trying to identify individual words
3. They may be less able to retain text in their memories and less likely to integrate those segments with other parts of the text

The simplest means of determining a student's reading rate is to have the student read aloud from a prescribed passage which is at the appropriate reading level for age and grade and contains a specified number of words. The passage should not be too familiar for the student (some will try to memorize or "work out" difficult bits ahead of time), and should not contain more words than can be read comfortably and accurately by a normal reader in one or two minutes. Count only the words <u>correctly</u> pronounced on first reading, and divide this word count into elapsed time to determine the student's reading rate. To determine the students standing and progress, compare this rate with the norm for the class and the average for all students who read fluently at that specific age/grade level.

The following general guidelines can be applied for reading lists of words with a speed drill and a 1-minute timing: 30 correct wpm for first- and second-grade children; 40 correct wpm for third- grade children; 60 correct wpm for mid-third-grade; and 80 wpm for students in fourth grade and higher.

Various techniques are useful with students who have acquired some proficiency in decoding skill but whose levels of skill are lower than their oral language abilities. Such techniques have certain, common features:

1. Students listen to text as they follow along with the book
2. Students follow the print using their fingers as guides
3. Reading materials are used that students would be unable to read independently.

Experts recommend that a beginning reading program should incorporate partner reading, practice reading difficult words prior to reading the text, timings for accuracy and rate, opportunities to hear books read, and opportunities to read to others.

Prosody concerns versification of text and involves such matters as which syllable of a word is accented. As regards fluency, it is that aspect which translates reading into the same experience as listening, within the reader's mind. It involves intonation and rhythm through such devices as syllable accent and punctuation.

In their article for *Perspectives* (Winter, 2002), Pamela Hook and Sandra Jones proposed that teachers can begin to develop awareness of the prosodic features of language by introducing a short three-word sentence with each of the three different words underlined for stress (e.g., *He is sick. He is sick. He is sick.*) The teacher can then model the three sentences while discussing the possible meaning for each variation. The students can practice reading them with different stress until they are fluent. These simple three-word sentences can be modified and expanded to include various verbs, pronouns, and tenses. (e.g., *You are sick. I am sick. They are sick.*) This strategy can also be used while increasing the length of phrases and emphasizing the different meanings (e.g., *Get out of bed. Get out of bed. Get out of bed now.*) Teachers can also practice fluency with common phrases that frequently occur in text. Prepositional phrases are good syntactic structures for this type of work (e.g., *on the _____, in the _____, over the _____ etc.*). Teachers can pair these printed phrases to oral intonation patterns that include variations of rate, intensity, and pitch. Students can infer the intended meaning as the teacher presents different prosodic variations of a sentence. For example, when speakers want to stress a concept they often slow their rate of speech and may speak in a louder voice (e.g., *Joshua, get-out-of-bed-NOW!*). Often, the only text marker for this sentence will be the exclamation point (!) but the speaker's intent will affect the manner in which it is delivered.

Practicing oral variations and then mapping the prosodic features onto the text will assist students in making the connection when reading. This strategy can also be used to alert students to the prosodic features present in punctuation marks. In the early stages using the alphabet helps to focus a student on the punctuation marks without having to deal with meaning. The teacher models for the students and then has them practice the combinations using the correct intonation patterns to fit the punctuation mark (e.g., ABC. DE? FGH! IJKL? or ABCD! EFGHI? KL.) Teachers can then move to simple two-word or three-word sentences. The sentences are punctuated with a period, question mark and exclamation point and the differences in meaning that occur with each different punctuation mark (e.g., *Chris hops. Chris hops? Chris hops!*) are discussed. It may help students to point out that the printed words convey the fact that someone named Chris is engaged in the physical activity of hopping, but the intonation patterns get their cue from the punctuation mark. The meaning extracted from an encounter with a punctuation mark is dependent upon a reader's prior experiences or background knowledge in order to project an appropriate intonation pattern onto the printed text. Keeping the text static while changing the punctuation marks helps students to attend to prosodic patterns.

Students who read word-for-word may benefit initially from practicing phrasing with the alphabet rather than words since letters do not tax the meaning system. The letters are grouped, an arc is drawn underneath, and students recite the alphabet in chunks (e.g., ABC DE FGH IJK LM NOP QRS TU VW XYZ). Once students understand the concept of phrasing, it is recommended that teachers help students chunk text into syntactic (noun phrases, verb phrases, prepositional phrases) or meaning units until they are proficient themselves. There are no hard and fast rules for chunking but syntactic units are most commonly used.

For better readers, teachers can mark the phrasal boundaries with slashes for short passages. Eventually, the slashes are used only at the beginning of long passages and then students are asked to continue "phrase reading" even after the marks end. Marking phrases can be done together with students or those on an independent level may divide passages into phrases themselves. Comparisons can be made to clarify reasons for differences in phrasing. Another way to encourage students to focus on phrase meaning and prosody in addition to word identification is to provide tasks that require them to identify or supply a paraphrase of an original statement.

Rate

A word count was obtained for each episode, then mean speed of words per second were computed within each episode and entire text. Participant miscue and accuracy rates were examined.

See also Skill 1.2

At some point it is crucial that, just as the nervous, novice bike rider finally relaxes and speeds happily off; so too must the early reader integrate graphophonic cues with semantic and structural ones and move toward fluency. Before this is done, the oral quality of early readers has a stilted beat to it, which of course, does not promote reading engagement and enjoyment.

The teacher needs to be at his/her most theatrical to model for children the beauties of voice and nuance that are contained in the texts whose print they are tracking so anxiously. Children love nothing more than to mimic their teacher and can do so legitimately and without hesitation if the teacher takes time each day to theatrically recite a poem with them. The poem might be posted on chart paper and be up on the board for a week.

First the teacher can model the fluent and expressive reading of this poem. Then with a pointer, the class can recite it with the teacher. As the week progresses, the class can recite it on their own.

Awareness of the challenges and supports in a text

Illustrations can be key supports for emergent and early readers. Teachers should not only use wordless stories (books which tell their narratives through pictures alone), but can also make targeted use of Big Books for read-alouds, so that young children become habituated in the use of illustrations as an important component for constructing meaning. The teacher should model for the child how to reference an illustration for help in identifying a word in the text the child does not recognize.

Of course, children can also go on a picture walk with the teacher as part of a mini-lesson or guided reading and anticipate the story (narrative) using the pictures alone to construct meaning,

Decoding

Use literature that contains examples of letter-sound correspondences you wish to teach. First, read the literature with the children or read it aloud to them. Then take a specific example from the text and have the children reread it as the teacher points out the letter-sound correspondence to the children. Then ask the children to go through the now familiar literature to find other letter-sound correspondences.

Once the children have correctly made the text sound correspondence, have them share other similar correspondences they find in other works of literature. The opportunity may also be used for repeated readings of various literature works which will enhance the children's ownership of their letter-sound correspondence ability and their pleasure in oral reading.

Cooper (2004) suggests that children can be told to become word detectives so that they can independently and fluently decode on their own. The child should learn the following word detective routines so that he or she can function as an independent fluent reader who can decode words on his/her own. First the child should read on to the end of the sentence. Then the child should search for word parts that he knows and also try to decode the word from the letter sounds. As a last resort, the child should ask someone for help or go to look up the word in the dictionary.

Techniques for determining students' independent, instructional and frustration reading levels

Instructional Reading is generally judged to be at the 95 percent accuracy level although Taberski places it at between 92 and 97 percent. Taberski tries to enhance the independent reading levels by making sure that readers on the instructional reading levels read a variety of genres and have a range of available and interesting books with a particular genre to read.

Taberski's availability for reading conferences helps her to both assess first hand her children's frustration levels and to model ongoing teacher/reader book conversations by scheduling child-initiated reading conferences where she personally replenishes their book bags.

In order to allay children's frustration levels in their reading and to foster their independent reading, it is important to some children that the teacher personally take time out to hear them read aloud and to check for fluency and expression. Children's frustration level can be immeasurably lessened if they are explicitly told by the teacher after they have read aloud that they need to read without pointing and that they should try chunking words into phrases that mimic their natural speech.

Assessment of the reading development of individual students-

For young readers who are from ELL backgrounds, even if they have been born in the United States, the use of pictures validates their story authoring and story telling skills and provides them with access and equity to the literary discussion and book talk of their native English speaking peers. These children can also demonstrate their story-telling abilities by drawing sequels or prequels to the story detailed in the illustrations alone. They might even be given the opportunity to share the story aloud in their native language or to comment on the illustrations in their native language.

Since many stories today are recorded in two or even three languages at once, discussing story events or analyzing pictures in a different native language is a beneficial practice.

Use of pictures and illustrations can also help the K-3 educator assess the capabilities of children who are struggling readers because they are children whose learning strength is spatial. Through targeted questions about how the pictures would change if different plot twists occurred or how the child might transform the story through changing the illustrations, the teacher can begin to assess struggling reader deficits and strengths.

Children from ELL backgrounds can benefit from listening to a recorded tape version of a particular story with which they can read along. This gives them another opportunity to "hear" the story correctly pronounced and presented and to begin to internalize its language structures. In the absence of taped versions of some key stories or texts, the teacher may want to make sound recordings.

Highly proficient readers can also be involved in creating these literature recordings for use with ELL peers or younger peers. This, of course, develops oral language proficiency, but also introduces these skilled readers into the intricacies of supporting ELL English language reading instruction. When they actually see their tapes being used by children they will be tremendously gratified.

Skill 20.6 Recognizing ways in which speaking, listening, spelling, and writing are essential components of reading development

Speaking, listening, spelling and writing are essential components of reading development and all four are interrelated. In order to learn to write a student needs to know how to spell words correctly and to read what has been written. The four components are essential for written communication.

When students speak they are communicating with others. However, all communication is not spoken and students must be able to not only read the textbooks but they must also be able to write the answers to questions and prepare reports. This requires reading and when engaging in the process of writing, they must be able to read what they write themselves in order to revise and edit their writing, as well as review notes they take when studying for exams.

Spelling often poses a difficulty for students because of the rules of spelling in the English language. It is quite normal for students to make repeated mistakes in spelling, even when the mistakes are pointed out to them. Teachers of young children quite often use word walls when children ask how words are spelled and direct the children to find the words they need.

Listening is a skill that is also hard for children to acquire. Through reading to children on a daily basis in the classroom, teachers can help instill in them a love of reading. A variety of topics and authors should be introduced to help students realize the many genres of literature that exist. Along with reading books to the students, one or more copies of the same book should be available in the classroom so that students who wish to do so can take the book and read it on their own.

COMPETENCY 0021   UNDERSTAND WORD RECOGNITION SKILLS
AND THE DEVELOPMENT OF VOCABULARY
SKILLS AND KNOWLEDGE.

Skill 21.1   Identifying decoding and word identification strategies,
including the use of structural analysis, spelling patterns, and
syllabication

Word analysis (a.k.a. phonics or decoding) is the process readers use to figure
out unfamiliar words based on written patterns. **Word recognition** is the process
of automatically determining the pronunciation and some degree of the meaning
of an unknown word. In other words, fluent readers recognize most written words
easily and correctly, without consciously decoding or breaking them down.

To **decode** means to change communication signals into messages. Reading
comprehension requires that the reader learn the code within which a message is
written and be able to decode it to get the message. **Encoding** involves
changing a message into symbols. Examples include encoding oral language
into writing (spelling), encoding an idea into words, or encoding a mathematical
or physical idea into appropriate mathematical symbols.

Although effective reading comprehension requires identifying words
automatically (Adams, 1990, Perfetti, 1985), children do not have to be able to
identify every single word or know the exact meaning of the every word in a text
to understand it. Indeed, Nagy (1988) says that children can read a work with a
high level of comprehension even if they do not fully know as many as 15 percent
of the words within a given text. Children develop the ability to decode and
recognize words automatically. They then can extend their ability to decode to
multi-syllabic words.

Spelling instruction should include learning the words that are misspelled in
daily writing, generalizing spelling knowledge, and mastering objectives in
progressive phases of development. The developmental stages of spelling
are as follows:

1) *Pre-phonemic spelling*—Children know that letters stand for a message,
    but they do not know the relationship between spelling and pronunciation.

2) *Early phonemic spelling*—Children are beginning to understand spelling.
    They usually write the beginning letter correctly, with the rest of the word
    being comprised of consonants or long vowels.

3) *Letter-name spelling*—Children spell some words consistently and correctly. The student is developing a sight vocabulary and a stable understanding of letters as representations of sounds. Long vowels are usually used accurately, but silent vowels are omitted. Unknown words are spelled by the child attempting to match the name of the letter to the sound.

4) *Transitional spelling*—This phase is typically entered in late elementary school. Short vowel sounds are mastered and some spelling rules are known. They are developing a sense of correct and incorrect spellings.

5) *Derivational spelling*—This is usually reached from high school to adulthood. This is the stage where spelling rules are being mastered.

How Words are Built

Knowledge of how words are built can help students with basic and more advanced decoding. A **root word** is the primary base of a word. A **prefix** is the affix (a morpheme that attaches to a base word) that is placed at the start of a root word, but that can't make a word on its own. Examples of prefixes include re-, pre-, and un-. A **suffix** follows the root word to which it attaches and appears at the end of the word. Examples of suffixes include –s, -es, -ed, -ly, and –tion. In the word unlikely, "un" is a prefix, "like" is the root work, and "ly" is a suffix.

Spelling Patterns

Concentration in this section will be on spelling plurals and possessives. The multiplicity and complexity of spelling rules based on phonics, letter doubling, and exceptions to rules that are not mastered by adulthood should be replaced by a good dictionary. As spelling mastery is also difficult for adolescents, the recommendation is the same; learning the use of a dictionary and thesaurus will be a more rewarding use of time.

Most plurals of nouns that end in hard consonant sounds followed by a silent *e* are made by adding *s*. Some words ending in vowels also only add an *s*.

fingers, numerals, banks, bugs, riots, homes, gates, radios, bananas

For nouns that end in the soft consonant sounds *s, j, x, z, ch,* and *sh,* add *es* to make them plural. Some nouns ending in *o* also add es.

dresses, waxes, churches, brushes, tomatoes, potatoes

Nouns ending in *y* preceded by a vowel are pluralized by just adding *s*.

boys, alleys

For nouns ending in *y* preceded by a consonant, change the *y* to *i* and add *es* to make them plural.

babies, corollaries, frugalities, poppies

Some noun plurals are formed irregularly or remain the same.

sheep, deer, children, leaves, oxen

Some nouns derived from foreign words, especially Latin, may make their plurals in two different ways. Sometimes, the meanings are the same; other times, the two plurals are used in slightly different contexts. It is always wise to consult the dictionary.

appendices, appendixes   criterion, criteria
indexes, indices   crisis, crises

Make the plurals of closed (solid) compound words in the usual way except for words ending in *ful*, which make their plurals on the root word.

timelines, hairpins, cupsful

Make the plurals of open or hyphenated compounds by adding the change in inflection to the word that changes in number.

fathers-in-law, courts-martial, masters of art, doctors of medicine

Make the plurals of letters, numbers, and abbreviations by adding *s.*

fives and tens, IBMs, 1990s, *p*s and *q*s (Note that letters are italicized.)

Skill 21.2   Recognizing methods of direct and indirect vocabulary instruction (e.g., specific word instruction, context clues)

SEE also Skill 21.1

Vocabulary in context

The National Reading Panel has put forth the following conclusions about vocabulary instruction.

1. There is a need for direct instruction of vocabulary items required for a specific text.
2. Repetition and multiple exposure to vocabulary items are important. Students should be given items that will be likely to appear in many contexts.

3. Learning in rich contexts is valuable for vocabulary learning. Vocabulary words should be those that the learner will find useful in many contexts. When vocabulary items are derived from content learning materials, the learner will be better equipped to deal with specific reading matter in content areas.

4. Vocabulary tasks should be restructured as necessary. It is important to be certain that students fully understand what is asked of them in the context of reading rather than to focus only on the words to be learned.

5. Vocabulary learning is effective when it entails active engagement in learning tasks.

6. Computer technology can be used effectively to help teach vocabulary.

7. Vocabulary can be acquired through incidental learning. Much of a student's vocabulary will have to be learned in the course of doing things rather than through explicit vocabulary learning. Repetition, richness of context, and motivation may also add to the efficacy of incidental learning of vocabulary.

8. Dependence on a single vocabulary instruction method will not result in optimal learning. A variety of methods can be used effectively with emphasis on multimedia aspects of learning, richness of context in which words are to be learned, and the number of exposures to words that learners receive.

• The National Reading Panel found that one critical feature of effective classrooms includes utilizing lessons and activities through which students apply their vocabulary knowledge and strategies to reading and writing. Included in the activities were discussions that allowed teachers and students to talk about words, their features, and strategies for understanding unfamiliar words.

There are many methods for directly and explicitly teaching words. In fact, the Panel found twenty-one methods that have been found effective in research projects. Many emphasize the underlying concept of a word and its connections to other words using graphics such as semantic mapping and diagrams. The keyword method uses words and illustrations that highlight salient features of meaning. Visualizing or drawing a picture either by the student or by the teacher was found to be effective. Many words cannot be learned in this way, so effective classrooms provide multiple ways for students to learn and interact with words. The Panel also found that computer-assisted activities can have a very positive role in the development of vocabulary.

Context Clues

Children who learn to read on schedule and who are avid readers have been seen to have superior vocabularies compared to other children their age. The reason for this is that in order to understand what they read, they often must determine the meaning for a word based on its context. Children who constantly turn to a dictionary for the meaning of a word they don't know will not have this advantage.

This is an important clue for providing students the kinds of exercises and helps they need in order to develop their vocabularies. Learning vocabulary lists is useful, of course, but much less efficient than exercises in determining meaning on the basis of context. It requires an entirely different kind of thinking and learning. Poetry is also useful for developing vocabulary exercises for children, especially rhymed poetry, where the pronunciation of a term may be deduced by what the poet intended for it to rhyme with. In some poets of earlier periods, the teacher may need to intervene because some of the words that would have rhymed when the poem was written do not rhyme in today's English. Even so, this is a good opportunity to help children understand some of the important principles about their constantly-changing language.

Another good exercise for developing vocabulary is the crossword puzzle. A child's ability to think in terms of analogy is a step upward toward mature language understanding and use. The teacher may construct crossword puzzles using items from the class such as students' names or the terms from their literature or language lessons.

Skill 21.3 Recognizing ways to help students identify and use references (e.g., dictionary, thesaurus) for various purposes

SEE Skill 21.1

Skill 21.4 Demonstrating an understanding of how prior knowledge, context clues, and graphic features of text can be used to predict, clarify, and expand word meanings

All children bring some level of background knowledge (e.g., how to hold a book, awareness of directionality of print) to beginning reading. Teachers can utilize children's background knowledge to help children link their personal literacy experiences to beginning reading instruction, while also closing the gap between students with rich and students with impoverished literacy experiences. Activities that draw upon background knowledge include incorporating oral language activities (which discriminate between printed letters and words) into daily read-alouds, as well as frequent opportunities to retell stories, look at books with predictable patterns, write messages with invented spellings, and respond to literature through drawing.

Reading aloud to children helps them acquire information and skills such as the meaning of words, how a book works, a variety of writing styles, information about their world, differences between conversations and written language, and the knowledge of printed letters and words along with the relationship between sound and print. Using different types of books assures that each child will find at least a few books that meet his or her interests and preferences.

Children's storybooks are traditional favorites for many young students. Some children may prefer to see books that have informational text such as those about animals, nature, transportation, careers, or travel. Alphabet books, picture dictionaries, and books with diagrams and overlays (such as those about the human body) catch the interest of children as well. Some children particularly enjoy books containing poetry, children's songs and verses, or folktales. Offering different types of books also gives flexibility in choosing one or two languages in which to read a story.

Illustrations for young children should support the meaning of the text and language patterns and predictable text structures should make these texts appealing to young readers. Illustrations can be key supports for emergent and early readers. Teachers should not only use wordless stories (books which tell their narratives through pictures alone), but can also make targeted use of Big Books for read-alouds, so that young children become habituated in the use of illustrations as an important component for constructing meaning. The teacher should model for the child, how to reference an illustration for help in identifying a word in the text the child does not recognize.

The content of the story should relate to the children's interests and experiences as the teacher knows them. The word should include lots of monosyllabic ones and lots of rhyming ones. Finally, children, particularly the emergent and beginning early readers, benefit from reading books with partners. The partners sit side by side and each one takes turns reading the entire text. Only after all these considerations have been addressed, can the teacher select "just right" books from an already leveled bin or list.

SEE also Skill 21.2

COMPETENCY 0022 **UNDERSTAND STRATEGIES FOR COMPREHENDING INFORMATIONAL/EXPOSITORY AND PERSUASIVE TEXTS.**

Skill 22.1 **Identifying characteristics of informational/expository and persuasive writing**

Discourse, whether in speaking or writing, falls naturally into four different forms: narrative, descriptive, expository, and persuasive.

The first question to be asked when *reading* a written piece, *listening* to a presentation, or *writing* is "What is the point?" The answer to this question is usually called the thesis. When you have finished reading an essay, you want to be able to say, "The point of this piece is that the foster-care system in America is a disaster." If it's a play, you should also be able to say, "The point of that play is that good overcomes evil." The same is true of any written document or performance. If it doesn't make a point, the reader/listener/viewer is likely to be confused or feel that it was not worth the effort.

Knowing that writing should make a point is very helpful when you are sitting down to write your own document, be it an essay, poem, or speech. What point do you want to make? We make these points in the forms that have been the structure of Western thinking since the Greek Rhetoricians.

Persuasion is a piece of writing, a poem, a play, or a speech whose purpose is to change the minds of the audience members or to get them to do something. This is achieved in many ways:

1) The credibility of the writer/speaker might lead the listeners/readers to a change of mind or a recommended action.

2) Reasoning is important in persuasive discourse. No one wants to believe that he or she accepts a new viewpoint or goes out and takes action just because he or she likes and trusts the person who recommended it. Logic comes into play in reasoning that is persuasive.

3) The third and most powerful force that leads to acceptance or action is emotional appeal. Even if audience members have been persuaded logically and reasonably that they should believe in a different way, they are unlikely to act on it unless moved emotionally. A person with resources might be convinced that people suffered in New Orleans after Katrina, but he or she will not be likely to do anything about it until he or she feels a deeper emotional connection to the disaster. Sermons are good examples of persuasive discourse.

got that wrong

Exposition is discourse whose only purpose is to inform. Expository writing is not interested in changing anyone's mind or getting anyone to take a certain action. It exists to give information. Some examples include directions to a particular place or the directions for putting together a toy that arrives unassembled. The writer doesn't care whether you do or don't follow the directions. He or she only wants to be sure you have the information in case you do decide to use it.

Narration is discourse that is arranged chronologically—something happened, and then something else happened, and then something else happened. It is also called a story. News reports are often narrative in nature, as are records of trips or experiences.

Description is discourse whose purpose is to make an experience available through one of the five senses—seeing, smelling, hearing, feeling (as with the fingers), and tasting. Descriptive words are used to make it possible for readers to "see" with their own mind's eye, hear through their own mind's ear, smell through their own mind's nose, taste with their own mind's tongue, and feel with their own mind's fingers. This is how language moves people. Only by experiencing an event can the emotions become involved. Poets are experts in descriptive language. Descriptive writing is typically used to make sure the point is established emotionally.

Nonfiction

Students often misrepresent the differences between fiction and nonfiction. They mistakenly believe that stories are always examples of fiction. The simple truth is that stories are both fiction and nonfiction. The primary difference is that fiction is imaginary, and nonfiction is generally true (or an opinion). It is harder for students to understand that non-fiction entails an enormous range of material from textbooks to true stories and newspaper articles to speeches. Fiction, on the other hand, is fairly simple—imaginary stories, novels, etc. But it is also important for students to understand that most of fiction throughout history has been based on true events. In other words, authors use their own life experiences to help them to create works of fiction.

The artistry in telling a story to convey a point is important in understanding fiction. When students see that an author's choice in a work of fiction is for the sole purpose of conveying a viewpoint, they can make better sense of the specific details.

Realizing what is truth and what is perspective is important in understanding nonfiction. Often, a nonfiction writer will present an opinion, and that opinion is very different from a truth. Knowing the difference between the two is very crucial.

In comparing fiction to nonfiction, students need to learn about the conventions of each. In fiction, students can generally expect to find plot, characters, setting, and themes. In nonfiction, students may find a plot, characters, settings, and themes, but they will also experience interpretations, opinions, theories, research, and other elements.

Overall, students can begin to see patterns that identify fiction from nonfiction. Often, the more fanciful or unrealistic a text or story is, the more likely it is fiction.

Nonfiction comes in a variety of styles. While many students simplify nonfiction as being true (as opposed to fiction, which is make-believe), nonfiction is much deeper than that. The following are various types of nonfiction; students should be exposed to all of these.

- *Informational texts:* These types of books explain concepts or phenomena. An informational text might explain the history of a state or the idea of photosynthesis. These types of text are usually based on research.
- *Newspaper articles:* These short texts rely completely on factual information and are presented in a very straightforward, sometimes choppy manner. The purpose of these texts is to present information to readers in a quick and efficient manner.
- *Essays:* Usually, essays take an opinion (whether it is about a concept, a work of literature, a person, or an event) and describe how the opinion was arrived at or why the opinion is a good one.
- *Biographies:* These texts explain the lives of individuals. They are usually based on extensive research.
- *Memoirs:* In a way, a memoir is like an autobiography, but memoirs tend to be based on a specific idea, concept, issue, or event in life. For example, most presidents of the United States write memoirs about their time in office.
- *Letters:* When letters are read and analyzed in the classroom, students are generally studying the writer's style or the writer's true opinions and feelings about certain events. Often, students will find letters of famous individuals in history reprinted in textbooks.
- *Journals:* Similar to letters, journals present very personal ideas. When available (as most people rarely want their journals published), they give students the opportunity to see peoples' thought processes about various events or issues.

In both fiction and nonfiction, authors portray ideas in very subtle ways through their skillful use of language. Style, tone, and point-of-view are the most basic of ways in which authors do this.

SEE also Skill 24.6.

Skill 22.2   Demonstrating knowledge of strategies for analyzing, interpreting, and evaluating a variety of informational/expository and persuasive texts

When analyzing, interpreting and evaluation informational and expository texts, the first question one has to ask is whether or not the information answers the questions that led to the search for information. One of the ways of organizing and planning for research, students should identify keywords that will help them narrow their search. As they locate different types of text containing these keywords, they can skim through the table of contents to find the specific pages that relate to what they are looking for. Then they scan the text to locate subheadings and titles to avoid having to read all the information to find a small section that applies to their search.

Students should identify the main ideas of the paragraphs of the text to determine the worthiness of the information to their quest. They should also summarize the paragraphs in their own words to show that they comprehend what they have read. They can also take notes on the reading to which they can refer later when studying or writing a report.

Analyzing, interpreting and evaluating persuasive text requires the use of different strategies. The text can be either negative or positive about the topic and presents an opinion of the author. The title should give a hint as to the slant that the author is taking in the text.

The first step is to analyze the title to determine whether or not the author is providing basic information in the persuasion or if the author wants to try to persuade you to adopt his/her way of thinking.

In order to determine how much of the text is fact and how much is the opinion of the author, students can make a list of all the facts they find in the text. They can then make a list of the information presented that is clearly opinion rather than fact.

Based on these lists, students can then discern the point or the argument that the author is trying to make and the evidence that is used to support this argument.

Propaganda techniques are often used in persuasive writing. These include quoting statements by experts in the field, the inclusion of statistics to prove a point, testimonials by those who are in agreement and can provide support as well as the use of bandwagon techniques. Once students recognize the use of these techniques in the text, they should ask three main questions:

- Who will benefit from agreeing with the author's point of view?
- Why does the author want to persuade readers to agree with the argument?
- Are the arguments based on sound evidence?

When students analyze the persuasive text in this manner, they are better able to interpret the message and determine whether or not the author's arguments are convincing.

Skill 22.3   Recognizing how tone, bias, and point of view influence meaning in informational/expository and persuasive texts

Style is the artful adaptation of language to meet various purposes. Authors can modify their word choice, sentence structure, and organization in order to convey certain ideas. For example, an author may write on a topic (such as the environment) in many different styles. In an academic style, the author uses long, complex sentences, advanced vocabulary, and very structured paragraphing. However, in an informal explanation in a popular magazine, the author may use a conversational tone in which simple words and simple sentence structures are utilized.

Tone is the attitude an author takes toward his or her subject. That tone is exemplified in the language of the text. For example, consider the topic of the environment. One author may dismiss the idea of global warming; the tone may be one of derision against environmentalists. A reader might notice this through the style (such as word choice), the details the author decides to present, and the order in which the details are presented. Another author may be angry about global warming and therefore use harsh words and other tones that indicate anger. Finally, yet another author may not care one bit about the issue of the environment either in a positive or negative light. Let's say this author is a comedian who likes to poke fun at political activists. His or her tone may be humorous; therefore, he or she will adjust the language used accordingly. In this example, all types of tones are about the same subject—they simply reveal, through language, different opinions and attitudes about the subject.

Finally, **point-of-view** is perspective. While most of us think of point-of-view in terms of first or third person in fiction (or even the points-of-view of various characters in stories), point-of-view also helps to explain much of language and the presentation of ideas in nonfiction texts. The above environmentalism example proves this. Three points-of-view are represented, and each creates a different style of language.

Students need to learn that language and text are changed dramatically by tone, style, and point-of-view. They can practice these concepts in everything they read. Doing so takes little time for each nonfiction or fiction text students read in class, and it goes a long way in helping them to comprehend text at a more advanced level.

Author's Tone and Point-of-View

The **author's tone** is his or her attitude as reflected in the statement or passage. His or her choice of words will help the reader to determine the overall tone of a statement or passage.

Consider the following paragraph.

I was shocked by your article, which said that sitting down to breakfast was a thing of the past. Many families consider breakfast time to be family time. Children need to realize the importance of having a good breakfast. It is imperative that they be taught this at a young age. I cannot believe that a writer with your reputation has difficulty comprehending this.

The author's tone in this passage is one of

(A) concern
(B) anger
(C) excitement
(D) disbelief

Since the author directly states that he or she "cannot believe" that the writer feels this way, the answer is (D).

Skill 22.4   **Recognizing how to apply comprehension strategies before, during, and after reading to promote understanding of informational/expository and persuasive texts**

Patterns of organization

Reading an essay should not take extraordinary effort for anyone. This is particularly true if the concepts are not too complex; reading an essay should not require extensive re-reading. The ideas should be clear and straightforward.

Anyone who has tried to write an essay knows that this sounds much easier than it really is! So how do teachers actually help students to become proficient at writing multi-paragraph essays in ways that allow them to clearly communicate their ideas? The trick is to help them to understand that various conventions of writing serve the purpose of making comprehension easier for readers. Those conventions include 1) good paragraphing; 2) transitions between paragraphs, ideas, and sentences; 3) topic sentences; 4) concluding sentences; 5) appropriate vocabulary; and 6) sufficient context.

1) Good paragraphing entails dividing up ideas into bite-sized chunks. A good paragraph typically includes a topic sentence that explains the content of the paragraph. A good paragraph also includes a sufficient explanation of that topic sentence. Thus, if a topic sentence suggests that the paragraph will be about the causes of the Civil War, the rest of the paragraph should actually explain specific causes of the Civil War.

2) As writers transition from one paragraph to another—or from one sentence to another—they will usually provide transitional phrases that give sign-posts to readers about what is coming next. Words like "however," "furthermore," "although," and "likewise," are good ways of communicating intention to readers. When ideas are thrown together on a page, it is hard to tell what the writer is actually doing with those ideas. Therefore, students need to become familiar with using transitional phrases.

3) As mentioned above, topic sentences are used at the beginning of paragraphs to provide structure for the information that the paragraph will contain. Topic sentences help both readers and writers in communicating and understanding.

4) Concluding sentences are often unnecessary; however, when done right, they provide a nice "farewell" or closing to a piece of writing. Students should be warned to not always use concluding sentences in paragraphs to avoid overexposure. However, they should also be alerted to their potential benefits.

5) When writers use appropriate vocabulary, they are sensitive to the audience and the purpose of what they are writing. For example, if writing an essay on a scientific concept to a group of non-scientists, it would not be a good idea to use specialized vocabulary to explain concepts. However, if writing for a group of scientists, not using that vocabulary may cause the writer to appear less credible. Vocabulary depends on what the writer intends with the piece of writing. Therefore, students need to learn early on that all writing has a purpose and that because of that purpose, good writers will make conscious decisions about how to arrange their texts, which words to use, and which examples and metaphors to include.

6) When writers provide sufficient context, they ensure that readers do not have to extensively question the text to figure out what is going on. Again, this has a lot to do with knowing the audience. Using the scientific concept example from above, the writer would need to provide more context if the audience were a group of non-scientists than if the audience were scientists. In other words, it would be necessary to provide more background so that the non-scientists could understand the basic concepts.

Some of the most common methods of teaching instruction are as follows:

• Summarization: This is where, either in writing or verbally, students go over the main point of the text, along with strategically chosen details that highlight the main point. This is not the same as paraphrasing, which is saying the same thing in different words. Teaching students how to summarize is very important, as it will help them look for the most critical areas in fiction and nonfiction. For example, in nonfiction, it will help them to distinguish between main arguments and examples. In fiction, it helps students to learn how to focus on the main characters and events in order to distinguish those from the lesser characters and events.

• Question answering: While this tends to be over-used in many classrooms, it is still a valid method of teaching students to comprehend. As the name implies, students answer questions regarding a text—either out loud, in small groups, or individually on paper. The best questions are those that cause students to have to think about the text (rather than just find an answer within the text).

• Question generating: This is the opposite of question answering, although students can later be asked to answer their own questions or the questions of peer students. In general, students should constantly question texts as they read. This is important because it causes students to become more critical readers. To teach students to generate questions helps them to learn the types of questions they can ask, and it gets them thinking about how best to be critical of texts.

• Graphic organizers: Graphic organizers are graphical representations of content within a text. For example, Venn Diagrams can be used to highlight the differences between two characters in a novel or two similar political concepts in a Social Studies textbook. A teacher can also use flow-charts with students to demonstrate the steps in a process (for example, the steps of setting up a science experiment or the chronological events of a story). Semantic organizers are similar in that they graphically display information. However, unlike flow-charts, semantic organizers usually focus on words or concepts. For example, a word web can help students to make sense of a word by mapping from the central word all the similar and related concepts to that word.

• Text structure: Many times in nonfiction (particularly in textbooks), and sometimes in fiction, text structures will give important clues to readers about what to look for. Students may not know how to make sense of all the types of headings in a textbook. For example, they may not realize that the side-bar story about a character in history is not the main text on a particular page in the history textbook. Teaching students how to interpret text structures gives them tools in which to tackle other similar texts. The most common text structures are comparison-contrast, cause-and-effect, chronological, and enumeration.

- Monitoring comprehension: Students need to be aware of their comprehension, or lack of it, in particular texts. Thus, it is important to teach students what to do when text suddenly stops making sense. For example, students can go back and re-read the description of a character, or they can go back to the table of contents or the first paragraph of a chapter to see where they are headed.

- Textual marking: This is where students interact with the text as they read. For example, armed with sticky notes, students can insert questions or comments regarding specific sentences or paragraphs within the text. This helps students to focus on the importance of the small things, particularly when they are reading larger works (such as young adult novels in middle school). It also gives students a reference point on which to go back into the text when they need to review something.

- Discussion: Small group or whole-class discussions stimulate thoughts about texts; they also give students a larger picture of the impact of those texts. More specifically, teachers can strategically encourage students to discuss concepts related to the text. Doing so helps students to learn to consider texts within larger societal and social concepts. Teachers can also encourage students to provide personal opinions in discussion. By listening to various students' opinions, all students in a class will better see the wide range of possible interpretations and thoughts regarding one text.

Many people mistakenly believe that the terms "research-based," "research-validated," or "evidence-based" relate mainly to specific programs, such as early reading textbook programs. While research does validate the efficacy of some of these programs, additional research has been conducted to test the effectiveness of other instructional strategies. On the subject of reading, many of these strategies have been documented in the report from the National Reading Panel (2000).

However, just because a strategy has not been validated as effective by research does not necessarily mean that it is not effective with certain students in certain situations. The number of strategies available far outweighs researchers' abilities to test their effectiveness. Some of the strategies listed above have been validated by rigorous research, while others have been shown consistently to help improve students' reading abilities in localized situations. There is simply not enough space to list all the strategies that have been proven effective; it is best to be aware that the above strategies are very commonly cited ones that work in a variety of situations.

SEE also Skill 20.4

COMPETENCY 0023   UNDERSTAND STRATEGIES FOR
                   COMPREHENDING LITERARY TEXTS.

Skill 23.1   Recognizing authors of literature written for children and
              young adults and characteristics of their works

Children's literature is a genre all its own. It has distinctive characteristics that
make it suitable for children and each author uses some of these in his/her work.

- the text is simple and straightforward
- the plot of the story is clearly stated
- it is about childhood and topics of interest to children
- it is usually written from a child's point of view
- often tends to be fantasy, but does include historical fiction as well
- some texts tend to be repetitious
- often has themes of good versus evil

Following are some authors who ~~have~~ are making significant contributions to
children's literature and some examples of their works:

Enid Blyton, British author, The Famous Five, The Secret Seven series.

J.K. Rowling, British author, Harry Potter series.

Jacqueline Wilson, British author, Tracy Beaker series.

Jane Yolen, American author, Owl Moon, Devil's Arithmetic.

Betsy Byars, American author, Summer of the Swans.

A great example of a fantasy book that was propelled into a 2006 movie is
Ronald Dahl's "Charlie and the Chocolate Factory. Both book and movie use the
fantasy of chocolate and living in a world of chocolate to show what would
happen if that world suddenly changed and was altered. The theme for young
readers is presenting ways for young children to adapt when their world is altered
and they must change to accommodate that adaptation.

Dick and Jane, along with Winnie the Pooh are early reader classics that have
been on bookshelves for decades. These books are fictionalized accounts using
human and animal characters to present morals and life lessons for readers who
are beginning to conceptualize the dynamics of actions and consequences.

In the juvenile genre, Barbara Holland's mystery and suspense thriller about a wealthy young girl and her best friend being kidnapped in "Prisoners at the Kitchen Table" is about creating a real problem needing real solutions. Readers are immediately drawn into a pressing issue and the need for a critical thinking solution to resolve the issue.

There are many historical novels that have been translated into various media mediums from the big screen to DVD classics. Charles Dickens's classic of "A Christmas Story" creates the moral of the wealthy protagonist with the struggling worker who has a handicapped son. The protagonist has a lot to give, but is seasonally stingy to his workers until he is visited by ghosts who represent his past, present and future. When he sees the light of his actions, the protagonist becomes a transformed man.

There are many books on the market that inspire and transform young readers. The ability of authors to create literature that educates and informs is historical. Books and stories are about magic and fantasy that allow readers to escape and engage imaginative activity that broadens cognitive thought and critical thinking development.

Other Titles

Dr. Seuss
Dr. Seuss's ABC: An Amazing Alphabet Book

An alphabet book is a book that utilizes letters of the alphabet in different ways that may or may not tell a story. These books often use rhyme and/or alliteration.

Alphabet books are usually organized in alphabetical order or reverse alphabetical order. There are pictures to accompany the words on each page that begin with the individual letters of the alphabet. One or two pages are devoted to each letter.

Most of the books by Dr. Seuss are written in anapestic tetrameter, a poetic technique employed by writers of the time. This consists of four rhyming units with a weak beat followed by a stronger one.

The books contain a lot of rhyme, which makes them easy for children to read and remember. They also contain numerous imaginary creatures and words that encourage students to make up their own characters for writing stories. There are also nonsensical words in the books, which children find amusing and are quick to point out as not being real words.

Another characteristic of Dr. Seuss books is the detailed drawings of the characters that appeal to all children.

Maurice Sendak
Where the Wild Things Are

Concept book—An informational book that introduces a single concept such as shape, color, size, or numbers.

This author has had a profound impact on the genre of Children's Literature both for the illustrations and the text. The book, Where the Wild Things Are, is realistic for children who have been sent to bed without supper and has become a favorite read aloud. It is a Caldecott book in which the text and the illustrations capture the emotions of the main character.

Some of the other titles by this author that are well-received by children are:
• Higglety, Pigglety Pop
• Outside Over There
• In the Night Kitchen

Bill Martin and Eric Carle
Brown Bear, Brown Bear, What Do You See?

Counting book—A picture book that focuses on numbers and counting.

The picture books of Bill Martin are known for their creative use of language. When the books are read aloud, students have the opportunity to hear rhyme, repetition and rhythm which helps them hear fluent reading. When teachers use choral reading using the books of this author, this helps students become fluent readers themselves when they read the books on their own.

Some of the other books by Bill Martin are:
• Hear are My Hands
• Chicka, Chicka, Boom, Boom
• Polar Bear, Polar Bear, What do you hear?
•   The Ghost Eye Tree

Eric Carle's books are often chosen as the subject of an author study in primary grade classrooms. They are filled with language learning skills, such as the use of repetition to support learning new vocabulary. They also span many different reading levels, which support Guided Reading in the classroom.

Popular books by Eric Carle include:
• The Very Hungry Caterpillar
• Pancakes! Pancakes!
• The Tiny Seed
• The Boastful Fisherman

Lois Ehlert
Fish Eyes: A Book You Can Count On

Early chapter book—Transitional fiction that is longer than a standard picture book, with fewer pictures. This type of book is generally written for grades 1-3.

The bright and colorful illustrations used by Lois Ehlert help bring the words on the page alive for the readers. When they can associate words to images that stand out in their mind it makes it easier for them to remember the words when they encounter them in other texts.

Mary Pope Osborne
The Tree House Series

Easy reader—A book that is written for grade levels 1-2 in which phrases or sentences are repeated in the text in easily recognizable patterns.

Mary Pope Osborne puts her own unique twist on heroes and heroines from the classical myths, legends and tall tales making them exciting adventures for children to read.

Stan and Jan Berenstein
The Berenstein Bears & The Honey Tree The Berenstein Bears Are A Family

Photo essay—A book that presents information on a concept or illustrates a story using photographs and text.

Stan and Jan Berenstein use bears in their stories that are more like humans than animals. These books are the biggest selling books in the genre or Children's Literature with timeless messages about the struggles of daily life and the challenges of responsibility.

Dorling Kindersley
My First Animal Book

Picture book—A book in which the message depends upon pictures as much or more than text.

Through the pages of the works by this author, children gain as much information about the world and animals through the pictures as they do from the words.

Margery Williams
The Velveteen Rabbit

Read aloud—A book that works well with children when presented orally.

This story appeals to children as it takes them through the dreams of toys as they want to become real. It is also a wonderful book to use with students when teaching drama and helping them learn how to act out the feelings of others.
Lucy Cousins
Flower in the Garden (My Cloth Book)

Young children and those with disabilities love the touchy-feely quality of cloth books along with the stories contained within.

Skill 23.2   Identifying characteristics of genres and recognizing themes of literature written for children and young adults

The major literary genres in adult literature include allegory, ballad, drama, epic, epistle, essay, fable, novel, poem, romance, and the short story. They are detailed below.

Allegory: A story in verse or prose with characters that represent virtues and vices. There are two meanings: symbolic and literal. John Bunyan's *The Pilgrim's Progress* is the most renowned of this genre.

Ballad: An *in medias res* story that is told or sung—usually in verse—and accompanied by music. Literary devices found in ballads include the refrain (repeated section) and incremental repetition (anaphora) for effect. Earliest forms were anonymous folk ballads. Later forms include Coleridge's Romantic masterpiece, "The Rime of the Ancient Mariner."

Drama: Plays (comedy, modern, or tragedy) that are typically performed in five acts. Traditionalists and neoclassicists adhere to Aristotle's unities of time, place, and action. Plot development is advanced through dialogue. Literary devices include asides, soliloquies, and the chorus, which represents public opinion. Considered by many to be the greatest of all dramatists/playwrights is William Shakespeare. Other dramaturges include Ibsen, Williams, Miller, Shaw, Stoppard, Racine, Moliére, Sophocles, Aeschylus, Euripides, and Aristophanes.

Epic: A long poem usually of book length that reflects values inherent in the generative society. Epic devices include an invocation to a Muse for inspiration, an overall purpose for writing, universal setting, a protagonist and antagonist who possess supernatural strength and acumen, and interventions of a God or the gods. Comparatively, there are few epics in literature: Homer's *Iliad* and *Odyssey*, Virgil's *Aeneid*, Milton's *Paradise Lost*, Spenser's *The Fairie Queene*, Barrett Browning's *Aurora Leigh*, and Pope's mock-epic, *The Rape of the Lock*.

Epistle: A letter that is not always originally intended for public distribution, but due to the fame of the sender and/or recipient, one that becomes public domain. For example, Paul wrote epistles that were later placed in the Bible.

Essay: Typically, a limited length prose work focusing on a topic and propounding a definite point-of-view and authoritative tone. Great essayists include Carlyle, Lamb, DeQuincy, Emerson, and Montaigne (who is credited with defining this genre).

Fable: A terse tale offering up a moral or exemplum. Chaucer's "The Nun's Priest's Tale" is a fine example of a *bete fabliau* (or beast fable) in which animals speak and act characteristically human, illustrating human foibles.

Legend: A traditional narrative or collection of related narratives, popularly regarded as historically factual but actually a mixture of fact and fiction.

Myth: Stories that are more or less universally shared within a culture to explain its history and traditions.

Novel: The longest form of fictional prose containing a variety of characterizations, settings, local color, and regionalism. Most have complex plots, expanded description, and attention to detail. Some of the great novelists include Austen, the Brontës, Twain, Tolstoy, Hugo, Hardy, Dickens, Hawthorne, Forster, and Flaubert.

Poem: The only requirement for a poem is rhythm. Sub-genres include fixed types of literature such as the sonnet, elegy, ode, pastoral, and villanelle. Unfixed types of literature include blank verse and dramatic monologue.

Romance: A highly imaginative tale set in a fantastical realm that deals with the conflicts between heroes, villains, and/or monsters. "The Knight's Tale" from Chaucer's *Canterbury Tales*, *Sir Gawain and the Green Knight,* and Keats' "The Eve of St. Agnes" are prime representatives.

Short Story: A concise narrative that has less background than a novel, but that typically includes many of the same plot developments and techniques. As mentioned before, some of the most notable short story writers include Hemingway, Faulkner, Twain, Joyce, Jackson, O'Connor, de Maupassant, Saki, Poe, and Pushkin.

Children's Literature

Children's literature is a genre of its own. Although it can share some of the same characteristics of adult literature, it emerged as a distinct and independent form in the second half of the seventeenth century. *The Visible World in Pictures* by John Amos Comenius, a Czech educator, was one of the first printed works in existence as well as the first picture book. After its publication, educators acknowledged that children are different from adults in many respects for the first time.

Modern educators acknowledge that introducing elementary students to a wide range of reading experiences plays an important role in their mental, social, and psychological development. Some of the most common forms of literature written specifically for children include:

Traditional Literature: Traditional literature opens up a world where right wins out over wrong, where hard work and perseverance are rewarded, and where helpless victims find vindication. These worthwhile values are ones that children identify with even as early as kindergarten.

In traditional literature, children are introduced to fanciful beings, humans with exaggerated powers, talking animals, and heroes that will inspire them. For younger elementary children, these stories in Big Book format are ideal for providing predictable and repetitive elements that are easily grasped.

Folktales/Fairy Tales: Adventures of animals or humans and the supernatural typically characterize these stories. The hero is usually on a quest aided by other-worldly helpers. More often than not, the story focuses on good and evil and reward and punishment. Some examples of folktales and fairy tales include: *The Three Bears, Little Red Riding Hood, Snow White, Sleeping Beauty, Puss-in-Boots, Rapunzel,* and *Rumpelstiltskin.*

Fables: Animals that act like humans are featured in these stories; the animals usually reveal human foibles or teach a lesson. Example: *Aesop's Fables.*

Myths: These stories about events from the earliest times, such as the origin of the world, are often considered true among various societies.

Legends: These are similar to myths except that they tend to deal with events that happened more recently. Example: Arthurian legends.

Tall tales: These are purposely exaggerated accounts of individuals with superhuman strength. Examples: Paul Bunyan, John Henry, and Pecos Bill.

Modern Fantasy: Many of the themes found in these stories are similar to those in traditional literature. The stories start out based in reality, which makes it easier for the reader to suspend disbelief and enter into worlds of unreality. Little people live in the walls in *The Borrowers,* and time travel is possible in *The Trolley to Yesterday.*

Including some fantasy tales in the curriculum often helps elementary-grade children to develop their imagination. The stories typically appeal to ideals of justice and issues having to do with good and evil; because children tend to identify with the characters, the message is more likely to be retained.

Science Fiction: Robots, spacecraft, mystery, and civilizations from other ages often appear in these stories. Most presume advances in science on other planets or in a future time. Most children like these stories because of their interest in space and the "what if" aspect of the stories. Examples: *Outer Space and All That Junk* and *A Wrinkle in Time.*

Modern Realistic Fiction: These stories are about real problems that real children face. By finding that their hopes and fears are shared by others, young children can find insight into their own problems. Young readers also tend to experience a broadening of interests as the result of this kind of reading. It is good for them to know that a child can be brave and intelligent and can solve difficult problems.

Historical Fiction: This type of literature provides the opportunity to introduce younger children to history in a beneficial way. *Rifles for Watie* is an example of this kind of story. Presented in a historically-accurate setting, it's about a sixteen year old boy who serves in the Union army. He experiences great hardships but discovers that his enemy is an admirable human being.

Biography: Reading about inventors, explorers, scientists, political and religious leaders, social reformers, artists, sports figures, doctors, teachers, writers, and war heroes helps children to see that one person can make a difference. They also open new vistas for children to think about when they choose a future occupation.

Informational Books: These are ways to learn more about something that children are interested in or something that they know little about. Encyclopedias are good resources, of course, but a book like *Polar Wildlife* by Kamini Khanduri also shows pictures and facts that will capture the imaginations of young children.

Skill 23.3   Analyzing story elements in works of fiction

The elements of fiction include plot, characters, settings, and point of view. The plot consists of five elements: the exposition, the rising action, the climax, the falling action, and the resolution. The exposition, or the beginning, typically introduces the main characters, the setting and the main conflict. Setting is important for students to comprehend as it should tell more than just the time and place. Setting also provides cultural, historical, political clues, as well as can set the mood and tone for a novel. For example, in Hawthorne's *The Scarlet Letter*, background knowledge of Puritan Boston would significantly help students comprehend other happenings in the story, as well as contribute to their understanding of the time period. A good study of the book's setting will contribute significant information to the student's knowledge of the story.

Character analysis tends to continue throughout the novel. The main characters are typically introduced at the beginning of the story, and then details and character traits tend to emerge as the story continues and they are challenged by the conflict. Students can analyze characters with ongoing character maps or trait analysis graphs or worksheets. Students can use these resources to record traits about the character and track how the character changes and develops throughout the story. Good character development is essential to a good novel because attachment to/interest in the character and their dealings with the conflict is often the main motivator for the reader to continue.

Point of view is from what perspective is the story told, and it is another important element of fiction. Point of view can typically be first person or third person. When the story is told in the first person, then the main character is telling the story using I, me and my. In the third person, an observer appears to be telling the story about the character using s/he, her, him, etc. In first person, the author can give the reader insight into the main characters thoughts and feelings, however, the author is limited to just the mind of the main character. In third person, the author can only describe words and actions that can be seen objectively and cannot get into character's thoughts. Analyzing point of view and why the author has chosen that point of view gains the reader insight into certain thoughts or feelings of the main character(s).

During the rising action, the characters and conflict continue to develop through the story telling, and it is during this time that the reader connects with the main character and the suspense of the conflict begins to arise. This leads to the climax, or turning point, of the story. Here the main character must face the conflict in some way, and the reader's interest is peaked to see how this confrontation will resolve. During the falling action, the loose ends are addressed and the climax is taken care of. Finally, the resolution, the story comes to a reasonable ending.

Figurative Language

Figurative language may also be called by its more familiar term: figures of speech. Poets and writers use figures of speech to sharpen the effect and meaning of their work and to help readers see things in ways they have never seen them before. Marianne Moore observed that a fir tree has "an emerald turkey-foot at the top." Her poem makes us aware of something we probably had never noticed before. The sudden recognition of the likeness yields pleasure in the reading.

Figurative language allows for the statement of truths that more literal language cannot. Skillfully used, a figure of speech will help the reader to see more clearly and to focus upon particulars. Figures of speech add many dimensions of richness to the reading and understanding of a poem; they also allow many opportunities for worthwhile analysis. The approach to take in analyzing a poem on the basis of its figures of speech is to ask pertinent questions: What does it do for the poem? Does it underscore meaning? Does it intensify understanding? Does it increase the intensity of our response?

Most of us are aware of a number of figures of speech; in fact, if all of them were listed, it would be a very long list! For the purpose of analyzing poetry or literature, the following list is fairly comprehensive and will allow for a suitable grasp.

Simile: A direct comparison between two things, often using the term "like" or "as" to foster the comparison. One very common example is "My love is like a red, red rose."

Metaphor: An indirect comparison between two things. It is the use of a word or phrase denoting one kind of object or action in place of another. While poets use metaphors extensively, they are also integral to understanding everyday speech. For example, chairs are said to have "legs" and "arms," even though they are typically unique to humans and other animals.

Symbolism:

Parallelism: This is the arrangement of ideas into phrases, sentences, and paragraphs that balance one element with another of equal importance and similar wording. An example from Francis Bacon's *Of Studies* is "Reading maketh a full man, conference a ready man, and writing an exact man."

Personification: This occurs when human characteristics are attributed to an inanimate object, an abstract quality, or an animal. For example, John Bunyan wrote characters named Death, Knowledge, Giant Despair, Sloth, and Piety in his *Pilgrim's Progress*. The earlier metaphor of the "arm" of a chair is also a form of personification.

Euphemism: This is the substitution of an agreeable or inoffensive term for one that might offend or suggest something unpleasant. Many euphemisms are used to refer to death, including "passed away," "crossed over," or even simply "passed."

Hyperbole: A deliberate exaggeration for effect. This passage from Shakespeare's *The Merchant of Venice* is an example:

> Why, if two gods should play some heavenly match
> And on the wager lay two earthly women,
> And Portia one, there must be something else
> Pawned with the other, for the poor rude world
> Hath not her fellow.

Irony: The expression of something other than and particularly opposite to the literal meaning, such as words of praise when blame is intended. In poetry, it is often used as a sophisticated or resigned awareness of contrast between what is and what ought to be; it expresses a controlled pathos without sentimentality. It is a form of indirection that avoids overt praise or censure. An early example is the Greek comic character Eiron, a clever underdog who, by his wit, repeatedly triumphs over the boastful character Alazon.

Alliteration: This is the repetition of consonant sounds in two or more neighboring words or syllables. In its simplest form, it reinforces one or two consonant sounds. For example, notice the repetition in Shakespeare's Sonnet #12:
When I do count the clock that tells the time.

Some poets have used more complex patterns of alliteration by creating similar consonant sounds both at the beginning of words and at the beginning of stressed syllables within words. For example, hear the sounds in Shelley's "Stanzas Written in Dejection Near Naples":

> The City's voice itself is soft like Solitude's

Onomatopoeia: The naming of a thing or action by a vocal imitation of the sound associated with it, such as "buzz" or "hiss." It is marked by the use of words whose sound suggests the sense. One good example is from "The Brook" by Tennyson:

> I chatter over stony ways,
> In little sharps and trebles,
> I bubble into eddying bays,
> I babble on the pebbles.

Malapropism: A verbal blunder in which one word is replaced by another that is similar in sound but different in meaning. The term itself comes from Sheridan's Mrs. Malaprop in *The Rivals* (1775). Thinking of the geography of contiguous countries, she spoke of the "geometry" of "contagious countries."

Skill 23.4   **Recognizing literary and narrative devices and historical contexts of literary works and analyzing their relationship to the meaning of the text**

Writers, from the time of the invention of the printing press, have played important roles in shaping public opinion, not only in their own countries but also around the world. Worldwide philosophical trends can be traced to the literature that was popular in a particular period of time. America has always been a nation of readers. With the development of theaters and ultimately movies and television that often dramatized popular novels, the power of the written word has increased.

Prior to twentieth century research on child development and child/adolescent literature's relationship to that development, books for adolescents were primarily didactic. They were designed to be instructive of history, manners, and morals.

Middle Ages

As early as the eleventh century, Anselm, the Archbishop of Canterbury, wrote an encyclopedia designed to instill in children the beliefs and principles of conduct acceptable to adults in medieval society. Early monastic translations of the *Bible* and other religious writings were written in Latin, for the edification of the upper class. Fifteenth century hornbooks were designed to teach reading and religious lessons. William Caxton printed English versions of *Aesop's Fables*, Malory's *Le Morte d'Arthur* and stories from Greek and Roman mythology. Though printed for adults, tales of adventures of Odysseus and the Arthurian knights were also popular with literate adolescents.

Renaissance

The Renaissance saw the introduction of the inexpensive chapbooks, small in size and 16-64 pages in length. Chapbooks were condensed versions of mythology and fairy tales. Designed for the common people, chapbooks were imperfect grammatically but were immensely popular because of their adventurous contents. Though most of the serious, educated adults frowned on the sometimes-vulgar little books, they received praise from Richard Steele of *Tatler* fame for inspiring his grandson's interest in reading and pursuing his other studies.

Meanwhile, the Puritans' three most popular reads were the *Bible*, John Foxe's *Book of Martyrs*, and John Bunyan's *Pilgrim's Progress*. Though venerating religious martyrs and preaching the moral propriety which was to lead to eternal happiness, the stories of the *Book of Martyrs* were often lurid in their descriptions of the fate of the damned. Not written for children and difficult reading even for adults, *Pilgrim's Progress* was as attractive to adolescents for its adventurous plot as for its moral outcome. In Puritan America, the *New England Primer* set forth the prayers, catechisms, *Bible* verses, and illustrations meant to instruct children in the Puritan ethic. The seventeenth-century French used fables and fairy tales to entertain adults, but children found them enjoyable as well.

Seventeenth century

The late seventeenth century brought the first concern with providing literature that specifically targeted the young. Pierre Perrault's *Fairy Tales*, Jean de la Fontaine's retellings of famous fables, Mme. d'Aulnoy's novels based on old folktales, and Mme. de Beaumont's "Beauty and the Beast" were written to delight as well as instruct young people. In England, publisher John Newbury was the first to publish a line for children. These include a translation of Perrault's *Tales of Mother Goose; A Little Pretty Pocket-Book*, "intended for instruction and amusement" but decidedly moralistic and bland in comparison to the previous century's chapbooks; and *The Renowned History of Little Goody Two Shoes*, allegedly written by Oliver Goldsmith for a juvenile audience.

Eighteenth century

By and large, however, into the eighteenth century adolescents were finding their reading pleasure in adult books: Daniel Defoe's *Robinson Crusoe*, Jonathan Swift's *Gulliver's Travels*, and Johann Wyss's *Swiss Family Robinson*. More books were being written for children, but the moral didacticism, though less religious, was nevertheless ever present. The short stories of Maria Edgeworth, the four-volume *The History of Sandford and Merton* by Thomas Day, and Martha Farquharson's twenty-six volume *Elsie Dinsmore* series dealt with pious protagonists who learned restraint, repentance, and rehabilitation from sin. Two bright spots in this period of didacticism were Jean Jacques Rousseau's *Emile* and *The Tales of Shakespear*, Charles and Mary Lamb's simplified versions of Shakespeare's plays. Rousseau believed that a child's abilities were enhanced by a free, happy life, and the Lambs subscribed to the notion that children were entitled to more entertaining literature in language comprehensible to them.

Nineteenth century

Child/adolescent literature truly began its modern rise in nineteenth century Europe. Hans Christian Andersen's *Fairy Tales* were fanciful adaptations of the somber revisions of the Grimm brothers in the previous century. Andrew Lang's series of colorful fairy books contain the folklores of many nations and are still part of the collections of many modern libraries. Clement Moore's "A Visit from St. Nicholas" is a cheery, non-threatening child's view of the "night before Christmas." The humor of Lewis Carroll's books about Alice's adventures, Edward Lear's poems with caricatures, Lucretia Nole's stories of the Philadelphia Peterkin family, were full of fancy and not a smidgen of morality. Other popular Victorian novels introduced the modern fantasy and science fiction genres: William Makepeace Thackeray's *The Rose and the Ring*, Charles Dickens' *The Magic Fishbone*, and Jules Verne's *Twenty Thousand Leagues Under the Sea*. Adventure to exotic places became a popular topic: Rudyard Kipling's *Jungle Books*, Verne's *Around the World in Eighty Days*, and Robert Louis Stevenson's *Treasure Island* and *Kidnapped*. In 1884, the first English translation Johanna Spyre's *Heidi* appeared.

North America was also finding its voices for adolescent readers. American Louisa May Alcott's *Little Women* and Canadian L.M. Montgomery's *Anne of Green Gables* ushered in the modern age of realistic fiction. American youth were enjoying the articles of Tom Sawyer and Huckleberry Finn. For the first time children were able to read books about real people just like themselves.

Twentieth century

The literature of the twentieth century is extensive and diverse, and as in previous centuries much influenced by the adults who write, edit, and select books for youth consumption. In the first third of the century, suitable adolescent literature dealt with children from good homes with large families. These books projected an image of a peaceful, rural existence. Though the characters and plots were more realistic, the stories maintained focus on topics that were considered emotionally and intellectually proper. Popular at this time were Laura Ingalls Wilder's Little House on the Prairie Series and Carl Sandburg's biography *Abe Lincoln Grows Up*. English author J.R.R. Tolkein's fantasy *The Hobbit* prefaced modern adolescent readers' fascination with the works of Piers Antony, Madelaine L'Engle, and Anne McCaffery.

John Steinbeck's *Grapes of Wrath* focused the attention of Americans on the plight of the common people who suffered more than anyone else because of the Great Depression. His revelation that Americans were starving to death in a land of great abundance still resonates with the public. Members of the "establishment" in the farms and towns of California are revealed as callous and greedy. Church members, particularly clergy and leaders, don't come off much better in his revealing story. Steinbeck lived with some of the migrants so he could write authentically and with first-hand knowledge. Many of the writers who have influenced public opinion write from personal experience.

The feminist movement has virtually been fueled by literature going back several hundred years. Although the organized movement began with the first women's rights convention at Seneca Falls, New York, in 1948, in 1869, John Stuart Mill had already published *The Subjection of Women* to demonstrate that the legal subordination of one sex to the other is wrong. Virginia Woolf's essay, *A Room of One's Own*, first published in 1929, had a strong influence on how women were beginning to see their roles.

However, in the crusade that was ignited by the Civil Rights movement of the 1960s, Betty Friedan's book, *The Feminine Mystique*, published in 1963, was very popular and influenced many women to become involved, both in changes in their own outlooks and behaviors, but also in the movement at large as activists. Feminism has been so much a part of the thinking throughout the world that it should always be included in the potential themes one looks for when writing a critique of a literary work.

Uncle Tom's Cabin broke new ground in literature on social injustice and was very powerful in influencing the thinking of American people about slavery. It was the best-selling novel of the 19th century and is credited with helping to fuel the abolitionist cause prior to the American Civil War. Written by Harriet Beecher Stowe and published in 1852, slavery is its central theme.

The Vietnam War inspired many novels although most were written after the war was over. However, the attitudes of Americans about the war have been influenced by these novels, and for many, they have formed the concept they carry with them about the conflict.

Some examples of novels about the Vietnam War:
- *Apocalypse Now*
- *Full Metal Jacket*
- *Platoon*
- *Good Morning Vietnam*
- *The Deer Hunter*
- *Born on the Fourth of July*
- *Hamburger Hill*

Skill 23.5 Analyzing a variety of literary texts, including how elements such as tone, style, and point of view influence meaning

Author's Purpose
An author may have more than one purpose in writing. An **author's purpose** may be to entertain, to persuade, to inform, to describe, or to narrate.

There are no tricks or rules to follow in attempting to determine an author's purpose. It is up to the reader to use his or her judgement.

Read the following paragraph.

Charles Lindbergh had no intention of becoming a pilot. He was enrolled in the University of Wisconsin until a flying lesson changed the entire course of his life. He began his career as a pilot by performing daredevil stunts at fairs.

The author wrote this paragraph primarily to:

(A) Describe
(B) Inform
(C) Entertain
(D) Narrate

Since the author is simply telling us or informing us about the life of Charles Lindbergh, the correct answer here is (B).

Author's Tone and Point of View
The **author's tone** is his or her attitude as reflected in the statement or passage. His or her choice of words will help the reader determine the overall tone of a statement or passage.

Read the following paragraph.

I was shocked by your article, which said that sitting down to breakfast was a thing of the past. Many families consider breakfast time, family time. Children need to realize the importance of having a good breakfast. It is imperative that they be taught this at a young age. I cannot believe that a writer with your reputation has difficulty comprehending this.

The author's tone in this passage is one of

(A) concern
(B) anger
(C) excitement
(D) disbelief

Since the author directly states that he "cannot believe" that the writer feels this way, the answer is (D) disbelief.

SEE also Skill 22.3

Skill 23.6   Recognizing the structural elements and essential attributes of poetic forms (e.g., rhyme scheme, meter, stanza)

People read poetry for many reasons, and they are often the very same reasons poets would give for writing it. Just the feel and sounds of the words that are turned by the artistic hands and mind of a poet into a satisfying and sometimes delightful experience is a good reason to read a poem. Good poetry constantly surprises.

The major purpose a writer of poetry has for creating his or her works of art is the sharing of an experience, a feeling, or an emotion; this is also the reason a reader turns to poetry rather than prose. Reading poetry is often a search for variety, joy, and satisfaction.

There is another important reason that poets create and that readers are drawn to their poems: they are interpreters of life. Poets feel deeply the things that others feel or even things that may be overlooked by others. Poets also have the skill and inspiration to recreate those feelings and interpret them in such a way that understanding and insight may come from the experience. They often bring understanding to life's big (or even not-so-big) questions.

Children can respond to poetry at very early stages. Elementary students are at the stage where the sounds of unusual words intrigue and entertain them. They are also very open to emotional meanings of passages. Teaching poetry to fifth graders can be an important introduction to seeking for meaning in literature. If a fifth grader enjoys reading poetry both silently and aloud, a habit may be formed that will last a lifetime.

When we speak of **structure** with regard to poetry, we usually mean one of three things:

1) The pattern of the sound and rhythm

It helps to know the background of this peculiarity of poetry. History was passed down in oral form almost exclusively until the invention of the printing press; it was often set to music. A rhymed story is much easier to commit to memory, and adding a tune makes it even easier to remember. Therefore, it is not surprising that much of the earliest literature—epics, odes, etc., are rhymed and were probably sung.

When we speak of the pattern of sound and rhythm, we are referring to two things: verse form and stanza form. The **verse form** is the rhythmic pattern of a single verse. An example is any meter; blank verse, for instance, is iambic pentameter. A **stanza** is a group of a certain number of verses (lines) having a rhyme scheme. If the poem is written, there is usually white space between the verses (although a short poem may be only one stanza). If the poem is spoken, there will be a pause between stanzas.

2) The visible shape it takes

In the seventeenth century, some poets shaped their poems on the page to reflect the theme. A good example is George Herbert's *Easter Wings*. Since that time, poets have occasionally played with this device; however, it is generally viewed as nothing more than a demonstration of ingenuity. The rhythm, effect, and meaning are often sacrificed by being forced into the visual contours of the poem's shape.

3) Rhyme and free verse

Poets also use devices that will underscore the meanings of their poems to establish form. A very common one is alliteration. When the poem is read (which poetry is usually intended to be), the repetition of a sound may not only underscore the meaning, it may also add pleasure to the reading.

Following a strict rhyming pattern can add intensity to the meaning of the poem in the hands of a skilled and creative poet. On the other hand, the meaning can be drowned out by the steady beat-beat-beat of it. Shakespeare very skillfully used the regularity of rhyme in his poetry, breaking the rhythm at certain points to very effectively underscore a point. For example, in Sonnet #130, "My mistress' eyes are nothing like the sun," the rhythm is primarily iambic pentameter. It lulls the reader (or listener) to accept that this poet is following the standard conventions for love poetry, which in that day reliably used rhyme and more often than not iambic pentameter to express feelings of romantic love along conventional lines. However, in Sonnet #130, the last two lines sharply break from the monotonous pattern, forcing reader or speaker to pause:

And yet, by heaven, I think my love as rare
As any she belied with false compare

Shakespeare's purpose is clear: he is not writing a conventional love poem; the object of his love is not the red-and-white conventional woman written about in other poems of the period. This is a good example of a poet using form to underscore meaning.

Poets eventually began to feel constricted by the rhyming conventions and began to break away and make new rules for poetry. When poetry was only rhymed, it was easy to define it. When free verse, or poetry written in a flexible form, came upon the scene in France in the 1880s, it quickly began to influence English-language poets such as T. S. Eliot, whose memorable poem, "The Wasteland," had an alarming but desolate message for the modern world; it is impossible to imagine that it could have been written in the soothing, lulling rhymed verse of previous periods.

Those who first began writing in free verse in English were responding to the influence of the French *vers libre.* However, it should be noted that free verse could also be loosely applied to the poetry of Walt Whitman, writing in the mid-nineteenth century, as can be seen in the first stanza of "Son of Myself."

I celebrate myself, and sing myself,
And what I assume you shall assume,
For every atom belonging to me as good belongs to you.

When poetry was no longer defined as a piece of writing arranged in verses that had a rhyme-scheme of some sort, distinguishing poetry from prose became a point of discussion. Merriam Webster's *Encyclopedia of Literature* defines poetry as "writing that formulates a concentrated imaginative awareness of experience in language chosen and arranged to create a specific emotional response through its meaning, sound and rhythm."

A poet chooses the form of poetry deliberately, based upon the emotional response he or she hopes to evoke and the meaning he or she wishes to convey. Robert Frost, a twentieth-century poet who chose to use conventional rhyming verse to make his point, is a memorable and often-quoted modern poet. Who can forget his closing lines in "Stopping by Woods"?

And miles to go before I sleep,
And miles to go before I sleep.

There are a number of literary techniques that make an appearance in poetry of all forms. It is important to understand the different mechanisms that poets use in order to fully understand the meaning of the poem. These include:

Slant Rhyme - This occurs when a rhyme is not exact; oftentimes, the final consonant sounds are the same, but the vowels are different. It occurs frequently in Irish, Welsh, and Icelandic verse. Examples include "green" and "gone," "that" and "hit," and "ill" and "shell."

Alliteration - Alliteration occurs when the initial sounds of a word, beginning either with a consonant or a vowel, are repeated in close succession. Examples include "Athena" and "Apollo," "Nate never knows," and "people who pen poetry."

The function of alliteration, like rhyme, might be to accentuate the beauty of language in a given context, or to unite words or concepts through a kind of repetition. Alliteration, like rhyme, can follow specific patterns. Sometimes the similar-sounding consonants aren't always the initial ones (although they are generally the stressed syllables). Alliteration is less common than rhyme, but because it is less common, it can call attention to a word or line in a poem that might not have the same emphasis otherwise.

Assonance - As alliteration typically occurs at the beginning of a word, and rhyme occurs at the end, assonance takes the middle territory. Assonance occurs when the vowel sound within a word matches the same sound in a nearby word, but the surrounding consonant sounds are different. "Tune" and "June" are rhymes; "tune" and "food" are assonant. The function of assonance is frequently the same as end rhyme or alliteration: all serve to give a sense of continuity or fluidity to the verse. Assonance is often especially effective when rhyme is absent, as it gives the poet more flexibility and it is not typically used as part of a predetermined pattern. Like alliteration, it does not so much determine the structure or form of a poem; rather, it is ornamental.

Onomatopoeia - These are words used to evoke meaning by their sounds. The early Batman series used *pow*, *zap*, *whop*, *zonk*, and *eek* in an onomatopoetic way.

Rhythm - In poetry, this refers to the recurrence of stresses at equal intervals. A stress (accent) is a greater amount of force given to one syllable in speaking than that which is given to another. For example, we put the stress on the first syllable of such words as father, mother, daughter, and children. The unstressed or unaccented syllable is sometimes called a slack syllable. All English words carry at least one stress (except articles and some prepositions such as by, from, at, etc.). Indicating where stresses occur is called scansion, or scanning. Very little is gained in understanding a poem or in making a statement about it by merely scanning it. The pattern of the rhythm—the meter—should be analyzed in terms of its overall relationship to the message and impression of the poem.

COMPETENCY 0024 UNDERSTAND THE PROCESS OF WRITING.

Skill 24.1 Demonstrating knowledge of the developmental stages of emergent writing (e.g., scribbling, letter strings, inventive spelling)

Role-Play Writing

In this stage, the child writes in scribbles and assigns a message to the symbols. Even though an adult would not be able to read the writing, the child can read what is written, although it may not be the same each time the child reads it. He/She will be able to read back the writing because of prior knowledge that print carries a meaning. The child will also dictate to adults, who can write a message or story.

The child gradually starts to emulate adult writing by graduating to wavy lines on a page instead of just random scribbles all over the page. Sometimes they have a picture on the page with the scribbles underneath to imitate what they see in picture books. They start to make letter shapes that resemble the letters of the alphabet, but they tend to be all over the page and vertical rather than horizontal.

As they become more used to making the letters in the proper way, they usually start with the letters of their own name. Then they write stories consisting of strings of letters across the page, which they can read as a story, but it illegible to anyone else.

Experimental Writing

In this stage the child writes in simple forms of language. Children usually write with letters according to the way the letters sound, such as the word "are" written as "r." However, the child does display a sense of sentence formation and writes in groups of words with a period at the end. He/she is aware of a correspondence between written words and oral language.

In both role-play and experimental writing, the child may simply have strings of letters put together that do not form words. They are however, in groups of letters that are separated in the same way as we see words written on a page.

For information on inventive spelling, **SEE** Skill 21.1

Skill 24.2   Identifying strategies for generating topics and developing ideas and for using organizational structures in writing

Structure

If there are two words synonymous with reading comprehension as far as the balanced literacy approach is concerned, they would be "Constructing Meaning." Cooper, Taberski, Strickland, and other theorists and classroom teachers conceptualize the reader as one who creates (constructs) a specific meaning based on both clues in the text and his or her own prior knowledge.

According to the leading theorists, comprehension for balanced literacy is a strategic process. The reader interacts with the text and brings his or her prior knowledge and experience to it. Writing is complementary to reading and is a mutually integrative and supportive parallel process. Hence, the division of literacy learning into reading workshops and writing workshops, with the same anchor "readings" or books being used for both, is particularly effective in teaching students.

Consider the sentence, "The test booklet was white with black print, but very scary looking."

According to the idea of constructing meaning as one reads the sentence above, readers' personal schemata (generic information stored in the mind) of tests will be activated by the author's ideas that tests are scary. The readers will remember emotions experienced during testing in themselves or in other people and use this information to comprehend the author's statement. Therefore, the ultimate meaning a reader derives from the page results from the interaction of the reader's own experiences with the ideas the author presents. The reader constructs a meaning that reflects the author's intent and also the reader's response to that intent.

It is also to be remembered that readings are generally fairly lengthy passages, comprised of paragraphs, which in turn are comprised of more than one sentence. With each successive sentence, and every new paragraph, the reader refocuses. The schemata are reconsidered, and a new meaning is constructed.

The purpose of reading is to convert visual images (the letters and words) into a message. Pronouncing the words is not enough; the reader must be able to extract the meaning of the text. When people read, they utilize four sources of background information to comprehend the meaning behind the literal text (Reid, pp.166-171).

These are:

1. *Word Knowledge:* This is information about words and letters. One's knowledge about word meanings is *lexical knowledge*—a sort of dictionary. Knowledge about spelling patterns and pronunciations is *orthographic knowledge.* Poor readers do not develop a high level of automaticity in using orthographic knowledge to identify words and to decode unfamiliar words.

2. *Syntax and Contextual Information:* When children encounter unknown words in a sentence, they rely on their background knowledge to choose a word that makes sense. Errors of younger children, therefore, are often substitutions of words in the same syntactic class. Poor readers often fail to make use of context clues to help them identify words or activate the background knowledge that would help them with comprehension. Poor readers also process sentences word by word, instead of by "chunking" phrases and clauses. This tendency results in a slow pace that focuses on the decoding rather than comprehension. Poor readers also have problems answering wh- (who, what, where, when, why) questions as a result of these problems with syntax.

3. *Semantic Knowledge:* This encompasses the reader's background knowledge about a topic, which is combined with the text information as the reader tries to comprehend the material. New information is compared to the background information and incorporated into the reader's schema. Poor readers have problems with using their background knowledge, especially with passages that require inference or cause-and-effect.

4. *Text Organization:* Good readers are able to differentiate types of text structure (e.g., story narrative, exposition, compare-contrast, or time sequence). They use their knowledge of text to build expectations and to construct a framework of ideas on which to build meaning. Poor readers may not be able to differentiate types of text and miss important ideas. They may also miss these same important ideas and details by concentrating on lesser or irrelevant details.

Research on reading development has yielded information on the behaviors and habits of good readers versus poor readers. Some of the characteristics of good readers:

- They think about the information that they will read in the text, formulate questions that they predict will be answered in the text, and confirm those predictions from the information in the text.
- When faced with unfamiliar words, they attempt to pronounce them using analogies to familiar words.

- Before reading, good readers establish a purpose for reading, anticipate possible text structure, choose a reading strategy, and make predictions about what will be in the reading.
- As they read, good readers test and confirm their predictions, go back when something does not make sense, and make new predictions.
The point of comprehension instruction is not necessarily to focus only on the text(s) that students are using at the very moment of instruction, but rather to help them learn the strategies that they can use independently with any other text.

Text Organization

In studies of professional writers and how they produce their successful works, it has been revealed that writing is a process that can be clearly defined (although in practice, it must have enough flexibility to allow for creativity). The teacher must be able to define the various stages that a successful writer goes through in order to make a statement that has value.

First of all, there must be a discovery stage when ideas, materials, supporting details, etc., are deliberately collected. These may come from many possible sources: the writer's own experience and observations, deliberate research of written sources, interviews of live persons, television presentations, or the Internet.

The next stage is the organization, during which the purpose, thesis, and supporting points are determined. Most writers will put forth more than one possible thesis; in the next stage, the writing of the paper, they will settle on one through the process trial and error.

Once the paper is written, the editing stage is necessary. This is probably the most important stage. This is not just about the polishing the paper; at this point, decisions must be made regarding whether the reasoning is cohesive: Does it hold together? Is the arrangement the best possible one or should the points be rearranged? Are there holes that need to be filled in? What form will the introduction take? Does the conclusion lead the reader out of the discourse, or is it inadequate or too abrupt?

Skill 24.3   Identifying strategies for prewriting, drafting, revising, editing, proofreading, and publishing materials

Stages of the writing process

Students should always gather ideas before writing. **Prewriting** may include clustering, listing, brainstorming, mapping, free writing, and charting. Providing many ways for a student to develop ideas on a topic in these ways will increase his or her chances for success.

Remind students that as they prewrite, they need to consider their audience. Prewriting strategies assist students in a variety of ways. Listed below are the most common prewriting strategies students can use to explore, plan, and write on a topic. It is important to remember when teaching these strategies that not all prewriting must eventually produce a finished piece of writing. In fact, in the initial lesson of teaching prewriting strategies, it might be more effective to have students practice prewriting strategies without the pressure of having to write a finished product.

- Keep an idea book so that they can jot down ideas that come to mind.
- Write in a daily journal.
- Write down whatever comes to mind; this is called free writing. Students do not stop to make corrections or interrupt the flow of ideas.

A variation of this technique is focused free writing—writing on a specific topic—to prepare for an essay.

- Make a list of all ideas connected with their topic; this is called brainstorming.
- Make sure students know that this technique works best when they let their mind work freely. After completing the list, students should analyze the list to see if a pattern or way to group the ideas emerges.
- Ask the questions Who? What? When? Where? Why? and How? Help the writer to approach a topic from several perspectives.
- Create a visual map on paper to gather ideas. Cluster circles and lines to show connections between ideas. Students should try to identify the relationships that exist between their ideas. If they cannot see the relationships, have them pair up, exchange papers, and have their partners look for some related ideas.
- Observe details of sight, hearing, taste, touch, and taste.
- Visualize by making mental images of something and write down the   details in a list.

After students have practiced with each of these prewriting strategies, ask them to pick out the ones they prefer and ask them to discuss how they might use the techniques to help them with future writing assignments. It is important to remember that they can use more than one prewriting strategy at a time. It is also important to reinforce that they may find that different writing situations may call for certain techniques.

When doing **research** in the library, note that most libraries will only allow the downloading and printing of seventy-five pages of information during any given month. The point is to provide the user with a hardcopy of specific information in a limited and environmentally friendly manner. Once the information is collected and categorized according to the research design and outline, the user can begin to take notes on the gathered information to create a cut and paste format for the final report.

For more information on note taking, **SEE** Skills 20.4 and 27.3.

To revise comes from the Latin word *revidere*, meaning "to see again." <u>**Revision**</u> is probably the most important step for the writer in the writing process. Here, students examine their work and make changes in <u>wording, details, and ideas.</u> All too often, students write a draft and then feel that they are done; on the contrary, students must be encouraged to develop, change, and enhance their writing as they go, as well as once they've completed a draft.

[handwritten: ★ got this wrong]

Effective teachers realize that revision and editing go hand-in-hand and that students often move back and forth between these stages during the course of one written work. These stages must be practiced in small groups, pairs, and/or individually. Students must learn to analyze and improve their own work as well as the works of their peers. Teachers should encourage the following activities:

1. Students work in pairs to analyze sentences for variety.
2. Students work in pairs or groups to ask questions about unclear areas in the writing or to help add details, information, etc.
3. Students perform final edit.

Many teachers introduce a Writer's Workshop to their students to maximize learning about the writing process. Writer's Workshops vary across classrooms, but the main idea is for students to become comfortable with the writing process. A basic Writer's Workshop will include a block of classroom time committed to focusing on various projects (e.g., narratives, memoirs, book summaries, fiction, book reports, etc). Students use this time to write, meet with others to review/edit writing, make comments on writing, revise their own work, proofread, meet with the teacher, and publish their work.

Teachers who facilitate effective Writer's Workshops are able to meet with students one at a time and can guide that student in his or her individual writing needs. This approach allows the teacher to differentiate instruction for each student's writing level.
Students need to be trained to become effective at proofreading, revising, and editing strategies. Begin by training them using both desk-side and scheduled conferences. Listed below are some strategies to use to guide students through the final stages of the writing process (and these can easily be incorporated into Writer's Workshop):

• Provide some guide sheets or forms for students to use during peer responses.
• Allow students to work in pairs and limit the agenda.
• Model the use of the guide sheet or form for the entire class.
• Give students a time limit or number of written pieces to be completed in a specific amount of time.

- Have the students read their partners' papers and ask at least three who, what, when, why, how questions. The students answer the questions and use them as a place to begin discussing the piece.
- At this point in the writing process, a mini-lesson that focuses on some of the problems your students are having would be appropriate.

To help students revise, provide students with a series of questions that will assist them in revising their writing.

1. Do the details give a clear picture? Add details that appeal to more than just the sense of sight.
2. How effectively are the details organized? Reorder the details if needed.
3. Are the thoughts and feelings of the writer included? When relevant, add personal thoughts and feelings about the subject.

Skill 24.4   Analyzing and identifying revisions of written work in relation to organization, unity, clarity, and style

When teaching revising and editing of written work, teachers need to analyze both the draft and the published piece in order to analyze how well the student has revised the writing. This involves comparing both pieces of writing to identify the changes that the student has made. There may simply be grammatical edits to correct mistakes in grammar, spelling and punctuation or the student may have made significant changes to the text so as to change the meaning of the writing.

The teacher should use a rubric that identifies features of an exceptional piece of writing all the way down to a piece that is very poor. A well written piece of writing should have outstanding content that is clear and focused on the topic. The organization should be seamless with each paragraph flowing into the next and there should be an easy flow and rhythm to the text. The sentence construction should be strong and varied and the reader should not have any difficulty discerning the voice of the writing. Word usage should be precise and present a picture for the reader in the words used to describe the topic. An excellent grasp of the standard writing conventions should be evident in this piece of writing.

Once the teacher has looked at the writing overall, then it is time to evaluate the individual aspects of the writing – organization, unity, clarity and style. This involves looking at the content of the piece, which involves looking at how well the student establishes a purpose for writing and selects the ideas to use to develop this purpose and the thesis of the text. It involves looking at the supporting details provided to make the content clear to the reader, showing that the writer has the reader in mind when writing.

Organization of a piece of writing refers to how well the student creates an effective opening and maintains this focus throughout. The details presented must be relevant to the topic and establishes relationships between the events and details presented. There should also be effective closure leading the reader to believe that the issue raised in the writing has been resolved. The writing should be divided into paragraphs with each paragraph having its own topic sentence and supporting details.

The sentence fluency makes it easy to read the text and to understand the message the writer is trying to portray in the words. This is the clarity of the writing, which should sound natural with each sentence flowing seamlessly into the next. Thus the unity of the writing is established with all sentences and paragraphs relating to each other and connected to the topic.

Students should also demonstrate knowledge of different styles of writing for different purposes. For example, if the purpose of the writing is to persuade the reader to take an opinion on an issue, then the supporting details should be used for this purpose.

Skill 24.5 Recognizing factors to consider when writing for various audiences and purposes

Author's Purpose

An author may have more than one purpose in writing. An **author's purpose** may be to entertain, to persuade, to inform, to describe, or to narrate.

There are no tricks or rules to follow in attempting to determine an author's purpose. It is up to the reader to use his or her own judgment.

Consider the following paragraph:

Charles Lindbergh had no intention of becoming a pilot. He was enrolled in the University of Wisconsin until a flying lesson changed the entire course of his life. He began his career as a pilot by performing daredevil stunts at fairs.

The author wrote this paragraph primarily to

> (A) describe
> (B) inform
> (C) entertain
> (D) narrate

Since the author is simply telling us (informing us) about the life of Charles Lindbergh, the correct answer here is (B).

The purpose of the writing dictates the organization of the text and the types of sentences and format of the writing. A student who wants to write a letter of complaint about an issue must include words, sentences and ideas in the writing that will convince the recipient of the letter that a mistake has been made. A piece of writing related to describing an event in one's life would revolve around using words and phrases that would bring that event to life in the mind of the reader.

Thus an important factor in writing is to consider the audience – who will read this piece of writing. Older students writing for younger students will have to use easy words and phrases as well as pictures in the work so that it will be interesting and easy to read for the younger students. The same students would not take the same format in the writing if they are writing a book report or a letter to an adult. The audience will determine the format and the focus of the writing.

Skill 24.6 Demonstrating knowledge of how form (e.g., research paper, editorial, memoir) and mode (e.g., expository, persuasive, narrative) shape writing

In order for students to determine which type of writing they need to use it is important that they have knowledge of the elements of each one and be exposed to different types of writing that fit within each.

Research reports are a special kind of expository writing. A topic is researched—explored by some appropriate means such as searching literature, interviewing experts, or even conducting experiments--and the findings are written up in such a way that a particular audience may know what was discovered. They can be very simple, such as delving into the history of an event or very complex, such as a report on a scientific phenomenon that requires complicated testing and reasoning to explain. A research report often reports possible conclusions, but puts forth one as the best answer to the question that inspired the research in the first place, which will become the thesis of the report.

Editorials are opinion pieces written for newspapers. The intention is that the message of the writing should be strong enough that it doesn't warrant the use of pictures or photos in order to convey the message or to contribute to the opinion presented in any way. They usually take the form of a thesis with supporting arguments to promote the point of view of the author. They are usually short, but there is no definite length that an editorial should take. This is an example of persuasive writing. All of the supporting details are related to the stance the writer takes on the issue.

Memoirs are autobiographical pieces that are shorter than a full autobiography of one's life. The goal is to capture highlights or meaningful moments in one's life. Descriptive words and phrases take the reader through the events that unfold in the writing. This is an example of narrative writing, but it is personal in nature and is usually written in the first person.

For information on mode, as well as more discussion on the topics in this skill,

SEE also Skill 22.1.

Other Forms

A **paraphrase** is the rewording of a piece of writing. The result will not necessarily be shorter than the original, but it will use different vocabulary and possibly a different arrangement of details. Paraphrases are sometimes written to clarify a complex piece of writing. Sometimes, material is paraphrased because it cannot be borrowed due to copyright restraints.

A **summary** is a "distilling" of the elements of a piece of writing or speech. It will be much shorter than the original. To write a good summary, the writer must determine what the "bones" of the original piece are. What is its structure? What is the thesis and what are the sub-points? A summary does not make judgments about the original; it simply reports the original in condensed form.

Letters are often expository in nature—their purpose is to give information. However, letters are also often persuasive, as the writer may want to persuade or get the recipient to do something. They are also sometimes descriptive or narrative, such as when the writer shares an experience or tells about an event.

COMPETENCY 0025 APPLY KNOWLEDGE OF GRAMMAR, USAGE, AND MECHANICS.

Skill 25.1 Applying knowledge of grammar and punctuation conventions for Standard American English

Because so many aspects of language change while others stay the same, teachers must be cognizant of the proper rules and conventions of punctuation, capitalization, and spelling in the modern oral and written language. Competency exams are designed to ensure that this is true; they generally test the ability to apply advanced language skills.

To aid in meeting the expectations of the competency exams, a limited number of the more frustrating rules are presented here. Rules should be applied according to the American style of English (i.e., spelling *theater* instead of *theatre* and placing terminal marks of punctuation almost exclusively within other marks of punctuation). The most common conventions are discussed below.

Sentence Completeness

Avoid fragments and run-on sentences. Recognizing sentence elements necessary to make a complete thought, properly using independent and dependent clauses, and using proper punctuation will correct such errors.

Capitalization

Capitalize all proper names of persons (including specific organizations or agencies of government); places (countries, states, cities, parks, and specific geographical areas); things (political parties, structures, historical and cultural terms, and calendar and time designations); and religious terms (any deity, revered person or group, sacred writings).

> Percy Bysshe Shelley, Argentina, Mount Rainier National Park, Grand Canyon, League of Nations, the Sears Tower, Birmingham, Lyric Theater, Americans, Midwesterners, Democrats, Renaissance, Boy Scouts of America, Easter, God, Bible, Dead Sea Scrolls, Koran

Capitalize proper adjectives and titles used with proper names.

> California gold rush, President John Adams, French fries, Homeric epic, Romanesque architecture, Senator John Glenn

Note: Some words that represent titles and offices are not capitalized unless used with a proper name.

Capitalized	Not Capitalized
Congressman McKay	the congressman from Florida
Commander Alger	commander of the Pacific Fleet
Queen Elizabeth	the queen of England

Capitalize all main words in titles of works of literature, art, and music. (See "Using Italics" in the Punctuation section.)

Punctuation

In a quoted statement that is either declarative or imperative, place the period inside the closing quotation marks.

> "The airplane crashed on the runway during takeoff."

If the quotation is followed by other words in the sentence, place a comma inside the closing quotations marks and a period at the end of the sentence.

> "The airplane crashed on the runway during takeoff," said the announcer.

In most instances in which a quoted title or expression occurs at the end of a sentence, the period is placed before either the single or double quotation marks.

> "The middle school readers were unprepared to understand Bryant's poem 'Thanatopsis.'"

> Early book-length adventure stories like *Don Quixote* and *The Three Musketeers* were known as "picaresque novels."

There is an instance in which the final quotation mark would precede the period: if the content of the sentence were about a speech or quote, and the understanding of the meaning would be confused by the placement of the period.

> The first thing out of his mouth was "Hi, I'm home."

but

> The first line of his speech began "I arrived home to an empty house".

In sentences that are interrogatory or exclamatory, the question mark or exclamation point should be positioned outside the closing quotation marks if the quote itself is a statement or command or cited title.

> Who decided to lead us in the recitation of the "Pledge of Allegiance"?

Why was Tillie shaking as she began her recitation, "Once upon a midnight dreary..."?

I was embarrassed when Mrs. White said, "Your slip is showing"!

In sentences that are declarative but the quotation is a question or an exclamation, place the question mark or exclamation point inside the quotation marks.

The hall monitor yelled, "Fire! Fire!"

"Fire! Fire!" yelled the hall monitor.

Cory shrieked, "Is there a mouse in the room?" (In this instance, the question supersedes the exclamation.)

Commas

Separate two or more coordinate adjectives that modify the same word and three or more nouns, phrases, or clauses in a list.

It was a dank, dark day.

Maggie's hair was dull, dirty, and lice-ridden.

Dickens portrayed the Artful Dodger as a skillful pickpocket, loyal follower of Fagin, and defendant of Oliver Twist.

Ellen daydreamed about getting out of the rain, taking a shower, and eating a hot dinner.

In Elizabethan England, Ben Johnson wrote comedy, Christopher Marlowe wrote tragedies, and William Shakespeare composed both.

Use commas to separate antithetical or complimentary expressions from the rest of the sentence.

The veterinarian, not his assistant, would perform the delicate surgery.

The more he knew about her, the less he wished he had known.

Randy hopes to, and probably will, get an appointment to the Naval Academy.

His thorough, though esoteric, scientific research could not easily be understood by high school students.

Using Semicolons

Use semicolons to separate independent clauses when the second clause is introduced by a transitional adverb. (These clauses may also be written as separate sentences, preferably by placing the adverb within the second sentence.)

> The Elizabethans modified the rhyme scheme of the sonnet; thus, it was called the English sonnet.
>   *or*
> The Elizabethans modified the rhyme scheme of the sonnet. Thus, it was called the English sonnet.

Use semicolons to separate items in a series that are long and complex or have internal punctuation.

> The Italian Renaissance produced masters in the fine arts: Dante Alighieri, author of the *Divine Comedy;* Leonardo da Vinci, painter of *The Last Supper;* and Donatello, sculptor of the *Quattro Coronati*, the four saints.

> The leading scorers in the WNBA were Zheng Haixia, averaging 23.9 points per game; Lisa Leslie, 22; and Cynthia Cooper, 19.5.

Using Colons

Place a colon at the beginning of a list of items. (Note its use in the sentence about Renaissance Italians on the previous page.)

> The teacher directed us to compare Faulkner's three symbolic novels: *Absalom, Absalom; As I Lay Dying;* and *Light in August.*

Do **not** use a colon if the list is preceded by a verb.

> Three of Faulkner's symbolic novels are *Absalom, Absalom; As I Lay Dying;* and *Light in August.*

Subject-Verb Agreement

A verb should always agree in number with its subject. Making them agree relies on the ability to properly identify the subject.

> One of the boys <u>was playing</u> too rough.

> <u>No one</u> in the class, not the teacher nor the students, <u>was listening</u> to the message from the intercom.

The <u>candidates</u>, including a grandmother and a teenager, <u>are debating</u> some controversial issues.

If two singular subjects are connected by *and*, the verb must be plural.

A man *and* his dog <u>were jogging</u> on the beach.

If two singular subjects are connected by *or* or *nor,* a singular verb is required.

Neither Dot *nor* Joyce <u>has missed</u> a day of school this year.

Either Fran *or* Paul <u>is</u> missing.

If one singular subject and one plural subject are connected by *or* or *nor,* the verb agrees with the subject nearest to the verb.

Neither the coach *nor* the <u>players</u> <u>were able</u> to sleep on the bus.

If the subject is a collective noun, its sense of number in the sentence determines the verb: singular if the noun represents a group or unit, and plural if the noun represents individuals.

The <u>House of Representatives</u> <u>has adjourned</u> for the holidays.

The <u>House of Representatives</u> <u>have failed</u> to reach agreement on the subject of adjournment.

Use of Verbs (Tense)

Present tense is used to express that which is currently happening or is always true.

Randy is playing the piano.

Randy plays the piano like a pro.

Past tense is used to express action that occurred in a past time.

Randy learned to play the piano when he was six years old.

Future tense is used to express action or a condition of future time.

Randy will probably earn a music scholarship.

Present perfect tense is used to express action or a condition that started in the past and is continued to or completed in the present.

Randy has practiced piano every day for the last ten years.

Randy has never been bored with practice

Past perfect tense expresses action or a condition that occurred as a precedent to some other action or condition.

Randy had considered playing clarinet before he discovered the piano.

Future perfect tense expresses action that started in the past or the present and will conclude at some time in the future.

By the time he goes to college, Randy will have been an accomplished pianist for more than half of his life.

Use of Verbs (Mood)

Indicative mood is used to make unconditional statements; subjunctive mood is used for conditional clauses or wish statements that pose untrue conditions. Verbs in subjunctive mood are plural with both singular and plural subjects.

If I were a bird, I would fly.

I wish I were as rich as Donald Trump.

Verb Conjugation

The conjugation of verbs follows the patterns used in the discussion of tense above. However, the most frequent problems in verb use stem from the improper formation of past and past participial forms.

Regular verb: believe, believed, (have) believed
Irregular verbs: run, ran, run; sit, sat, sat; teach, taught, taught

Other problems stem from the use of verbs that are the same in some tenses but have different forms and different meanings in other tenses.

I lie on the ground. I lay on the ground yesterday. I have lain down.
I lay the blanket on the bed. I laid the blanket there yesterday. I have laid the blanket every night.

The sun rises. The sun rose. The sun has risen. He raises the flag. He raised the flag. He had raised the flag.

I sit on the porch. I sat on the porch. I have sat in the porch swing.
I set the plate on the table. I set the plate there yesterday. I had set the table before dinner.

Two other common verb problems stem from misusing the preposition *of* for the verb auxiliary *have* and misusing the verb *ought* (now rare).

Incorrect:	I should of gone to bed.
Correct:	I should have gone to bed.

Incorrect:	He hadn't ought to get so angry.
Correct:	He ought not to get so angry.

Use of Pronouns

A pronoun used as a subject of predicate nominative is in nominative case.

She was the drum majorette. The lead trombonists were Joe and he.
The band director accepted whoever could march in step.

A pronoun used as a direct object, indirect object, or object of a preposition is in objective case.

The teacher praised him. She gave him an A on the test. Her praise of him was appreciated. The students whom she did not praise will work harder next time.

Some common pronoun errors occur from the misuse of reflexive pronouns:

Singular: *myself, yourself, herself, himself, itself*
Plural: *ourselves, yourselves, themselves*

Incorrect:	Jack cut hisself shaving.
Correct:	Jack cut himself shaving.

Incorrect:	They backed theirselves into a corner.
Correct:	They backed themselves into a corner.

Use of Adjectives

An adjective should agree with its antecedent in number.

Those apples are rotten. This one is ripe. These peaches are hard.

Comparative adjectives end in -er and superlatives in -est, with some exceptions like *worse* and *worst*. Some adjectives that cannot easily make comparative inflections are preceded by *more* and *most*.

> Mrs. Carmichael is the better of the two basketball coaches.

> That is the hastiest excuse you have ever contrived.

Avoid double comparisons.

Incorrect:	This is the worstest headache I ever had.
Correct:	This is the worst headache I ever had.

When comparing one thing to others in a group, exclude the thing under comparison from the rest of the group.

Incorrect:	Joey is larger than any baby I have ever seen. (Since you have seen him, he cannot be larger than himself.)
Correct:	Joey is larger than any other baby I have ever seen.

Include all the words necessary to make a comparison clear in meaning.

> I am as tall as my mother. I am as tall as she (is).

> My cats are better behaved than those of my neighbor.

Skill 25.2 Applying knowledge of orthographic patterns and usage rules for Standard American English

Orthography is a method of representing a spoken language through the use of written symbols (commonly referred to as **spelling**). It involves the application of letters and their sequencing within words. Fundamentally, English orthography is made up of four basic word types:

1. Regular, for reading and spelling (e.g., cat, print)
2. Regular, for reading but not for spelling (e.g. float, brain - could be spelled "flote" or "brane," respectively)
3. Rule based (e.g., canning - doubling rule, faking - drop e rule)
4. Irregular (e.g., beauty).

Students must be taught to recognize all four types of words automatically in order to be effective readers. Repeated practice in pattern recognition is often necessary. Practice techniques for student development can include speed drills in which they read lists of isolated words with contrasting vowel sounds that are signaled by the syllable type.

The study of word structure is another important reading skill. When readers develop morphemic skills, they are developing an understanding of patterns they see in words. For example, English speakers realize that cat, cats, and caterpillar share some similarities in structure. This understanding helps readers to recognize words at a faster and easier rate, since each word doesn't need individual decoding.

Skill 25.3   Recognizing a variety of sentence structures and their uses

Types of Sentences

Sentences are made up of two parts: the subject and the predicate. The **subject** is the "do-er" of an action or the element that is being joined. Any adjectives describing this do-er or element are also part of the subject. The **predicate** is made up of the verb and any other adverbs, adjectives, pronouns, or clauses that describe the action of the sentence.

A **simple sentence** contains one independent clause (which contains one subject and one predicate).

In the following examples, the subject is underlined once and the predicate is underlined twice.

> The dancer bowed.

> Nathan skied down the hill.

A **compound sentence** is made up of two independent clauses that are joined by a conjunction, a correlative conjunction (e.g., either-or, neither-nor), or a semicolon. Both of these independent clauses are able to stand on their own, but for sentence variety, authors will often combine two independent clauses.

In the following examples, the subjects of each independent clause are underlined once, and the predicates of each independent clause are underlined twice. The conjunction is in bold.

> Samantha ate the cookie, **and** she drank her milk.

> Mark is excellent with computers; he has worked with them for years.

> **Either** Terry runs the project **or** I will not participate.

A **complex sentence** is made up of one independent clause and at least one dependent clause. In the following examples, the subjects of each clause are underlined once, and the predicates are underlined twice. The independent clause is in plain text, and the dependent clause is in italics.

When *Jody saw how clean the house was*, she was happy.

Brian loves taking diving lessons, *which he has done for years*.

Skill 25.4   Recognizing a variety of paragraph formats and their uses

Main Idea

A **topic** of a paragraph or story is what the paragraph or story is about. The **main idea** of a paragraph or story states the important idea(s) that the author wants the reader to know about a given topic. The topic and main idea of a paragraph or story are sometimes directly stated; however, there are times when the topic and main idea are not directly stated but simply implied.

Look at this paragraph:

Henry Ford was an inventor who developed the first affordable automobile. The cars that were being built before Mr. Ford created his Model-T were very expensive. Only rich people could afford to have cars.

The topic of this paragraph is cars. The main idea is that Henry Ford built the first affordable automobile.

Readers can find the main ideas by looking at the way in which paragraphs are written. A paragraph is a group of sentences about one main idea. Paragraphs usually have two types of sentences: a topic sentence, which contains the main idea, and two or more detail sentences which support, prove, provide more information, explain, or give examples.

The **topic sentence** indicates what the passage is about. It is the subject of that portion of the narrative. The ability to identify the topic sentence in a passage will enable the student to focus on the concept being discussed and to better comprehend the information provided.

You can only tell if you have a detail or topic sentence by comparing the sentences with each other.

Look at this sample paragraph:

Fall is the best of the four seasons. The leaves change colors to create a beautiful display of golds, reds, and oranges. The air turns crisp and windy. The scents of pumpkin muffins and apple pies fill the air. Finally, Halloween marks the start of the holiday season. Fall is my favorite time of year!

Breakdown of sentences:
Fall is the best of the four seasons. (TOPIC SENTENCE)
The leaves change colors to create a beautiful display of golds, reds, and oranges. (DETAIL)
The air turns crisp and windy. (DETAIL)
The scents of pumpkin muffins and apple pies fill the air. (DETAIL)
Finally, Halloween marks the start of the holiday season. (DETAIL)
Fall is my favorite time of year! (CLOSING SENTENCE – Often a restatement of the topic sentence.)

The first sentence introduces the main idea, and the other sentences support and give the many uses for the product.

Tips for Finding the Topic Sentence

- The topic sentence is usually first one in a paragraph, but it could be in any position in the paragraph.

- A topic is usually more "general" than the other sentences; that is, it covers many things and looks at the big picture. Sometimes it refers to more that one thing. Plurals and the words "many," "numerous," or "several" often signal a topic sentence.

- Detail sentences are usually more "specific" than the topic; that is, they usually cover one single idea or a small part or side of an idea. The words "for example," "i.e.," "that is," "first," "second," "third," and "finally" often signal a detail.

- Most of the detail sentences support, give examples, prove, talk about, or point toward the topic in some way.

How can you be sure that you have a topic sentence? Try this trick: Switch the sentence you think is the topic sentence into a question. If the other sentences seem to "answer" the question, then that is probably the topic sentence.

For example:

Reword the topic sentence "Fall is the best of the four seasons" in one of the following ways:

"Why is fall the best of the four season?"
"Which season is the best season?"
"Is fall the best season of the year?"

Then, as you read the remaining sentences (the ones you didn't pick), you will find that they answer (support) your question.

If you attempt this with a sentence other than the topic sentence, it won't work.

For example:

Suppose you select "Halloween marks the start of the holiday season," and you reword it in the following way:

"Which holiday is the start of the holiday season?"

You will find that the other sentences fail to help you answer (support) your question.

Summary Statements

The introductory statement should be at the beginning of the passage. An introductory statement will provide a bridge between any previous, relevant text and the content to follow. It will provide information about, and set the tone and parameters for, the text to follow. The old axiom regarding presenting a body of information suggested that you should always "tell them what you are going to tell them; tell it to them; tell them what you just told them." The introductory statement is where the writer will tell the readers what he or she is going to tell them.

The summary statement should be at or near the end of the passage, and is a concise presentation of the essential data from that passage. In terms of the old axiom, the content portion (the main body of the narrative) is where the writer will "tell it to them." The summary statement is where the writer will tell the readers what he or she has just told them.

Restating the Main Idea

An accurate restatement of the main idea from a passage will usually summarize the concept in a concise manner, and it will often present the same idea from a different perspective. A restatement should always demonstrate complete comprehension of the main idea.

To select an accurate restatement, identifying the main idea of the passage is essential. Once you comprehend the main idea of a passage, evaluate your choices to see which statement restates the main idea while eliminating statements that restate a supporting detail. Walk through the steps below the sample paragraph to see how to select the accurate restatement.

Sample Paragraph:

Fall is the best of the four seasons. The leaves change colors to create a beautiful display of golds, reds, and oranges. The air turns crisp and windy. The scent of pumpkin muffins and apple pies fill the air. Finally, Halloween marks the start of the holiday season. Fall is my favorite time of year!

Steps:

1. Identify the main idea. (Answer: "Fall is the best of the four seasons.")
2. Decide which statement below restates the topic sentence:
3. The changing leaves turn gold, red, and orange.
4. The holidays start with Halloween.
5. Of the four seasons, fall is the greatest of them all.
6. Crisp wind is a fun aspect of fall.

The answer is (C) because it rewords the main idea of the first sentence, the topic sentence.

Supporting Details

The **supporting details** are sentences that give more information about the topic and the main idea.

The supporting details in the aforementioned paragraph about Henry Ford would be that he was an inventor and that before he created his Model-T, only rich people could afford cars because they were too expensive.

COMPETENCY 0026 **UNDERSTAND THE INTERRELATIONSHIPS AMONG READING, WRITING, SPELLING, LISTENING, VIEWING AND THINKING.**

Skill 26.1 **Demonstrating knowledge of the role of metacognition in reading and writing and in listening and speaking**

Aspects of speaking and listening

Listening is a very specific skill for very specific circumstances. There are two aspects to listening that warrant attention: comprehension and purpose. **Comprehension** is simply understanding what someone says, the purposes behind the message, and the contexts in which it is said. **Purpose** comes in to play when considering that while someone may completely understand a message, they must also know what to do with it. Are they expected to just nod and smile? Go out and take action?

While listening comprehension is indeed a significant skill in itself—one that deserves a lot of focus in the classroom (much in the same way that reading comprehension does), we will focus on purpose here. Often, when we understand the purpose of listening in various contexts, comprehension will be much easier. Furthermore, when we know the purpose of listening, we can better adjust our comprehension strategies.

Purpose

When complex or new information is provided to us orally, we must analyze and interpret that information. What is the author's most important point? How do the figures of speech impact meaning? How can we arrive at conclusions? Often, making sense of this information can be difficult for oral presentations—first, because we have no way to go back and review material already stated; secondly, because oral language is so much less predictable than written language. However, when we focus on extracting the meaning, message, and speaker's purpose, rather than just "listening" and waiting for things to make sense for us—in other words, when we are more "active" in our listening—we have greater success in interpreting speech.

Listening is often done for the purpose of enjoyment. We like to listen to stories, we enjoy poetry, and we like radio dramas and theater. Listening to literature can also be a great pleasure. The problem today is that students have not learned how to extract great pleasure on a wide-spread scale from simply listening. Perhaps that is because we have not done a good enough job of showing students how listening to literature, for example, can indeed be more interesting than television or video games. In the classrooms of exceptional teachers, we will often find that students are captivated by the reading aloud of good literature. It is refreshing and enjoyable to just sit and soak in the language, story, and poetry of literature being read aloud. Therefore, we must teach students *how* to listen and enjoy such work. We do this by making it fun and giving many possibilities and alternatives to capture the wide array of interests in each classroom.

Let us consider listening in large and small group conversations. The difference here is that conversation requires more than just listening: it involves feedback and active involvement. This can be particularly challenging, as in our culture, we are trained to move conversations along, to discourage silence in a conversation, and to always get the last word in. This poses significant problems for the art of listening. In a discussion, for example, when we are instead preparing our next response—rather than listening to what others are saying—we do a large disservice to the entire discussion. Students need to learn how listening carefully to others in discussions actually promotes better responses on the part of subsequent speakers. One way teachers can encourage this in both large and small group discussions is to expect students to respond *directly* to the previous student's comments before moving ahead with their new comments. This will encourage them to pose their new comments in light of the comments that came just before them.

Making Sense of Oral Language

Oral speech can also be much less structured than written language. Yet, aside from re-reading, many of the skills and strategies that help us in reading comprehension can help us in listening comprehension. For example, as soon as we start listening to something new, we should tap into our prior knowledge in order to attach new information to what we already know. This will not only help us to understand the new information more quickly, but it will also assist us in remembering the material.

We can also look for transitions between ideas. Sometimes, in oral speech, this is pretty simple, such as when voice tone or body language changes; as listeners, we have access to the animation that comes along with live speech. Human beings have to try very hard to be completely non-expressive in their speech. Listeners should take advantage of this and notice how the speaker changes character and voice in order to signal a transition of ideas.

Listeners can also better comprehend the underlying intent of the author when they notice nonverbal cues. In oral speech, unlike written text, elements like irony are not indicated by the actual words, but rather by the tone and nonverbal cues. Simply looking to see expression on the face of a speaker can often do more to signal irony than trying to extract irony from actual words.

One good way to follow oral speech is to take notes and outline major points. Because oral speech can be more circular (as opposed to linear) than written text, it can be of great assistance to keep track of an author's message. Students can learn this strategy in many ways in the classroom: they can take notes during the teacher's oral messages as well as other students' presentations and speeches.

Other classroom methods can also be used to help students to learn good listening skills. For example, teachers can have students practice following complex directions. They can also have students orally retell stories—or retell (in writing or in oral speech) oral presentations of stories or other materials. These activities give students direct practice in the very important skills of listening. They provide students with outlets in which they can slowly improve their abilities to comprehend oral language and take decisive action based on oral speech.

Utilizing Appropriate Communication

In public speaking, not all speeches deserve the same type of speaking style. For example, when providing a humorous speech, it is important to utilize body language that accents the humorous moments. However, when giving instructions, it is extremely important to speak clearly and slowly, carefully noting the mood of the audience, so that if there is general confusion on peoples' faces, you can go back and review something. In group discussions, it is important to ensure that you are listening to others carefully and tailoring your messages so that what you say fits into the general mood and location of the discussion at hand. When giving an oral presentation, the mood should be both serious and friendly; you should focus on ensuring that the content is covered, while also relating to audience members as much as possible.

It used to be that we thought of speaking and communication only in terms of what is effective and what is not effective. Today, we realize that there is more to communication than just good and bad. We must take into consideration that we must adjust our communication styles for various audiences. While we should not stereotype audiences, we can still recognize that certain methods of communication are more appropriate with certain people than with others. Age is an easy one to consider: Adults know that when they talk to children, they should come across as pleasant and non-threatening, and they should use vocabulary that is simple for children to understand. On the other hand, teenagers realize that they should not speak to their grandmothers they way the speak with their peers. When dealing with communications between cultures and genders, people must be sensitive, considerate, and appropriate.

How do teachers help students to understand these "unspoken" rules of communication? Well, these rules are not easy to communicate in regular classroom lessons. Instead, teachers must model these behaviors, and they must have high expectations for students (clearly communicated, of course) inside and outside the classroom walls.

Teachers must also consider these aspects as they deal with colleagues, parents, community members, and even students. They must realize that all communication should be tailored so that it conveys appropriate messages and tones to listeners.

The differences between **informal** and **formal language** are distinctions made on the basis of the occasion as well as the audience. At a "formal" occasion (for example, a meeting of executives or of government officials), even conversational exchanges are likely to be formal. At a cocktail party or a golf game, the language is likely to be much more informal. Formal language uses fewer or no contractions, less slang, longer sentences, and more organization in longer segments. Speeches delivered to executives, college professors, government officials, etc., are likely to be formal. Speeches made to fellow employees are likely to be informal. Sermons tend to be formal; Bible lessons tend to be informal.

Combining Oral and Written Communication

The art of debating, discussion, and conversation is different from the basic writing forms of discourse. The ability to use language and logic to convince the audience to accept your reasoning and to side with you is an art. This form of writing/speaking is extremely confined and structured, logically sequenced, and contains supporting reasons and evidence. At its best, it is the highest form of propaganda. Position statements, evidence, reason, evaluation, and refutation are integral parts of this writing schema.

Interviewing provides opportunities for students to engage in expository and informative communication. It teaches them how to structure questions to evoke fact-filled responses. Compiling the information from an interview into a biographical essay or speech helps students to list, sort, and arrange details in an orderly fashion.

Speeches that encourage them to describe persons, places, or events in their own lives as well as oral interpretations of literature help students to sense the creativity and effort used by professional writers.

Skill 26.2 Analyzing ways in which the integration of reading, writing, speaking, listening, viewing, and thinking is necessary for constructing knowledge and communicating effectively

The Language Arts program in schools consists of six strands – reading, writing, listening, speaking, viewing and thinking. All of these are interrelated and are necessary for students to be able to construct knowledge and communicate effectively. These components, when taught together in the classroom, make up the components of a balanced literacy program.

Reading is the process of learning how to construct meaning from text. Young students use picture cues to help them discover this meaning, which brings viewing into the instruction. The teacher who is helping a student overcome difficulty with reading may often ask the student to refer to the picture on the page in order to try to determine what words would fit naturally in the text. After the reading has finished, the teacher spurs higher –level thinking by having the student respond to the text either by speaking, writing or drawing.

Reading is a constructive process that requires frequent practice in order for the student to become a fluent reader. It is continually developing and the reading material must be motivating for the student in order to sustain interest. Students view non-print material, read texts and listen to other students, the teacher and guest speakers in order to gain information and to gain the skills necessary to perform specific tasks.

Writing allows the students to put their thoughts into written words and to generate ideas for writing stories and poems. In order for students to have the prior knowledge that they need in order to carry out such activities they need to be exposed to various forms of literary experiences through listening to stories, viewing various types of media and speaking with others. Writing is a way of putting their thoughts on paper and through revising and editing, they learn how to read their own writing in order to correct mistakes.

Through listening, students make sense of the spoken word and learn the nuances of the English language. Young students may not speak clearly or use the proper grammatical structures in their speech, but through listening to others, reading and through instruction they become competent speakers. This knowledge also helps them in their writing as they transfer their thoughts to paper.

Skill 26.3   Recognizing how features of spoken language and nonverbal cues affect communication

Listening is not a skill that is talked about much, except when someone clearly does not listen. The truth is, though, that listening is a very specific skill for very specific circumstances. There are two aspects to listening that warrant attention. The first is comprehension or understanding what someone says; the purposes behind the message; and the contexts in which it is said. The second is purpose. While someone may completely understand a message, what is the listener supposed to do with it? Just nod and smile? Go out and take action? While listening comprehension is indeed a significant skill in itself that deserves a lot of focus in the classroom (much in the same way that reading comprehension does), we will focus on purpose here. Often, when we understand the purpose of listening in various contexts, comprehension will be much easier. Furthermore, when we know the purpose of listening, we can better adjust our comprehension strategies.

When complex or new information is provided to us orally, we must analyze and interpret that information. What is the author's most important point? How do the figures of speech impact meaning? How are conclusions arrived at? Often, making sense of this information can be tough when presented orally—first, because we have no way to go back and review material already stated; second, because oral language is so much less predictable and even than written language. However, when we focus on extracting the meaning, message, and speaker's purpose, rather than just "listen" and wait for things to make sense for us—in other words, when we are more "active" in our listening, then we have greater success in interpreting speech.

The tone of voice used in speaking conveys one's thoughts about a topic. The intonation used on certain words and phrases will give the listener an idea of how the speaker feels about the topic of the conversation. Feelings are evident in speech, such as expressions of doubt, emotion and confidence in the tone of voice a person uses. When a speaker is really surprised by something, for example, the voice tends to become higher and perhaps stronger than the normal speaking voice. A person who is angry is easily identified by loud words whereas a person who is very calm speaks in a low tone of voice.

The tone of voice used in asking a question is different from that used to state a fact. Even when stating a fact, the intonation can determine whether the speaker is emphatic about the statement. The four types of sentences – statement, question, command and exclamation – can all be understood for what they are by the tone of voice.

One can also discern how a person feels about a subject by the nonverbal cues that the person gives off. A person who is bored with the conversation usually has a stance that tells he/she is ready to leave or the facial expressions may be such that the speaker knows this person is not really listening.

As teachers get to know the students in their class they will learn who is listening and who is not by their nonverbal cues. A student who is playing with a toy or one who is reading something completely different from what the teacher is discussing is not listening to what is going on in the classroom.

In the classrooms of exceptional teachers, we will often find that students are captivated by the reading-aloud of good literature. It is refreshing and enjoyable to just sit and soak in the language, stories, and poetry of literature being read aloud. Therefore, we must teach students how to listen and enjoy such work. We do this by making it fun and giving many possibilities and alternatives to appeal to the wide array of interests in each classroom.

Finally, we will discuss listening in large and small group conversation. The difference here is that conversation requires more than just listening: It involves feedback and active involvement. This can be particularly challenging because, in our culture, we are trained to move conversations along, to avoid silences in a conversation, and to always get the last word in. This poses significant problems for the art of listening. In a discussion, for example, when we are preparing our next response instead of listening to what others are saying, we do a large disservice to the entire discussion. Students need to learn how listening carefully to others in discussions actually promotes better responses on the part of subsequent speakers. One way teachers can encourage this in both large and small group discussions is to expect students to respond directly to previous comments before moving ahead with their new comments. This will encourage them to pose their new comments in light of the comments that came before their turn.

Skill 26.4   Identifying strategies for planning, organizing, delivering, and evaluating oral presentations for a variety of audiences and purposes

Analyzing the speech of others is a very good technique for helping students to improve their own public speaking abilities. In most circumstances, students cannot view themselves as they give speeches and presentations; however, when they get the opportunity to critique, question, and analyze others' speeches, they begin to learn what works and what doesn't work in effective public speaking.

However, a very important word of warning: DO NOT have students critique each others' public speaking skills.

It could be very damaging to a student to have his or her peers point out what did not work in a speech. Instead, video is a great tool teachers can use. Any appropriate source of public speaking can be used in the classroom for students to analyze and critique.

Some of the things students can pay attention to include the following:

- Volume: A speaker should use an appropriate volume—not too loud to be annoying, but not too soft to be inaudible.
- Pace: The rate at which words are spoken should be appropriate—not too fast to make the speech incomprehensible, but not too slow so as to put listeners to sleep.
- Pronunciation: A speaker should make sure words are spoken clearly. Listeners do not have a text to go back and re-read things they didn't catch.
- Body language: While animated body language can help a speech, too much of it can be distracting. Body language should help convey the message, not detract from it.
- Word choice: The words speakers choose should be consistent with their intended purpose and the audience.
- Visual aids: Visual aids, like body language, should enhance a message. (However, remember that many visual aids can be distracting and can detract from the message.)

Overall, instead of telling students to keep these above factors in mind when presenting information orally, have them view speakers who do these things well and poorly. This will help them to remember what to do the next time they give a speech.

There are a number of factors that must be taken into consideration when giving or listening to a speech. Although some of these have been touched upon in the above passages, we have included a detailed list of tips to keep in mind:

Voice: Many people fall into one of two traps when speaking: using a monotone or talking too fast. These are both typically caused by anxiety. A monotone restricts your natural inflection, but can be remedied by releasing tension in the upper and lower body muscles. Talking too fast on the other hand, is not necessarily a bad thing if the speaker is exceptionally articulate. However, if the speaker is not articulate, or if the speaker is talking about very technical things, it becomes far too easy for the audience to become lost.

If you talk too fast and begin tripping over your words, it is important to consciously pause after every sentence. Don't be afraid of brief silences. The audience needs time to absorb what you are saying.

Volume: Problems with volume, whether too soft or too loud, can usually be combated with practice. If you tend to speak too softly, have someone stand in the back of the room and give you a signal when your volume is strong enough. If possible, have someone in the front of the room as well to make sure you're not overcompensating with excessive volume. In this same vein, if you have a problem with speaking too loudly, have the person in the front of the room signal you when your voice is soft enough and check with the person in the back to make sure it is still loud enough to be heard. In both cases, note your volume level for future reference. Don't be shy about asking your audience, "Can you hear me in the back?" Suitable volume is beneficial for both you and the audience.

Pitch: Pitch refers to the length, tension, and thickness of a person's vocal bands. As your voice gets higher, the pitch gets higher. In an oral performance, pitch reflects upon the emotional arousal level. More variation in pitch typically corresponds to more emotional arousal, but can also be used to convey sarcasm or to highlight specific words.

Posture: Maintain a straight but not stiff posture. Instead of shifting weight from hip to hip, point your feet directly at the audience and distribute your weight evenly. Keep shoulders orientated towards the audience. If you have to turn your body to use a visual aid, turn 45 degrees and continue speaking towards the audience.

Movement: Instead of staying glued to one spot or pacing back and forth, stay within four to eight feet of the front row of your audience; take maybe a step or half-step to the side every once in a while. If you are using a lectern, feel free to move to the front or side of it to engage your audience more. Avoid distancing yourself from the audience. You want them to feel involved and connected.

Gestures: Gestures are a great way to keep a natural atmosphere when public speaking. Use them just as you would when speaking to a friend. They shouldn't be exaggerated, but they should be utilized for added emphasis. Avoid keeping your hands in your pockets or locked behind your back, wringing your hands, fidgeting nervously, or keeping your arms crossed.

Eye Contact: Many people are intimidated by using eye contact when speaking to large groups. Interestingly, eye contact usually *helps* the speaker to overcome speech anxiety by allowing him or her to connect with the attentive audience and by easing feelings of isolation. Instead of looking at a spot on the back wall or at your notes, scan the room and make eye contact for one to three seconds for each person.

Attending to messages

Speech can be very difficult to follow. First, we have no written record in which to "re-read" things we didn't hear or understand. Second, it can be much less structured and can feature far more variation in volume, tone, and rate than written language. Yet, aside from re-reading, many of the skills and strategies that help us in reading comprehension can help us in listening comprehension. For example, as soon as we start listening to something new, we should tap into our prior knowledge in order to attach new information to what we already know. This will not only help us understand the new information more quickly, it will also assist us in remembering the material.

We can also look for transitions between ideas. Sometimes, in speech, this is pretty simple because we can notice voice-tone or body-language changes. Of course, we don't have the luxury of looking at paragraphs in oral language, but we do have the animation that comes along with live speech. Human beings have to try very hard to be completely non-expressive in their speech. Listeners should take advantage of this and notice how the speakers change character and voice in order to signal a transition of ideas.

Speaking of animation of voice and body language, listeners can also better comprehend the underlying intents of speakers when they attend to the nonverbal cues of those speakers. Simply looking to see the expression on the face of speakers can do more to comprehend irony, for example, than trying to extract it from the actual words. And often, in speech, elements like irony are not indicated at all by the actual words, but rather through the tone and nonverbal cues.

One good way to follow speech is to take notes and outline major points. Because speech can be less linear than written text, it can be of great assistance in keeping track of a speaker's message. Students can practice this strategy in the classroom by taking notes of teachers' oral messages and of other students' presentations and speeches.

Other classroom methods can help students learn good listening skills. For example, teachers can have students practice following complex directions. They can also have students retell stories—or retell oral presentations of stories or other materials. These activities give students direct practice in very important skills of listening. They provide students with outlets in which they can slowly improve their abilities to comprehend oral language and take decisive action based on interpreting speech.

Teachers should tell students the specific purpose of their reading assignments. This will help them to:

- ASSOCIATE: Relate ideas to each other.
- VISUALIZE: Try to see pictures in their mind as they read.
- CONCENTRATE: Have a specific purpose for reading.
- REPEAT: Remind themselves of important points, and to associate details with these points.

Oral language (listening and speaking) involves receiving and understanding messages sent by other people and also expressing our own feelings and ideas. Students must learn that listening is a communication process and, in order to be useful, must be an active process. In other words, they must be an active participant in this communication process. In active listening, meaning and evaluation of a message must take place before students can respond appropriately.

Responding to messages

How students respond to messages is more than communication going from a student's mouth to a teacher's ear. In addition to the words, messages are transferred by eye contact, physical closeness, the tone of voice, visual cues, and overall body language. Speech employs gestures, visual clues, and vocal dynamics to convey information between teachers and students. Children first learn to respond to messages by listening to and understanding what they hear (supported by overall body language); next, they experiment with expressing themselves through speaking.

As children become proficient in language, they expect straight messages from teachers. A straight message is one in which words, vocal expression, and body movements are all congruent. Students need to feel secure and safe. If the message is not straight; if the words say one thing but the tone and facial expression say another, children get confused. When they are confused, they often feel threatened.

Remembering message content

Reading is more than pronouncing words correctly; readers have to gain meaning from the words. A competent reader can pronounce the words on a page, remember what the words mean, and learn from them.

The processes that increase student ability to remember.

- ASSOCIATION: When you associate, you remember things be relating them to each other in some way.
- VISUALIZATION: Visualization helps you to create a strong, vivid memory. Try to picture in your mind what you wish to remember.
- CONCENTRATION: Concentration can be defined as focusing attention on one thing only. How can you learn to concentrate better? Visualizing will help because it forces attention to one thing only. If you try to see specific pictures as you read, it will help you to concentrate. Making sure of your purpose in a third way to force concentration. When you read for a particular purpose, you will concentrate on what you read.
- REPETITION: When you have difficulty remembering textbook information, you should repeat the procedures for associating, visualizing, and concentration. The repetition will help store the information in your memory.

Skill 26.5   Analyzing the influence of media on culture and on people's actions and communications

Media plays a huge role in influencing people's actions and communications with one another, as well as a way of displaying the various cultures of the world. Through the medium of television and movies, it is possible to see how the people in other parts of the world live. News reports have a great effect on how people feel about the various cultures of the world in the way in which they present the information they bring to the public.

Books and magazines relating cultural stories are also important ways of learning about people from other cultures. However, it is important for teachers to carefully choose the resources that they bring into the classroom so that they will not unintentionally cause any bias towards any one culture or ethnic group. They also have a responsibility for teaching the students how to identify instances of bias in what they read and view in the media.

Bias in the information that one reads, views and listens to can lead to discriminating acts against ethnic groups, even though the people directly affected may not have anything to do with the situation. One example of this is racially motivated attacks in innocent people because of events that take place in a part of the world far removed from where the attackers live.

COMPETENCY 0027   UNDERSTAND INQUIRY AND RESEARCH
METHODS IN LANGUAGE ARTS.

Skill 27.1   Identifying strategies for locating information from a variety of
sources (e.g., table of contents, indexes, newspaper, the
Internet)

Resource and research material

Locating information for research projects and compiling research sources using
both print and electronic resources is vital in the construction of written
documents. The resources that are available in today's school communities
include a large database of Internet resources and World Wide Web access that
provide individual navigation for print and electronic information. Research
sources include traditional commercial databases and The Electronic Library,
both of which can be used to print and cite a diversity of informational resources.

One vital aspect of the research process includes learning to analyze the
applicability and validity of the massive amounts of information in cyberspace.
Verifying and evaluating electronic resources are just two parts of the process of
sorting through downloaded hardcopies or electronic databases. In using a
diversity of research sources, the user must be able to discern authentic sources
of information from the mass collections of websites and information databases
available.

In primary research, selecting a topic and setting up an outline for research
information are the most important steps. They should precede using the
secondary research of both print and electronic resources. Using conceptual
Venn diagrams to center the topic and brainstorm the peripheral information
pertaining to the topic will clarify the purpose of the research.

There are two aspect of the secondary research: using print sources and using
electronic research tools. Print sources provide guides on locating specific or
general information resources. Libraries have floors or designated areas
dedicated to the collection of encyclopedias, specific resource manuals, card
catalogs, and periodical indexes that provide information on the projected topic.
Electronic research tools includes a listing of the latest and most effective search
engines like Google, Microsoft, AOL, Infotrac, and Yahoo to find the topic of
research, along with peripheral support information. Electronic databases that
contain extensive resources will assist the user in selecting resources, choosing
effective keywords, and constructing search strategies. The world of electronic
research opens up a global library of resources for both print and electronic
information.

to find African animals in book
do you look table of contents or index?

Major online services such as Microsoft, Prodigy, and CompuServe provide users with information on specialized information that is either free or has a minimal charge assessed for that specific service or website. Online resources teach effective ways to bookmark sites of interest and to cut and paste relevant information onto word documents for citation and reference.

Bookmarking favorite Internet searches that contain correct sources for reference can save a lot of research time. On AOL, bookmarking is known as "Favorites"; with one click of the mouse, a user can type in the URL on the browser's location bar to create instant access to that location. Netscape uses the terminology of "bookmarks" to save browser locations for future research.

Online search engines and web portals create avenues of navigating the World Wide Web. Web portals provide linkages to other websites and are typically subdivided into other categories for searching. Portals are also specific to certain audience interests that index parts of the web. Search engines can provide additional strategic site searches.

Students should be taught about plagiarizing sources directly from the World Wide Web without attribution. This is a difficult concept for elementary-aged students to grasp. If the teacher does not attend to teaching at least a basic notion of "giving credit" to sources, he or she can expect student reports to be nothing more than cut and paste essays written by someone other than the typical fourth grader handing in the material.

Skill 27.2 Demonstrating knowledge of appropriate source citations for bibliographies, footnotes, and endnotes

A **bibliography** is a listing of resources used for information in writing a research paper or a report. This will give the readers a resource to use when checking the information that is presented in the writing as well as a listing of books and magazines they may be interested in reading on their own for more information. The list of resources should be presented beginning with the name of the author(s) in alphabetical order. All entries should be double-spaced with single spacing used within each listing following punctuation.

The purpose of a bibliography is to give credit to the authors of works you have read in order to write the report. It shows that you have not plagiarized any of the material. It is placed at the end of the report. It must include, in this order:

- the name of the author(s)
- the title of the book or magazine.
- the place of publication
- the name of the publisher
- the date of publication and in the case of magazines the issue number
- the pages referenced in the report

Footnotes occur throughout the report. They are used to cite direct references to information you have taken from the resources used for information when writing the document. A footnote must be included whenever one or more of the following are used:

- a direct quote from one of the resources
- statistics
- a precise idea or group of ideas taken from another work

There is a very precise method involved in writing a footnote. The author's full name goes first and then the title of the document, which is written in italicized font. Then, you must give the city in which this work was published, the name of the editor and publishing house, the year that it was published and finally the page(s) in the work where this information can be found.

Since footnotes vary throughout a report, they are found on the bottom of the page containing the information quoted from a text. The first time a work is quoted, you need to include all this information. If the second quote is from the same text, you do not have to repeat all the information. Instead you write, Ibid, and then the page number. If, however, there is a quote from a different source in between quotes you use from the first quote, you simply have to give the author's name and the page number.

Endnotes are footnotes, but instead of including them on each page of the document where there is a quote from another text, they are compiled at the end of the report before the bibliography. They are written in the same way as footnotes, but they must include the page of the document where readers can find these quotes.

Skill 27.3   Identifying effective note-taking strategies

Being an effective note taker requires consistent techniques, whether the mode of note taking is on 5x7 note cards, lined notebook paper, or on a computer. Organizing all collected information according to a research outline will allow the user to take notes on each section and begin the writing process. If the computer is used, then the actual format of the report can be word processed and information inputted to speed up the writing process of the final research report. Creating a title page and the bibliography page will allow each downloaded report to have its resources cited immediately in that section.

Note taking involves the identification of specific resources that include the author's or organization's name, year of publication, title, publisher location, and publisher. When taking notes—whether on the computer or using note cards—use the author's last name and page number on cited information. In citing information for major categories and subcategories on the computer, create a file for notes that includes summaries of information and direct quotes. When direct quotes are put into a word file, the cut and paste process for incorporation into the report is quick and easy.

In outline information, it is crucial to identify the headings and subheadings for the topic being researched. When researching information, it is easier to cut and paste information under the indicated headings in creating a visual flow of information for the report. In the actual drafting of the report, the writer is able to lift direct quotations and citations from the posted information to incorporate in the writing.

SEE also Skill 20.4

Skill 27.4 Demonstrating knowledge of the appropriate use of quotations as well as methods for summarizing and paraphrasing source information

Oftentimes, statements in students' writing or oral reports will require a quotation as support for an idea or statements or for dramatic effect. When you quote a section of a resource for use in your own research report, it must be documented by either a footnote or endnote in your report. There is a specific method for including such quotations. If the quotation you take directly from another text is less than three lines, then you write it as part of the normal document, inserting quotation marks around it and noting the footnote or endnote number.

If the size of the quotation is more than three lines, you must indent and start a new paragraph with quotation marks. The quoted section will then occupy a space in the middle of the page and will be separate from the rest of the text on the page.
When you summarize or paraphrase the ideas of another author, this means you are taking the ideas of this person and putting them in your own words. This must be cited in the report you are writing so as not to give the idea that these are your ideas.

Paraphrasing means that you condense the ideas and make the paragraph or section of the text smaller than the original. Summarizing means that you put the main ideas and the main points into your own words. In both cases, you do have to give credit to the author by adding a footnote or endnote after the words in the document you are writing.

Skill 27.5   Identifying methods for formulating research topics and essential questions

One of the problems that most students have in formulating research topics is that they choose too broad a topic and then become bogged down in the writing when they realize that there is too much information for them to incorporate into one report. The first thing that teachers should do is to teach students how to narrow down a topic by giving them instruction on this and practice in narrowing down broader topics into manageable chunks. In this way they can see that it is possible for several people to do a research paper on similar topics and take a different approach.

As part of this process, teachers can show students how to use a K-W-L chart on which they list what they **know** about a topic and what information they **want** to find. This will help them formulate the questions they need to ask as well as help them determine the types of resources they will need to use in order to find this information.

DOMAIN   SOCIAL STUDIES

COMPETENCY 0028   DEMONSTRATE KNOWLEDGE OF CONCEPTS
                       RELATED TO CITIZENSHIP AND GOVERNMENT

Skill 28.1   Recognizing basic purposes and concepts of government and
              laws, the organization of federal, state, and local government
              in the United States, and how stakeholders influence public
              policy

Historically, the functions of government (or people's concepts of government
and its purpose and function) have varied considerably. In the theory of political
science, the function of government is to secure the common welfare of the
members of the given society over which it exercises control. In different
historical eras, governments have attempted to achieve the common welfare by
means in accordance with the traditions and ideologies of the given society.

Among primitive peoples, systems of control were rudimentary at best. They
arose directly from the ideas of right and wrong that had been established in the
group and that were common in that particular society. Control was exercised
most often by means of group pressure, typically in the forms of taboos and
superstitions—and in many cases by ostracism, or banishment from the group.
Thus, in most cases, because of the extreme tribal nature of society in those
early times, this led to very unpleasant circumstances for the individual so
treated. Without the protection of the group, a lone individual did not survive long.

Among civilized peoples, governments began to assume more institutional forms.
They rested on a well-defined legal basis. They imposed penalties on violators of
the social order. They used force, which was supported and sanctioned by their
people. The government was charged to establish the social order and was
supposed to do so in order to be able to discharge its functions.

Eventually, the ideas of government, such as who should govern and how, came
to be considered by various thinkers and philosophers. The most influential of
these were the ancient Greek philosophers Plato and Aristotle. Aristotle's
conception of government was based on a simple idea. The function of
government was to provide for the general welfare of its people. A good
government, and one that should be supported, was one that did so in the best
way possible, with the least pressure on the people. Bad governments were
those that subordinated the general welfare to that of the individuals who ruled.
At no time should any function of any government be that of personal interest of
any one individual, no matter who that individual is. This does not mean that
Aristotle had no sympathy for the individual or individual happiness (as at times
Plato has been accused). Rather, Aristotle believed that a society is greater than
the sum of its parts, or that "the good of the many outweighs the good of the few
and also of the one."

Yet, a good government and one that carries out its functions well will always weigh the relative merits of what is good for a given individual in society and what is good for the society as a whole. This basic concept has continued to our own time and has found its fullest expression in the idea of representative democracy and political and personal freedom. In addition, the most ideal government is one that maintains good social order while allowing the greatest possible exercise of autonomy for individuals.

Skill 28.2   Demonstrating knowledge of the core values and democratic principles of the United States as set forth in foundational documents, including the Constitution and the Declaration of Independence, and of key ideals of U.S. democracy

The United States Government has three distinct branches: the Executive, the Legislative, and the Judicial. Each has its own function and its own "check" on the other two.

The Legislative Branch consists primarily of the House of Representatives and the Senate. Each house has a set number of members, the House with 435 apportioned according to national population trends and the Senate with 100 (two from each state). House members serve two-year terms; Senators serve six-year terms. Each house can initiate a bill, but that bill must be passed by a majority of both houses in order to become a law. The House is primarily responsible for initiating spending bills; the Senate is responsible for ratifying treaties that the president might sign with other countries.

The Executive Branch has the president and vice-president as its two main figures. The president is the commander-in-chief of the armed forces and the person who can approve or veto all bills from Congress. (Vetoed bills can become law anyway if two-thirds of each house of Congress votes to pass them over the president's objections.) The president is elected to a four-year term by the electoral college, which usually mirrors the popular will of the people. The president can serve a total of two terms. The Executive Branch also has several departments consisting of advisors to the president. These departments include State, Defense, Education, Treasury, and Commerce, among others. Members of these departments are appointed by the president and approved by Congress.

The Judicial Branch consists of a series of courts and related entities, with the top body being the Supreme Court. The Court decides whether laws of the land are constitutional; any law invalidated by the Supreme Court is no longer in effect. The Court also regulates the enforcement and constitutionality of the Amendments to the Constitution. The Supreme Court is the highest court in the land. Cases make their way to it from federal Appeals Courts, which hear appeals of decisions made by federal District Courts. These lower two levels of courts are found in regions around the country. Supreme Court justices are appointed by the president and confirmed by the Senate. They serve for life. Lower-court judges are elected in popular votes within their states.

The **United States Constitution** is the written document that describes and defines the system and structure of the United States government. Ratification of the Constitution by the required number of states (nine of the original thirteen), was completed on June 21, 1788, and thus the Constitution officially became the law of the land.

The Constitution binds the states in a governmental unity in everything that affects the welfare of all. At the same time, it recognizes the rights of the people of each state to independence of action in matters that relate only to them. Since the Federal Constitution is the law of the land, all other laws must conform to it.

An **amendment** is a change or addition to the United States Constitution. To date, there are only twenty-seven amendments to the Constitution that have passed. An amendment may be used to cancel out a previous one (such as the Eighteenth Amendment of 1919, known as Prohibition, and canceled by the Twenty-First Amendment in 1933). Amending the United States Constitution is an extremely difficult thing to do.

An amendment must start in Congress. One or more lawmakers propose it, and then each house votes on it in turn. The amendment must have the support of two-thirds of each house separately in order to progress on its path into law. (It should be noted here that this two-thirds need be only two-thirds of a quorum, which is just a simple majority. Thus, it is theoretically possible for an amendment to be passed and be legal even though it has been approved by less than half of one or both houses.)

The final and most difficult step for an amendment is the ratification of the state legislature. A total of three-fourths of those must approve the amendment. Approvals there need be only a simple majority, but the number of states that must approve the amendment is thirty-eight. Hundreds of amendments have been proposed through the years.

that was a question

A key element in some of those failures has been the time limit that Congress has the option to put on amendment proposals. A famous example of an amendment that got close but didn't reach the threshold before the deadline expired was the Equal Rights Amendment, which was proposed in 1972 but couldn't muster enough support for passage, even though its deadline was extended from seven to ten years.

The first ten Amendments are called the **Bill of Rights**; they were approved at the same time, shortly after the Constitution was ratified. The Eleventh and Twelfth Amendments were ratified around the turn of the nineteenth century and, respectively, voided foreign suits against states and revised the method of presidential election. The Thirteenth, Fourteenth, and Fifteenth Amendments were passed in succession after the end of the Civil War. Slavery was outlawed by the Thirteenth Amendment. The Fourteenth and Fifteenth Amendments provided for equal protection and for voting rights, respectively, without consideration of skin color.

The first amendment of the twentieth century was the Sixteenth Amendment, which provided for a federal income tax. Providing for direct election to the Senate was the Seventeenth Amendment. (Before this, Senators were appointed by state leaders, not elected by the public at large.)

The Eighteenth Amendment prohibited the use or sale of alcohol across the country. The long battle for voting rights for women ended in success with the passage of the Nineteenth Amendment. The date for the beginning of terms for the President and the Congress was changed from March to January by the Twentieth Amendment. With the Twenty-first Amendment came the only instance in which an Amendment was repealed. In this case, it was the Eighteenth Amendment and its prohibition of alcohol consumption or sale.

The Twenty-second Amendment limited the number of terms that a President could serve to two. Presidents since George Washington had followed Washington's practice of not running for a third term; this changed when Franklin D. Roosevelt ran for re-election a second time, in 1940. He was re-elected that time and a third time, too, four years later. He didn't live out his fourth term, but he did convince Congress and most of the state legislature that some sort of term limit should be in place.

The little-known Twenty-third Amendment provided for representation of Washington, D.C., in the Electoral College. The Twenty-fourth Amendment prohibited poll taxes, which people had had to pay in order to vote.

Presidential succession is the focus of the Twenty-fifth Amendment, which provides a blueprint of what to do if the president is incapacitated or killed. The Twenty-sixth Amendment lowered the legal voting age for Americans from twenty-one to eighteen. The final Amendment, the Twenty-seventh, prohibits members of Congress from substantially raising their own salaries. This Amendment was one of twelve originally proposed in the late eighteenth century. Ten of those twelve became the Bill of Rights, and one has yet to become law.

A host of potential amendments have made news headlines in recent years. A total of six amendments have been proposed by Congress and passed muster in both houses but have not been ratified by enough state legislatures. The aforementioned Equal Rights Amendment is one. Another one, which would grant the District of Columbia full voting rights equivalent to states, has not passed; like the Equal Rights Amendment, its deadline has expired. A handful of others remain on the books without expiration dates, including an amendment to regulate child labor.

Skill 28.3   Demonstrating knowledge of the principles of democratic civic involvement and the roles, rights, and responsibilities of citizenship at the federal, state, local, and neighborhood levels

It is presumed that all citizens of the United States will recognize their responsibilities to the country and that the surest way of protecting their rights is by exercising those rights, which also entail a responsibility. Some examples include the *right* to vote and the *responsibility* to be well-informed on various issues, the *right* to a trial by jury and the *responsibility* to ensure the proper working of the justice system by performing jury duty (rather than avoiding it). In the end, it is only by the mutual recognition of the fact that an individual has both rights and responsibilities in society that enables the society to function in order to protect those very rights.

State governments are mirror images of the federal government, with a few important exceptions: Governors are not technically commanders-in-chief of armed forces; state supreme court decisions can be appealed to federal courts; terms of state representatives and senators vary; judges, even of the state supreme courts, are elected by popular vote; and governors and legislators have term limits that vary by state.

Local governments vary widely across the country, although none of them has a judicial branch per se. Some local governments consist of a city council, of which the mayor is a member and has limited powers; in other cities, the mayor is the head of the government and the city council members are the chief lawmakers. Local governments also have fewer strict requirements for people running for office than do the state and federal governments.

The format of the governments of the various Native American tribes varies as well. Most tribes have governments along the lines of the U.S. federal or state governments. An example is the Cherokee Nation, which has a fifteen-member Tribal Council as the head of the Legislative branch; a Principal Chief and Deputy Chief who head up the Executive branch and carry out the laws passed by the Tribal Council; and a Judicial branch made up of the Judicial Appeals Tribunal and the Cherokee Nation District Court. Members of the Tribunal are appointed by the Principal Chief. Members of the other two branches are elected by popular vote of the Cherokee Nation.

Skill 28.4 **Demonstrating knowledge of the political organization of the world, characteristics of past and present forms of government, and factors that affect international relationships and the development of foreign policy**

Anarchism – A political movement believing in the elimination of all government and its replacement by a cooperative community of individuals. It has sometimes involved political violence, such as assassinations of important political or governmental figures. The historical banner of this movement is a black flag.

Communism – A belief as well as a political system characterized by a classless, stateless social organization. It calls for the common ownership of national goods. This ideology is the same as Marxism. The historical banner of the movement is a red flag and variation of stars, hammer and sickles, representing the various types of workers.

Dictatorship – Also called an Oligarchy, it is the rule by an individual or small group of individuals; it centralizes all political control in itself and enforces its will with a strong police force.

Fascism – A belief as well as a political system opposed ideologically to Communism, though similar in basic structure, with a one-party state and centralized political control. Unlike Communism, it tolerates private ownership of the means of production, though it maintains tight overall control. Central to its belief is the idolization of the Leader, a "Cult of the Personality," and most often an expansionist ideology. Examples have been German Nazism and Italian Fascism.

Monarchy – The rule of a nation by a monarch (a non-elected usually hereditary leader), most often a king or queen. This form of government may or may not be accompanied by some measure of democratically open institutions and elections at various levels. A modern example is Great Britain, which is called a Constitutional Monarchy.

Parliamentary System – A system of government with a legislature, usually involving a multiplicity of political parties and often coalition politics. There is division between the head of state and head of government. The head of government is usually known as a prime minister, who is also usually the head of the largest party. The head of government and cabinet usually both sit and vote in the parliament. The head of state is most often an elected president (though in the case of a constitutional monarchy, like Great Britain, the sovereign may take the place of a president as head of state). A government may fall when a majority in parliament votes "no confidence" in the government.

Presidential System – A system of government with a legislature, involving few or many political parties, with no division between head of state and head of government: the president serves in both capacities. The president is elected either by direct or indirect election. A president and cabinet usually do not sit or vote in the legislature, and the president may or may not be the head of the largest political party. A president can thus rule even without a majority in the legislature. He can only be removed from office for major infractions of the law.

Socialism – A political belief and system in which the state takes a guiding role in the national economy and provides extensive social services to its population. It may or may not own outright means of production, but even where it does not, it exercises tight control. It usually promotes democracy (Democratic-Socialism), though the heavy state involvement produces excessive bureaucracy and usually inefficiency. Taken to an extreme it may lead to Communism as government control increases and democratic practice decreases. Ideologically, the two movements are very similar in both belief and practice, as Socialists also preach the superiority of their system to all others and that it will become the eventual natural order. It is also considered for that reason a variant of Marxism. It also has used a red flag as a symbol.

COMPETENCY 0029   DEMONSTRATE KNOWLEDGE OF ECONOMIC
                   CONCEPTS AND SYSTEMS

Skill 29.1   Recognizing basic terminology and concepts related to economics

Economic systems refer to the arrangements a society has devised to answer what are known as the "three questions": 1) <u>what</u> goods to produce, 2) <u>how</u> to produce the goods, and 3) <u>for whom</u> the goods are being produced (or how the allocation of the output is determined). Different economic systems answer these questions in different ways.

A **market** is defined as the mechanism that brings buyers and sellers in contact with each other so that they can buy and sell. Buyers and sellers do not have to meet face to face; for example, when the consumer buys a good from a catalog or through the Internet, the buyer never comes face to face with the seller, yet both buyer and seller are part of a bona fide market.

Markets exist in both the input and output sides of the economy. The **input market** is the market in which factors of production, or resources, are bought and sold. Factors of production, or inputs, fall into four broad categories: land, labor, capital, and entrepreneurship. Each of these four inputs is used in the production of every good and service. **Output markets** refer to the market in which goods and services are sold. When the consumer goes to the local shoe store to buy a pair of shoes, the shoes are the output, and the consumer is taking part in the output market. However, the shoe store is a participant in both the input and output market. The sales clerk and workers are hiring out their resource of labor in return for a wage rate. Therefore they are participating in the input market.

In a **market oriented economy**, all of these markets function on the basis of supply and demand. The **equilibrium price** is determined as the overlap of the buying decisions of buyers with the selling decision of sellers. This is true whether the market is an input market, with a market rate of wage, or an output market, with a market price of the output. A market oriented economy results in the most efficient allocation of resources.

The best place to see **supply and demand** and markets in action is at a stock exchange or at a commodity futures exchange. Buyers and sellers come face to face in the trading pit and accomplish trades by open outcry. Sellers who want to sell stocks or futures contracts call out the prices at which they will sell. Buyers who want to buy stocks or futures contracts call out the prices at which they will buy. When the two sides agree on price, a trade is made. This process goes on throughout trading hours. It is easiest to see how markets and supply and demand function in this kind of setting because it is open and very obvious.

The same kinds of forces are at work at your local shopping mall or grocery store, even though the price appears as a given to you the consumer. The price you see was arrived at through the operation of supply and demand. In this way, the **equilibrium price** is the price that clears the markets. The term "clears the market" means that there are no shortages or surpluses. If the price is too high, consumers won't buy the product and the store will have a surplus of the good. The stores then have to lower prices to eliminate the surplus merchandise. If the price is too low, consumers will buy so much that there will be a shortage. The shortage is then alleviated as the price goes up, rationing the good to those that are willing and able to pay the higher price for the good.

In cases where government imposes legally mandated prices, the results can either be a shortage, with a price imposed below the market price, or a surplus, with a price imposed below the market price. The existence of price supports in agriculture is the reason for the surplus in agricultural products.

Finally, **opportunity cost** is essentially the value of the sacrificed alternative: the value of what had to be given up in order to have the output of good X. Opportunity cost does not just refer to production. Your opportunity cost of studying with this guide is the value of what you are not doing because you are studying, whether it is watching TV, spending time with family, or working. Every choice has an opportunity cost.

The **supply curve** represents the selling and production decisions of the seller and is based on the costs of production. The costs of production of a product are based on the costs of the resources used in its production. The costs of resources are based on the scarcity of the resource. The scarcer a resource is, relatively speaking, the higher its price. A diamond costs more than paper because diamonds are scarcer than paper is. All of these concepts are embodied in the seller's supply curve.

The same thing is true on the buying side of the market. The buyer's preferences, taste, and income—all of his or her buying decisions—are embodied in the **demand curve**. Where the demand and supply curves intersect is where the buying decisions of buyers are equal to the selling decisions of sellers. The quantity that buyers want to buy at a particular price is equal to the quantity that sellers want to sell at that particular price. This is where the market is in equilibrium, which is evident in the chart below.

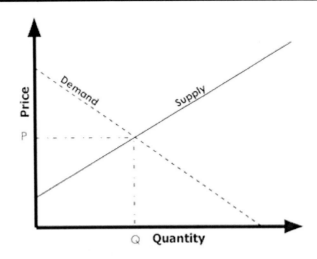

What happens when there is a change? Technological developments result in newer and more efficient ways of doing things. Technology means more efficient production techniques that allow for larger output at lower costs. Suppose a new big oil field is found. Also, suppose there is a technology that allows its recovery and refining at a fraction of the present costs. The result is a big increase in the supply of oil at lower costs, as reflected by a rightward shifting oil supply curve. Oil is used as an input into almost all production. Firms now have lower costs. This means that the firm can produce the same amount of output at a lower cost or can produce a larger amount of output at the same cost. The result is a rightward shift of the firm's, and therefore, the industry supply curve. This means that sellers are willing and able to offer for sale larger quantities of output at each price. Assuming buyers' buying decisions stay the same, there is a new market equilibrium, or new point of intersection of the shifted supply curve with the buyers' demand curve. The result is a lower price with a larger quantity of output. The market has achieved a new equilibrium based on the increase in the quantity of a resource.

Technological progress and innovation allow for the production of more output at lower prices. This leads to increased consumption for consumers. Technology can also result in unemployment by displacing workers. This is referred to as **structural unemployment**. The displaced workers must be retrained to find jobs in other industries.

supply & demand
competition   business → expands
↑ wages   sell car ↑

Skill 29.2   Recognizing characteristics of economic systems and that economic choice involve costs and consequences

A **market economy** answers these questions in terms of demand and supply and the use of markets. Consumers vote for the products they want with their dollar spending. Goods acquiring enough dollar votes are profitable, signaling to the producers that society wants its scarce resources used in this way. This is how the <u>what</u> question is answered. The producer then hires inputs in accordance with the goods consumers want, looking for the most efficient or lowest cost method of production. The lower the firm's costs for any given level of revenue, the higher the firm's profits. This is the way in which the <u>how</u> question is answered in a market economy. The <u>for whom</u> question is answered in the marketplace by the determination of the equilibrium price. Price serves to ration the goods to those who can and will transact at the market price or better. Those who can't or won't are excluded from the market. The United States has a market economy.

The opposite of the market economy is called the **centrally planned economy**. This used to be called Communism, even though the term is not correct in a strict Marxian sense. In a planned economy, the means of production are publicly owned, with little, if any private ownership. Instead of the "three questions" being solved by markets, there is a planning authority that makes the decisions. The planning authority decides what will be produced and how. Since most planned economies direct resources into the production of capital and military goods, there is little remaining for consumer goods; the result is often chronic shortages. Price functions as an accounting measure and does not reflect scarcity. The former Soviet Union and most of the Eastern Bloc countries were planned economies of this sort.

In between the two extremes is **market socialism**. This is a mixed economic system that uses both markets and planning. Planning is usually used to direct resources at the upper levels of the economy, with markets used to determine the prices of consumer goods and wages. This kind of economic system answers the "three questions" with planning and markets. The former Yugoslavia was a market socialist economy.

You can put each nation of the world on a continuum in terms of these characteristics and rank them from most capitalistic to the most planned. The United States would probably rank as the most capitalistic and North Korea would probably rank as the most planned, but this doesn't mean that the United States doesn't engage in planning or that economies like mainland China don't use markets.

SEE also Skill 29.1

Skill 29.3   Demonstrating knowledge of the purposes and functions of currency and financial institutions and the role of government as participant in the economy through taxation, spending, and policy

The scarcity of resources is the basis for the existence of economics. Economics is defined as a study of how scarce resources are allocated to satisfy unlimited wants. In this sense, "resources" refer to the four factors of production mentioned above: **labor, capital, land,** and **entrepreneurship**.

- *Labor* refers to anyone who sells his or her ability to produce goods and services.
- *Capital* is anything that is manufactured to be used in the production process.
- *Land* refers to the land itself and everything occurring naturally on it (such as oil, minerals, and lumber).
- *Entrepreneurship* is the ability of an individual to combine the three inputs with his or her own talents to produce a viable good or service. The entrepreneur takes the risk and experiences the losses or profits.

The fact that the supply of these resources is finite means that society cannot have as much of everything that it wants. There is a constraint on production and consumption as well as on the kinds of goods and services that can be produced and consumed. Scarcity means that choices have to be made. If society decides to produce more of one good, this means that there are fewer resources available for the production of other goods. For example, assume that a society can produce two goods: good X and good Y. The society uses resources in the production of each good. If producing one unit of good X requires the same amount of resources used to produce three units of good Y, then producing one more unit of good X results in a decrease in three units of good Y. In effect, one unit of good X "costs" three units of good Y. This cost is referred to as **opportunity cost (SEE** Skill 29.1).

If wants were limited and/or if resources were unlimited, the concepts of choice and opportunity cost would not exist, and neither would the field of economics. There would be enough resources to satisfy the wants of consumers, businesses, and governments. The allocation of resources wouldn't be a problem. Society could have more of both good X and good Y without having to give up anything. There would be no opportunity cost. However, this isn't the situation that societies are faced with.

Because resources are scarce, society doesn't want to waste them. Society wants to obtain the most satisfaction it can from the consumption of the goods and services produced with its scarce resources. The members of the society don't want their scarce resources wasted through inefficiency. This means that producers must choose an efficient production process, which is the lowest cost means of production. High costs mean wasted resources.

Consumers also don't want society's resources to be wasted by producing goods that they don't want. Producers reduce this kind of inefficiency by determining which goods their consumers want. They do this by watching how consumers spend their money, essentially "voting" with their dollar spending. A desirable good, one that consumers want, earns profits. A good that incurs losses is a good that society doesn't want its resources wasted on. This signals the producer that society, as a whole, wants its resources used in another way.

The role of government in economics

Even in a capitalist economy, there is a role for government. Government is required to provide the framework for the functioning of the economy. This requires a legal system, a monetary system, and a "watch dog" authority to protect consumers from bad or dangerous products and practices. Society needs a government to correct for the misallocation of resources when the market doesn't function properly, as in the case of externalities, like pollution. Another function of the government is to correct for the unequal distribution of income that results from a market oriented system. Government functions to provide public goods, like national defense, and to correct for macro-instability like inflation and unemployment through the use of monetary and fiscal policies. Although there are countless more ways in which the government acts on the economy, these are the more important roles.

In the same way, economics impacts government. First, the government has to respond to economic situations. Inflation and unemployment call on the government to implement various economic policies. The business cycle and the policies implemented to counter the business cycle affect the level of tax revenues that the government receives. This affects the budget and the amount of dollars that government has to spend on various programs. A government that has lower tax revenues due to economic conditions has to postpone certain discretionary spending programs until the economy improves. Unlike individuals, government can spend more tax dollars than it receives and operate in a debt condition financed by selling bonds. These are dollars that have to be repaid at some future date. Different economic conditions and situations call on the government to respond with different policies; the government has to figure out what to do and how much to do in each situation.

Skill 29.4 Demonstrating knowledge of the economic issues that all societies face

The world is becoming more global in its economy, requiring societies to adapt their production and economic strategies to suit these changing conditions. As some countries are able to capitalize on the emergence of new markets, the gap between poor countries that cannot participate is widening. Economic forces are also attracting immigrants from poorer countries to those with job opportunities, creating social stresses.

International organizations such as the U.N. and the World Bank have programs to assist developing nations with loans and education so they might join the international economy. Many countries are taking steps to regulate immigration.

Current national and international issues and controversies involve employment and trade issues. In today's world, markets are international. Nations are all part of a global economy. No nation exists in isolationism or is totally independent of other nations. Isolationism is referred to as autarky or a closed economy. No one nation has all of the resources needed to be totally self-sufficient in everything it produces and consumes. Even a nation with such a well-diversified resource base as the United States has to import items like coffee, tea and other staples. The United States is not as dependent on trade as are other nations, but we still need to trade for goods and items that we either can't produce domestically or that we can't produce as cheaply as other nations can.

Membership in a global economy means that what one nation does affects other nations because economies are linked through international trade, commerce, and finance. They all have open economies. International transactions affect the levels of income, employment and prices in each of the trading economies. The relative importance of trade is based on what percentage of Gross Domestic Product trade constitutes. In a country like the United States, trade represents only a few percent of GDP. In other nations, trade may represent over fifty percent of GDP. For those countries changes in international transactions can cause many economic fluctuations and problems.

Trade barriers are a way in which economic problems are caused in other countries. Suppose the domestic government is confronted with rising unemployment in the domestic industry due to cheaper foreign imports. Consumers are buying the cheaper foreign import instead of the higher priced domestic good. In order to protect domestic labor, government imposes a tariff, thus raising the price of the more efficiently produced foreign good. The result of the tariff is that consumers buy more of the domestic good and less of the foreign good. The problem is that the foreign good is the product of the foreign nation's labor. A decrease in the demand for the foreign good means foreign producers don't need as much labor, so they lay off workers in the foreign country. The result of the trade barrier is that unemployment has been exported from the domestic country to the foreign country. Treaties like NAFTA are a way of lowering or eliminating trade barriers on a regional basis. As trade barriers are lowered or eliminated, this causes changes in labor and output markets. Some grow; some shrink. These adjustments are taking place now for Canada, the United States, and Mexico. Membership in a global economy adds another dimension to economics, in terms of aiding developing countries and in terms of national policies that are implemented.

COMPETENCY 0030 UNDERSTAND MAJOR PRINCIPLES, CONCEPTS AND PHENOMENA OF GEOGRAPHY

Skill 30.1 Demonstrating knowledge of major geographic concepts and themes

The five themes of geography are:

Location – This includes relative and absolute location. A **relative location** refers to the surrounding geography (e.g., on the banks of the Mississippi River). **Absolute location** refers to a specific point, such as 41 degrees North latitude, 90 degrees West longitude, or 123 Main Street.

Place – This is something that has both human and physical characteristics. Physical characteristics include features such as mountains, rivers, and deserts. Human characteristics are the features created by human interaction with the environment (such as canals and roads).

Human-Environmental Interaction – The theme of human-environmental interaction has three main concepts: humans adapt to the environment (wearing warm clothing in a cold climate); humans modify the environment (planting trees to block a prevailing wind); and humans depend on the environment (for food, water, and raw materials).

Movement – The theme of movement covers how humans interact with one another through trade, communications, emigration, and other forms of contact.

Regions – A region is an area that has some kind of unifying characteristic, such as a common language or a common government. There are three main types of regions. **Formal regions** are areas defined by actual political boundaries, such as a city, county, or state. **Functional regions** are defined by a common function, such as the area covered by a telephone service. **Vernacular regions** are less formally defined areas that are formed by people's perception (e.g., "the Middle East" or "the South").

Skill 30.2 **Recognizing major geographic features of the United States and the world and their historical and contemporary significance**

The United States contains a large variety of geographical features. Mountains are landforms with rather steep slopes at least 2,000 feet or more above sea level. Mountains are found in groups called mountain chains or mountain ranges. At least one range can be found on six of the earth's seven continents. North America has the Appalachian and Rocky Mountains. The Appalachian Mountains, for example, served as a boundary as the earliest "frontier" line for the colonies, whereas later on in American settlement, the Rocky Mountains became the "frontier" in the 1800s. Today, distinct cultures have formed in these areas, and they also serve as beautiful additions to outdoor vacations and lanscapes.

Hills are elevated landforms rising to an elevation of about 500 to 2000 feet. They are found everywhere on Earth—including Antarctica, where they are covered by ice. Many regions of the United States contain this geographical feature.

Plateaus are elevated landforms that are usually level on top. Some plateaus are dry because they are surrounded by mountains that keep out any moisture. Plateaus can be formed by underground volcanic activity, erosion, or colliding tectonic plates.

Plains are described as areas of flat or slightly rolling land, usually lower than the landforms next to them. Sometimes called **lowlands** (and often located along **seacoasts**), they support the majority of the world's people. Many have been formed by large rivers, which provided extremely fertile soil for successful cultivation of crops and numerous large settlements of people. In North America, the vast plains areas extend from the Gulf of Mexico north to the Arctic Ocean and between the Appalachian and Rocky Mountains. It was this area that served as the frontier point for much of the early 1800s. Today and in more recent history, the plains serve as a great agricultural contributor.

Valleys are land areas that are found between hills and mountains. Some have gentle slopes containing trees and plants; others have very steep walls and are referred to as canyons. One famous example is Arizona's Grand Canyon of the Colorado River, which was formed by erosion.

Deserts are large dry areas of land receiving ten inches or less of rainfall each year. Deserts are found mainly in the tropical latitudes and are formed when surrounding features such as mountain ranges extract most of the moisture from the prevailing winds

Mesas are the flat tops of hills or mountains, usually with steep sides. Mesas are similar to plateaus, but smaller.

Foothills are generally considered a low series of hills found between a plain and a mountain range.

Marshes and swamps are wet lowlands providing growth of such plants as rushes and reeds.

Oceans are the largest bodies of water on the planet. Five major oceans are usually recognized: Pacific, Atlantic, Indian, Arctic, and Southern; the last two listed are sometimes consolidated into the first three. The **Atlantic Ocean** is one-half the size of the Pacific and separates North and South America from Africa and Europe; the **Pacific Ocean** covers almost one-third of the entire surface of the earth and separates North and South America from Asia and Australia.

A **lake** is a body of water surrounded by land. The Great Lakes in North America are a good example.

Rivers, considered a nation's lifeblood, usually begin as very small streams, formed by melting snow and rainfall. They flow from higher to lower land, emptying into a larger body of water—usually a sea or an ocean. Civilizations often settle at first near rivers because rivers provided water, a way to travel, and attracted game for hunters. The Mississippi River is a great example of important rivers in the United States, as it served as the starting point to the West, as well as a tremendous trade contributor.

Skill 30.3   Deriving information from maps, charts, and other geographic tools

Studying the geographic features of the earth is essential to understand the history of the physical environment and the history of humanity. Only when a comprehensive worldview is obtained through extensive geographical research can we have a complete understanding of the earth, its lands, and its peoples throughout time. In this way, geography is useful as a historical and evaluative tool.

At the same time, geography is also useful for looking toward the future. To understand the world we live in today and the world we will inhabit in the future, we have to be aware of the geographic concepts that drive world events. This includes, but is not limited to, environmental concerns.

Maps

Physical locations of the earth's surface features include the four major hemispheres and the parts of the earth's continents in them. **Political locations** are the political divisions, if any, within each continent. Both physical and political locations are precisely determined in two *ways:* (1) Surveying determines boundary lines and distance from other features. (2) Exact locations are precisely determined by imaginary lines of **latitude (parallels)** and **longitude (meridians).** The intersection of these lines at right angles forms a grid, making it possible to pinpoint an exact location of any place using any two grid coordinates.

The process of putting the features of the Earth onto a flat surface is called **projection**. All maps are really map projections. There are many different types. Each one deals in a different way with the problem of distortion. Map projections are made in a number of ways. Some are done using complicated mathematics. However, the basic ideas behind map projections can be understood by looking at the three most common types:

(1)　**Cylindrical Projections** - These are done by taking a cylinder of paper and wrapping it around a globe. A light is used to project the globe's features onto the paper. Distortion is least where the paper touches the globe. For example, suppose that the paper was wrapped so that it touched the globe at the equator, the map from this projection would have just a little distortion near the equator.

However, in moving north or south of the equator, the distortion would increase as you moved further away from the equator. The best known and most widely used cylindrical projection is the **Mercator Projection.** It was first developed in 1569 by Gerardus Mercator, a Flemish cartographer.

(2)　**Conical Projections** - The name for these maps come from the fact that the projection is made onto a cone of paper. The cone is made so that it touches a globe at the base of the cone only. It can also be made so that it cuts through part of the globe in two different places. Again, there is the least distortion where the paper touches the globe. If the cone touches at two different points, there is some distortion at both of them. Conical projections are most often used to map areas in the **middle latitudes**. Maps of the United States are most often conical projections. This is because most of the country lies within these latitudes.

(3)　**Flat-Plane Projections** - These are made with a flat piece of paper. It touches the globe at one point only. Areas near this point show little distortion. Flat-plane projections are often used to show the areas of the north and south poles. One such flat projection is called a **Gnomonic Projection**. On this kind of map all meridians appear as straight lines, Gnomonic projections are useful because any straight line drawn between points on it forms a Great-Circle Route.

Great-Circle Routes can best be described by thinking of a globe and when using the globe the shortest route between two points on it can be found by simply stretching a string from one point to the other. However, if the string was extended in reality, so that it took into effect the globe's curvature, it would then make a great-circle. A great-circle is any circle that cuts a sphere, such as the globe, into two equal parts. Because of distortion, most maps do not show great-circle routes as straight lines, Gnomonic projections, however, do show the shortest distance between the two places as a straight line, because of this they are valuable for navigation. They are called Great-Circle Sailing Maps.

To properly analyze a given map one must be familiar with the various parts and symbols that most modern maps use. For the most part, this is standardized, with different maps using similar parts and symbols, these can include:

The Title - All maps should have a title, just like all books should. The title tells you what information is to be found on the map.

The Legend - Most maps have a legend. A legend tells the reader about the various symbols that are used on that particular map and what the symbols represent, (also called a **map key**).

The Grid - A grid is a series of lines that are used to find exact places and locations on the map. There are several different kinds of grid systems in use however most maps do use the longitude and latitude system, known as the **Geographic Grid System**.

what is an absolute location of Pasco

Directions - Most maps have some directional system to show which way the map is being presented. Often on a map, a small compass will be present, with arrows showing the four basic directions, north, south, east, and west.

The Scale - This is used to show the relationship between a unit of measurement on the map versus the real world measure on the Earth. Maps are drawn to many different scales. Some maps show a lot of detail for a small area. Others show a greater span of distance, whichever is being used one should always be aware of just what scale is being used. For instance the scale might be something like 1 inch = 10 miles for a small area or for a map showing the whole world it might have a scale in which 1 inch = 1,000 miles. The point is that one must look at the map key in order to see what units of measurements the map is using.

Maps have four main properties. They are: (1) the size of the areas shown on the map, (2) The shapes of the areas, (3) Consistent scales, and (4) Straight line directions. A map can be drawn so that it is correct in one or more of these properties. No map can be correct in all of them.

Equal areas - One property which maps can have is that of equal areas. In an equal area map, the meridians and parallels are drawn so that the areas shown have the same proportions as they do on the Earth. For example, Greenland is about 118th the size of South America, thus it will be show as 118th the size on an equal area map. The **Mercator projection** is an example of a map that does not have equal areas. In it, Greenland appears to be about the same size of South America. This is because the distortion is very bad at the poles and Greenland lies near the North Pole.

Conformal Map - A second map property is conformal, or correct shapes. There are no maps which can show very large areas of the earth in their exact shapes. Only globes can really do that, however Conformal Maps are as close as possible to true shapes. The United States is often shown by a Lambert Conformal Conic Projection Map.

Consistent Scales - Many maps attempt to use the same scale on all parts of the map. Generally, this is easier when maps show a relatively small part of the earth's surface. For example, a map of Florida might be a Consistent Scale Map. Generally maps showing large areas are not consistent-scale maps. This is because of distortion. Often such maps will have two scales noted in the key. One scale, for example, might be accurate to measure distances between points along the Equator. Another might be then used to measure distances between the North Pole and the South Pole.

Maps showing physical features often try to show information about the elevation or **relief** of the land. **Elevation** is the distance above or below the sea level. The elevation is usually shown with colors, for instance, all areas on a map which are at a certain level will be shown in the same color.

Relief Maps - Show the shape of the land surface, flat, rugged, or steep. Relief maps usually give more detail than simply showing the overall elevation of the land's surface. Relief is also sometimes shown with colors, but another way to show relief is by using **contour lines**. These lines connect all points of a land surface which are the same height surrounding the particular area of land.

Thematic Maps - These are used to show more specific information, often on a single **theme**, or topic. Thematic maps show the distribution or amount of something over a certain given area in topics of interest such as population density, climate, economic information, cultural, political information, etc.

Photographs and Globes

Photographs and globes are useful as well, but as they are limited in what kind of information that they can show, they are rarely used. Unless, as in the case of a photograph, it is of a particular political figure or a time that one wishes to visualize.

Although maps have advantages over globes and photographs, they do have a major disadvantage. This problem must be considered as well. The major problem of all maps comes about because most maps are flat and the Earth is a sphere. It is impossible to reproduce exactly on a flat surface an object shaped like a sphere. In order to put the earth's features onto a map they must be stretched in some way. This stretching is called **distortion.**

Graphs

Most often used are those known as **bar graphs** and **line graphs**. Graphs themselves are most useful when one wishes to demonstrate the sequential increase, or decrease of a variable or to show specific correlations between two or more variables in a given circumstance.

Most common is the **bar graph** because it has an easy to see and understand way of visually showing the difference in a given set of variables. However it is limited in that it can not really show the actual proportional increase, or decrease, of each given variable to each other. (In order to show a decrease, a bar graph must show the "bar" under the starting line, thus removing the ability to really show how the various different variables would relate to each other).

Thus in order to accomplish this, one must use a **line graph**. Line graphs can be of two types: a **linear** or **non-linear** graph. A linear line graph uses a series of straight lines; a non-linear line graph uses a curved line. Though the lines can be either straight or curved, all of the lines are called **curves**.

A line graph uses a number line or **axis.** The numbers are generally placed in order, equal distances from one another, the number line is used to represent a number, degree or some such other variable at an appropriate point on the line. Two lines are used, intersecting at a specific point. They are referred to as the X-axis and the Y-axis. The Y-axis is a vertical line the X-axis is a horizontal line. Together they form a **coordinate system.** The difference between a point on the line of the X-axis and the Y-axis is called the **slope** of the line, or the change in the value on the vertical axis divided by the change in the value on the horizontal axis. The Y-axis number is called the **rise** and the X-axis number is called the **run**, thus the equation for slope is:

SLOPE = $\underline{\text{RISE}}$ - (Change in value on the vertical axis)
$\quad\quad\quad\quad$ RUN - (Change in value on the horizontal axis)

The slope tells the amount of increase or decrease of a given specific variable. When using two or more variables one can plot the amount of difference between them in any given situation. This makes presenting information on a line graph more involved. It also makes it more informative and accurate than a simple bar graph. Knowledge of the term slope and what it is and how it is measured helps us to describe verbally the pictures we are seeing visually. For example, if a curve is said to have a slope of "zero", you should picture a flat line. If a curve has a slope of "one", you should picture a rising line that makes a 45-degree angle with the horizontal and vertical axis lines.

The preceding examples are of **linear** (straight line) curves. With **non-linear** curves (the ones that really do curve) the slope of the curve is constantly changing, so as a result, we must then understand that the slope of the non-linear curved line will be at a specific point. How is this done? The slope of a non-linear curve is determined by the slope of a straight line that intersects the curve at that specific point. In all graphs, an upward sloping line represents a direct relationship between the two variables. A downward slope represents an inverse relationship between the two variables. In reading any graph, one must always be very careful to understand what is being measured, what can be deduced and what cannot be deduced from the given graph.

Charts

To use **charts** correctly, one should remember the reasons one uses graphs. The general ideas are similar. It is usually a question as to which, a graph or chart, is more capable of adequately portraying the information one-wants to illustrate. One can see the difference between them and realize that in many ways graphs and charts are interrelated. One of the most common types is the **Pie-chart** because it is easy to read and understand, even for the lay person. You can see pie-charts used often, especially when one is trying to illustrate the differences in percentages among various items, or when one is demonstrating the divisions of a whole.

Demography is the branch of science of statistics most concerned with the social well being of people. **Demographic tables** may include: (1) Analysis of the population on the basis of age, parentage, physical condition, race, occupation and civil position, giving the actual size and the density of each separate area. (2) Changes in the population as a result of birth, marriage, and death. (3) Statistics on population movements and their effects and their relations to given economic, social and political conditions. (4) Statistics of crime, illegitimacy and suicide. (5) Levels of education and economic and social statistics.

Such information is also similar to that area of science known as **vital statistics** and as such is indispensable in studying social trends and making important legislative, economic, and social decisions. Such demographic information is gathered from census, and registrar reports and the like, and by state laws such information, especially the vital kind, is kept by physicians, attorneys, funeral directors, member of the clergy, and similar professional people.

Skill 30.4 **Demonstrating knowledge of settlement patterns around the world and the natural processes and human activities that create them**

Social scientists use the term **culture** to describe the way of life of a group of people. This term includes not only art, music, and literature but also beliefs, customs, languages, traditions, and inventions—in short, any way of life, whether complex or simple. Although term **geography** is defined as the study of the earth's features, it also includes the study of living things as it pertains to their location, the relationships of these locations with each other, how they came to be there, and what impact these have on the world.

Physical geography is concerned with the locations of such features as climate, water, and land as well as how these relate to and affect each other. It includes how they affect human activities and what forces shaped and changed them.

All three of these earth features (climate, water, and land) affect the lives of all humans, ultimately having a direct influence on what is made and produced, where this production occurs, how it occurs, and what makes it possible. The combination of the different climatic conditions and types of landforms and other surface features work together all around the earth to give the many varied cultures their unique characteristics and distinctions.

Cultural geography studies the location, characteristics, and influence of the physical environment on different cultures around the earth. Also included in these studies are comparisons and influences of the many varied cultures.

Physical locations of the earth's surface features include the four major hemispheres and the parts of the earth's continents in them. **Political locations** are the political divisions, if any, within each continent. Both physical and political locations are precisely determined in two ways: 1) surveying is done to determine boundary lines and distance from other features, and 2) exact locations are precisely determined by imaginary lines of latitude (**parallels**) and longitude (**meridians**). The intersection of these lines at right angles forms a grid, making it possible to pinpoint an exact location of any place using any two grid coordinates.

The **Eastern Hemisphere** is located between the North and South Poles, between the Prime Meridian (0 degrees longitude) east to the International Date Line (180 degrees longitude). It consists of most of Europe, all of Australia, most of Africa, and all of Asia (except for a tiny piece of the easternmost part of Russia that extends east of 180 degrees longitude).

The **Western Hemisphere** is located between the North and South Poles, between the Prime Meridian (0 degrees longitude) west to the International Date Line (180 degrees longitude). It consists of all of North and South America, a tiny part of the easternmost part of Russia that extends east of 180 degrees longitude, and a part of Europe that extends west of the Prime Meridian.

The **Northern Hemisphere,** located between the North Pole and the Equator, contains all of the continents of Europe and North America and parts of South America, Africa, and most of Asia.

The **Southern Hemisphere,** located between the South Pole and the Equator, contains all of Australia, a small part of Asia, about one-third of Africa, most of South America, and all of Antarctica.

Spatial organization is a description of how things are grouped in a given space. In geographical terms, this can describe people, places, and environments anywhere and everywhere on earth.

The most basic form of spatial organization for people is where they live. The vast majority of people live near other people in villages, towns, cities, and settlements. These people live near others in order to take advantage of the goods and services that naturally arise from cooperation. These villages, towns, cities, and settlements are, to varying degrees, near bodies of water. Water is a staple of survival for every person on the planet; it is also a good source of energy for factories and other industries, as well as a form of transportation for people and goods.

Another way to describe where people live is by the **geography** and **topography** around them. The vast majority of people on the planet live in areas that are very hospitable. Yes, people live in the Himalayas and in the Sahara, but the populations in those areas are very small when compared to the plains of China, India, Europe, and the United States. People naturally want to live where they do not have to work really hard just to survive, and world population patterns reflect this.

We can examine the spatial organization of the places where people live. For example, in a city, where are the factories and heavy industry buildings? Are they near airports or train stations? Are they on the edge of town, near major roads? What about housing developments? Are they near these industries, or are they far away? Where are the other industry buildings? Where are the schools and hospitals and parks? What about the police and fire stations? How close are homes to each of these things?

Towns and especially cities are routinely organized into neighborhoods so that each house or home is near most things that its residents might need on a regular basis. This means that large cities have multiple schools, hospitals, grocery stores, fire stations, etc.

The distances between cities, towns, villages, or settlements are also related to settlement patterns. In certain parts of the United States and in many European countries, population settlement patterns achieve megalopolis standards, with no clear boundaries from one town to the next. Other, more sparsely populated areas have towns that are few and far between with relatively few people in them. Some exceptions to this exist, of course, like oases in the deserts; for the most part, however, population centers tend to be relatively near one another or at least near smaller towns.

Most populated places in the world also tend to be close to agricultural lands. Food makes the world go round. Although some cities are more agriculturally inclined than others, it is rare to find a city that grows absolutely no crops. The kind of food grown is almost entirely dependent on the kind of available land and the climate surrounding that land. Rice doesn't grow well in the desert, for instance, nor do bananas grow well in snowy lands. Certain crops are easier to transport than others, and the ones that aren't are usually grown near ports or other areas of export.

Skill 30.5   Analyzing the cultural and physical characteristics that define specific areas as regions

Major cultural regions of the United States

By far, the nation's immigrants were an important reason for America's phenomenal industrial growth from 1865 to 1900. They came seeking work and better opportunities for themselves and their families than what life in their native country could give them. What they found in America was suspicion and distrust because they were competitors with Americans for jobs, housing, and decent wages. Their languages, customs, and ways of living were different, especially between the different national and ethnic groups. Until the early 1880s, most immigrants were from parts of northwestern Europe such as Germany, Scandinavia, the Netherlands, Ireland, and Great Britain. After 1890, the new arrivals increasingly came from eastern and southern Europe. Chinese immigrants on the Pacific coast, so crucial to the construction of the western part of the first transcontinental railroad, were the first to experience this increasing distrust that eventually erupted into violence and bloodshed. From about 1879 to the present time, the U.S. Congress made, repealed, and amended numerous pieces of legislation concerning quotas, restrictions, and other requirements pertaining to immigrants. The immigrant laborers, both skilled and unskilled, were the foundation of the modern labor union movement as a means of gaining recognition, support, respect, rights, fair wages, and better working conditions.

New England is located in the northeastern part of the United States and includes the states of Maine, New Hampshire, Vermont, Massachusetts, Rhode Island and Connecticut. It was the first region of the US to be heavily settled by Europeans, beginning in the seventeenth century. The largest city in the region is Boston. New Englanders, or "Yankees" as they are often called, share a tradition of direct involvement in government through small town meetings where local decisions are made. The Democratic Party is the dominant political group in the region. Education is highly regarded, and several of the nation's top universities are located in New England.

Ireland came to US because?
1800's+h
Disease
potatoe

The **Mid-Atlantic** region is located in the central part of the east coast of the US, and includes the states of New York, New Jersey, Pennsylvania, Delaware and Maryland. Virginia and West Virginia are usually included in this region, but are sometimes considered southern states. Some of the country's most densely settled urban areas are in this region, including New York City, Philadelphia, and Washington, D.C. The Mid-Atlantic region has always been more ethnically diverse than other east coast regions, with settlers from a wider range of the world. The political feelings are mainly liberal within the urban areas, but political opinions of all types come together in Washington, D.C., which is the capital of the nation. The Mid-Atlantic area has provided much of the heavy industry and manufacturing for the country, and has a large working class population. From colonial times through the nineteenth century, this region has served as a kind of buffer zone between the northern and southern states, which is one of the reasons it was chosen for the site of the capital.

The **South** is one of the country's most distinctive cultural regions, and includes the states of North Carolina, South Carolina, Tennessee, Georgia, Florida, Alabama, Mississippi, Louisiana, Texas and Arkansas. Also sometimes considered part of the South are the states of Oklahoma, Missouri, Kentucky, Virginia and West Virginia. Major urban centers in the South include Atlanta, Miami, New Orleans, Dallas and Houston.

With the exception of some French and Latin-settled regions such as in Louisiana and Florida, the South is predominantly Protestant Christian in religion, and is the location of the area sometimes called the Bible Belt. Texas, which was one of the Confederate States, extends westward into the Southwest region of the US. Oklahoma, which is sometimes considered part of the South, also has a large population of Native Americans who were moved to the area from other parts of the eastern US. Florida's warm climate has made it a popular retirement area for people from all over the US, and its proximity to Cuba and other Latino-settled islands has contributed a large Hispanic population to the region.

The **Midwest** is located in the northern central part of the United States, and traditionally includes the states of Minnesota, Wisconsin, Iowa, Illinois, Indiana, Ohio and Michigan. North Dakota, South Dakota, Nebraska, Kansas and Missouri are also sometimes thought of as being Midwestern States. Major Midwestern cities include Chicago, Minneapolis, Cincinnati, St. Louis and Detroit. Outside the urban areas, the region is characterized by many small towns that grew around agriculture. Early settlers found rich soil drained by the Ohio, Missouri and Mississippi Rivers. The western portions of the region contain rolling, grassy range land suitable for ranching.

Beginning in the 1790s, the Midwest was settled mainly by pioneers of western European heritage. They found several Native American peoples in the area, who were gradually pushed westward and eventually removed to reservations. European Americans make up most of the population of the central Midwestern states. In the twentieth century, African Americans from the South migrated northwards to industrial areas such as St. Louis, Chicago, Indianapolis and Detroit. Traditionally, Midwesterners are thought of as hard working and stoic, embodying the values of the American pioneer. Religion plays an important role in the social relationships of many Midwesterners, who are mainly Christian. The region extends westward to include what is considered Western cultural areas, and borders on the Mid-Atlantic States to the east, where parts of Ohio are perhaps more closely associated with the industrial East than the more agricultural Midwest.

The **Southwest** cultural region of the US is an area where Native and Latin American culture has had the most influence. Arizona and New Mexico are the two states that make up the main part of the Southwest, with some of the surrounding states of California, Nevada, Utah, Colorado, Oklahoma and Texas extending into the region. Major cities in the region include Phoenix and Albuquerque. Once a part of Spanish territory, then a part of Mexico, the Southwest has retained its cultural connection to these countries. Native American cultures established settlements in this region thousands of years ago, and their influence is still seen. Arizona has the largest population of Native Americans in the US.

The **West** region extends from the Pacific Coast of the US eastward to the Rocky Mountain States, and includes the states of California, Colorado, Idaho, Montana, Nevada, Oregon, Utah, Washington, and Wyoming. Major western cities include Los Angeles, San Francisco, Denver, Salt Lake City, Portland and Seattle. The West has some of the least densely populated areas in the country, particularly in the desert regions of the southwest and areas of Montana and Wyoming. Immigration from the eastern US began seriously in the 1840s, along the Oregon Trail to the Pacific Northwest region. Mormons also settled in Utah at around this time, and are still prevalent in that state. In 1849, the discovery of gold near San Francisco brought thousands of new people to the area.

Situated along the Pacific Rim, the West has a high concentration of Asian immigrants especially evident in the coastal cities. It is a very diverse region with wide influence on American culture, especially from California, where most American television programs and movies are produced.

Major cultural regions of the world

North America includes the countries of the United States and Canada. Mexico, while geographically part of North America, is often thought of as being closer to Latin and South America culturally. English is the primary language of North America, with large sections of French speakers in Quebec, Canada, and Spanish speakers in the southwestern US. Because of its history of immigration from wide areas, North America contains people of many cultures, with people of western European descent in the majority. Christianity is the primary religion, with significant populations practicing other religions such as Judaism and Islam.

Latin America includes the mainly Spanish and Portuguese speaking countries of Mexico, Central America and South America. Culturally, this area has been heavily influenced by Spain and Portugal, who explored and conquered much of the region in the 16th Century. Catholicism, introduced by the conquistadors and through subsequent missions, is the primary religious observance. Native practices are still observed in many areas, and several groups of indigenous peoples still inhabit the interior of South America.

Europe is a diverse collection of independent countries who have banded together economically. Primarily Christian in observance, Europe contains several significant groups that observe other religions. Turkey, a Muslim nation, is often considered to be part of Europe culturally owing to its long history of interaction with the western countries.

Middle East and North Africa includes the countries of Saudi Arabia, Egypt, Libya, Iran, Iraq, Lebanon, Jordan and Syria. This region is largely Islamic in faith, and once extended well into present day Europe. Arabic is the primary language. Israel is located in this region, but is officially a Jewish state with a sizable Arabic-speaking Palestinian population.

Sub Saharan Africa is that portion of Africa located south of the great Sahara desert and includes the countries of South Africa, Kenya, Rwanda, and Ghana as well as 38 other nations. This is a culturally diverse area, stemming from the widespread colonization of the region by European countries upon whom many African countries still rely for assistance.

The region of **Russia and Central Asia** is made up of many of the former states of the Soviet Union, which was dominated by the Russian language and culture. Russia observes the Eastern Orthodox religion, and is renowned for its contributions to the arts, especially ballet and music. Since the breakup of the Soviet Union, several of the smaller states in Central Asia have re-established cultural connections with the Muslim nations of the Middle East and South Asia.

East Asia includes China, North and South Korea and Japan. Historically, China has dominated this region, with the Korean and Japanese cultures developing independent from the Chinese. Presently China and North Korea are communist countries, however China has developed a hybrid system that allows some free enterprise. Japan and South Korea are democratic countries with thriving economies. Religion is varied within the region, and includes Buddhism, Taoism, Shinto and the philosophy of Confucianism.

South Asia includes the countries of India, Pakistan, Bangladesh, Nepal, and Sri Lanka. This area is the most densely populated region of the world, and contains around 1.6 billion people. The predominant religion is Hinduism, especially in India, although there is a long and rich Muslim culture as well, particularly in Pakistan. India, the largest nation in the region, came under British rule in the 19th Century and gained independence in 1947. British culture has contributed to the region significantly. Movies are a popular form of entertainment, and India is the second largest producer of motion pictures after the US.

Southeast Asia includes the countries of Thailand, Vietnam, Cambodia, and Laos on the mainland of Asia, and Indonesia, the Philippines, Malaysia and Singapore off the shore of Asia. The mainland countries have been heavily influenced by the proximity of China and are mainly Buddhist, with several other faiths observed. Indonesia is the world's most populous Muslim country, and the Philippines is mainly Christian.

Australia and New Zealand are two former British colonies that have much in common with western European and American cultures. Aboriginal culture has influenced the region, but these people are now in the minority.

For additional information on physical characteristics, **SEE** Skills 30.2 and 30.4

COMPETENCY 0031   UNDERSTAND MAJOR FORMS OF INTERACTION BETWEEN PEOPLE, ENVIRONMENTS, AND CULTURES

Skill 31.1   Recognizing basic concepts related to the structure and organization of human societies

Anthropology is the scientific study of human culture and humanity: the relationship between humans and their cultures. Anthropologists study different groups, patterns of behavior, how they relate to one another, and their similarities and differences. Their research is two-fold: it is cross-cultural and comparative. The major method of study is referred to as "participant observation." In it, the anthropologist studies and learns about the culture's members by living among them and participating with them in their daily lives. Other methods may be used, but this is the most common. For example, in the 1920s, Margaret Mead lived among the Samoans, observing their ways of life. Her study resulted in the book *Coming of Age in Samoa*. The Leakey family, comprised of Louis, his wife Mary, and their son Richard, were anthropologists who did much field work to further the study of human origins.

Many aspects of anthropology and the study of human cultures interact with the study of geography. Because the earth's physical features contribute to the actions and livelihoods of all cultures around the globe, the two fields of study are inexorably linked. Therefore, it is not uncommon to find discussions of geography interspersed in cultural studies.

Socialization is the process by which humans learn the expectations their society has for their behavior, in order that they might successfully function within that society. Socialization takes place primarily in children as they learn and are taught the rules and norms of their culture. For example, children grow up eating the common foods of a culture and develop a "taste" for these foods. By observing adults and older children, they learn about gender roles and appropriate ways to interact. Socialization also takes place among adults who change their environment and are expected to adopt new behaviors. Joining the military, for example, requires a different type of dress and behavior than civilian culture. Taking a new job or going to a new school are other examples of situations where adults must re-socialize.

Two primary ways that socialization takes place are through positive and negative **sanctions**. Positive sanctions are rewards for appropriate or desirable behavior, and negative sanctions are punishments for inappropriate behavior. Recognition from peers and praise from a parent are examples of positive sanctions that reinforce expected social behaviors. Negative sanctions might include teasing by peers for unusual behavior or punishment by a parent. Sanctions can be either formal or informal. Public awards and prizes are ways a society formally reinforces positive behaviors. Laws that provide for punishment of specific infractions are formal negative sanctions.

Innovation is the introduction of new ways of performing work or organizing societies; they can spur drastic changes in a culture. Prior to the innovation of agriculture, for instance, human cultures were largely nomadic and survived by hunting and gathering their food. Agriculture led directly to the development of permanent settlements and instigated a radical change in social organization. Likewise, technological innovations in the Industrial Revolution of the nineteenth century changed the way work was performed and transformed the economic institutions of Western cultures. Recent innovations in communications are changing the way cultures interact today.

Cultural diffusion is the movement of cultural ideas or materials between populations independent of the movement of those populations. Cultural diffusion can take place when two populations are close to one another through direct interaction, or across great distances through mass media and other routes. For example, American movies are popular all over the world. Within the United States, hockey, traditionally a Canadian pastime, has become a popular sport. These are both examples of cultural diffusion.

Adaptation is the process through which individuals and societies change their behaviors and organization to cope with social, economic, and environmental pressures.

Acculturation is the exchange or adoption of cultural features when two cultures come into regular direct contact. An example of acculturation is the adoption of Christianity and Western dress by many Native Americans in the United States.

Assimilation is the process of a minority ethnic group adopting the culture of the larger group it exists within. These groups are typically immigrants moving to a new country, as with the European immigrants who traveled to the United States at the beginning of the twentieth century.

Extinction is the complete disappearance of a culture. Extinction can occur suddenly (from disease, famine, or war) when the people of a culture are completely destroyed, or slowly over time as a culture adapts, acculturates, or assimilates to the point where its original features are lost.

Skill 31.2 **Recognizing basic concepts related to the transmission and diffusion of culture, interactions among cultures, and the global interdependence of societies**

A **population** is a group of people living within a certain geographic area. Populations are usually measured on a regular basis by a census, which also measures age, economic, ethnic, and other data.

Populations change over time due to many factors, and these changes can have significant impact on cultures. When a population grows in size, it becomes necessary for it to either expand its geographic boundaries to make room for new people or to increase its density. **Population density** is simply the number of people in a population divided by the geographic area in which they live. Cultures with a high population density are likely to have different ways of interacting with one another than those with low density, as people in the former category live in closer proximity.

As a population grows, its economic needs change. More basic needs are required, and more workers are needed to produce them. If a population's production or purchasing power does not keep pace with its growth, its economy can be adversely affected. The age distribution of a population can also impact the economy if the number of young and old people who are not working is disproportionate to those who are.

Growth in some areas may spur **migration** to other parts of a population's geographic region that are less densely populated. This redistribution of population also places demands on the economy, as infrastructure is needed to connect these new areas to older population centers, and land is put to new use.

Populations can grow naturally (when the rate of birth is higher than the rate of death) or by adding new people from other populations through **immigration**. Immigration is often a source of societal change, as people from other cultures bring their institutions and language to a new area. Immigration also impacts a population's educational and economic institutions, as they enter the workforce and place their children in schools. Populations can also decline in number naturally (when the death rate exceeds the birth rate) or when people migrate to another area. War, famine, disease, and natural disasters can also dramatically reduce a population. The economic problems arising from population decline can be similar to those from overpopulation because economic demands may be higher than can be met. In extreme cases, a population may decline to the point where it can no longer perpetuate itself; its members and their culture either disappear or are absorbed into another population.

Cultural identity is the identification of individuals or groups as they are influenced by their particular group or culture. This term refers to the sense of who one is, what values are important, what racial or ethnic characteristics are important in one's self-understanding, and the manner of interacting with the world and with others. In the United States, a nation with a well-deserved reputation as a "melting pot," the attachment to cultural identities can become a divisive factor in communities and societies. **Cosmopolitanism**, its alternative, tends to blur those cultural differences in the creation of a shared new culture.

Throughout the history of the nation, groups have defined themselves and/or assimilated into the larger population to varying degrees. In order for a society to function as a cohesive and unifying force, there must be some degree of enculturation of all groups. The alternative is a competing, and often conflicting, collection of sub-groups that are not able to cohere into a society. This failure to assimilate will often result in culture wars, as values and lifestyles come into conflict. Cross-cultural exchanges, however, can enrich every involved group of persons with the discovery of shared values and needs, as well as an appreciation for unique cultural characteristics of each. For the most part, the history of this nation has been a story of successful enculturation and cultural enrichment. The notable failures often resulted from prejudice or intolerance. For example, **cultural biases** led to the oppression of the Irish or the Chinese immigrants in various parts of the country. **Racial biases** have led to various kinds of suppressive and oppressive activities. For example, the bias of the European settlers against the civilization and culture of the Native peoples of North America caused mass extermination, relocation, and isolation.

SEE also Skill 31.1

Skill 31.3   Analyzing the nature and implications of the effects of human activities on the environment

By nature, people are essentially social creatures. They generally live in communities or settlements of some kind and of some size. Settlements are the cradles of culture, political structure, education, and the management of resources. The relative placement of these settlements or communities are shaped by the proximity to natural resources, the movement of raw materials, the production of finished products, the availability of a work force, and the delivery of finished products. Shared values, language, culture, religion, and subsistence will at least to some extent, determine the composition of communities.

Settlements begin in areas that offer the natural resources to support life – food and water. With the ability to manage the environment one finds a concentration of populations. With the ability to transport raw materials and finished products, comes mobility. With increasing technology and the rise of industrial centers comes a migration of the workforce.

Cities are the major hubs of human settlement. Almost half of the population of the world now lives in cities. These percentages are much higher in developed regions. Established cities continue to grow. The fastest growth, however, is occurring in developing areas. In some regions there are "metropolitan areas" made up of urban and sub-urban areas. In some places cities and urban areas have become interconnected into "megalopoli" (e.g., Tokyo-Kawasaki-Yokohama).

The concentrations of populations and the divisions of these areas among various groups that constitute the cities can differ significantly. North American cities are different from European cities in terms of shape, size, population density, and modes of transportation. While in North America, the wealthiest economic groups tend to live outside the cities, the opposite is true in Latin American cities.

There are significant differences among the cities of the world in terms of connectedness to other cities. While European and North American cities tend to be well linked both by transportation and communication connections, there are other places in the world in which communication between the cities of the country may be inferior to communication with the rest of the world.

Rural areas tend to be less densely populated because of the needs of agriculture. More land is needed to produce crops or for animal husbandry than for manufacturing, especially in a city in which the buildings tend to be taller. Rural areas, however, must be connected via communication and transportation in order to provide food and raw materials to urban areas.

Environmental and geographic factors have affected the pattern of urban development in the world. In turn, urban infrastructure and development patterns are interrelated factors.

The growth of urban areas is often linked to the advantages provided by its geographic location. Before the advent of efficient overland routes of commerce such as railroads and highways, water provided the primary means of transportation of commercial goods. Most large cities are situated along bodies of water.

As **transportation** technology advanced, the supporting infrastructure was built to connect cities with one another and to connect remote areas to larger communities. The railroad, for example, allowed for the quick transport of agricultural products from rural areas to urban centers. This newfound efficiency not only further fueled the growth of urban centers it changed the economy of rural America. Where once farmers had practiced only subsistence farming – growing enough to support one's own family – the new infrastructure meant that one could convert agricultural products into cash by selling them at market.

For urban dwellers, improvements in building technology and advances in transportation allowed for larger cities. Growth brought with it a new set of problems unique to each location. The bodies of water that had made the development of cities possible in their early days also formed natural barriers to growth. Further infrastructure in the form of bridges, tunnels and ferry routes were needed to connect central urban areas with outlying communities.

In the modern age, advancements in **telecommunications** infrastructure may have an impact on urban growth patterns as information can pass instantly and freely between almost any two points on the globe, allowing access to some aspects of urban life to those in remote areas.

Cities are the major hubs of human settlement. Almost half of the population of the world now lives in cities. These percentages are much higher in developed regions. Established cities continue to grow. The fastest growth, however, is occurring in developing areas. While European and North American cities tend to be well linked both by transportation and communication connections, there are other places in the world in which communication between the cities of the country may be inferior to communication with the rest of the world.

Deforestation or clear cutting is of particular concern in rainforest regions, which hold most of the Earth's natural biodiversity - irreplaceable genetic natural capital. Conservation of natural resources is the major focus of Natural Capitalism, environmentalism, the ecology movement, and Green Parties. Some view this depletion as a major source of social unrest and conflicts in developing nations.

Environmental policy is concerned with the sustainability of the earth, the region under the administration of the governing group or individual or a local habitat. The concern of environmental policy is the preservation of the region, habitat or ecosystem. Because humans, both individually and in community, live upon the earth, draw upon the natural resources of the earth, and affect the environment in many ways, environmental and social policy must be mutually supportive.

If modern societies have no understanding of the limitations on natural resources or how their actions affect the environment, and they act without regard for the sustainability of the earth, it will become impossible for the earth to sustain human existence. At the same time, the resources of the earth are necessary to support the human welfare. Environmental policies must recognize that the planet is the home of humans and other species.

For centuries, social policies, economic policies, and political policies have ignored the impact of human existence and human civilization on the environment. Human civilization has disrupted the ecological balance, contributed to the extinction of animal and plant species, and destroyed ecosystems through uncontrolled harvesting.

In an age of global warming, unprecedented demand on natural resources, and a shrinking planet, social and environmental policies must become increasingly interdependent if the planet is to continue to support life and human civilization.

SEE also Skill 12.8

Skill 31.4 **Analyzing the nature and implications of the effects of the environment and environmental changes on people**

SEE Skill 31.3

COMPETENCY 0032 **UNDERSTAND MAJOR CONCEPTS, ISSUES, PEOPLE, EVENTS, AND DEVELOPMENTS IN THE HISTORY OF THE UNITED STATES**

Skill 32.1 **Identifying and comparing the characteristics and interactions of cultures during different periods of U.S. history**

European exploration and colonization

Colonists from England, France, Holland, Sweden, and Spain all settled in North America on lands once frequented by Native Americans. Spanish colonies were mainly in the south, French colonies were mainly in the extreme north and in the middle of the continent, and the rest of the European colonies were in the northeast and along the Atlantic coast. These colonists got along with their new neighbors to varying degrees of success.

Of all of them, the French colonists seemed the most willing to work with the Native Americans. Even though their pursuit of animals to fill the growing demand for the fur trade was overpowering, they managed to find a way to maintain a relative peace with their new neighbors; the French and Native Americans even fought on the same side of the war against England. The Dutch and Swedish colonists were interested mostly in surviving in their new homes. However, they didn't last long in their struggles against England.

The English and Spanish colonists had the worst relations with the Native Americans, mainly because the Europeans made a habit of taking land, signing and then breaking treaties, massacring, and otherwise abusing their new neighbors. The Native Americans were only too happy to share their agriculture and jewel-making secrets with the Europeans; what they got in return was grief and deceit. The term "Manifest Destiny" meant nothing to the Native Americans, who believed that they lived on land loaned to them by the gods above.

The colonies were generally divided into three regions: New England, Middle Atlantic, and Southern. The culture of each was distinct and affected attitudes, ideas towards politics, religion, and economic activities. The geography of each region also contributed to their unique characteristics.

The **New England** colonies consisted of Massachusetts, Rhode Island, Connecticut, and New Hampshire. Life in these colonies was centered on the towns. Each family farmed its own plot of land, but a short summer growing season and limited amount of good soil gave rise to other economic activities such as manufacturing, fishing, shipbuilding, and trade. The vast majority of the settlers shared similar origins, mostly arriving from England and Scotland. Towns were carefully planned and laid out in similar fashions. The form of government was the town meeting where all adult males met to make the laws. The legislative body, the General Court, consisted of an upper and lower house.

The **Middle or Middle Atlantic** colonies included New York, New Jersey, Pennsylvania, Delaware, and Maryland. New York and New Jersey were at one time the Dutch colony of New Netherland, and Delaware was at one time New Sweden. These five colonies, from their beginnings, were considered "melting pots," with settlers from many different nations and backgrounds. The main economic activity was farming; the settlers were scattered over the countryside cultivating rather large farms. The Indians were not as much of a threat as they were in New England so the colonists did not have to settle in small farming villages. The soil was very fertile, the land was gently rolling, and a milder climate provided a longer growing season. These farms produced a large surplus of food, not only for the colonists themselves but also for sale. This colonial region became known as the "breadbasket" of the New World, and the New York and Philadelphia seaports were constantly filled with ships being loaded with meat, flour, and other foodstuffs for the West Indies and England.

There were other economic activities such as shipbuilding, iron mining, and producing paper, glass, and textiles in factories. The legislative body in Pennsylvania was unicameral or consisted of one house. In the other four colonies, the legislative body had two houses. Units of local government were found in counties and towns.

The **Southern** colonies were Virginia, North and South Carolina, and Georgia. Virginia was the first permanent successful English colony and Georgia was the last. The year 1619 was a very important year in the history of Virginia as well as the United States, with the occurrence of three very significant events. First, sixty women were sent to Virginia to marry and establish families; second, twenty Africans, the first of thousands, arrived; and third and most importantly, the Virginia colonists were granted the right to self-government. They began by electing their own representatives to the House of Burgesses—their own legislative body.

The major economic activity in this region was farming. Here too the soil was very fertile, and the climate was very mild with an even longer growing season than farther north. The large plantations, eventually requiring large numbers of slaves, were found in the coastal or tidewater areas. Although the wealthy slave-owning planters set the pattern of life in this region, most of the people lived inland away from coastal areas. They were small farmers and very few, if any, owned slaves.

The settlers in these four colonies came from diverse backgrounds and cultures. Virginia was colonized mostly by people from England, while Georgia was started as a haven for debtors from English prisons. Pioneers from Virginia settled in North Carolina, while South Carolina welcomed people from England and Scotland, French Protestants, Germans, and emigrants from islands in the West Indies.

Products from farms and plantations included rice, tobacco, indigo, cotton, some corn, and wheat. Other economic activities included lumber and naval stores (tar, pitch, rosin, and turpentine) from the pine forests and fur trade on the frontier. Cities such as Savannah and Charleston were important seaports and trading centers.

The American Revolution

Causes for the War for Independence

- With the end of the French and Indian War (The Seven Years' War), England decided to reassert control over the colonies in America. They particularly needed the revenue from the control of trade to pay for the recent war and to defend the new territory obtained as a result of the war.
- English leaders decided to impose a tax that would pay for the military defense of the American lands. The colonists rejected this idea for two reasons: 1) They were undergoing an economic recession, and 2) They believed it unjust to be taxed unless they had representation in the Parliament.
- England passed a series of laws that provoked fierce opposition:
  - The Proclamation Act prohibited English settlement beyond the Appalachian Mountains to appease the Native Americans.
  - The Sugar Act imposed a tax on foreign molasses, sugar, and other goods imported into the colonies.
  - The Currency Act prohibited colonial governments from issuing paper money.

Opposition melded in Massachusetts. Leaders denounced "taxation without representation" and a boycott was organized against imported English goods. The movement rapidly spread to other colonies.

The Stamp Act placed a tax on newspapers, legal documents, licenses, almanacs, and playing cards. This was the first instance of an "internal" tax on the colonies. In response, the colonists formed secret groups called "the Sons of Liberty" and staged riots against the agents who collected the taxes and marked items with a special stamp. In October of 1765, representatives of nine colonies met in the Stamp Act Congress. They drafted resolutions stating their reasons for opposing the Act and sent them to England. Merchants throughout the colonies applied pressure with a large boycott of imported English goods. The Stamp Act was repealed three months later.

England then had a dual concern: to generate revenue and to regain control of the colonists. They passed the Townshend Acts in 1767. These acts placed taxes on lead, glass, paint, paper, and tea.
This led to another very successful boycott of English goods. England responded by limiting the tax to tea. This ended the boycotts of everything except tea.
The situation between colonists and British troops was becoming increasingly strained. Despite a skirmish in New York and the "Boston Massacre" in 1770, tensions abated over the next few years.

The Tea Act of 1773 gave the British East India Company a monopoly on sales of tea. The colonists responded with the "Boston Tea Party." England responded with the "Coercive Acts" (called the "Intolerable Acts" by the colonists) in 1774. This closed the port of Boston, changed the charter of the Massachusetts colony, and suppressed town meetings. Eleven colonies sent delegates to the first Continental Congress in 1774. The group issued the "Declaration of Rights and Grievances" which vowed allegiance to the king but protested the right of Parliament to tax the colonies. The boycotts resumed at the same time.

Massachusetts mobilized its colonial militia in anticipation of difficulties with England. The British troops attempted to seize their weapons and ammunition. The result was two clashes with "minute men" at Lexington and Concord. The Second Continental Congress met a month later. Many of the delegates recommended a declaration of independence from Britain. The group established an army and commissioned George Washington as its commander.

British forces attacked patriot strongholds at Breed's Hill and Bunker Hill. Although the colonists withdrew, the loss of life for the British was nearly fifty percent of the army. The next month King George III declared the American colonies to be in a state of rebellion. The war quickly began in earnest. On July 3, 1776, British General Howe arrived in New York Harbor with 10,000 troops to prepare for an attack on the city. The following day, the Second Continental Congress accepted the final draft of the Declaration of Independence by unanimous vote.

Although the colonial army was quite small in comparison to the British army, and although it was lacking in formal military training, the colonists had learned a new method of warfare from the Indians. To be sure, many battles were fought in the traditional style of two lines of soldiers facing off and firing weapons, but the advantage the patriots had was the understanding of guerilla warfare–fighting from behind trees and other defenses. When the war began, the colonies began to establish state governments. To a significant extent, the government that was defined for the new nation was intentionally weak. The colonies/states feared centralized government; however, the lack of continuity between the individual governments was confusing and economically damaging.

Expanding a Nation

In the United States, territorial expansion occurred in the expansion westward under the banner of **Manifest Destiny**. In addition, the United States was involved in the War with Mexico, the Spanish-American War, and the support of the Latin American colonies of Spain in their revolt for independence. In Latin America, the Spanish colonies were successful in their fight for independence and self-government

After the United States purchased the Louisiana Territory, Jefferson appointed Captains Meriwether Lewis and William Clark to explore it, to find out exactly what had been bought. The expedition, called the Corps of Discovery, eventually included a slave named York, a dog, forty young men, a female Indian named Sacagawea and her infant son. They went all the way to the Pacific Ocean, returning two years later with maps, journals, and artifacts. This led the way for future explorers to make available more knowledge about the territory; it also resulted in the Westward Movement and the later belief in the doctrine of Manifest Destiny.

Initially, the United States and Britain shared the Oregon country. By the 1840s, with the increase in the free and slave populations and the demand of the settlers for control and government by the United States, the conflict had to be resolved. In a treaty signed in 1846 by both nations, a peaceful resolution occurred with Britain giving up its claims south of the 49th parallel.

In the American Southwest, the results were exactly the opposite. Spain had claimed this area since the 1540s, had spread northward from Mexico City, and, in the 1700s, had established missions, forts, villages, towns, and very large ranches. After the purchase of the Louisiana Territory in 1803, Americans began moving into Spanish territory. A few hundred American families in what is now Texas were allowed to live there but had to agree to become loyal subjects to Spain. In 1821, Mexico successfully revolted against Spanish rule, won independence, and chose to be more tolerant towards American settlers and traders. The Mexican government encouraged and allowed extensive trade and settlement, especially in Texas. Many of the new settlers were southerners who brought their slaves with them. Slavery was outlawed in Mexico and technically illegal in Texas, although the Mexican government often looked the other way.

Friction increased between land-hungry Americans swarming into western lands and the Mexican government that controlled these lands. The clash was not only political but also cultural and economic. The Spanish influence permeated all parts of southwestern life: law, language, architecture, and customs. By this time, the doctrine of Manifest Destiny was in the hearts and on the lips of those seeking new areas of settlement and a new life. Americans were demanding U.S. control of not only the Mexican Territory but also of Oregon. Although peaceful negotiations with Great Britain secured Oregon, it took two years of war to gain control of the southwestern United States.

To make the tensions worse, the Mexican government owed debts to U.S. citizens whose property was damaged or destroyed during its struggle for independence from Spain. By the time war broke out in 1845, Mexico had not paid its war debts. The government was weak, corrupt, irresponsible, torn by revolutions, and not in decent financial shape. Mexico was also bitter over American expansion into Texas and the 1836 revolution, which resulted in Texas' independence. In the 1844 presidential election, the Democrats pushed for the annexation of Texas and Oregon and after winning, they started the procedure to admit Texas to the Union.

When statehood occurred, diplomatic relations between the United States and Mexico were ended. President Polk wanted U.S. control of the entire southwest, from Texas to the Pacific Ocean. He sent a diplomatic mission with an offer to purchase New Mexico and Upper California, but the Mexican government refused to even receive the diplomats. Consequently, in 1846, each nation claimed aggression on the part of the other and war was declared. The treaty signed in 1848 and a subsequent one in 1853 completed the southwestern boundary of the United States, reaching to the Pacific Ocean, as President Polk wished.

The impact of the entire westward movement resulted in the completion of the borders of the present-day contiguous United States. Overall, the major contributing factors included the bloody war with Mexico; the ever-growing controversy over slave versus free states, which affected the balance of power in the U.S. Congress, especially the Senate; and the Civil War.

The Civil War began through a series of events that spanned decades. Tensions between the southern states and the northern states were increasing; in 1833, Congress lowered tariffs, this time at a level acceptable to South Carolina, which had been growing increasingly dissatisfied with the federal government. Although President Jackson believed in states' rights, he also firmly believed in and was determined to preserve the Union. Through Jackson's efforts, a constitutional crisis had been averted, but sectional divisions were getting deeper and more pronounced. The abolition movement was also growing rapidly, becoming an important issue in the North. The slavery issue was at the root of every problem, crisis, event, decision, and struggle from then on.

The next crisis involved the issue concerning Texas. By 1836, Texas was an independent republic with its own constitution. During its fight for independence, Americans were sympathetic to and supportive of the Texans, and some individuals recruited volunteers who crossed into Texas to help the struggle. Problems arose when the state petitioned Congress for statehood. Texas wanted to allow slavery, but Northerners in Congress opposed admission to the Union because it would disrupt the balance between free and slave states and give Southerners in Congress increased influence.

A few years later, Congress took up consideration of new territories between Missouri and present-day Idaho. Again, heated debate over permitting slavery in these areas flared up. Those opposed to slavery used the **Missouri Compromise** to prove their point showing that the land being considered for territories was part of the area the Compromise had been designated as banned to slavery. On May 25, 1854, Congress passed the infamous **Kansas-Nebraska Act** which nullified the provision creating the territories of Kansas and Nebraska. This allowed the people of these two territories to decide for themselves whether or not to permit slavery to exist there. Feelings were so deep and divided that any further attempts to compromise met with little, if any, success. Political and social turmoil swirled everywhere. Kansas was called "Bleeding Kansas" because of the extreme violence and bloodshed throughout the territory due to the two governments that existed there: one pro-slavery and the other anti-slavery.

In 1857, the Supreme Court handed down a decision guaranteed to cause explosions throughout the country. Dred Scott was a slave whose owner had taken him from slave state Missouri, then to free state Illinois, into Minnesota Territory (free under the provisions of the Missouri Compromise), and finally back to slave state Missouri. Abolitionists pursued the dilemma by presenting a court case, stating that since Scott had lived in a free state and free territory, he was in actuality a free man.

Two lower courts ruled before the Supreme Court became involved: one ruling in favor and one against. The Supreme Court decided that residing in a free state and free territory did not make Scott a free man because Scott (and all other slaves) was not a U.S. citizen or a state citizen of Missouri. Therefore, he did not have the right to sue in state or federal courts. The Court went a step further and ruled that the old Missouri Compromise was now unconstitutional because Congress did not have the power to prohibit slavery in the Territories.

In 1858, Abraham Lincoln and Stephen A. Douglas were running for the office of U.S. Senator from Illinois; they participated in a series of debates that directly affected the outcome of the 1860 presidential election. Douglas, a Democrat, was up for re-election and knew that if he won this race, he had a good chance of becoming president in 1860. Lincoln, a Republican, was not an abolitionist but he believed that slavery was morally wrong. He firmly believed in and supported the Republican Party principle that slavery must not be allowed to extend any further. The final straw came with the election of Lincoln to the Presidency the next year. Due to a split in the Democratic Party, there were four candidates from four political parties. With Lincoln receiving a minority of the popular vote and a majority of electoral votes, the Southern states, one by one, voted to secede from the Union, as they had promised they would do if Lincoln and the Republicans were victorious. The die was cast.

The Civil War

Both sides quickly prepared for war. The North had more in its favor: a larger population; superiority in finances and transportation facilities; and manufacturing, agricultural, and natural resources. The North possessed most of the nation's gold, had about 92 percent of all industries, and had almost all the known supplies of copper, coal, iron, and various other minerals. Most of the nation's railroads were in the North and mid-West; men and supplies could be moved wherever needed and food could be transported from the farms of the mid-West to workers in the East as well as to soldiers on the battlefields. Trade with nations overseas could go on as usual due to control of the navy and the merchant fleet.

The Northern states numbered twenty-four and included western (California and Oregon) and border (Maryland, Delaware, Kentucky, Missouri, and West Virginia) states. The Southern states numbered eleven and included South Carolina, Georgia, Florida, Alabama, Mississippi, Louisiana, Texas, Virginia, North Carolina, Tennessee, and Arkansas, making up the Confederacy.

Although outnumbered in population, the South was completely confident of victory. They knew that all they had to do was fight a defensive war and protect their own territory. The North had to invade and defeat an area almost the size of Western Europe. Another advantage of the South was that a number of its best officers had graduated from the U.S. Military Academy at West Point and had long years of army experience. Many had exercised varying degrees of command in the Indian Wars and the war with Mexico. Men from the South were conditioned to living outdoors and were more familiar with horses and firearms than men from northeastern cities. Since cotton was such an important crop, Southerners felt that British and French textile mills were so dependent on raw cotton that they would be forced to help the Confederacy in the war.

The South won decisively until the **Battle of Gettysburg**, July 1 - 3, 1863. Until Gettysburg, Lincoln's commanders, McDowell and McClellan, were less than desirable; Burnside and Hooker, not what was needed. Lee, on the other hand, had many able officers; Jackson and Stuart were depended on heavily by him. Jackson died at Chancellorsville and was replaced by Longstreet. Lee decided to invade the North and depended on J.E.B. Stuart and his cavalry to keep him informed of the location of Union troops and their strengths.

The day after Gettysburg, on July 4, Vicksburg, Mississippi surrendered to Union General Ulysses Grant, thus severing the western Confederacy from the eastern part. In September 1863, the Confederacy won its last important victory at Chickamauga. In November, the Union victory at Chattanooga made it possible for Union troops to go into Alabama and Georgia, splitting the eastern Confederacy in two. Lincoln gave Grant command of all Northern armies in March of 1864. Grant led his armies into battles in Virginia while Phil Sheridan and his cavalry did as much damage as possible. In a skirmish at a place called Yellow Tavern, Virginia, Sheridan's and Stuart's forces met, with Stuart being fatally wounded.

The Civil War took more American lives than any other American war in history, the South losing one-third of its soldiers in battle compared to about one-sixth for the North. More than half of the total deaths were caused by disease and the horrendous conditions of field hospitals. Destruction was pervasive in towns, farms, trade, and industry. The lives and homes of men, women, and children were almost entirely destroyed and an entire Southern way of life lost. The South had no voice in the political, social, and cultural affairs of the nation, lessening to a great degree the influence of the more traditional Southern ideals. The Northern Yankee Protestant ideals of hard work, education, and economic freedom became the standard of the United States and helped influence the development of the nation into a modem, industrial power.

The effects of the Civil War were tremendous. It changed the methods of waging war and has been called the first modern war. It introduced weapons and tactics that, when improved later, were used extensively in wars of the late 1800s and 1900s. Civil War soldiers were the first to fight in trenches, the first to fight under a unified command, and the first to wage a defense called "major cordon defense" (a strategy of advance on all fronts). They were also the first to use repeating and breech loading weapons. Observation balloons were first used during the war along with submarines, ironclad ships, and mines. Telegraphy and railroads were also first put to use during this time.

By executive proclamation and constitutional amendment, slavery was officially ended, although there remained deep prejudice and racism (which is still apparent today). The Union was preserved and the states were finally truly united. Sectionalism, especially in the area of politics, remained strong for another 100 years but not to the degree and with the violence as existed before 1861.

It has been noted that the Civil War may have been American democracy's greatest failure, as calm reason, which is basic to democracy, fell victim to human passion. Yet democracy did survive. The victory of the North established that no state has the right to end or leave the Union. Because of this unity, the United States became a major global power. It is important to remember that Lincoln never proposed to punish the South. He was most concerned with restoring the South to the Union in a program that was flexible and practical rather than rigid and unbending. In fact, he never really felt that the states had succeeded in leaving the Union, but that they had left the 'family circle" for a short time.

The conclusion of the Civil War opened the floodgates for **westward migration** and the settlement of new land. The availability of cheap land and the expectation of great opportunities prompted thousands to travel across the Mississippi River and settle the Great Plains and California. The primary activities of the new western economy were farming, mining, and ranching. Both migration and the economy were facilitated by the expansion of the railroad and the completion of the transcontinental railroad in 1869.

Industrialization

The United States underwent significant social and economic changes during the twentieth century, and it became a dominant world power internationally. Economically, the United States saw periods of great prosperity, as well as severe depression, emerging as primary economic forces.

The **industrialization** that had started following the end of the Civil War in the mid-nineteenth century continued into the early decades of the twentieth century. A huge wave of immigration at the turn of the century provided industry with a large labor pool and established millions of immigrants and their families in the working class.

Populism is a philosophy concerned with the common sense needs of average people. Populism often finds expression as a reaction against perceived oppression of the average people by the wealthy elite in society. The prevalent claim of populist movements is that they will put the people first. Populist movements claim to represent the majority of the people and call them to stand up to institutions or practices that seem detrimental to their well-being.

Populism flourished in the late nineteenth and early twentieth centuries in the United States. Several political parties were formed out of this philosophy, including the Greenback Party, the Populist Party, the Farmer-Labor Party, the Single Tax movement of Henry George, the Share Our Wealth movement of Huey Long, the Progressive Party, and the Union Party.

The tremendous changes caused by the Industrial Revolution led to a demand for reform that would control the power wielded by big corporations. The gap between the industrial moguls and the working people was growing; this disparity resulted in a public outcry for reform at the same time that there was an outcry for governmental reform that would end the political corruption and elitism of the day.

The reforms initiated by leaders and the spirit of **Progressivism** were far-reaching. Politically, many states enacted initiatives and referendums for progressive movements. The adoption of the recall occurred in many states, and several states enacted legislation that would undermine the power of political machines. On a national level, the two most significant political changes were: 1) the ratification of the Seventeenth Amendment, which required that all U.S. Senators be chosen by popular election, and 2) the ratification of the Nineteenth Amendment, which granted women the right to vote.

Major economic reforms of the period included the aggressive enforcement of the Sherman Antitrust Act and the passage of the Elkins Act and the Hepburn Act, which gave the Interstate Commerce Commission greater power to regulate the railroads. The Pure Food and Drug Act prohibited the use of harmful chemicals in food; the Meat Inspection Act regulated the meat industry to protect the public against tainted meat; over two-thirds of the states passed laws prohibiting child labor; workmen's compensation was mandated; and the Department of Commerce and Labor was created.

Responding to concern over the environmental effects of the timber, ranching, and mining industries, Roosevelt set aside 238 million acres of federal lands to be protected from development. Wildlife preserves were established, the national park system was expanded, and the National Conservation Commission was created. The Newlands Reclamation Act also provided federal funding for the construction of irrigation projects and dams in semi-arid areas of the country.

The Wilson Administration carried out additional reforms. The Federal Reserve Act created a national banking system, providing a more stable money supply. The Sherman Act and the Clayton Antitrust Act defined unfair competition, made corporate officers liable for the illegal actions of employees, and exempted labor unions from antitrust lawsuits. The Federal Trade Commission was established to enforce these measures. Finally, the Sixteenth Amendment was ratified, establishing an income tax. This measure was designed to relieve the poor of a disproportionate burden in funding the federal government and to make the wealthy pay a greater share of the nation's tax burden.

Before 1800, most manufacturing activities were done in small shops or in homes. However, starting in the early 1800s, factories with modern machines were built, making it easier to produce goods faster. The eastern part of the country became a major industrial area, although some industry was developed in the west. At about the same time, improvements began to be made in building roads, railroads, canals, and steamboats. The increased ease of travel facilitated the westward movement as well as boosted the economy with faster and cheaper shipment of goods and products, covering larger and larger areas. Some of the innovations arising from these changes included the Erie Canal, which connects the interior and Great Lakes with the Hudson River and the coastal port of New York. Many other natural waterways were connected by canals during this time.

Robert Fulton's Clermont, the first commercially successful steamboat, led the pack as the fastest way to ship goods, making it the most important means to do so. Later, steam-powered railroads became the biggest rival of the steamboat as a means of shipping, eventually becoming the most important transportation method opening the west.

With expansion into the interior of the country, the United States became the leading agricultural nation in the world. The hardy pioneer farmers produced a vast surplus, and emphasis went to producing products with a high-sale value. Implements such as the cotton gin and the reaper aided in higher production. Travel and shipping were greatly assisted in areas not yet reached by railroad; they were also facilitated by improved and new roads, such as the National Road in the east and the Oregon and Santa Fe Trails in the west.

As travel and communication became faster, people became more exposed to works of literature, art, newspapers, drama, live entertainment, and political rallies. More information was desired about previously unknown areas of the country, especially the west, and the discovery of gold and other mineral wealth resulted in a literal surge of settlers.

Public schools were established in many of the states, and more and more children were able to get an education. With higher literacy and more participation in literature and the arts, the young nation was developing its own unique culture, and becoming less and less influenced by and dependent on that of Europe.

At the same time, more industries and factories required more labor. Women, children, and, at times, entire families worked dangerously long hours until the 1830s. By that time, factories were getting even larger and employers began hiring immigrants who were coming to America in huge numbers. Before then, efforts were made to organize a labor movement to improve working conditions and increase wages. It never really caught on until after the Civil War.

The prosperity of industrial and economic changes was interrupted by America's entry into the **First World War** in 1917. While reluctant to enter the hostilities, the United States played a decisive role in ending the war and in the creation of the League of Nations that followed, establishing its central position in international relations that would increase in importance through the century.

World War I

The **World War I** effort required a massive production of weapons, ammunition, radios, and other equipment of war. During wartime, work hours were shortened, wages were increased, and working conditions improved. When the war ended, and business and industrial owners attempted to return to pre-war conditions, the workers revolted. These conditions contributed to the establishment of new labor laws.

Roosevelt and The New Deal

The years between WWI and WWII produced significant advancements in aircraft technology, and the pace of aircraft development and production was dramatically increased during WWII. Major developments included flight-based weapon delivery systems, the long-range bomber, the first jet fighter, the first cruise missile, and the first ballistic missile. Although they were invented, cruise and ballistic missiles were not widely used during the war. Glider planes were heavily used in WWII because they were silent upon approach. Another significant development was the broad use of paratrooper units. Hospital planes also came into use to extract the seriously wounded from the front and to transport them to hospitals for treatment.

The United States resumed its prosperous industrial growth in the years after WWI, but even as industrial profits and stock market investments skyrocketed, farm prices and wages fell, creating an unbalanced situation that caused an economic collapse in 1929, when the stock market crashed. The United States plummeted into economic depression with high unemployment. This period is known as the **Great Depression**.

President Franklin Roosevelt proposed that the federal government assist in rebuilding the economy, something his predecessor, President Hoover, thought the government should not do. Roosevelt's **New Deal** policies were adopted to wide success, and marked an important shift in the role that the U.S. government plays in economic matters and social welfare.

World War II

The nation's recovery was underway when, in late 1941, it entered the Second World War to fight against Japan and Germany and their allied Axis powers. Fifty-nine nations became embroiled in **World War II**, which began September 1, 1939 and ended September 2, 1945. These dates include both the European and Pacific Theaters of war. The horribly tragic results of this second global conflagration were more deaths and more destruction than those of any other armed conflict. It completely uprooted and displaced millions of people. The end of the war brought renewed power struggles, especially in Europe and China; many Eastern European nations as well as China came under the control and domination of the communists, supported and backed by the Soviet Union.

The war began with essentially the same weaponry that had been used in WWI. However, as the war progressed, so did technology. The aircraft carrier joined the battleship; the Higgins boat, the primary landing craft, was invented; light tanks were developed to meet the needs of a changing battlefield; and other armored vehicles were developed. Submarines were also perfected during this period. With the development of atomic bombs and their deployment against two Japanese cities, the world found itself in the nuclear age. The peace settlement established by the United Nations Organization after the war still exists and operates today.

The war industry fueled another period of economic prosperity that lasted through the post-war years. The 1950s saw the emergence of a large consumer culture in the United States, which has bolstered not only the American economy ever since, but has been an important development for other countries that produce goods for the U.S. market.

The United States first established itself as an important world military leader at the turn of the twentieth century during the Spanish American War; it cemented this position during the two World Wars. Following WWII, with Europe struggling to recover from the fighting, the United States and the Soviet Union emerged as the two dominant world powers. This remained the situation for three decades while the two super powers engaged in a Cold War between the ideals of communism and capitalism. In the 1980s, the Soviet Union underwent a series of reforms that resulted in the collapse of the country and the end of the Cold War, leaving the United States as the true world power. Thus, the United States changed from a reluctant participant in international affairs into a central leader.

Major technological developments in the post WWII era:
- Discovery of penicillin (1945)
- Detonation of the first atomic bombs (1945)
- Xerography process invented (1946)
- Exploration of the South Pole
- Studies of X-ray radiation
- U.S. airplane first flies at supersonic speed (1947)
- Invention of the transistor (1947)
- Long-playing record invented (1948)
- Studies begin in the science of chemo-genetics (1948)
- Mount Palomar reflecting telescope created (1948)
- Idlewild Airport (now known as JFK International Airport) opens in NY City
- Cortisone discovered (1949)
- USSR tests first atomic bomb (1949)
- U.S. guided missile launched and traveled 250 miles (1949)
- Plutonium separated (1950)
- Tranquilizer meprobamate comes into wide use (1950)
- Antihistamines become popular in treating colds and allergies (1950)
- Electric power produced from atomic energy (1951)
- First heart-lung machine devised (1951)
- First solo flight over the North Pole (1951)
- Yellow fever vaccine developed (1951)
- Isotopes used in medicine and industry (1952)
- Contraceptive pill produced (1952)
- First hydrogen bomb exploded (1952)
- Nobel Prize in medicine for discovery of streptomycin (1952)
- Cave Cougnac discovered with prehistoric paintings (1953)
- USSR explodes hydrogen bomb (1953)
- Hillary and Tenzing reach the summit of Mount Everest (1953)
- Lung cancer connected to cigarette smoking (1953)
- First U.S. submarine converted to nuclear power (1954)
- Polio vaccine invented (1954)
- Discovery of Vitamin B12 (1955)
- Discovery of the molecular structure of insulin (1955)
- First artificial manufacture of diamonds (1955)
- Beginning of development of "visual telephone" (1956)
- Beginning of Transatlantic cable telephone service (1956)
- USSR launches first earth satellites (Sputnik I and II) (1957)
- Mackinac Straits Bridge in Michigan opens as the longest suspension bridge (1957)
- Stereo recordings introduced (1958)
- NASA created (1958)
- USSR launches rocket with two monkeys aboard (1959)
- Nobel Prize for Medicine for synthesis of RNA and DNA (1959)

Skill 32.2 **Demonstrating knowledge of major issues, people, events, and cause-and-effect relationships during different periods of U.S. history, their influence on the present, and how they affect planning for the future**

SEE Skill 33.3

Skill 32.3 **Analyzing various perspectives and interpretations of issues and events in the history of the United States**

An important task teachers face in the social science classroom is aiding students in becoming mindful readers and independent/analytical thinkers. Teachers must guide students in their learning how to formulate independent thoughts and not just accepting what is written in textbooks and on web sites as the sole truth.

History is filled with wonderful facts, intriguing stories, and innumerous combinations of perspectives and interpretations on just about every major event in its history. These problems and issues encountered in the past have affected history in immeasurable ways. It is nearly impossible to consider all of the thoughts, values, ideas and perspectives involved. When studying a time period of United States history, students and teachers should decide on broad key questions that relate to major impacts, nature of social change, urbanization, cultural effects and so on when entering into an historical analysis. These questions can serve as a foundation to the study, providing a focus for students as they explore the related perspectives.

From here, students can explore one or more of these key questions by creating subtopics beneath them as they consider the major elements such as time period, cultural impacts, various viewpoints, previous and concurrent events and so on. This is a great place in which to introduce "primary resources" in the field of social science. Diaries, field trips, field trips to historic sites and museums, historical documents, photos, artifacts, and other records of the past provide students with an alternative voices and accounts of events. It is within primary resources, first-hand accounts of events, that provide the richest and least "processed" information. For example, a letter from a freed slave would provide more valuable information about attitudes toward African Americans in the North in 1860 than a textbook entry. Things to consider when analyzing historical resources include:

- Who is the author? What motivated this author? Why did they create this resource? Is he or she representing a group?
- The time frame – when was this resource produced? How has it reached us? Was it contemporary at the time of production?
- The location – where was this document produced?
- The type of document – is it a letter, a poem, a report, a song, a study?

- The audience – who was intended to see this piece?

When engaging in higher-ordered thinking skills, students should develop their skills through enthusiastic experiences where they can:

- Examine a situation
- Raise questions
- Compare differing ideas, interests, perspectives, actions, and institutions represented in these sources
- Elaborate upon what they read and see to develop interpretations, explanations, or solutions to the questions they have raised
- Analyze historical fiction, nonfiction, and historical illustrations
- Distinguish between fact and fiction
- Consider multiple perspectives
- Explain causes in analyzing historical actions
- Challenge arguments of historical inevitability
- Hypothesize the influence of the past

Teachers must also create an open and engaging learning environment rich where students can examine data. Use of libraries, historical collections, museums, newspapers, collections, students' families and artifacts, professional and community resources, historians, local colleges, and more allow students to see history for themselves – the first step in truly teaching them how to analyze history.

Skill 32.4 Recognizing the influence of individuals, movements, culture, cultural groups, ideas, and technology on history and social change in the United States

SEE Skill 32.1

COMPETENCY 0033   UNDERSTAND MAJOR CONCEPTS, ISSUES, PEOPLE, EVENTS, AND DEVELOPMENTS IN WORLD HISTORY

Skill 33.1   Recognizing ways in which historical events are organized into time periods and eras, the chronological relationships within those periods and eras, and the ways in which different cultures perceive and record the passage of time

The Calendar

Recording of time is an ancient challenge. In the earliest days, ancient people connected the heavens and their calendars for the purpose of agriculture, religion and celebrations. By using familiar or repeating patterns of celestial objects, such as the rising and setting sun, the cycle of the moon, and the sun's position (high or low) against the stars' position, ancient cultures utilized these natural clocks for a respective concept of days, months, and years. The week, however, is said to have evolved from names of the seven bright bodies in the sky that man observed: the sun, the moon, Mars, Mercury, Jupiter, Venus, and Saturn.

The most ancient of civilizations had their own versions of calendars. The Babylonians (and in later years, the Greeks) possessed a lunisolar calendar of 12 months with 30 days each. They would add months to round their calendar out for a year when needed. In ancient Egypt, the lunar calendar was replaced with one based on the sun when the Egyptians noticed a connection to Canis Major and the annual Nile flood. With this knowledge, they created a calendar with 365 days starting in 4236 B.C., the earliest recorded year. This calendar also had 12 months with 30 days, and they had 5 extra added days at the end of the year. So, around 238 B.C., King Ptolemy III commanded an extra day be added to every fourth year like our modern day leap year. Ancient Incan and Mayan (and later the Aztec) cultures in South American also relied on the sun and moon, and even more so on Venus to devise their calendar.

Our modern calendar was first adopted by the Egyptians and then the Romans under the ruler, Julius Caesar. Caesar determined the current calendar to be wrong and extended the year to consist of 445 days. However, the calendar returned to the 365 ¼ days under the advice of the astronomer, Sosigenes. To "fix" the ¼ day, an extra day was added every fourth year – our leap year.

Clocks

Various tools were used to record the passage of time. 20,000 years ago, scratched lines and gouged holes was an Ice-age hunters' method. Egyptian obelisks divided the day into two halves, and then sundials, and then later hemicycles, emerged to display hours. The earliest clocks used water to track time, and these were discovered in Greek tombs dating back to 1500 B.C.

Large weight-driven (and inaccurate) clocks were first used by the early-to-mid-14th century. Spring-powered clocks were invented between 1500 and 1510 by Peter Henlein of Nuremberg, and pendulum clocks emerged in 1656 when Christiaan Huygens, a Dutch scientist, made the first pendulum clock.

Time Periods

When time is categories, these categories are referred to as per iodization. Major periods include cosmological (the time period concerning the origin of the universe): geological (the time period within which the earth was formed and evolved); and historical (the time period marking the evolution of man).

In the social science, the areas of paleontology and archaeology study ancient historical time periods. A supereon is the largest defined time unit, and this is broken down into eons which are subdivided into eras, then, periods, then epochs, and finally ages. The earliest considered time is the Precambrian Supereon which is followed by the Phanerozoic eon, which contains the Paleozoic, Mesozoic (time of dinosaurs) and Cenozoic eras.

Human prehistory is divided into three main times: The Stone Age, The Bronze Age, and the Iron Age. Humans are thought to have evolved starting back 265,000 years ago during the Stone Age (2.5 million years ago – 3000 B.C.) when use of stone tools predominated the culture. This time period is broken into three main phases. The Paleolithic Age, or Old Stone Age, extends from 2.5 million years ago with the earliest use of stone tools to 10000 B.C. when agriculture was introduced. This Age is made up of three sub periods, Lower, Middle, and Upper Paleolithic, and the Upper Paleolithic ended with the last ice age 10,000 years ago. The Mesolithic Age (10,000 years ago - 6,000 years ago) was followed by the Neolithic Age (starting anywhere from 9,500 - 6,000 years ago – 3,000 years ago). The Bronze Age (3,300 B.C. – 1,200 B.C.) refers to the ancient age when metalworking evolved as a way of life to survive, and finally, the Iron Age (1200 – 1000 B.C.) marks the time period when people made tools and weapons primarily with iron.

From here, time periods pick up to what is considered "civilized" times. The earliest civilizations from 3,500 B.C. to year zero, or 0 A.D. include the Mesopotamians, ancient Egypt, the first dynasties of China (Shang and Zhou), and ancient Greece. The Middle Ages in Europe covered the time between 400 A.D. and the 15th century and this time included the Early Middle Ages, the Dark Age, and the Viking Age. Chinese dynasties such as the Sui, Tang, Liao, Jin, and Ming are some of the periods in early Chinese history from 420 A.D. to 1644. Europe experienced a major military expansion between 1000 and 1450 A.D., which evolved into the Renaissance era in the 14th – 16th centuries.

The earliest modern period is considered to have begun with 16th – 18th century Europe with the Age of Discovery, the Elizabethan period, the Protestant Reformation, the Age of Enlightenment, and many other empires in Japan, China, Islam and other Asian countries. The Modern era includes Europe in the 18th – 20th centuries, the Industrial Revolutions in both Europe and the United States, Colonialism, the Napoleonic Era, the Georgian Era, the Victorian Era, the Romantic Era, the Edwardian period, the Machine Age, World Wars I and II, the Atomic Age, the Cold War, and the Space Age.

We are currently situated in the Information Age (1990 – Present), the Net Generation and Generation Z eras and the .com age.

Skill 33.2   Demonstrating knowledge of early civilizations and cultures and their lasting influence

Prehistory and early civilizations

The earliest known civilizations developed in the Tigris-Euphrates Valley of Mesopotamia (modern Iraq) and the Nile Valley of Egypt between 4000 BCE and 3000 BCE. Because these civilizations arose in river valleys, they are known as **fluvial civilizations**. Geography and the physical environment played a critical role in the rise and the survival of both of these civilizations.

The Fertile Crescent was bounded on the west by the Mediterranean Sea, on the south by the Arabian Desert, on the north by the Taurus Mountains, and on the east by the Zagros Mountains.

The rivers provided a source of water that sustained life, including animal life. The hunters of the society had ample access to a variety of animals, which were hunted to provide food, as well as hides, bones, and antlers from which clothing, tools, and art was made. The proximity to water provided a natural attraction to animals, which could be herded and husbanded to provide a stable supply of food and animal products. The rivers of these regions also overflowed their banks each year, leaving behind a deposit of very rich soil. As these early people began to experiment with growing crops rather than gathering food, they discovered that the soil was fertile and that water was readily available to produce sizeable harvests. In time, the people developed systems of irrigation that channeled water to the crops without significant human effort on a continuing basis.

The designation "Fertile Crescent" was applied to the part of the Near East that extended from the Persian Gulf to the Sinai Peninsula by the famous historian and Egyptologist James Breasted. It included Mesopotamia, Syria, and Palestine. In early years, this region was marked by almost constant invasions and migrations. These invaders and migrants seemed to have destroyed the culture and civilization that existed; however, upon taking a longer view, it is apparent that they actually absorbed and supplemented the civilization that existed before their arrival. This is one of the reasons the civilization developed so quickly and created such an advanced culture.

The culture of Mesopotamia was definitely autocratic in nature. The various civilizations spread throughout the Fertile Crescent were very much top-heavy, with a single ruler as the head of the government who, in many cases, also served as the head of the religion. The people followed his strict instructions or faced the consequences, which were usually dire and often life-threatening.

The civilizations of the Sumerians, Amorites, Hittites, Assyrians, Chaldeans, and Persians controlled various areas of the land we now call Mesopotamia. With few exceptions, tyrants and military leaders controlled the vast majority of aspects of society, including trade, religions, and laws. Each Sumerian city-state (of which there were many) had its own god, with the city-state's leader doubling as the high priest of worship of that local god. Subsequent cultures had a handful of gods as well, although they had more of a national worship structure, with high priests centered in the capital city as advisors to the leader.

Trade was vastly important to these civilizations, since they had access to some but not all of the things that they needed to survive. Some trading agreements led to occupation, as was the case with the Sumerians, who didn't bother to build walls to protect their wealth of knowledge. Egypt and the Phoenician cities were powerful and regular trading partners of the various Mesopotamian cultures.

Legacies handed down to us from these people include:

- The first use of writing, the wheel, and banking (Sumeria);
- The first written set of laws (Code of Hammurabi);
- The first epic story (*Gilgamesh*);
- The first library dedicated to preserving knowledge (instituted by the Assyrian leader Ashurbanipal);
- The Hanging Gardens of Babylon (built by the Chaldean Nebuchadnezzar)

The ancient civilization of the **Sumerians** invented the wheel; developed irrigation through the use of canals, dikes, and devices for raising water; devised the system of cuneiform writing; learned to divide time; and built large boats for trade. The Babylonians devised the famous **Code of Hammurabi**, a code of laws.

Egypt made numerous significant contributions, including construction of the great pyramids; development of hieroglyphic writing; preservation of bodies after death; creation of paper from papyrus; contributions to developments in arithmetic and geometry; invention of the method of counting in groups of 1-10 (the decimal system); completion of a solar calendar; and formation of the foundation for science and astronomy.

The earliest historical record of the **Kush** civilization is in Egyptian sources. They describe a region upstream from the first cataract of the Nile as "wretched." This civilization was characterized by a settled way of life in fortified mud-brick villages. They subsisted on hunting and fishing, herding cattle, and gathering grain. Skeletal remains suggest that the people were a blend of Negroid and Mediterranean peoples. This civilization appears to be the second-oldest in Africa (after Egypt).

During the period of Egypt's Old Kingdom (ca. 2700-2180 BCE), this civilization was essentially a diffused version of Egyptian culture and religion. When Egypt came under the domination of the Hyksos, Kush reached its greatest power and cultural energy (1700-1500 BCE). When the Hyksos were eventually expelled from Egypt, the New Kingdom brought Kush back under Egyptian colonial control.

The ancient **Assyrians** were warlike and aggressive due to a highly organized military; they also used horse-drawn chariots.

The **Hebrews**, also known as the ancient Israelites, instituted "monotheism," which is the worship of one God (as opposed to many). The Hebrew Scriptures became the Old Testament of the Christian Bible.

The **Minoans** had a system of writing using symbols to represent syllables in words. They built palaces with multiple levels containing many rooms, water and sewage systems with flush toilets, bathtubs, hot and cold running water, and bright paintings on the walls.

The **Mycenaeans** changed the Minoan writing system to aid their own language and used symbols to represent syllables.

The **Phoenicians** were sea traders well-known for their manufacturing skills in glass and metals as well as the development of their famous purple dye. They became so proficient in the skill of navigation that they were able to sail by the stars at night. Furthermore, they devised an alphabet using symbols to represent single sounds, which was an improved extension of the Egyptian principle and writing system.

China is considered by some historians to be the oldest, uninterrupted civilization in the world; it was in existence around the same time as the ancient civilizations found in Egypt, Mesopotamia, and the Indus Valley. The Chinese studied nature and weather; stressed the importance of education, family, and a strong central government; followed the religions of Buddhism, Confucianism, and Taoism; and invented such things as gunpowder, paper, printing, and the magnetic compass. China began building the Great Wall; practiced crop rotation and terrace farming; increased the importance of the silk industry; and developed caravan routes across Central Asia for extensive trade. They also increased proficiency in rice cultivation and developed a written language based on drawings or pictographs.

The ancient **Persians** developed an alphabet; contributed the religions and philosophies of **Zoroastrianism**, **Mithraism**, and **Gnosticism**; and allowed conquered peoples to retain their own customs, laws, and religions.

The classical civilization of **Greece** reached the highest levels in human achievement based on the foundations already laid by such ancient groups as the Egyptians, Phoenicians, Minoans, and Mycenaeans.

Among the more important contributions of Greece was the Greek alphabet derived from the Phoenician letters, which formed the basis for the Roman alphabet and our present-day alphabet. Extensive trading and colonization resulted in the spread of Greek civilization. The love of sports, with emphasis on a physically sound body, led to the tradition of the Olympic Games. Greece was responsible for the rise of independent, strong city-states. Other important areas that the Greeks are credited with influencing include drama, epic and lyric poetry, fables, myths centered on the many gods and goddesses, science, astronomy, medicine, mathematics, philosophy, art, architecture, and recording historical events.

The conquests of Alexander the Great spread Greek ideas to the areas he conquered and brought many ideas from Asia to the Greek world. The desire to learn as much about the world as possible was a major objective of the conquests.

The ancient civilization of **Rome** lasted approximately 1,000 years (including the periods of the Republic and the Empire), although its lasting influence on Europe and its history was for a much longer period. There was a very sharp contrast between the curious, imaginative, inquisitive Greeks and the practical, simple, down-to-earth Romans, who spread and preserved the ideas of ancient Greece and other cultural groups. The contributions and accomplishments of the Romans are numerous, but their greatest included language, engineering, building, law, government, roads, trade, and the "Pax Romana." Pax Romana was the long period of peace enabling free travel and trade, spreading people, cultures, goods, and ideas all over a vast area of the known world.

In **India**, Hinduism was a continuing influence along with the rise of Buddhism. Industry and commerce developed along with extensive trading with the Near East. Outstanding advances in the fields of science and medicine were made, and the civilization was one of the first to be active in navigation and maritime enterprises during this time. In India, the caste system was developed and the principle of zero in mathematics was discovered.

The civilization in **Japan** appeared during this time, having borrowed much of its culture from China. It was the last of the classical civilizations to develop. Although they used, accepted, and copied Chinese art, law, architecture, dress, and writing, the Japanese refined these into their own unique way of life, including incorporating the religion of Buddhism into their culture.

During this time, the civilizations in **Africa** south of the Sahara were developing the refining and use of iron, especially for farm implements and later for weapons. Trading happened over land by using camels and over sea at important seaports. The Arab influence was extremely important, as was the Arabs' later contact with Indians, Christian Nubians, and Persians. In fact, these trading activities were probably the most important factor in the spread and assimilation of different ideas as well as stimulation of cultural growth.

The people who lived in the Americas before Columbus arrived had a thriving, connected society. The civilizations in North America tended to be spread farther and were in occasional conflict; however, for the most part, they each maintained their sovereignty. On the contrary, the South American civilizations tended to migrate into empires, with the strongest city or tribe assuming control of the lives and resources of the rest of the nearby peoples.

Native Americans in North America had a spiritual and personal relationship with the various spirits of nature and a keen appreciation of the ways of woodworking and metalworking. Various tribes dotted the landscape of what is now the United States. They struggled against one another for control of resources such as food and water but had no concept of ownership of land, since they believed that they were living on the land with the permission of the spirits. The North Americans mastered the art of growing many crops and, to their credit, were willing to share that knowledge with the various Europeans who eventually immigrated to their land. Artwork made of hides, beads, and jewels were popular at this time within various Native American cultures.

The most well-known empires of South America were the **Aztec, Inca,** and **Maya** civilizations. Each of these empires had a central capital which housed the emperor. The emperor controlled all aspects of the lives of his subjects. The empires traded with other peoples; if the relations soured, the results were usually absorption of the trading partners into the empire. These empires, especially the Aztecs, had access to large numbers of metals and jewels, and they created weapons and artwork that continue to impress historians today. The Incan Empire stretched across a vast period of territory down the western coast of South America and was connected by a series of roads. A series of messengers ran along these roads, carrying news and instructions from the capital, Cusco. The Mayas are most well-known for their famous pyramids and calendars, as well as their language, which still stumps archaeologists.

Classical Civilizations

Ancient Greece is often called the Cradle of Western Civilization because of the enormous influence it had not only on the time in which it flourished, but on western culture ever since.

Early Greek institutions have survived for thousands of years and have influenced the entire world. The Athenian form of democracy, with all citizens having an equal vote in their own government, is a philosophy upon which all modern democracies are based. In the United States, the Greek tradition of democracy was honored in the choice of Greek architectural styles for the nation's government buildings. The modern Olympic Games are a revival of an ancient Greek tradition, and many of the events are re-creations of original contests.

The works of the Greek epic poet Homer, author of the Iliad and the Odyssey, are considered the earliest in western literature, and are still read and taught today. The tradition of the theater was born in Greece, with the plays of Aristophanes and others. In philosophy, Aristotle developed an approach to learning that emphasized observation and thought, and Socrates and Plato contemplated the nature of being and the origins and ideals of government and political relations. Greek mythology has been the source of inspiration for literature into the present day.

In the field of mathematics, Pythagoras and Euclid laid the foundation of geometry and Archimedes calculated the value of pi. Herodotus and Thucydides were the first to apply research and interpretation to written history.

In the arts, Greek sensibilities were held as perfect forms to which others might strive. In sculpture, the Greeks achieved an idealistic aesthetic that had not been perfected before that time.

The Greek civilization served as an inspiration to the Roman Republic, which followed in its tradition of democracy and was directly influenced by its achievements in art and science. Later, during the Renaissance, European scholars and artists would rediscover ancient Greece's love for dedicated inquiry and artistic expression, leading to a surge in scientific discoveries and advancements in the arts.

The ancient civilization of **Rome** owed much to the Greeks. Romans admired Greek architecture and arts, and built upon these traditions to create a distinct tradition of their own that would influence the western world for centuries.

In government, the Romans took the Athenian concept of democracy and built it into a complex system of a representative government that included executive, legislative, and judicial functions. In the arts, Romans created a realistic approach to portraiture, in contrast to the more idealized form of the Greeks. In architecture, Rome borrowed directly from the Greek tradition, but also developed the dome and the arch, allowing for larger and more dramatic forms. The Romans continued the Greek tradition of learning, often employing Greeks to educate their children.

The Roman Republic flourished in the centuries leading up to the advent of the Christian era. An organized bureaucracy and active political population provided elite Roman citizens with the means to ascend to positions of considerable authority. During the first century BCE, Gaius Julius Caesar ambitiously began to gather support among the ruling authorities of the Republic, eventually being named one of the two Consuls who were elected annually. Caesar was ultimately named dictator for life, and was the transitional leader between the Roman Republic and what would become the Roman Empire.

Like the Republic, the Roman Empire also looked to the east, to Greece, for inspiration. The Macedonian conqueror Alexander, who had unified Greece and introduced the culture throughout the eastern world, provided many Roman emperors with a role model.

The Roman Empire extended through much of Europe, and Roman culture extended with it. Everywhere the Romans went, they built roads, established cities, and left their mark on the local population. The Roman language, Latin, spread as well and was transformed into the Romance languages of French and Spanish. The Roman alphabet, which was based on the Greek transformation of Phoenician letters, was adopted throughout the empire and is still used today. The empire itself has served as a model for modern government, especially in federal systems such as that found in the United States. The eventual decline and fall of the empire has been a subject that has occupied historians for centuries.

The rise of non-European civilizations

Between the fourth and ninth centuries, Asia was a story of religions and empires, of kings and wars, and of increasing and decreasing contact with the West.

India began this period recovering from the invasion of Alexander the Great. One strong man who met the great Alexander was Chandragupta Maurya, who began one of his country's most successful dynasties. Chandragupta conquered most of what we now call India. His grandson, Asoka, was a more peaceful ruler, but powerful nonetheless. He was also a great believer in the practices and power of Buddhism, sending missionaries throughout Asia to preach the ways of the Buddha. Succeeding the Mauryas were the Guptas, who ruled India for a longer period of time and brought prosperity and international recognition to their people.

The Guptas were great believers in science and mathematics, especially as they pertained to the production of goods. They invented the decimal system and had a concept of zero, two things that put them ahead of the rest of the world on the mathematics timeline. They were the first to make cotton and calico, and their medical practices were much more advanced than those in Europe and elsewhere in Asia at the time. These inventions and innovations created high demand for Indian goods throughout Asia and Europe.

The idea of a united India continued after the Gupta Dynasty ended. It was especially favorable to the invading Muslims, who took over in the eleventh century, ruling the country for hundreds of years through a series of sultanates. The most famous Muslim leader of India was Tamerlane, who founded the Mogul Dynasty and began a series of conquests that expanded the borders of India. Tamerlane's grandson Akbar is considered the greatest Mogul. He believed in freedom of religion and is perhaps most well-known for the series of buildings that he had built, including mosques, palaces, forts, and tombs—some of which are still standing today. During the years that Muslims ruled India, Hinduism continued to be respected, although it was a minority religion; however, Buddhism died out almost entirely from the country that begot its founder.

The story of **China** during this time is one of dynasties controlling various parts of what is now China and Tibet. The Tang Dynasty was one of the most long-lasting and the most proficient, inventing the idea of civil service and the practice of block printing. The Sung Dynasty was also very influential, as it produced some of the world's greatest paintings and porcelain pottery. However, it failed to unify China in a meaningful way; this would prove instrumental in the takeover of China by the Mongols, led by Genghis Khan and his most famous grandson, Kublai.

Genghis Khan was known as a conqueror, and Kublai was known as a "uniter". However, they both extended the borders of their empire; at its height, the Mongol Empire was the largest the world has ever seen, encompassing all of China, Russia, Persia, and central Asia. Following the Mongols were the Ming and Manchu Dynasties, both of which focused on isolation. As a result, China at the end of the eighteenth century knew very little of the outside world, and vice versa. Ming artists created beautiful porcelain pottery, but not much of it saw its way into the outside world until much later. The Manchus were known for their focus on farming and road-building, two practices that were instituted in greater numbers in order to try to keep up with expanding population. Confucianism, Taoism, and ancestor worship—the staples of Chinese society for hundreds of years—continued to flourish during all this time.

The other major power in Asia was **Japan**, which developed independently and tried to keep itself that way for hundreds of years. Early Japanese society focused on the emperor and the farm, in that order. Japan was often influenced early on by China, from which it borrowed many things, including religion (Buddhism), a system of writing, a calendar, and even fashion. The Sea of Japan protected Japan from outside invasion, including the famous campaign of the Mongols.

The power of the emperor declined as it was usurped by the era of the Daimyo and his loyal soldiers, the samurai. Japan flourished economically and culturally during many of these years, although the policy of isolation the country developed kept the rest of the world from knowing such things. Buddhism and local religions were joined by Christianity in the sixteenth century, but it wasn't until the mid-nineteenth century that Japan rejoined the world community.

African civilizations during these centuries were few and far between. Most of northern coastal Africa had been conquered by Moslem armies. The preponderance of deserts and other inhospitable lands restricted African settlements to a few select areas. The city of Zimbabwe became a trading center in south-central Africa in the fifth century, but it didn't last long. More successful was **Ghana**, a Muslim-influenced kingdom that arose in the ninth century and lasted for nearly 300 years. Ghanaians had large farming areas and also raised cattle and elephants. They traded with people from Europe and the Middle East. Eventually overrunning Ghana was Mali, whose trade center Timbuktu survived its own empire's demise and blossomed into one of the world's caravan destinations.

Iron, tin, and leather came out of **Mali** in abundance. The succeeding civilization of the Songhai had relative success in maintaining the accomplishments of their predecessors. Religion in all of these places was mostly Muslim. Even after extended contact with other cultures, technological advancements were few and far between.

The **North American** and **South American Native Americans** were vastly different cultures. Differences in geography, economic focus, and the preponderance of visitors from overseas produced differing patterns of occupation, survival, and success.

In North America, the landscape was much more hospitable to settlement and exploration. The North American continent, especially in what is now the United States, had few mountain ranges and a handful of wide rivers but nothing near the dense jungles and staggeringly high mountains that South America had. The area that is now Canada was cold but otherwise conducive to settlement. As a result, the Native Americans in the northern areas of the Americas were more spread out and their cultures more diverse than their South American counterparts.

One of the best known North American tribes were the Pueblo, who lived in what is now the American Southwest. They are remembered for the challenging vista-based villages that they constructed from the sheer faces of cliffs and rocks as well as for their *adobes*, mud-brick buildings that housed their living and meeting quarters. The Pueblos chose their own chiefs. This was perhaps one of the oldest representative governments in the world. Known also for their organized government were the Iroquois, who lived in the American Northeast. The famous Five Nations of the Iroquois made treaties among themselves and shared leadership of their peoples.

Religion was a personal affair for nearly all of these tribes, with beliefs in higher powers extending to spirits in the sky and elsewhere in nature. Native Americans had none of the one-god-only mentality that developed in Europe and the Middle East, nor did they have the wars associated with the conflict that those monotheistic religions had with one another. Those people who lived in North America had large concentrations of people and houses, but they didn't have the kind of large civilization centers like cities elsewhere in the world. These people did not have an exact system of writing, either. These were two technological advances that were found in many other places in the world, including, to varying degrees, South America.

We know the most about the empires of South America: the Aztec, Inca, and Maya. However, people lived in South America before the advent of these empires; one of the earliest people of record was the Olmecs, who left behind little to prove their existence except a series of huge carved figures.

The **Aztecs** dominated Mexico and Central America. They weren't the only people living in these areas, just the most powerful ones. The Aztecs had many enemies, some of whom were only too happy to help Hernán Cortés precipitate the downfall of the Aztec society. The Aztecs had access to large numbers of metals and jewels; they used many of the metals to make weapons and the jewels to trade for items they didn't already possess. On the whole, however, the Aztecs didn't do a whole lot of trading; rather, they conquered neighboring tribes and demanded tribute from them, providing the source of much of the Aztec riches.

They also believed in a handful of gods and that these gods demanded human sacrifice in order to continue to smile on the Aztecs. The center of Aztec society was the great city of Tenochtitlan, which was built on an island so as to be easier to defend. It boasted a population of 300,000 at the time of the arrival of the conquistadors. Tenochtitlan was known for its canals and its pyramids, none of which survive today.

The **Inca** Empire stretched across a vast period of territory down the western coast of South America and was connected by a series of roads. A series of messengers ran along these roads, carrying news and instructions from the capital, Cusco, another large city along the lines of but not as spectacular as Tenochtitlan. The Incas are known for inventing the *quipu*, a string-based device that provided them with a method of keeping records. The Inca Empire, like the Aztec Empire, was very much a centralized state, with all income going to the state coffers and all trade going through the emperor. The Incas worshiped the dead, their ancestors, and nature.

The most advanced Native American civilization was the **Maya**, who lived primarily in Central America. They were the only Native American civilization to develop writing, which consisted of a series of symbols that has still not been deciphered. The Mayas also built huge pyramids and other stone figures and sculptures, mostly of the gods they worshiped. The Mayas are most famous, however, for their calendars and mathematics. The Mayan calendars were the most accurate on the planet until the sixteenth century. The Mayas also invented the idea of zero, something that no other culture had thought of except for India. Mayan worship resembled the practices of the Aztec and Inca, although human sacrifices were rare. The Mayas also traded heavily with their neighbors.

Cross-cultural comparisons

As the main civilizations grew and came into contact with each other, cultural exchanges took place at an increasing rate. Nevertheless, distinct religions, governments, and technological differences existed among the major civilizations during the first millennium CE.

Following the collapse of the Roman Empire and the division of the Christian Church in the fifth century, much of Europe became Christian, including the Visigoths who had taken control of Rome and much of the continent. The western Christian church became the Roman Catholic Church, and the Christian sect centered at Constantinople became the Eastern Orthodox Church. In Asia at this time, Confucianism was spreading from China as a religious and moral philosophy, and was adopted in China as the official core of the educational system. During the seventh century, the religion of Islam arose in the Middle East following the prophet Muhammad. In India, the already ancient religion of Hinduism was widely practiced.

Government among the various peoples during the first millennium was largely vested in a single leader: a king or emperor. Religion also played an important part in government and was often tightly connected to the figure of the king. In Europe, the concept of the divine right of kings emerged; it held that kings received authority to rule from God and held absolute power. Kings ruled through military power and by granting authority to other royal supporters. The system of feudalism arose as a method of ensuring military strength while providing a social order. In China, a vast bureaucracy was established to exercise control over the large area covered by the country. Confucianism was adopted as the basis for the exams given to those applying to enter the government service. In the Muslim areas of the Middle East, law was based on the Koran, the primary religious text of Islam. In the eighth century, the Pala Empire arose in India, a monarchical administration of Buddhist leaders who restored the Buddhist faith from near extinction in India.

In the area of science and technology, India was the first civilization to begin refining iron into steel around the third century CE. China developed printing and papermaking technologies that allowed information to be widely distributed. Muslim scholars made great strides in the fields of astronomy and mathematics, developing algebra and naming several stars. In Europe, Vikings were extending the range of boats and small ships, allowing for greater movement over the sea and setting the stage for the Age of Exploration that would follow in the next millennium.

The rise and expansion of Europe

As civilizations progressed through the Middle Ages and into early modern times, the ways in which people communicated, explored, fought, and traded expanded. Methods of transportation were being updated all the time, with land-based vehicles growing ever larger and ships increasing in size and purpose. Ways to build, as in cities and towns, were increasing technologically as well.

At the same time that an emphasis was being put on connecting with the outside world, people were increasingly looking inward, both in their pursuit of "the next life," as most religions would style it, and in their desire to protect what they had earned. The same groups of people who worked together to build ships to sail the high seas also worked together to build tall castles to watch over their houses and towns. Advances in technology extended to warfare as well, with powerful new weapons like gunpowder making old ways of fighting obsolete. It was a turbulent time throughout the world.

Mountains and rivers still formed formidable boundaries for countries and civilizations as well. The ways that men killed other men had advanced, but the ways in which men crossed rivers and mountains hadn't kept pace. Mountains still had to be marched over, and rivers still had to be ferried or rafted across. If the defender was at the top of the mountain or on the other side of the river, it didn't matter how many advanced weapons the attackers had; the defender still had the edge. This was true in the high mountains of Asia and South America, in the delta-dotted plains of India and Central Asia, and in Europe, which boasted more than its fair share of high mountains (Alps and Pyrenees) and wide rivers (like the Rhine and the Rhone). This was the case everywhere around the world, except, of course, in the sands of sub-Saharan Africa, where struggles took the form of wars of attrition, with the victors being those who weathered the sandstorms and lack of water the best.

As in the earliest days of civilization, people lived near waterways because they depended on those waterways for trade. The larger the boats, the more they could carry; this certainly increased the efficiency of trade. Foods and spices that previously were nonexistent in the markets of Europe because they would spoil before they ever reached their destination were increasingly for sale, since travel times had dramatically decreased due to improvements in travel technology. Following the stunningly successful example of the Roman Empire, more and more people built serviceable roads, making land-based trade less of a desperate adventure and more of a viable alternative to water trading.

Especially in Europe during this period, the castle was a dominant feature on the landscape of towns, villages, and countries. Castles housed kings, soldiers, retinues, and peasants. They also served as watchtowers, guardhouses, and barracks. It was commonly known that if you wanted to take over a country, you had to take over the castles so your enemy couldn't stockpile soldiers and resources to make a counterstrike when you least expected it. Some conquerors made a habit of targeting castles, taking them over and then razing them, in order to eliminate the enemy's ability to fight back. Other conquerors felt compelled to build castles every few miles as guard towers or, more likely, as symbols of their newfound authority. In a way, the castle was the new "high ground." In battles of old, the army that held the high ground had the advantage because its opponents would tire themselves out running uphill just to engage, while the high ground holders could pepper them with rocks, arrows, and other airborne weapons. Walled cities were certainly popular as defensible positions throughout history, but they weren't as easy to create as castles were and they couldn't be as easily defended. By building castles, the people of these periods changed the landscape in their favor, in effect creating a huge advantage where none had been before.

This was perhaps the way that the landscapes of the world changed the most—the way that people changed it. Where broad plains had been before, towns and villages, castles and fortifications, and ports and trade centers dotted the landscape. Despite such episodes as the devastating Black Plague and a seemingly endless series of wars, the populations of the world continued to expand, with people always seeking to expand their living spaces. More people meant not only more living space, but also more demand for basic and exotic goods. As civilization spread outward from its beginnings in the Fertile Crescent, ancient Africa, and along the rivers Indus and Yangtze, the needs and signatures of mankind spread with it.

Skill 33.3   Demonstrating knowledge of major issues, people, events, and cause-and-effect relationships in historical periods of the world, their influence on the present, and how they affect planning for the future

Historic causation is the concept that events in history are linked to one another by an endless chain of cause and effect. The root causes of major historical events cannot always be seen immediately, and are only apparent when looking back from many years later.

In some cases, individual events can have an immediate, clear effect. In 1941, Europe was embroiled in war. On the Pacific Rim, Japan was engaged in military occupation of Korea and other Asian countries. The United States took a position of isolation, choosing not to become directly involved with the conflicts. This position changed rapidly, however, on the morning of December 7, 1941, when Japanese forces launched a surprise attack on a US naval base at Pearl Harbor in Hawaii. The United States immediately declared war on Japan, and became involved in Europe shortly afterwards. The entry of the United States into the Second World War undoubtedly contributed to the eventual victory of the Allied forces in Europe, and the defeat of Japan after two atomic bombs were dropped there by the US. The surprise attack on Pearl Harbor affected the outcome of the war and the shape of the modern world.

Interaction between cultures, either by exploration and migration or war, often contribute directly to major historical events, but other forces can influence the course of history, as well. Religious movements such as the rise of Catholicism in the Middle Ages created social changes throughout Europe and culminated in the Crusades and the expulsion of Muslims from Spain. Technological developments can lead to major historical events, such as the Industrial Revolution, which was driven by the replacement of water power with steam.

Social movements can also cause major historical shifts. Between the Civil War and the early 1960s in the United States, racial segregation was practiced legally in many parts of the country through "Jim Crow" laws. Demonstrations and activism opposing segregation began to escalate during the late 1950s and early 1960s, eventually leading to the passage in the US Congress of the Civil Rights Act of 1964, which ended legal segregation in the United States.

The **Agricultural Revolution**, initiated by the invention of the plow, led to a thoroughgoing transformation of human society by making large-scale agricultural production possible and facilitating the development of agrarian societies. During the period during which the plow was invented, the wheel, numbers, and writing were also invented. Coinciding with the shift from hunting wild game to the domestication of animals, this period was one of dramatic social and economic change.

The **Scientific Revolution** and the Enlightenment were two of the most important movements in the history of civilization, resulting in a new sense of self-examination and a wider view of the world than ever before. The Scientific Revolution was, above all, a shift in focus from belief to evidence. Scientists and philosophers wanted to see the proof, not just believe what other people told them. It was an exciting time, if you were a forward-looking thinker.

The **Industrial Revolution** of the eighteenth and nineteenth centuries resulted in even greater changes in human civilization and even greater opportunities for trade, increased production, and the exchange of ideas and knowledge. The first phase of the Industrial Revolution (1750-1830) saw the mechanization of the textile industry, vast improvements in mining, with the invention of the steam engine, and numerous improvements in transportation, with the development and improvement of turnpikes, canals, and the invention of the railroad.

The Information Revolution refers to the sweeping changes during the latter half of the twentieth century as a result of technological advances and a new respect for the knowledge or information provided by trained, skilled and experienced professionals in a variety of fields. This approach to understanding a number of social and economic changes in global society arose from the ability to make computer technology both accessible and affordable. In particular, the development of the computer chip has led to such technological advances as the Internet, the cell phone, Cybernetics, wireless communication, and the related ability to disseminate and access a massive amount of information quite readily.

During the twentieth century, the world witnessed unprecedented strides in communications, a major expansion of international trade, and significant international diplomatic and military activity, including two world wars.

The rise of **nationalism** in Europe at the end of the nineteenth century led to a series of alliances and agreements among European nations. These agreements eventually led to the First World War, as nations called on their military allies to provide assistance and defense.

A new model of international relations was proposed following the devastation of WWI, one based on the mission to preserve peace. The **League of Nations** was formed to promote this peace, but it ultimately failed, having no way to enforce its resolutions. When Germany, led by Adolph Hitler, rebelled against the restrictions placed on it following WWI and began a campaign of military expansion through Europe, World War II ensued. Great Britain, the United States, and other allied nations combined forces to defeat Germany and the Axis powers.

Taking a lesson from the failure of the League of Nations, the world's nations organized the **United Nations**, an international assembly given the authority to arrange and enforce international resolutions.

World War II left Europe in ruins. As a result, the United States and the Soviet Union emerged as the two major world powers. Although allies in the war, tension arose between the two powers as the United States engaged in a policy of halting the spread of communism sponsored by the Soviets and China. The United States and the Soviet Union never engaged in direct military conflict during this "**Cold War**," but they were each involved in protracted conflicts in Korea and Vietnam. The threat of nuclear war increased as each power produced more and more weapons in an extended arms race. The threat of the spread of nuclear weapons largely diminished after the fall of the Soviet Union in the early 1990s, which ended the Cold War.

In Asia, new economies matured and the formerly tightly-controlled Chinese market became more open to foreign investment, increasing China's influence as a major economic power. In Europe, the **European Union** made a bold move to a common currency, the Euro, in a successful effort to consolidate the region's economic strength. In South America, countries such as Brazil and Venezuela showed growth despite political unrest, as Argentina suffered a near complete collapse of its economy. As the technology sector expanded, so did the economy of India, where high-tech companies found a highly educated work force.

Conflict between the Muslim world and the United States increased during the last decade of the twentieth century, culminating in a terrorist attack on New York City and Washington, D.C., in 2001. These attacks, sponsored by the radical group Al-Qaeda, prompted a military invasion by the United States into Afghanistan, where the group is based. Shortly afterwards, the United States, England, and several smaller countries addressed further instability in the region by ousting Iraqi dictator Saddam Hussein in a military campaign. In the eastern Mediterranean, tension between Israelis and Palestinians continued to build, regularly erupting into violence.

Skill 33.4   Recognizing the causes and consequences of major world conflicts

Individuals and societies have divided the earth's surface through conflict for a number of reasons:

- The domination of peoples or societies, e.g., colonialism
- The control of valuable resources, e.g., oil
- The control of strategic routes, e.g., the Panama Canal

Religion, political ideology, national origin, language, and race can spur conflicts. Conflicts can result from disagreement over how land, ocean or natural resources will be developed, shared, and used. Conflicts have resulted from trade, migration, and settlement rights. Conflicts can occur between small groups of people, between cities, between nations, between religious groups, and between multi-national alliances.

Today, the world is primarily divided by political/administrative interests into state sovereignties. A particular region is recognized to be controlled by a particular government, including its territory, population and natural resources. The only area of the earth's surface that today is not defined by state or national sovereignty is Antarctica.

Alliances are developed among nations on the basis of political philosophy, economic concerns, cultural similarities, religious interests, or for military defense. Some of the most notable alliances today are:

- The United Nations
- The North Atlantic Treaty Organization
- The Caribbean Community
- The Common Market
- The Council of Arab Economic Unity
- The European Union

Large companies and multi-national corporations also compete for control of natural resources for manufacturing, development, and distribution.

Throughout human history there have been conflicts on virtually every scale over the right to divide the Earth according to differing perceptions, needs and values. These conflicts have ranged from tribal conflicts to urban riots, to civil wars, to regional wars, to world wars. While these conflicts have traditionally centered on control of land surfaces, new disputes are beginning to arise over the resources of the oceans and space.

On smaller scales, conflicts have created divisions between rival gangs, use zones in cities, water supply, school districts; economic divisions include franchise areas and trade zones.

Skill 33.5   Analyzing various perspectives and interpretations of issues and events in world history

SEE Skill 32.3

Skill 33.6   Recognizing the influence of individuals, movements, culture, cultural groups, ideas, and technology on history and social change in the world

Human characteristics of a place include the architecture, roads, patterns of settlement and land use. These characteristics can be shaped by conditions of the past that affect how humans interact with the geography of their home. The relative wealth and poverty of a person or a community can determine the type of architecture encountered, for example. A formerly poor area that finds prosperity may demolish older, less desirable buildings and replace them with newer ones. Likewise, a formerly prosperous area that falls on hard times may still be living among older buildings, lacking the resources to replace them.

Land use in the past can affect settlement patterns. Small villages often arose among open agricultural areas, and as agriculture gave way to industry, these villages emerged into towns and cities even though their original reason for existing had passed. The narrow, wandering streets of Greenwich Village in Manhattan, for instance, are remnants of the country lanes that existed before New York City expanded into the area, replacing the lanes with paved streets.

Language and religion are also human characteristics that define a place. These social aspects of a place are greatly affected by traditions of the region, but can also be influenced by other regions through colonial settlement or conquest. For example, present day Central and South America are largely Spanish-speaking and Roman Catholic, a result of the region having been conquered and colonized by Spain in the sixteenth century.

The Industrial Revolution of the eighteenth and nineteenth centuries resulted in even greater changes in human civilization and even greater opportunities for trade, increased production, and the exchange of ideas and knowledge.

The first phase of the Industrial Revolution (1750-1830) saw the mechanization of the textile industry, vast improvements in mining, with the invention of the steam engine, and numerous improvements in transportation, with the development and improvement of turnpikes, canals, and the invention of the railroad.

The second phase (1830-1910) resulted in vast improvements in a number of industries that had already been mechanized through such inventions as the Bessemer steel process and the invention of steam ships. New industries arose as a result of the new technological advances, such as photography, electricity, and chemical processes. New sources of power were harnessed and applied, including petroleum and hydroelectric power. Precision instruments were developed, and engineering was launched. It was during this second phase that the Industrial Revolution spread to other European countries, to Japan, and to the United States.

The direct results of the Industrial Revolution, particularly as they affected industry, commerce, and agriculture, included:

- Enormous increase in productivity
- Huge increase in world trade
- Specialization and division of labor
- Standardization of parts and mass production
- Growth of giant business conglomerates and monopolies
- A new revolution in agriculture facilitated by the steam engine, machinery, chemical fertilizers, processing, canning, and refrigeration

The political results included:

- Growth of complex government by technical experts
- Centralization of government, including regulatory administrative agencies
- Advantages to democratic development, including extension of franchise to the middle class, and later to all elements of the population, mass education to meet the needs of an industrial society, the development of media of public communication, including radio, television, and cheap newspapers
- Dangers to democracy included the risk of manipulation of the media of mass communication, facilitation of dictatorial centralization and totalitarian control, subordination of the legislative function to administrative directives, efforts to achieve uniformity and angles, and social depersonalization.

The economic results were numerous:

- The conflict between free trade and low tariffs and protectionism
- The issue of free enterprise against government regulation
- Struggles between labor and capital, including the trade-union movement
- The rise of socialism

- The rise of the utopian socialists
- The rise of Marxian or scientific socialism

The social results of the Industrial Revolution include:

- Increase of population, especially in industrial centers
- Advances in science applied to agriculture, sanitation and medicine
- Growth of great cities
- Disappearance of the difference between city dwellers and farmers
- Faster tempo of life and increased stress from the monotony of the work routine
- The emancipation of women
- The decline of religion
- Rise of scientific materialism
- Darwin's theory of evolution

Increased mobility produced a rapid diffusion of knowledge and ideas. Increased mobility also resulted in wide-scale immigration to industrialized countries. Cultures clashed and cultures melded.

The **microscope** first appeared about 1590, and was steadily improved upon. The microscope revealed an entire world of invisible activity by bacteria and fungus, and laid bare the cell structure of complex organisms. Advancements in microscopy led directly to important discoveries concerning germs, viruses and the cause of disease, greatly aiding the field of medicine.

Electrical power is a phenomenon that has been known for centuries, but not until the late nineteenth century had understanding and technology advanced to the point where it could be reliably produced and transmitted. The ability to transmit power by wire over distances changed the nature of industry, which previously had relied on other sources, such as steam plants or water power to move machinery.

The **Theory of Relativity** was proposed by Albert Einstein, and revolutionized physics. Einstein proposed that the measurement of time and space changed relative to the position of the observer, implying that time and space were not fixed but could warp and change. This had radical implications for Newtonian physics, as it related to gravity, and opened new fields of scientific study.

Penicillin was developed in the mid twentieth century, and rapidly became an important drug, saving countless lives. Penicillin is derived from a mold, which, it was discovered, inhibited and even killed many kinds of germs. In drug form, it could be used to fight infections of various kinds in humans. Penicillin and similarly derived drugs are called antibiotics.

The **microchip** was developed in the 1950s as a way to reduce the size of transistor-based electronic equipment. By replacing individual transistors with a single chip of semiconductor material, more capability could be included in less space. This development led directly to the microprocessor, which is at the heart of every modern computer and most modern electronic products.

The religious beliefs and institutions of a culture can greatly influence scientific research and technological innovation. Political factors have affected scientific advancement, as well, especially in cultures that partially support scientific research with public money. Warfare has traditionally been a strong driver of technological advancement as cultures strive to outpace their neighbors with better weapons and defenses. Technologies developed for military purposes often find their way into the mainstream. Significant advances in flight technology, for example, were made during the two World Wars.

Socially, many cultures have come to value innovation and welcome new products and improvements to older products. This desire to always be advancing and obtaining the latest, newest technology creates economic incentive for innovation.

The list of major social problems facing the world is long, with each culture approaching them based on their own values and beliefs. Four broad areas where social problems are affecting the world are the global economy, the environment, education, and health.

Economic - The world is becoming more global in its economy, requiring societies to adapt their production and economic strategies to suit these changing conditions. As some countries are able to capitalize on the emergence of new markets, the gap between poor countries that cannot participate is widening. Economic forces are also attracting immigrants from poorer countries to those with job opportunities, creating social stresses.

International organizations such as the U.N. and the World Bank have programs to assist developing nations with loans and education so they might join the international economy. Many countries are taking steps to regulate immigration.

Environmental - The impact a growing world population is having on the world environment is a subject of great concern and some controversy. Increased demand for food and fuel are creating environmental stresses that may have worldwide consequences.

The use of fossil fuels such as coal and natural gas, for instance, are widely thought to be contributing to the gradual warming of the planet by creating "greenhouse gases." The effects of this warming may include the rising of world sea levels and adverse changes in climate. Because oil and gas are non-renewable resources, continual exploration must take place to identify new sources. This drilling itself impacts the environment and presents potential pollution danger from pipelines and oil spills.

The international community has attempted to place limits on the production of greenhouse gases, but not all developed countries have agreed to these protocols. Many countries have placed limits on emissions from factories and automobiles in an effort to reduce the amount of pollution that enters the atmosphere. Alternative, "clean" energy resources are being researched.

Education - As the world's economy changes, educational needs change to provide a skilled workforce, and a society's ability to educate its people is crucial to participating in this economy. Likewise, educational institutions contribute to the artistic, cultural, and academic advancement of a nation.

Disparity in educational opportunities within and between nations can contribute to social and economic disparities. Failure to keep pace with international demands for certain fields of education can leave a country at a disadvantage.

Health - In most developed countries, the population is living longer and placing a higher demand on health care systems. This in turn places a burden on the larger society as taxes used to support the healthcare system rise, in the case of socialized medicine, or health insurance costs increase, as in private systems. In the U.S., people who are unemployed or otherwise unable to obtain health insurance are sometimes unable to meet the high costs of health care.

Diseases such as AIDS and other viruses are rampant in some parts of the world. Treatments can be difficult to come by either because of their high costs, or lack of organization to distribute them. International aid organizations exist to provide treatment to disease victims and to assist local governments in developing plans to reduce disease transmission.

COMPETENCY 0034   UNDERSTAND INQUIRY AND INFORMATION SKILLS IN SOCIAL STUDIES

Skill 34.1   Demonstrating knowledge of strategies for locating information from a variety of social studies resources and of creating graphic representations of textual information

SEE Skill 30.3

Skill 34.2   Identifying time, place, audience, purpose, and form of a source and distinguishing between primary and secondary sources

Primary sources include the following kinds of materials:

1. Documents that reflect the immediate and everyday concerns of people. They should be understood the context in which it was produced.
2. Do not read history blindly; but be certain that you understand both explicit and implicit referenced in the material.
3. Read the entire text you are reviewing; do not simply extract a few sentences to read.
4. Although anthologies of materials may help you identify primary source materials, the full original text should be consulted.

Secondary sources include the following kinds of materials:

- Books written on the basis of primary materials about the period of time,
- Books written on the basis of primary materials about persons who played a major role in the events under consideration,
- Books and articles written on the basis of primary materials about the culture, the social norms, the language, and the values of the period,
- Quotations from primary sources,
- Statistical data on the period,
- The conclusions and inferences of other historians, and
- Multiple interpretations of the ethos of the time.

Guidelines for the use of secondary sources:

- Do not rely upon only a single secondary source.
- Check facts and interpretations against primary sources whenever possible.
- Do not accept the conclusions of other historians uncritically.
- Place greatest reliance on secondary sources created by the best and most respected scholars.
- Do not use the inferences of other scholars as if they were facts.
- Ensure that you recognize any bias the writer brings to his/her interpretation of history.

- Understand the primary point of the book as a basis for evaluating the value of the material presented in it to your questions.

Skill 34.3   Recognizing stereotypes, clichés, bias, and propaganda techniques and distinguishing between fact and opinion

Making a decision based on a set of given information requires a careful interpretation of the information to decide the strength of the evidence supplied and what it means.

A chart showing that the number of people of foreign birth living in the U.S. has increased annually over the last ten years might allow one to make conclusions about population growth and changes in the relative sizes of ethnic groups in the U.S. The chart would not give information about the reason the number of foreign-born citizens increased, or address matters of immigration status. Conclusions in these areas would be invalid based on this information.

Analyzing an event or issue from multiple perspectives involves seeking out sources that advocate or express those perspectives, and comparing them with one another. Listening to the speeches of Martin Luther King, Jr. provides insight to the perspective of one group of people concerning the issue of civil rights in the U.S. in the 1950s and 1960s. Public statements of George Wallace, an American governor opposed to desegregation provides another perspective from the same time period. Looking at the legislation that was proposed at the time and how it came into effect offers a window into the thinking of the day.

Comparing these perspectives on the matter of civil rights provides information on the key issues that each group was concerned about, and gives a fuller picture of the societal changes that were occurring at that time. Analysis of any social event, issue, problem or phenomenon requires that various perspectives be taken into account in this way.

One way to analyze historical events, patterns and relationships is to focus on historical themes. There are many themes that run throughout human history, and they can be used to make comparisons between different historical times as well as between nations and peoples. While new themes are always being explored, a few of the widely recognized historical themes are as follows:

Politics and political institutions can provide information of prevailing opinions and beliefs of a group of people and how they change over time. Historically, Texas has produced several important political figures and was a traditional supporter of the Democratic Party for nearly a century. This has changed in recent years, with the Republican Party gaining more influence and control of Texas politics. Looking at the political history of the state can reveal the popular social ideals that have developed in Texas, and how they have changed over time.

Race is a term used most generally to describe a population of people from a common geographic area that share certain common physical traits. Skin color and facial features have traditionally been used to categorize individuals by race. The term has generated some controversy among sociologists, anthropologists and biologists as to what if anything, is meant by race and racial variation. Biologically speaking, a race consists of people who share a common genetic lineage. Socially, race can be more complicated to define, with many people identifying themselves as part of a racial group that others might not. This self-perception of race, and the perception of race by others, is perhaps more crucial than any genetic variation when trying to understand the social implications of variations in race.

An **ethnic group** is a group of people who identify themselves as having a common social background and set of behaviors, and who perpetuate their culture by traditions of marriage within their own group. Ethnic groups will often share a common language and ancestral background, and frequently exist within larger populations with which they interact. Ethnicity and race are sometimes interlinked, but differ in that many ethnic groups can exist within a population of people thought to be of the same race. Ethnicity is based more on common cultural behaviors and institutions than common physical traits.

The study of **gender** issues is a theme that focuses on the relative places men and women hold in a society, and is connected to many other themes such as politics and economics. In the United States, for many years women were not allowed to vote, for example. In economic matters, married women were expected not to hold jobs. For women who did work, a limited number of types of work were available. Investigating the historical theme of gender can reveal changes in public attitudes, economic changes and shifting political attitudes, among other things.

Economic factors drive many social activities such as where people live and work and the relative wealth of nations. As a historical theme, economic history can connect events to their economic causes and explore the results. Mexican immigration is a national political issue currently. Economic imbalances between the U.S. and Mexico are driving many Mexicans to look for work in the United States. As a border state with historic ties to Mexico, Texas receives a large number of these immigrants and has the second largest Hispanic population in the country, which plays a crucial role in Texas' current economy. The subject of immigration in Texas is an example of how the historical themes of politics, economics and race can intersect, each providing a line of historic interpretation into Texas' past.

Historical concepts are movements, belief systems or other phenomena that can be identified and examined individually or as part of a historical theme. Capitalism, communism, democracy, racism and globalization are all examples of historical concepts. Historical concepts can be interpreted as part of larger historical themes and provide insight into historical events by placing them in a larger historical context.

The historic concept of colonialism, is that a nation should seek to control areas outside of its borders for economic and political gain by establishing settlements and controlling the native inhabitants. Beginning in the seventeenth century, France and Spain were both actively colonizing North America, with the French establishing a colony at the mouth of the Mississippi River. Spain moved into the area to contain the French and keep them away from their settlements in present-day Mexico. These colonial powers eventually clashed, with Spain maintaining its hold over the region. France finally sold its holdings to the United States in the Louisiana Purchase, which positioned the U.S. at New Spain's frontier. The eighteenth and early nineteenth centuries were a time of revolutionary movements in many parts of the world. The American and French Revolutions had altered the balance of world power in the 1770s and 1780s, and by the 1820s Mexicans living under Spanish colonial control won independence and Texas became part of the new independent state of Mexico. Texas would itself declare independence from Mexico and survive as an independent country for a decade before being annexed by the United States as a state.

Skill 34.4 Demonstrating knowledge of strategies for evaluating the accuracy and reliability of information, including identifying the message and target audience of narrative documents

Reference sources can be of great value and by teaching students how to access these first, they will later have skills that will help them access more in—depth databases and sources of information.

Encyclopedias are reference materials that appear in book or electronic form and can be considered general or specific. General encyclopedias peripherally cover most fields of knowledge; specific encyclopedias cover a smaller amount of material in greater depth. Encyclopedias are good first sources of information for students. While their scope is limited, they can provide a quick introduction to topics so that students can get familiar with the topics before exploring the topics in greater depth.

Almanacs provide statistical information on various topics. Typically, these references are rather specific. They often cover a specific period of time. One famous example is the *Farmer's Almanac.* This annual publication summarizes among many other things weather conditions for the previous year among many other things.

Bibliographies contain references for further research. Bibliographies are usually organized topically. They point people to the in-depth resources they will need for a complete review of a topic.

Databases, typically electronic, are collections of material on specific topics. For example, teachers can go online and find many databases of science articles for students in a variety of topics.

The Internet and other research resources provide a wealth of information on thousands of interesting topics for students preparing presentations or projects. Using search engines like Google and Yahoo!, student can search multiple Internet resources or databases on one subject search. Students should have an outline of the purpose of a project or research presentation that includes:

- Purpose - identify the reason for the research information.
- Objective - having a clear thesis for a project will allow the students opportunities to be specific on Internet searches.
- Preparation - when using resources or collecting data, students should create folders for sorting through the information. Providing labels for the folders will create a system of organization that will make construction of the final project or presentation easier and less time consuming.
- Procedure - organized folders and a procedural list of what the project or presentation needs to include will create A+ work for students and A+ grading for teachers.
- Visuals or artifacts - choose data or visuals that are specific to the subject content or presentation. Make sure that poster boards or Power Point presentations can be visually seen from all areas of the classroom. Teachers can provide laptop computers for Power Point presentations.

When a teacher models and instructs students in the proper use of search techniques, the teacher can minimize wasted time in preparing projects and wasted paper from students who print every search. In some school districts, students are allowed a minimum number of printed pages per week. Since students have Internet accounts for computer usage, the monitoring of printing is easily done by the school's librarian and teachers in classrooms.

Having the school's librarian or technology expert as a guest speaker in classrooms provides another method of sharing and modeling proper presentation preparation using technology. Teachers can also appoint technology experts from the students in a classroom to work with students on projects and presentations. In high schools, technology classes provide students with upper-class teacher assistants who fill the role of technology assistants.

Internet usage agreements define a number of criteria of technology use that a students must agree to in order to have access to school computers. Students must exercise responsibility and accountability in adhering to technology usage during the school day. Students who violate any parts of the computer usage agreement are subject to have all access to school computers or other educational technology denied or blocked, which, for the student needing to print a paper using the school computer and printer, could make the difference in handing assignments in on time or receiving a lower grade for late assignments.

Atlases are visual representations of geographic areas. Often they serve different functions. Some atlases demonstrate geologic attributes, while others emphasize populations of various areas.

An **atlas** is a collection of maps usually bound into a book and contain geographic features, political boundaries, and perhaps social, religious and economic statistics. Atlases can be found at most libraries but they are widely available on the Internet. The United States Library of Congress holds more than 53,000 atlases, most likely the largest and most comprehensive collection in the world.

Finally, periodical guides categorize articles and special editions of journals and magazines to help archive and organize the vast amount of material that is put in periodicals each year.

Statistical **surveys** are used in social sciences to collect information on a sample of the population. With any kind of information, care must be taken to accurately record information so the results are not skewed or distorted.

Opinion Polls are used to represent the opinions of a population by asking a number of people a series of questions about a product, place, person, event or perhaps the president and then using the results to apply the answers to a larger group or population. Polls, like surveys are subject to errors in the process. Errors can occur based on who is asked the question, where they are asked, the time of day or the biases one may hold in relevance to the poll being taken.

DOMAIN V.   **THE ARTS**

COMPETENCY 0035   UNDERSTAND THE CONCEPTS, TECHNIQUES, MATERIALS, FUNCTIONS, AND PROCESSES OF MUSIC AND THE VISUAL ARTS.

Skill 35.1   Demonstrating knowledge of basic elements, techniques, concepts, skills, and foundations in music and basic elements, principles of design, concepts, and skills in the visual arts

Basics in Music   ☆ *what is a rest?*

Melody, harmony, rhythm, timbre, dynamics and texture are some of the basic components of music.

Melody is the tune – a specific arrangement of sounds in a pleasing pattern. Melody is often seen as the horizontal aspect of music, because melodic notes on a page travel along horizontally.

Harmony refers to the vertical aspect of music, or the musical chords related to a melody. So, when looking at a piece of music, the harmony notes are the ones lined up below each note of the melody, providing a more complex, fuller sound to a piece of music.

Rhythm refers to the duration of musical notes. Rhythms are patterns of long and short music note durations. A clear way to describe rhythm to young students is through percussion instruments. A teacher creates a rhythmic pattern of long and short drum beats and asks the students to repeat the rhythm.

Timbre is the quality of a sound. If a clarinet and a trumpet play the same exact note, they will still have a different timbre, or unique quality of sound. You can also describe different timbres using the same instrument. You may have two singers, but one has a harsh timbre and the other has a warm or soothing timbre to their voice. Timbre is subjective and lends itself to a number of creative exercises for early childhood students to describe what they hear in terms of the timbre of the sound.

Dynamics refer to the loudness or softness of music. Early Childhood students should develop a basic understanding of music vocabulary for dynamics. Piano describes soft music. Forte describes loud music. Pianissimo is very soft music. Double Forte refers to very loud music. Mezzo piano is kind of soft, while mezzo forte is kind of loud. These definitions can be organized on a continuum of soft to loud, with music examples for each.

Texture in music usually refers to the number of separate components making up the whole of a piece. A monophonic texture is a single melody line, such as a voice singing a tune. Polyphonic texture denotes two or more music lines playing at the same time. A single melodic line with harmonic accompaniment is called homophonic texture.

Music is an integral part of dance and is also often included in dramatic productions, either as background or as a central element in the story. Music is a terrific historian, as well, and much may be learned of cultures by listening to their popular music. American history is charted by the styles of music brought to the United States and then combined into new musical forms as people from different countries and cultures learn to live together.

Basics for Visual Arts

Students should have an early introduction to the principles of visual art and should become familiar with the basic level of the following terms:

abstract
an image that reduces a subject to its essential visual elements, such as lines, shapes, and colors.

background
portions or areas of composition that are behind the primary or dominant subject matter or design areas

balance
the arrangement of one or more elements in a work of art so that they appear symmetrical or asymmetrical in design and proportion

contrast
juxtaposing one or more elements in opposition, to show their differences

emphasis
making one or more elements in a work of art stand out in such a way as to appear more important or significant

sketch
an image-development strategy; a preliminary drawing

texture
the way something feels by representation of the tactile character of surfaces

unity
the arrangement of one or more of the elements used to create a coherence of parts and a feeling of completeness or wholeness

After learning the above terms and how they relate to the use of line, color, value, space, texture and shape, an excellent opportunity is to have students create an "art sample book." Such books could include a variety of materials that would serve as examples, such as sandpaper and cotton balls to represent texture elements. Samples of square pieces of construction paper designed into various shapes could represent shape. String samples could represent the element of lines.

The sampling of art should also focus clearly on colors necessary for the early childhood student. Color can be introduced more in-depth when discussing **intensity**, the strength of the color, and **value**, the lightness or darkness of the colors. Another valuable tool regarding color is the use of a color wheel, and allowing students to experiment with the mixing of colors to create their own art experience.

It is vital that students learn to identify characteristics of visual arts that include materials, techniques and processes necessary to establish a connection between art and daily life. Early ages should begin to experience art in a variety of forms. It is important to reach many areas at an early age to establish a strong artistic foundation for young students. Students should be introduced to the simple recognition of simple patterns found in the art environment. They must also identify art materials such as clay, paint and crayons. Each of these types of material should be introduced and explained for use in daily lessons with young children.

Skill 35.2 Recognizing types and characteristics of musical instruments, including the human voice, and methods, processes, and philosophies of creating music

Vocal music is probably the oldest form of music, since it does not require any instrument besides the human voice. Unaccompanied music is referred to as acappella. The human voice consists of sound made by using the vocal folds (vocal chords) used for talking. The vocal folds, in combination with the lips, the tongue, the lower jaw, and the palate, are capable of producing highly intricate sound. The tone (i.e., pitch, intensity, and modulation) of voice may be modified to suggest various emotions, such as happiness and sadness. Tone quality is the quality of a note or sound that distinguishes different types of musical instruments. Tone quality is what people use to distinguish the saxaphone from a trumpet, even when both instruments are playing notes at the same pitch.

Vocalists use the human voice as an instrument to create music and is complex. The vocal folds can loosen, tighten, or change their thickness, transferring breath at various pressures. The position of the tongue and tightening of the muscles in the neck can result in changes of pitch and volume. Breath control, tone, and posture all require different techniques.

Breathing technique is very important for proper voice projection. To talk we use air from the top of the lungs and the muscles from the back of the throat. To properly project our voices, we pull air from the bottom of the lungs, and the diaphragm (or stomach area) is used to push it out. Finding ways to exercise and lift the diaphragm such as singing musical scales can help singers reach higher or lower notes. Stance is also important. It is recommended to stand up straight with your feet shoulder width apart, and your foot slightly forward. This improves your balance. This also improves your breathing.

Types of Musical Instruments

Instruments are categorized by the mechanism that creates its sound. Musical instruments can be divided into four basic categories.

1. String
2. Percussion
3. Brass
4. Wind

String Instruments

String instruments all make their sounds through strings. The sound of the instrument depends on the thickness and length of the strings. The slower a string vibrates, the lower the resulting pitch. Also, the way the strings are manipulated varies among string instruments. Some strings are plucked (e.g., guitar) while others use a bow to cause the strings to vibrate (e.g., violin). Some are even connected to keys (e.g., piano). Other common string instruments include the viola, double bass, cello and piano.

Wind Instruments

The sound of wind instruments is caused by wind vibrating in a pipe or tube. Air blows into one end of the instrument, and in many wind instruments, air passes over a reed which causes the air to vibrate. The pitch depends on the air's frequency as it passes through the tube, and the frequency depends on the tube's length or size. Larger tubes create deeper sounds in a wind instrument. The pitch is also controlled by holes or values. As fingers cover the holes or press the valve, the pitch changes for the notes the musician intends. Other common wind instruments include pipe organ, oboe, clarinet and saxophone.

Brass Instruments

Brass instruments are similar to wind instruments since music from brass instruments also results from air passing through an air chamber. They are called brass instruments, however, because they are made from metal or brass. Pitch on a brass instrument is controlled by the size or length of the air chamber. Many brass instruments are twisted or coiled which lengthens the air chamber without making the instrument unmanageably long. Like wind instruments, larger air chambers create deeper sounds, and the pitch can be controlled by valves on the instrument. In addition, some brass instruments also control the pitch by the musician's mouth position on the mouthpiece. Common brass instruments include the French horn, trumpet, trombone and tuba.

Percussion Instruments

To play a percussion instrument, the musician hits or shakes the instrument. The sound is created from sound vibrations as a result of shaking or striking the instrument. Many materials, such as metal or wood, are used to create percussion instruments, and different thicknesses or sizes of the material help control the sound. Thicker or heavier materials like drum membranes make deeper sounds, while thinner, metal materials (e.g., triangle) make higher-pitched sounds. Other common percussion instruments include the cymbals, tambourine, bells, xylophone and wood block.

Skill 35.3 **Recognizing types and characteristics of materials, tools, techniques, methods, and processes used to create a variety of visual arts (e.g., painting, drawing, sculpting)**

Young students may need to be introduced to items that are developmentally appropriate for their age and for their fine motor skills. Many Pre-Kindergarten and Kindergarten students use oversized pencils and crayons for the first semester. Typically, after this first semester, development occurs to enable children to gradually develop into using smaller sized materials.

Students should begin to explore artistic expression at this age using colors and mixing. The color wheel is a vital lesson for young children and students begin to learn the uses of primary colors and secondary colors. By the middle of the school year students should be able to explain this process. For example, a student needs orange paint, but only has a few colors. Students should be able to determine that by mixing red and yellow that orange is created.

Teachers should begin to plan and use variation using line, shape, texture and many different principles of design. By using common environmental figures such as people, animals and buildings teachers can base many art lessons on characteristics of readily available examples. Students should be introduced to as many techniques as possible to ensure that all strands of the visual arts and materials are experienced at a variety of levels.

By using original works of arts students should be able to identify visual and actual textures of art and based their judgments of objects found in everyday scenes. Other examples that can be described as subjects could include landscapes, portraits and still life.

The major areas that young students should experience should include the following:

1. Painting-using tempra or watercolors.
2. Sculpture-typically using clay or play-dough.
3. Architecture-building or structuring design using 3D materials such as cardboard and poster board to create a desired effect.
4. Ceramics- another term for pottery using a hollow clay sculpture and pots made from clay and fired in a kiln using high temperature to strengthen them.
5. Metalworking-another term for engraving or cutting design or letters into metal with a sharp tool printmaking.
6. Lithography is an example of planographics, where a design is drawn on a surface and then the print is lifted from the surface.

Skill 35.4   Recognizing methods and processes of creating, performing, and responding to music and to the visual arts

The process of creating art is a discovery process. As soon as early childhood, students are exposed to the basic elements of the arts, the process of discovery begins. As students increase their knowledge base, they question their basic assumptions, and the creative process evolves with each new creation. Fingers and toes are added to stick figures; what once was a melody, now also includes harmony; basic movements are coordinated into a dance combination; pretending to be an old woman evolves to a storytelling piece about an old woman who lives in a house by the sea and makes dolls for little children. Students begin to use the arts as a language to reflect on the world as they see it.

The process of performing is slightly different. The performer may not be the original creator. For instance, a singer may be performing a song written by Mozart hundreds of years ago. Dancers perform a piece created and choreographed by their teacher. Performers must understand the intent of the original creator. This means researching the history of performance techniques from the period in which the artwork was originally performed, or it may require careful study of the notes of the author. A performer understands that he or she is only a vessel bringing someone else's creation to light.

Creating, performing and responding are three points of an artistic triangle, which flow from one to the other. The artist creates, the performer brings the creation to an audience, and the audience responds, giving the feedback to the creator and commenting on what that particular work of art means to them.

Music

Core skills such as reading and writing music notation; composing, arranging and improvising music are continuously improved and complimented by other musical activities and information. Students become part of the musical process by ascertaining the natural evolution of their capabilities by the experience the teacher provides.

The increase of substance in the students' performance, both instrumental and vocal, is connected to the context provided by the teacher. Relating the students' musical inclinations to a working context of existing and current musical production creates a viable pathway for motivation and progress.

Amplifying the context in which music is performed through exercises and analysis that is grounded through knowledge of the historical and cultural context; aesthetic value; connections, relationships and applications of music lends the broad appreciation that is intrinsic in successfully interpreting the performer's role. Success in the music industry is appreciated according to the knowledge absorbed about the function of music in the social and cultural environment.

Visual Arts

Western Principles of design in western art include the following:

1) Unity
2) Balance
3) Center of Interest
4) Movement
5) Repetition
6) Variation
7) Rhythm
8) Contrast
9) Space
10) Tension

These principles are apparent in artistic works throughout all historical time periods, although emphasis may shift from period to period, or from location to location, or from artist to artist.

There are different types of visual balance and artists use these types to create art work that convey a particular message or idea to a view. Balance is a fundamental of design seen as a visual weight and counterweight. That is apparent in a single image or in the organization of images and objects in a composition. Examples of balance are:

- **Symmetrical Balance** - The same objects or arrangement are on both sides.
- **Asymmetrical Balance** - Objects or arrangements on are on different sides.
- **Radial Balance** - The axis design or pattern appear to radiate from the center axis.
- **Horizontal Balance** - Works which utilize the picture plane from left to right.

Lines are the marks left by the painting tools that define the edges of objects in artwork. Their shape and thickness may express movement or tone. Texture in a painting is the "feel" of the canvas based on the paint used and its method of application. There are two forms of texture in painting, visual and tactile. Because texture uses two different senses it is a unique element of art.

Color refers to the hue (e.g., red vs. orange) and intensity or brightness (e.g., neon-green vs. yellow-green) of the colors used. Shapes are formed from the meeting of lines and the enclosing of areas in a two-dimensional space.

Students are expected to fine tune observation skills and be able to identify and recreate the experiences that teachers provide for them as learning tools. For example, students may walk as a group on a nature hike taking in the surrounding elements and then begin to discuss the repetition found in the leaves of trees, or the bricks of the sidewalk, or the size and shapes of the buildings and how they may relate. They may also use such an experience to describe lines, colors, shapes, forms and textures. Beginning elements of perspective are noticed at an early age. The questions of why buildings look smaller when they are at a far distance and bigger when they are closer are sure to spark the imagination of early childhood students. Students can then take their inquiry to higher level of learning with some hands-on activities such as building three dimensional buildings and construction using paper and geometric shapes. Eventually students should acquire higher level thinking skills such as analysis, in which they will begin to question artists, art work, and analyze many different aspects of visual art.

An excellent opportunity is to have students create an "art sample book." Such books could include a variety of materials that would serve as examples, such as sandpaper and cotton balls to represent texture elements. Samples of square pieces of construction paper designed into various shapes could represent shape. String samples could represent the element of lines.

The sampling of art should also focus clearly on colors necessary for the early childhood student. Color can be introduced more in-depth when discussing **intensity**, the strength of the color, and **value**, the lightness or darkness of the colors. Another valuable tool regarding color is the use of a color wheel, and allowing students to experiment with the mixing of colors to create their own art experience.

Skill 35.5 **Demonstrating knowledge of how music and the visual arts are used to communicate and to express ideas and feelings for specific purposes and of how aesthetic and cultural diversity are reflected in music and in the visual arts**

Music and the visual arts have always been part of world cultures and are a way of illustrating the diversity that exists between cultures. People create music and visual arts for different purposes – one of which is for enjoyment and beauty. In many cultures music is a way of telling stories through song, such as in ballads. Visual art helps to portray pictures of daily life and to provide a sense of the people who make up a culture.

Visual arts provide historical proof of various cultures. Andy Warhol's Campbell's Soup Can of the sixties is a comment on American society and a glimpse of life at the time in the United States. Prehistoric Venus figurines combine art and religion and show us about the beliefs of a particular culture. Visual art is also used to enhance and strengthen music, dance and drama, by providing a beautiful backdrop or aesthetic surroundings to portray a specific time or place.

When we listen to certain music styles, they often connect us to a memory, a time in the past, or even an entire historical period. Very often, classical pieces, such as Bach or Beethoven, create a picture in our minds of the Baroque Period. The historical perspective of music can deepen one's musical understanding.

Throughout history, different cultures have developed different styles of music. Most of the written records of music developed from Western civilization.

Music styles varied across cultures as periods in history. As in the opening discussion, classical music, although still popular and being created today, is often associated with traditional classical periods in history such as the Renaissance.

As world contact merged more and more as civilizations developed and prospered, more and more influence from various cultural styles emerged across music styles. For example, African drums emerged in some Contemporary and Hip Hop music. Also, the Bluegrass music in the United States developed from the "melting pot" contributions from Irish, Scottish, German and African-American instrumental and vocal traditions.

In addition, the purposes for music changed throughout cultures and times. Music has been used for entertainment, but also for propaganda, worship, ceremonies, and communication.

Call-and-response songs are a form of verbal and non-verbal interaction between a speaker and a listener, in which statements by a speaker are responded to by a listener. In West African cultures, call-and-response songs were used in religious rituals, gatherings, and are now used in other forms such as gospel, blues, and jazz as a form of musical expression. In certain Native American tribes, call-and-response songs are used to preserve and protect the tribe's cultural heritage and can be seen and heard at modern-day "pow-wows". The men would begin the song as the speaker with singing and drumming, and the women would respond with singing and dancing.

A ballad is a song that contains a story. Instrumental music forms a part of folk music, especially dance traditions. Much folk music is vocal, since the instrument (the voice) that makes such music is usually handy. As such, most folk music has lyrics and is descriptive about something. Any story form can be a ballad, such as fairy tales or historical accounts. It usually has simple repeating rhymes and often contains a refrain (or repeating section) that is played or sung at regular intervals throughout. Ballads could be called hymns when they are based on religious themes. In the 20th century, "ballad" took on the meaning of a popular song "especially of a romantic or sentimental nature".

Folk music is music that has endured and been passed down by oral tradition and emerges spontaneously from ordinary people. In early societies, it arose in areas that were not yet affected by mass communication. It was normally shared by the entire community and was transmitted by word of mouth. A folk song is usually seen as an expression of a way of life now past or about to disappear. In the 1960's, folk songs were sung as a way of protest.

The work song is typically a song sung a cappella by people working on a physical and, often, repetitive task. It was probably intended to reduce feelings of boredom. Rhythms of work songs also serve to synchronize physical movement in a gang or the movement in marching. Frequently, the verses of work songs are improvised and sung differently each time. Examples of work songs could be heard from slaves working in the field, prisoners on chain gangs, and soldiers in the military.

The Visual Arts curriculum consists of six main strands, each of which represents a way in which students can explore their own creative talents as well as that of others. These strands are:

- drawing
- painting and coloring
- printmaking
- working with clay
- constructing
- working with fabric and fibre

As students view works of art by famous artists throughout history they can gain a sense of time and space. They will be able to see how art has developed over time and the differences between artists of different periods.

Young students draw and color pictures to represent the world around them, and mainly concentrate on drawing their families and friends. They are also introduced to pictures in books and use visual art to represent their thoughts and feelings about what they read.

Skill 35.6   **Recognizing vocal and instrumental musical styles and visual arts styles and achievements from various artists, cultures, and periods of history and how music and the visual arts shape and reflect culture and history**

Music

Music is a form of art that involves organized and audible sounds (notes) and silence (rests). It is normally expressed in terms of pitch, rhythm and tone. Musical style is the basic musical language. A musical genre is a collection of music that shares a style.

Classical music is a class of music covering compositions and performances by professionally trained artists. Classical music is written traditionally. It is composed and written using music notation (see Skill VOID #12), and as a rule is performed exactly as written. Classical music often refers to instrumental music in general, although opera is also considered classical.

Jazz is a form of music that grew out of a combination of folk music, ragtime, and band music. It has been called the first native art form to develop in the United States. The music has gone through a series of developments since its inception. In rough chronological order they are: Dixieland, swing, big band, bebop, cool jazz, and smooth jazz.

☆ where did reggae & calypso originate

Blues is a vocal and instrumental music form which came from West African spirituals, work songs, and chants. This musical form has been a major influence on later American popular music, finding expression in jazz, rock and roll, and country music. Due to its powerful influence that originated from America, blues can be regarded as the root of pop as well as American music. Elvis Presley and Eric Clapton feel they found their niche in the music industry from their predecessors in the blues industry.

Rock and roll, in its broadest sense, can refer to almost all pop music recorded since the early 1950's. Its main features include an emphasis on rhythm, and the use of percussion and amplified instruments like the bass and guitar. Elvis Presley in the 1950's shocked the nation with his rhythm and gyrating hips in what was the early stages of rock and roll. Starting the mid-1960s, a group of British bands, sometime referred to as the British Invasion, formed folk rock, as well as a variety of less-popular genres. The British Invasion evolved into psychedelic rock, which in turn gave birth to jam bands and progressive rock.

The resources available to man to make music has varied throughout different ages and eras and has given the chance for a musical style or type to be created or invented due to diverse factors. Social changes, cultural features and historical purpose have all shared a part in giving birth to a multitude of different musical forms in every part of the earth.

Music can be traced to the people who created it by the instruments, melodies, rhythms and records of performance (songs) that are composed in human communities. Starting from early musical developments, as far back as nomadic cave dwellers playing the flute and beating on hand drums, to the different electric instruments and recording technology of the modern music industry, the style and type music produced has been closely related to the human beings who choose it for their particular lifestyle and way of existence.

Western music, rising chiefly from the fusion of classical and folkloric forms, has always been the pocket of a large variety of instruments and music generating new techniques to fit the change in expression provided by the expansion of its possibilities. Instruments such as the piano and the organ; stringed instruments like the violin, viola, cello, guitar and bass; wind instruments like the flute, saxophone, trumpet, trombone, tuba and saxophone; electronic instruments like the synthesizer and electric guitar have all provided for the invention of new styles and types of music created and used by different people in different times and places.

The rites of Christianity during the early middle ages were the focus of social and cultural aspiration and became a natural meeting place for communities to come together consistently for the purpose of experiencing God, through preaching and music. Composers and performers fulfilled their roles with sacred music with Gregorian chants and Oratorios. The art patron's court in the 15th and 14th centuries; the opera house of the 19th century satisfied the need of nascent, progressive society looking to experience grander and more satisfying music. New forms were generated such as the *concerto*, *symphony*, *sonata* and *string quartet* that employed a zeal and zest for creation typical of the burgeoning intellect at the end of the middle ages and the beginning of modern society.

Traditional types and styles of music in America, India, China, throughout the Middle East and Africa, using a contrasting variety of stringed instruments and percussion to typical Western instruments, began a long and exciting merging to the Western musical world with the beginning of widespread colonialism and the eventual integration it would achieve between disparate cultures. Western musical instruments were adopted to play the traditional musical styles of different cultures. Blues music, arising from the southern black community in the United States would morph into *Rock n' Roll* and *Hip Hop*, alongside the progression of the traditional folk music of European settlers. Hispanic music would come about by Western musical instruments being imbued with African rhythms throughout the Caribbean in different forms like *Salsa*, *Merengue*, *Cumbia* and *Son Cubano*.

Below is a list of some of the most common categories of musical styles.

Common Musical Styles

Medieval
Classical Music (loosely encompassing Renaissance and Baroque)
Gospel Music
Jazz
Latin Music
Rhythm and Blues
Funk
Rock
Country
Folk
Bluegrass
Electronic (Techno)
Melodic
Island (Ska, Reggae and other)
Hip Hop
Pop
African
Contemporary

Visual Arts

The greatest works in art, literature, music, theater, and dance, all mirror universal themes. Universal themes are themes which reflect the human experience, regardless of time period, location, or socio-economic standing. Universal themes tend to fall into broad categories, such as Man vs. Society, Man vs. Himself, Man vs. God, Man vs. Nature, and Good vs. Evil, to name the most obvious. The general themes listed below all fall into one of these broad categories.

Prehistoric Arts, (circa 1,000,000-circa 8,000 B.C)
Major themes of this vast period appear to center around religious fertility rites and sympathetic magic, consisting of imagery of pregnant animals and faceless, pregnant women.

Mesopotamian Arts, (circa 8,000-400 B.C.)
The prayer statues and cult deities of the period point to the theme of polytheism in religious worship.

Egyptian Arts, (circa 3,000-100 B.C.)
The predominance of funerary art from ancient Egypt illustrates the theme of preparation for the afterlife and polytheistic worship. Another dominant theme, reflected by artistic convention, is the divinity of the pharaohs. In architecture, the themes were monumentality and adherence to ritual.

Greek Arts, (800-100 B.C.)
The sculpture of ancient Greece is replete with human figures, most nude and some draped. Most of these sculptures represent athletes and various gods and goddesses. The predominant theme is that of the ideal human, in both mind and body. In architecture, the theme was scale based on the ideal human proportions.

Roman Arts, (circa 480 B.C.- 476 A.D.)
Judging from Roman arts, the predominant themes of the period deal with the realistic depiction of human beings, and how they relate to Greek classical ideals. The emphasis is on practical realism. Another major theme is the glory in serving the Roman state. In architecture, the theme was rugged practicality mixed with Greek proportions and elements.

Middle Ages Arts, (300-1400 A.D.)
Although the time span is expansive, the major themes remain relatively constant. Since the Roman Catholic Church was the primary patron of the arts, most work was religious in nature. The purpose of much of the art was to educate. Specific themes varied from the illustration of Bible stories to interpretations of theological allegory, to lives of the saints, to consequences of good and evil. Depictions of the Holy Family were popular. Themes found in secular art and literature centered around chivalric love and warfare. In architecture, the theme was glorification of God, and education of congregation to religious principles.

Renaissance Arts, (circa 1400-1630 A.D.)
Renaissance themes include Christian religious depiction (see Middle Ages), but tend to reflect a renewed interest in all things classical. Specific themes include Greek and Roman mythological and philosophic figures, ancient battles and legends. Dominant themes mirror the philosophic beliefs of Humanism, emphasizing individuality and human reason, such as those of the High Renaissance which center around the psychological attributes of individuals. In architecture, the theme was scale based on human proportions.

Baroque Arts, (1630-1700 A.D.)
The predominant themes found in the arts of the Baroque period include the dramatic climaxes of well-known stories, legends and battles, and the grand spectacle of mythology. Religious themes are found frequently, but it is drama and insight that are emphasized and not the medieval "salvation factor". Baroque artists and authors incorporated various types of characters into their works, careful to include minute details. Portraiture focused on the psychology of the sitters. In architecture, the theme was large scale grandeur and splendor.

Eighteenth Century Arts, (1700-1800 A.D.)
Rococo themes of this century focused on religion, light mythology, portraiture of aristocrats, pleasure and escapism, and occasionally, satire. In architecture, the theme was artifice and gaiety, combined with an organic quality of form. Neo-classical themes centered on examples of virtue and heroism, usually in classical settings and historical stories. In architecture, classical simplicity and utility of design was regained.

Nineteenth Century Arts, (1800-1900 A.D.)
Romantic themes include human freedom, equality, and civil rights, a love for nature, and a tendency toward the melancholic and mystic. The underlying theme is that the most important discoveries are made within the self, and not in the exterior world. In architecture, the theme was fantasy and whimsy, known as "picturesque". Realistic themes included social awareness, and a focus on society victimizing individuals. The themes behind Impressionism were the constant flux of the universe and the immediacy of the moment. In architecture, the themes were strength, simplicity, and upward thrust as skyscrapers entered the scene.

Twentieth Century Arts, (1900-2000 A.D.)
Diverse artistic themes of the century reflect a parting with traditional religious values, and a painful awareness of man's inhumanity to man. Themes also illustrate a growing reliance on science, while simultaneously expressing disillusionment with man's failure to adequately control science. A constant theme is the quest for originality and self-expression, while seeking to express the universal in human experience. In architecture, "form follows function".

Genres By Historical Periods

Ancient Greek Art, (circa 800-323 B.C.)
Dominant genres from this period were vase paintings, both black-figure and red-figure, and classical sculpture.

Roman Art, (circa 480 B.C.- 476 A.D.)
Major genres from the Romans include frescoes (murals done in fresh plaster to affix the paint), classical sculpture, funerary art, state propaganda art, and relief work on cameos.

Middle Ages Art, (circa 300-1400 A.D.)
Significant genres during the Middle Ages include Byzantine mosaics, illuminated manuscripts, ivory relief, altarpieces, cathedral sculpture, and fresco paintings in various styles.

Renaissance Art, (1400-1630 A.D.)
Important genres from the Renaissance included Florentine fresco painting (mostly religious), High Renaissance painting and sculpture, Northern oil painting, Flemish miniature painting, and Northern printmaking.

Baroque Art, (1630-1700 A.D.)
Pivotal genres during the Baroque era include Mannerism, Italian Baroque painting and sculpture, Spanish Baroque, Flemish Baroque, and Dutch portraiture. Genre paintings in still-life and landscape appear prominently in this period.

Eighteenth Century Art, (1700-1800 A.D.)
Predominant genres of the century include Rococo painting, portraiture, social satire, Romantic painting, and Neoclassic painting and sculpture.

Nineteenth Century Art, (1800-1900 A.D.)
Important genres include Romantic painting, academic painting and sculpture, landscape painting of many varieties, realistic painting of many varieties, impressionism, and many varieties of post-impressionism.

Twentieth Century Art, (1900-2000 A.D.)
Major genres of the twentieth century include symbolism, art nouveau, fauvism, expressionism, cubism (both analytical and synthetic), futurism, non-objective art, abstract art, surrealism, social realism, constructivism in sculpture, Pop and Op art, and conceptual art.

Skill 35.7   Demonstrating knowledge of how music and the visual arts make connections within and across the arts and to other disciplines, life, cultures, and work

The evolution of how and why artworks are created is complicated, but in general historical terms; arts were originally part of religious ritual. Early religious artworks are evident in the cave drawings from the Paleolithic Era in Chauvet-Pont-d'Arc in France.

As time progressed, dance, theatre, music and visual arts were used to commemorate events, such as the ordination of a king. George F. Handel composed four coronation anthems in 1727 for the coronation of King George II, and these anthems are still widely performed today.

Courtly dances of the Renaissance period were an art form that reflected values in society and provided entertainment and romance. This example of the arts combined dance and music.

The arts are often used to record or comment on a time in history. We receive much of our knowledge of history from surviving artworks. The portrait "American Gothic," by Grant Wood, is one of the most familiar depictions of American regionalism from the 1930s. The musical "South Pacific" by Rogers & Hammerstein, written in 1949, depicts life in the U.S. Navy during World War II. Theatre often combines all of the arts into one performance. Music, dance, drama and the visual arts in the backdrops and scenery come together into one experience in American Musical Theatre.

Additionally, the arts provide social commentary, tell a story or convey intense emotion. Artworks are also created simply to provide something that is pleasing to the senses. Whatever the reason why artworks are created, they have become an interpreter of the world around us. The arts provide a unique language to express individual and societal values and reflect on culture.

The process of creating art is a discovery process. As soon as early childhood students are exposed to the basic elements of the arts, the process of discovery begins. As students increase their knowledge base, they question their basic assumptions, and the creative process evolves with each new creation. Fingers and toes are added to stick figures; what once was a melody, now also includes harmony; basic movements are coordinated into a dance combination; pretending to be an old woman evolves to a storytelling piece about an old woman who lives in a house by the sea and makes dolls for little children. Students begin to use the arts as a language to reflect on the world as they see it.

Creating, performing and responding are three points of an artistic triangle, which flow from one to the other. The artist creates, the performer brings the creation to an audience, and the audience responds, giving the feedback to the creator and commenting on what that particular work of art means to them.

The arts provide essential opportunities to explore connections among all disciplines. Content areas are unique, but they share common themes and terms and ideas. Skills developed in the arts enhance learning across content areas. Conversely, increased knowledge in curriculum content areas enhance the depth of knowledge and experience in the arts.

Charles Fowler effectively argues in his book, *Strong Arts, Strong Schools: the Promising Potential and Shortsighted Disregard of the Arts in American Schooling,* that the best schools have the best arts programs. He explains that we need to utilize every possible way to represent and interpret our world, and that means combining content areas, not isolating them. Science, Math, Literature, History or the Arts by themselves only convey a part of the subject. Charles Fowler believes that integrating these programs to provide students with a more complete picture is crucial. He uses the Grand Canyon as an example. A teacher can discuss mathematically the dimensions of the Grand Canyon or the science behind how it was formed, but this lesson is taken a step further by providing examples of artistic renderings of the Grand Canyon or asking students to write a poem describing the canyon. This integration provides a more three dimensional understanding of the subject.

Using African cultural history as another example, a teacher begins with a short history lesson on select African cultures. Geography may also come into play in the lesson, as the teacher chooses a specific region, such as Senegal-Gambia in West Africa, to describe to the children what an area of Africa looks like. This may be expanded to a music lesson on African musical styles and how they influenced Western music, such as gospel, jazz, spirituals, hip hop and rap. The teacher can introduce various African instruments, and discuss what the instruments are made of and how they are played. Students will learn several drum techniques and experiment with creating their own unique drum beats. Again, at the end of this lesson students have experienced Africa through an integrated teaching approach, and they come away with a more complete understanding.

Lynn Hallie Najem provides further evidence of the importance of integrating the arts into standard curriculum in her research article, "Sure It's Fun, But Why Bother With It During the School Day? The Benefits of Using Drama with Primary Students" A copy of this article may be found on the following website: http://www.madison.k12.wi.us/ . In her research, she found that integrating the arts into primary school curriculum had a very positive effect on the self-esteem of students and opened them up to learning in all subject areas.

COMPETENCY 0036   **UNDERSTAND THE CONCEPTS, TECHNIQUES, MATERIALS, METHODS, AND PROCESSES RELATED TO DANCE AND THEATRE.**

Skill 36.1   **Demonstrating knowledge of basic elements, techniques, and principles of composition in dance**

Dance is an artistic form of self expression that uses the various elements of dance, such as use of **space**, **time**, **levels**, and **force**, to form a composition.

The primary grades have a gross understanding of their motor movements whereas older children are more apt to have a refined concept of their bodies. Individual movements are developed by the instructor when attention is given to various aspects such as:

- the range of movement or gestures through **space**
- the **direction** of the action or imaginary lines the body flows through space
- the **timing** of when movements form the dramatic effects
- the awareness of the **planes** formed by any two areas such as height and width or width and depth
- **levels** that are introduced so that the composition incorporates sit, stand, and kneeling, etc.
- The **elevation** or the degree of lift as in leaping and the movements that are done under that allusion of suspension
- the **force** and energy of dance that reflects the music, such as adagio (slow music) or allegro (quickening steps).

Rhythm is the basis of dance. A child can sit in a chair and clap or tap their hands on their legs to express thoughts of rhythm. With older children, imagery enables a dancer to visualize and internalize the particular qualities of a specific movement.

Because the younger child is more unsteady the initial level emphasis is not on gracefulness but rather to develop **body awareness**. The uniqueness of dance is that it is self-expression that can be guided through instruction. The student is taught the elements that are available such as **time and space.** Therefore, the student is incorporating **listening skills** to develop a sense of tempo.

Creative dance is the one that is most natural to a young child. Creative dance depicts feelings through movement. It is the initial reaction to sound and movement. The older elementary student will incorporate mood and expressiveness. Stories can be told to release the dancer into imagination.

Isadora Duncan is credited with being the mother of modern dance. **Modern dance** today refers to a concept of dance where the expressions of opposites are developed such as fast-slow, contract- release, vary height and level to fall and recover. Modern dance is based on four principles which are substance, dynamism, metakinesis, and form.

Skill 36.2   Demonstrating knowledge of basic concepts, skills, foundations, and techniques in theatre

Drama comes from the Greek word "dran", meaning "to do." Therefore, drama is the acting out of a written story. Theater itself has several aspects, such as speech, gesture, dance, music, sound and spectacle. This art form combines many of the arts into a single live performance.

[handwritten margin note: technology?, lighting, director, actor]

The basic elements of drama include:

Acting - Acting requires the student to demonstrate the ability to effectively communicate using skillful speaking, movement, rhythm, and sensory awareness.

Directing - Direction requires the management skills to produce and perform an onstage activity. This requires guiding and inspiring students as well as script and stage supervision.

Designing - Designing involves creating and initiating the onsite management of the art of acting.

Scriptwriting - Scriptwriting demands that a leader be able to produce original material and staging an entire production through the writing and designing a story that has performance value.

Each of the above mentioned skills should be incorporated in daily activities with young children. It is important that children are exposed to character development through stories, role-play, and modeling through various teacher guided experiences. Some of the experiences that are age appropriate for early childhood level include puppet theatre, paper dolls, character sketches, storytelling, and re-telling of stories in a student's own words.

Drama and dance both tell stories, and they are often combined as art forms. Drama and dance provide clues to cultures. Through the dances and the stories that unfold in dramas, we discover what is important to a particular culture, what they value, what they enjoy, what issues they face. Music and visual arts are also very often intertwined in drama and dance. Dance is certainly greatly enhanced by music, and visual backdrops and decorations displayed in a dramatic presentation help audience members to better imagine the artistic creation or representation before them.

Skill 36.3   Demonstrating knowledge of dance forms (e.g., ballet, folk, modern) and their characteristic forms of movement, expressive qualities, and cultural origins

The various *styles* of dance can be explained as follows:

- Creative dance
- Modern dance
- Social dance
- Dance of other cultures
- Structured dance
- Ritual Dance
- Ballet
- Folk

For information on modern dance, **SEE** Skill 36.1

Social dance requires a steadier capability that the previous levels. The social aspect of dance, rather than romantic aspect, represents customs and pastimes. Adults laugh when they hear little ones go "eweeee". Changing partners frequently within the dance is something that is subtly important to maintain. Social dance refers to a cooperative form of dance with respect to one sharing the dance floor with others and to have respect for ones partner. Social dance may be in the form of marches, waltz, and the two-step.

The upper level elementary student can learn dance in connection with historical **cultures** such as the minuet. The minuet was introduced to the court in Paris in 1650, and it dominated the ballroom until the end of the eighteenth century. The waltz was introduced around 1775 and was an occasion of fashion and courtship. The pomp and ceremony of it all makes for fun classroom experiences. Dance traditionally is central to many cultures and the interrelatedness of teaching history such as the Native American Indians dance, or the Mexican hat dance, or Japanese theater that incorporates both theater of masks and dance are all important exposures to dance and culture.

Structured dances are recognized by particular patterns such as the Tango, or waltz and were made popular in dance studios and gym classes alike. Arthur Murray promoted dance lessons for adults.

Ritual dance are often of a religious nature that celebrate a significant life event such as a harvest season, the rain season, glorifying the gods, asking for favors in hunting, birth and death dances. Many of these themes are carried out in movies and theaters today but they have their roots in Africa where circle dances and chants summoned the gods and sometimes produced trance like states where periods of divine contact convey the spiritual cleansing of the experience.

Dancing at weddings today is a prime example of ritual dance. The father dances with the bride. Then the husband dances with the bride. The two families dance with each other.

Ballet uses a barre to hold onto to practice the five basic positions used in ballet. Alignment is the way in which various parts of the dancer's body are in line with one another while the dancer is moving. It is very precise and executed with grace and form. The mood and expressions of the music are very important to ballet and form the canvas upon which the dance is performed.

Folk dance is a term used to describe a large number of dances, mostly of European origin. Folk originally danced around 19th century or earlier. Performances were typically dominated by and inherited tradition rather than by innovation. Most dances of folk were danced by common people not just exclusive to aristocracy. Folk dances have developed spontaneously and there isn't a governing body that has the final say over what "the dance" is or who may teach it to others. It is also permissible for any age to participate in the dance and no true definition of what the actual folk dance is. Folk dances are traditionally performed during social events by people with little or no professional training. New dancers often learn informally by observing others and/or receiving help from others. Folk dancing is viewed as more of a social activity rather than competitive, although there are professional and semi-professional folk dance groups, and occasional folk dance competitions

Skill 36.4   Demonstrating knowledge of dramatic and theatrical forms and their characteristics (e.g., pantomime, improvisation)

Students must be able to create, perform, and actively participate in theatre. Classes must be able to apply processes and skills involved in dramatic and theatre.
From acting, designing, script writing, creating formal and informal theatre, and media productions there is a wide variety of skills that must encompass the theatre expression.

Literature in the classroom opens many doors for learning. Reading and rehearsing stories with children allows them to explore the area of imagination and creative play. Students can take simple stories such as "The Three Little Pigs" and act out such tales. Acting allows students to experience new found dramatic skills and to enhance their creative abilities. A school curriculum incorporating dramatic and theatrical forms should include the vocabulary for theatre and the development of a criterion for evaluation of dramatic events. Students must understand and appreciate a dramatic work.

A good drama curriculum should include the following:

- Acting - involves the students' ability to skillfully communicate with an audience. It requires speaking, movement, sensory awareness, rhythm and great oral communication skills.
- Improvisation- actors must be able to respond to unexpected stimuli and be spontaneous, creative, and must adapt to any scene that may be previously unscripted.
- Drama- a reenactment of life and life situations for entertainment purposes.
- Theatre-theatre involves a more formal presentation in front of an audience. Typically it involves a script, set, direction and production.
- Production- this often includes arranging for the entire theatre performance and the production of the whole process.
- Direction- Coordinating and directing or guiding the onstage activities.
- Playmaking - this involves creating an original script and staging a performance without a set or formal audience.
 - Pantomime- a form of communication by means of gesture and facial expressions; telling a story without the use of words.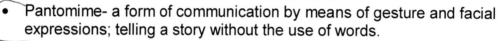

Various areas of art framework should be addressed including but not limited to the following:

- Direction of theatrical productions
- Auditions
- analyzing script
- demonstrating vision for a project
- knowledge of communication skills
- social group skills
- creativity
- principles of production
- applying scheduling, budget, planning, promotion, roles and responsibilities of others
- knowledge of legal issues such as copyright etc
- selection of appropriate works

Skill 36.5   Recognizing methods and processes of creating, performing, and responding to dance and theatre

Movement

Dance is an artistic form of self expression that uses the various elements of dance, such as use of space, time, levels, and force, to form a composition.

The primary grades have a gross understanding of their motor movements whereas older children are more apt to have a refined concept of their bodies. Individual movements are developed by the instructor when attention is given to various aspects such as:

- the range of movement or gestures through space
- the direction of the action or imaginary lines the body flows through space
- the timing of when movements form the dramatic effects
- the awareness of the planes formed by any two areas such as height and width or width and depth
- levels that are introduced so that the composition incorporates sit, stand, and kneeling, etc.
- The elevation or the degree of lift as in leaping and the movements that are done under that allusion of suspension
- the force and energy of dance that reflects the music, such as adagio (slow music) or allegro (quickening steps).

Drama

Students come to the classroom with a basic knowledge of drama through their own games of make-believe. Extending that game of pretend or make-believe through improvisation is a starting point in building knowledge, language and concepts related to drama.

The **ten elements of acting** can be incorporated immediately into improvisation exercises. These elements begin with the questions: Who? What? Where? When? Why? Then, rounding out the ten elements are the senses: sight, hearing, smell, taste and touch. Discussing the ten elements within acting exercises begins a pattern of thought or a checklist for the students.

In a sample exercise, the students pretend to be at the beach. What do they see? What do they smell? Who are they? Why are they there? After these guided questions become more familiar, the student will take the ten elements and apply them to future dramatic creations. The ten elements will also be used as a barometer to critique dramatic performances. Do you know where that actor is located? What are they doing? Why? Did they hear something? What do you think they heard? Who are they?

The teacher further builds the drama language of a student by setting up an improvisation and placing actors **center stage**, **downstage** or **upstage** to begin the exercise. The teacher may also use drama vocabulary such as **stage left**, **stage right** when guiding actors. Incorporating the language of drama into hands-on activities, where the students are up and moving around, helps to cement the new vocabulary.

The next step for students is to increase their roles from actors to directors, script writers, set designers and audience members. Each one of these roles will build knowledge of drama and the various aspects that come together to create a dramatic piece, as well as reinforce the language of drama. Directors must tell their actors to move downstage or stage right. Audience members must sit quietly until the end of the exercise or performance and then clap for their fellow students to show appreciation. What materials do set designers use to create the illusion of a particular place or time? How does a script writer put into words what they would like the actors to portray?

Encouraging students with exercises such as writing their own scripts and performing them for each other is a hands-on activity that builds knowledge of the elements of acting, reinforces the language of theatre through writing down stage directions and dialogue, and adds a piece of the puzzle that will come together as a dramatic production.

Skill 36.6 Demonstrating knowledge of how dance and theatre are used to communicate and to express ideas and feelings for specific purposes and of how aesthetic and cultural diversity are reflected in dance and theatre

Dance is a form of nonverbal communication which takes place through the various types of movements in different dances, the space between the partners and the facial expressions and eye contact. Throughout history, dance has been used as a means of celebrating achievements and special events, as part of religious rituals or to demonstrate culture, such as in the Break dancing developed by Black youth.

The speed and tempo of the music determines the dance style and the type of communication. Waltzes, for example, are generally dance styles in which partners stand very close together and usually denote a relationship of some kind. Fast dances where the dancers either dance alone or at some distance from the partners, are more casual in nature.

SEE Skill 36.7

Skill 36.7 **Recognizing dance and theatre styles and achievements from various artists, cultures, and periods of history and how dance and theatre shape and reflect culture and history**

Greek History

The history of theatre can be dated back to early sixth century B.C. in Greece. The Greek theatre was the earliest known theater experience. Drama was expressed in many Greek spiritual ceremonies. There are two main forms of dramatic forms that have both evolved in their own time.

Tragedy- typically conflict between characters

Comedy- typically paradoxical relationships between humans and the unknown gods such as Sophocles and Euripides

Comedies and Tragedies were seldom mixed playwrights. Plays such as these were designed to entertain and contained little violence and were based on knowledge and the teachings of Aristotle.

Roman History

The history of theatre in Roman times was discovered in the third century. These theatre shows were too based on religious aspects of the lives of Roman gods and goddesses. Drama wasn't able to withstand the fall of the Roman Empire in 476 A.D. By the end of the sixth century drama was nearly dead in Rome.

Medieval Drama

Medieval theatre was a new revelation of drama that appeared in around the tenth century. New phases of religion were introduced in many holiday services such as Christmas and Easter. In the church itself drama was noticed in many troupes that toured churches presenting religious narratives and life stories of moral deeds. Over time the once small traveling groups grew into full sized plays, presentations, and elaborate passions. Performances became spectacles at outdoor theaters, marketplaces, and any place large audiences could gather. The main focus of these presentations of drama was to glorify God and humanity and to celebrate local artisan trades.

Puritan Commonwealth

The Puritan Commonwealth was ruled by Oliver Cromwell who outlawed dramatic performances and that ban lasted for nearly twenty years. Following the Puritan era was the restoration of the English monarchy and new more well rounded plays became the focus of art. For the first time in history women were allowed to participate.

Melodrama

Melodrama eventually took over the stage of acting, in which the good always triumphed over the evil. This form of acting was usually pleasing to the audience yet sometimes unrealistic.

Serious Drama

Serious Drama emerged late in the nineteenth and twentieth centuries it came following the movement of realism. Realism attempted to combine the dealings of nature with realistic and ordinary situations on stage.

Realism

Today realism is the most common form of stage presence. The techniques used today to stage drama combine many of the past histories and cultures of drama.

Dance has been an important part of world cultures since the beginning of time. It was used to celebrate the changing of seasons, to celebrate tribal victory in battle and to celebrate the stages of life. As cultures developed and became more refined so did the dance styles. Two main types of styles emerged – social dance and religious dances. Both took different forms and had different purposes. At first the dancers were accompanied by only rhythmic sounds and later melodies were added. The movements in the dances of primitive peoples reflected the actions of their daily lives – such as using their arms to plant seeds. They also imitated the actions of animals in their environment.

To the Ancient Egyptians, dance was an important part of the culture and was considered an integral part of daily life. In Ancient Greece, it was regarded as a physical activity and therefore important to the health of the people. In these societies, dances were performed in circles and the dancers did not touch one another. The movements were almost like gymnastic moves. In all there were about 200 different Greek dances developed to suit various themes and occasions.

Social dancing as we know it today dates back to the courts of European kingdoms. The waltz, for example, originated in Austria in the 17th century and because it was deemed immoral, the dance was banned in Germany in the 18th century. At the time, this dance represented freedom of expression and freedom of movement because it contrasted with the restricted steps of the commonly used dances at the time.

The influence of dances from the Caribbean and South America, such as the tango, brought about different styles of dancing, such as the Jitterbug and the Twist. Each of these had a craze faze in which everyone wanted to try the new steps. The Irish immigrants, in the mid 1800's, introduced tap dancing and clog dancing to the US.

Theatre was also a popular form of entertainment throughout history. The courts of kings and queens always had court jesters and troupes of actors to provide amusement for social gatherings. These were almost always men, who did play the part of women when needed as part of the performance. Sometimes the act involved a parody on some aspect of life or as a veiled ridicule of the rulers.

The greatest known theatrical performances are those of William Shakespeare. He and his group of actors performed a wide variety of theatrical performances in England in the 1500's written by Shakespeare himself. They covered the gamut of tragedies, comedies and romance.

Italian opera is a theatrical performance that includes acting and music with soprano voices. There were many operas written by famous musicians, such as Mozart and Hayden. They are usually performed in the Italian language.

Theatre evolved into movies, but is still an important part of the entertainment industry. Drama in schools uses the age-old techniques developed by early actors and many of the old plays are still being performed on stage.

Skill 36.8   Demonstrating knowledge of how dance and theatre make connections within and across the arts and to other disciplines, life, cultures, and work

SEE Skill 35.7

SAMPLE TEST

DIRECTIONS: Read each item and select the best response.

1. **Deductive reasoning is:**
   (Average Rigor) (Skill 2.1)

   A. The process of finding a pattern from a group of examples.

   B. The process of arriving at a conclusion based on other statements that are known to be true.

   C. Both A and B

   D. Neither A nor B

2. **Find the inverse of the following statement: If I like dogs, then I do not like cats.**
   (Rigorous) (Skill 2.2)

   A. If I like dogs, then I do like cats.

   B. If I like cats, then I like dogs.

   C. If I like cats, then I do not like dogs.

   D. If I do not like dogs, then I like cats.

3. **Find the converse of the following statement: If I like math, then I do not like science.**
   (Average Rigor) (Skill 2.2)

   A. If I do not like science, then I like math.

   B. If I like math, then I do not like science.

   C. If I do not like math, then I do not like science.

   D. If I like math, then I do not like science.

4. **Which of the following is an irrational number?**
   (Rigorous) (Skill 4.1)

   A. .36262626262...

   B. 4

   C. 8.2

   D. -5

5. The number "0" is a member of all the following groups of numbers EXCEPT:
(Rigorous) (Skill 4.1)

A. Whole numbers

B. Real numbers

C. Natural numbers

D. Integers

6. An item that sells for $375 is put on sale at $120. What is the percent of decrease?
(Average Rigor) (Skill 4.2)

A. 25%

B. 28%

C. 68%

D. 34%

7. 0.16 is equivalent to:
(Average Rigor) (Skill 4.2)

A. 16

B. 16%

C. 16/10

D. 1.6

8. 4,087,361
What number represents the ten-thousands place?
(Easy) (Skill 4.4)

A. 4

B. 6

C. 0

D. 8

9. What is the greatest common factor of 16, 28, and 36?
(Easy) (Skill 4.4)

A. 2

B. 4

C. 8

D. 16

10. **The order of mathematical operations is done in the following order:**
(Average Rigor) (Skill 5.1)

   A. Simplify inside grouping characters such as parentheses, brackets, square root, fraction bar, etc.; multiply out expressions with exponents; do multiplication or division, from left to right; do addition or subtraction, from left to right.

   B. Do multiplication or division, from left to right; simplify inside grouping characters such as parentheses, brackets, square root, fraction bar, etc.; multiply out expressions with exponents; do addition or subtraction, from left to right.

   C. Simplify inside grouping characters such as parentheses, brackets, square root, fraction bar, etc.; do addition or subtraction, from left to right; multiply out expressions with exponents; do multiplication or division, from left to right.

   D. None of the above

11. **Which of the following is an example of the associative property?**
(Average Rigor) (Skill 5.2)

   A. $a(b + c) = ab + bc$

   B. $a + 0 = a$

   C. $(a + b) + c = a + (b + c)$

   D. $a + b = b + a$

12. **What is the absolute value of the number -5?**
(Rigorous) (Skill 6.2)

   A. -5

   B. 10

   C. 1/5

   D. 5

13. $3x + 2y = 12$
$12x + 8y = 15$
Solve for x and y.
(Average Rigor) (Skill 6.2)

   A. All real numbers

   B. $x = 4, y = 4$

   C. $x = 2, y = -1$

   D. None of the above

14. Two mathematics classes have a total of 410 students. The 8:00 a.m. class has 40 more than the 10:00 a.m. class. How many students are in the 10:00 a.m. class? *(Average rigor) (Skill 6.4)*

A. 123.3

B. 370

C. 185

D. 330

D. 5

15. Three-dimensional figures in geometry are called: *(Rigorous) (Skill 7.1)*

A. Solids

B. Cubes

C. Polygons

D. Blocks

16. If a right triangle has legs with the measurements of 3 cm and 4 cm, what is the measure of the hypotenuse? *(Average Rigor) (Skill 7.3)*

A. 6 cm

B. 1 cm

C. 7 cm

D. 5 cm

17. What is a translation? *(Rigorous) (Skill 7.4)*

A. To turn a figure around a fixed point.

B. The object has the same shape and same size, but figures face in different directions.

C. To "slide" an object a fixed distance in a given direction.

D. The transformation that "shrinks" or "makes it bigger."

18. If the radius of a right circular cylinder is doubled, how does its volume change?
(Rigorous) (Skill 8.1)

A. No change

B. Also is doubled

C. Four times the original

D. Pi times the original

19. Find the area of a rectangle if you know that the base is 8 cm and the diagonal of the rectangle is 8.5 cm:
(Rigorous) (Skill 8.1)

A. 24 cm²

B. 30 cm²

C. 18.9 cm²

D. 24 cm

20. All of the following are examples of obtuse angles EXCEPT:
(Average Rigor) (Skill 8.1)

A. 110 degrees

B. 90 degrees

C. 135 degrees

D. 91 degrees

21. What measures could be used to report the distance traveled in walking around a track?
(Easy) (Skill 8.2)

A. Degrees

B. Square meters

C. Kilometers

D. Cubic feet

22. The mass of a cookie is closest to:
(Easy) (Skill 8.2)

A. 0.5 kg

B. 0.5 grams

C. 15 grams

D. 1.5 grams

23. Given the formula d = rt, (where d = distance, r = rate, and t = time), calculate the time required for a vehicle to travel 585 miles at a rate of 65 miles per hour.
(Average Rigor) (Skill 8.3)

A. 8.5 hours

B. 6.5 hours

C. 9.5 hours

D. 9 hours

24. In probability, the sample space represents:
(Average Rigor) (Skill 9.1)

A. An outcome to an experiment

B. A list of all possible outcomes of an experiment.

C. The amount of times you must flip a coin.

D. The amount of room needed to conduct an experiment.

25. Corporate salaries are listed for several employees. Which would be the best measure of central tendency?
(Average Rigor) (Skill 9.2)

$24,000	$24,000
$26,000	$28,000
$30,000	$120,000

A. Mean

B. Median

C. Mode

D. No difference

26. Permutation is:
(Rigorous) (Skill 9.3)

A. The number of possible arrangements, without repetition, where order of selection is not important.

B. The number of possible arrangements, with repetition, where order of selection is not important

C. The number of possible arrangements of items, without repetition, where order of selection is important.

D. The number of possible arrangements of items, with repetition, where order of selection is important.

27. Given a drawer with 5 black socks, 3 blue socks, and 2 red socks, what is the probability that you will draw two black socks in two draws in a dark room?
(Rigorous) (Skill 9.5)

A. 2/9

B. 1/4

C. 17/18

D. 1/18

28. **Suppose you have a bag of marbles that contains 2 red marbles, 5 blue marbles, and 3 green marbles. If you replace the first marble chosen, what is the probability you will choose 2 green marbles in a row?**
   (Average Rigor) (Skill 9.5)

   A. 2/5

   B. 9/100

   C. 9/10

   D. 3/5

29. **The volume is:**
   (Easy) (Skill 10.1)

   A. Area of the faces excluding the bases

   B. Total area of all the faces, including the bases

   C. The number of cubic units in a solid

   D. The measure around the object

30. **The following are examples of chemical reactions EXCEPT:**
   (Average Rigor) (Skill 10.1)

   A. Melting ice into water

   B. Dissolving a seltzer tablet in water

   C. Using a fire-cracker

   D. Burning a piece of plastic

31. **The transfer of heat by electromagnetic waves is called _____:**
   (Easy) (Skill 10.3)

   A. Conduction

   B. Convection

   C. Phase change

   D. Radiation

32. **In the following equation, what does *G* represent?**
(Rigorous) (Skill 11.2)

$$F_{\text{gravity}} = G \frac{m_1 m_2}{d^2}$$

A. The distance between the two masses

B. The universal gravitational constant

C. Coulomb's constant

D. The speed of the object

33. **The theory of "sea floor spreading" explains** _____

(Average Rigor) (Skill 12.1)

A. The shapes of the continents.

B. How continents got named.

C. How continents move apart.

D. How continents sink to become part of the ocean floor.

34. **Which of the following types of rock are made from magma?**
(Rigorous) (Skill 12.1)

A. Fossils

B. Sedimentary

C. Metamorphic

D. Igneous

35. **Which statement is true when describing the stratosphere?**
(Rigorous) (Skill 12.5)

A. This layer contains a subarea called the ionosphere.

B. This is the coldest layer.

C. This layer is closest to the earth's surface.

D. This layer contains very little water, and clouds are rare.

36. **The most abundant gas in the atmosphere is:**
(Rigorous) (Skill 12.7)

A. Oxygen

B. Nitrogen

C. Carbon dioxide

D. Methane

37. **Which of the following is the best definition for 'meteorite'?**
(Rigorous) (Skill 12.7)

   A. A meteorite is a mineral composed of mica and feldspar.

   B. A meteorite is material from outer space that has struck the earth's surface.

   C. A meteorite is an element that has properties of both metals and nonmetals.

   D. A meteorite is a very small unit of length measurement.

38. **All of the following are natural resources EXCEPT:**
(Average Rigor) (Skill 12.8)

   A. Trees

   B. Coal

   C. Fish

   D. Paper

39. **Which of the following is the most accurate definition of a nonrenewable resource?**
(Average Rigor) (Skill 12.8)

   A. A nonrenewable resource is never replaces once used.

   B. A nonrenewable resource is replaced on a timescale that is very long relative to human life spans.

   C. A nonrenewable resource is a resource that can only be manufactured by humans.

   D. A nonrenewable resource is a species that has already become extinct.

40. **What cell organelle contains the cell's stored food?**
(Rigorous) (Skill 13.1)

   A. Vacuoles

   B. Golgi Apparatus

   C. Ribosome

   D. Lysosome

41. **Identify the correct sequence of organization of living things from lower to higher order:**
(Rigorous) (Skill 13.1)

A. Cell, Organelle, Organ, Tissue, System, Organism

B. Cell, Tissue, Organ, Organelle, System, Organism

C. Organelle, Cell, Tissue, Organ, System, Organism

D. Organelle, Tissue, Cell, Organ, System, Organism

42. **Which kingdom is comprised of organisms made of one cell with no nuclear membrane?**
(Average Rigor) (Skill 13.2)

A. Monera

B. Protista

C. Fungi

D. Algae

43. **Heterozygous refers to:**
Average Rigor) (Skill 13.7)

A. Having 2 dominant genes

B. Having 2 recessive genes

C. Having neither a recessive nor a dominant gene

D. Having 1 recessive gene and 1 dominant gene

44. **Which of the following is a correct explanation for scientific evolution?**
(Rigorous) (Skill 13.7)

   A. Giraffes need to reach higher leaves to eat, so their necks stretch. The giraffe babies are then born with longer necks. Eventually, there are more long-necked giraffes in the population.

   B. Giraffes with longer necks are able to reach more leaves, so they eat more and have more babies than other giraffes. Eventually, there are more long-necked giraffes in the population.

   C. Giraffes want to reach higher for leaves to eat, so they release enzymes into their bloodstream, which in turn causes fetal development of longer-necked giraffes. Eventually, there are more long-necked giraffes in the population.

   D. Giraffes with long necks are more attractive to other giraffes, so they get the best mating partners and have more babies. Eventually, there are more long-necked giraffes in the population.

45. **In an experiment measuring the growth of bacteria at different temperatures, what is the independent variable?**
(Rigorous) (Skill 14.1)

   A. Number of bacteria

   B. Growth rate of bacteria

   C. Temperature

   D. Size of bacteria

46. **Which is the correct order of methodology?**
(Average Rigor) (Skill 14.3)

   1. Collecting data

   2. Planning a controlled experiment

   3. Drawing a conclusion

   4. Hypothesizing a result

   5. Re-visiting a hypothesis to answer a question

   A. 1,2,3,4,5

   B. 4,2,1,3,5

   C. 4,5,1,3,2

   D. 1,3,4,5,2

47. **This following formula depicts:**
(Rigorous) (Skill 15.2)

$$s = \sqrt{\frac{\left(x_i - \bar{x}\right)^2}{n-1}}$$

A. Newton's law of motion

B. Standard deviation

C. Pythagoras' theorem

D. None of the above

48. **Which scientist is credited with launching the Scientific Revolution in the 16ᵗʰ century?**
(Rigorous) (Skill 16.1)

A. Roger Bacon

B. Nicolaus Copernicus

C. Johannes Kepler

D. Isaac Newton

49. **All of the following professions are classified under 'earth sciences' EXCEPT:**
(Average Rigor) (Skill 16.4)

A. Geologist

B. Meteorologist

C. Seismologist

D. Biochemist

50. **The period of development which includes children learning more complex motor patterns including running, jumping, climbing and balancing describes which stage of motor development?**
(Average rigor) (Skill 17.1)

A. Stage 1

B. Stage 2

C. Stage 3

D. Stage 4

51. **According to Piaget's stages of development, in which stage is a child thought to be able to utilize logic?**
(Average rigor) (Skill 17.1)

A. Preoperational

B. Formal operational

C. Concrete operational

D. Sensorimotor

52. **The alleged benefit of this substance is an increase in muscle mass and strength; however, it produces harmful side effects. Such as premature closure of growth plates in bones.**
(Rigorous) (Skill 17.6)

A. Cocaine

B. Alcohol

C. Nicotine

D. Steroids

53. **Gross motor development is:**
(Easy) (Skill 18.2)

A. the movement of the large muscles of the body

B. the movement of the small muscles of the body.

C. an essential skill for learning to write.

D. A & C.

54. **_____ is a tough band of fibrous connective tissue that connects muscle to bone or muscle to muscle.**
(Rigorous) (Skill 18.5)

A. A joint

B. A tendon

C. A ligament

D. Cartilage

55. **Target Hearth Rate (THR) is determined by which following formula?**
(Rigorous) (Skill 18.5)

A. 220-height multiplied by .75 to .80.

B. 220-age multiplied by .60 to .80.

C. 210 – age multiplied by .65 to .90.

D. 220-age multiplied by .75 to .80.

56. **The arrangement and relationship of words in sentences or sentence structure best describes:**
(Average Rigor) (Skill 19.1)

A. Style

B. Discourse

C. Thesis

D. Syntax

57. **All of the following are true about phonological awareness EXCEPT?**
(Average Rigor) (Skill 19.1)

A. It may involve print.

B. It is a prerequisite for spelling and phonics.

C. Development of phonological skills may begin during the pre-kindergarten years.

D. Students have the ability to recognize the sounds of spoken language.

58. **Which of the following is NOT one of the metalinguistic abilities acquired by children from early involvement in reading activities?**
(Rigorous) (Skill 20.1)

A. Conventions of print

B. Word consciousness

C. Spelling fluency

D. Functions of print

59. **Which of the following is NOT a strategy of teaching reading comprehension?**

(Rigorous) (Skill 20.4)

A. Summarization

B. Utilizing graphic organizers

C. Manipulating sounds

D. Having students generate questions

60. **Which of the following indicates that a student is a fluent reader?**
(Easy) (Skill 20.5)

   A. Reads texts with expression or prosody

   B. Reads word-to-word and haltingly

   C. Must intentionally decode a majority of the words

   D. In a writing assignment, sentences are poorly-organized structurally

61. **To decode is to:**
(Easy) (Skill 21.1)

   A. Construct meaning

   B. Sound out a printed sequence of letters

   C. Use a special code to decipher a message

   D. None of the above

62. **If a student has a poor vocabulary, the teacher should recommend that:**
(Average Rigor) (Skill 21.2)

   A. The student read newspapers, magazines, and books on a regular basis.

   B. The student enroll in a Latin class.

   C. The student write the words repetitively after looking them up in a dictionary.

   D. The student use a thesaurus to locate synonyms and incorporate them into his/her vocabulary.

63. **Which of the following is an example of nonfiction literature?**
(Average Rigor) (Skill 22.1)

   A. Letters

   B. Biographies

   C. Journals

   D. All of the above

64. **The use of steroids in professional baseball is ruining the sport. Which of the following does NOT support this thesis?**
(Rigorous) (Skill 22.2)

A. Steroids are performance enhancers and give players who take steroids an unfair advantage.

B. Steroids are physically harmful to the players.

C. Steroids make baseball more exciting because more players hit home runs.

D. Kids in high school and college are taking steroids because they want to give themselves a better shot to make it into the major leagues.

65. **Which is NOT a true statement concerning an author's literary tone?**
(Rigorous) (Skill 22.3)

A. Tone is partly revealed through the selection of details.

B. Tone is the expression of the author's attitude toward his/her subject.

C. Tone in literature is usually satiric or angry.

D. Tone in literature corresponds to the tone of voice a speaker uses

66. **All of the following are examples of transitional phrases EXCEPT:**
(Easy) (Skill 22.4)

A. The

B. However

C. Furthermore

D. Although

67. A sixth-grade science teacher has given her class a paper to read on the relationship between food and weight gain. The writing contains signal words such as "because," "consequently," "this is how," and "due to." This paper has which text structure?
(Average Rigor) (Skill 22.4)

A. Cause & effect

B. Compare & contrast

C. Description

D. Sequencing

68. All of the following are common types of narratives EXCEPT:
(Rigorous) (Skill 23.2)

A. Legends

B. Short stories

C. Poems

D. Memoirs

69. Which of the following is NOT a characteristic of a fable?
(Average Rigor) (Skill 23.2)

A. Animals that feel and talk like humans

B. Happy solutions to human dilemmas

C. Teaches a moral or standard for behavior

D. Illustrates specific peoples or groups without directly naming them

70. Which of the following is a ballad?
(Average Rigor) (Skill 23.2)

A. "The Knight's Tale"

B. *Julius Ceasar*

C. *Paradise Lost*

D. "The Rime of the Ancient Mariner"

71. Which of the following is an epic?
(Rigorous) (Skill 23.2)

A. *On the Choice of Books*

B. *The Faerie Queene*

C. *Northanger Abbey*

D. *A Doll's House*

72. The children's literature genre came into its own in the:
     (Average Rigor) (Skill 23.2)

     A. Seventeenth century

     B. Eighteenth century

     C. Nineteenth century

     D. Twentieth century

73. A simile is:
     (Average Rigor) (Skill 23.3)

     A. A direct comparison between two things.

     B. An indirect comparison between two things.

     C. When human characteristics are applied to things that are not human, such as animals.

     D. Deliberate exaggeration for effect or comic effect.

74. A student has written a paper with the following characteristics: written in first person; characters, setting, and plot; some dialogue; and events organized in chronological sequence with some flashbacks. In what genre has the student written?
     (Easy) (Skill 23.3)

     A. Expository writing

     B. Narrative writing

     C. Persuasive writing

     D. Technical writing

75. **Alliteration is a poetic device where:**
   (Average Rigor) (Skill 23.3)

   A. The words used (*Pow, Zap,* etc...) evoke meaning by their sounds.

   B. The final consonant sounds are the same, but the vowels are different.

   C. The vowel sound within a word matches the vowel sound within a nearby word, but the surrounding consonant sounds are different (Ex. *June* and *Tune*).

   D. The initial sound of a word, beginning in either a consonant of a vowel, in repeated in succession (Ex. *People* who *pen* poetry).

76. **Which of the following reading strategies is NOT associated with fluent reading abilities?**
   (Average rigor) (Skill 24.2)

   A. pronouncing unfamiliar words by finding similarities with familiar words

   B. establishing a purpose for reading

   C. formulating questions about the text while reading

   D. reading sentences word by word

77. **Which of the following is NOT a technique of prewriting?**
   (Average Rigor) (Skill 24.3)

   A. Clustering

   B. Listing

   C. Brainstorming

   D. Proofreading

78. **All of the following are correctly capitalized EXCEPT:**
(Rigorous) (Skill 25.1)

A. Queen Elizabeth

B. Congressman McKay

C. commander Alger

D. the president of the United States

79. **All of the following are correctly punctuated EXCEPT:**
(Rigorous) (Skill 25.1)

A. "The book is on the table," said Bill's mother.

B. "Who would like to sing 'The Star Spangled Banner'?" the teacher asked.

C. I was embarrassed when Joanne said, "The meeting started an hour ago!"

D. "The policeman apprehended the criminals last night."

80. **Orthography is:**
(Rigorous) (Skill 25.2)

A. The study of word structure.

B. A method of representing a spoken language through the use of written symbols.

C. The complete set of related word-forms associated with a given lexeme.

D. A process of word-formation that involves combining complete word-forms into a single compound form.

81. **When students present information orally, they should keep the following in mind:**
(Average Rigor) (Skill 26.1)

A. Volume

B. Pace

C. Body language

D. All of the above

82. **Which of the following is NOT an advisable strategy for making sense of oral language?**
(Easy) (Skill 26.1)

A. Observing body language and other nonverbal cues

B. Take notes to outline major points

C. Critique, question, and evaluate others' as well as students' own oral presentations

D. Ignore prior knowledge of the topic as it does not help understand what is being presented

83. **Which of the following are examples of research materials that are available to use?**
(Easy) (Skill 27.1)

A. Encyclopedias

B. Internet search engines

C. Card catalogues

D. All of the above

84. **The Bill of Rights consists of which Amendments?**
(Average Rigor) (Skill 28.2)

A. Amendments 1-5

B. Amendments 1-10

C. Amendments 1 and 2

D. Amendments 1-22

85. **All of the following are examples of why the first known civilizations developed by water EXCEPT:**
(Average Rigor) (Skill 30.2)

A. Rivers provided water, which both the humans and animals needs.

B. Rivers allowed the settlers to travel so they could trade goods.

C. The rivers attracted animals so hunters had a continuous supply of food.

D. The rivers overflowed, which left a deposit of very rich soil.

86. **All of the following are oceans EXCEPT:**
(Easy) (Skill 30.2)

A. Pacific

B. Atlantic

C. Mediterranean

D. Indian

87. **Which term best defines the customs, traditions, and arts of a group of people?**
(Easy) (Skill 30.4)

A. Culture

B. Democracy

C. Interdependence

D. Geography

88. **Cultural diffusion is:**
(Rigorous) (Skill 31.1)

A. The process that individuals and societies go through in changing their behavior and organization to cope with social, economic and environmental pressures.

B. The complete disappearance of a culture.

C. The exchange or adoption of cultural features when two cultures come into regular direct contact.

D. The movement of cultural ideas or materials between populations independent of the movement of those populations

89. **Which one of the following is not a reason why Europeans came to the New World?**
(Average Rigor) (Skill 32.1)

A. To find resources in order to increase wealth.

B. To establish trade.

C. To increase a ruler's power and importance.

D. To spread Christianity.

90. **The year 1619 was memorable for the colony of Virginia. Three important events occurred, resulting in lasting effects on U.S. history. Which one of the following is not one of events?**
(Rigorous) (Skill 32.1)

A. Twenty African slaves arrived.

B. The London Company granted the colony a charter making it independent.

C. The colonists were given the right by the London Company to govern themselves through representative government in the Virginia House of Burgesses.

D. The London Company sent to the colony 60 women who were quickly married, establishing families and stability in the colony.

91. **The belief that the United States should control all of North America was called:**
(Easy) (Skill 32.1)

A. Westward Expansion

B. Pan Americanism

C. Manifest Destiny

D. Nationalism

92. **All of the following were causes of the American Revolution EXCEPT:**
(Average Rigor) (Skill 32.1)

A. The Tea Act of 1773

B. The Stamp Act

C. The colonists were forced to house English troops

D. The colonists wanted more schools

93. **The English placed taxes on the colonies for two reasons. What were they?**
(Easy) (Skill 32.1)

A. To generate revenue and to gain control over the colonists

B. To stimulate the colonists' economy while gaining control over the colonists

C. To generate revenue and encourage freedom in the colonies

D. To turn the colonists toward other trade markets and to gain control over the colonists

94. **The Westward expansion occurred for a number of reasons; however, the most important reason was:** *(Average Rigor) (Skill 32.1)*

    A. Colonization

    B. Slavery

    C. Independence

    D. Economics

95. **Which war took the most American lives in American history?** *(Easy) (Skill 32.1)*

    A. The Civil War

    B. The Revolutionary War

    C. World War I

    D. World War II

96. **The economic collapse of the United States in 1929 is known as the:** *(Easy) (Skill 32.1)*

    A. Cold War

    B. New Deal

    C. Unhappy times

    D. Great Depression

97. **Which civilization invented the wheel?** *(Rigorous) (Skill 33.2)*

    A. Egyptians

    B. Romans

    C. Assyrians

    D. Sumerians

98. **What is the "Pax Romana"?** *(Rigorous) (Skill 33.2)*

    A. Long period of peace enabling free travel and trade, spreading people, cultures, goods, and ideas all over the world

    B. A period of war where the Romans expanded their empire

    C. The Roman government

    D. A time where the government was over-ruled

99. **Who wrote the *Iliad* and the *Odyssey*?** *(Rigorous) (Skill 33.2)*

    A. Aristotle

    B. Homer

    C. Pythagoras

    D. Herodotus

100. **The "divine right" of kings was the key political characteristic of:**
(Rigorous) (Skill 33.2)

A. The Age of Absolutism

B. The Age of Reason

C. The Age of Feudalism

D. The Age of Despotism

101. **Which one of the following would not be considered a result of World War II?**
(Average Rigor) (Skill 33.3)

A. Economic depressions and slow resumption of trade and financial aid

B. Western Europe was no longer the center of world power

C. The beginnings of new power struggles not only in Europe but in Asia as well

D. Territorial and boundary changes for many nations, especially in Europe

102. **The cold war involved which two countries who both emerged as world powers?**
(Rigorous) (Skill 33.3)

A. China and Japan

B. United States and the Soviet Union

C. England and Brazil

D. Afghanistan and the United States

103. **Which of the following is an opinion?**
(Easy) (Skill 34.3)

A. The sky is blue.

B. Albany is the capital of New York State.

C. A dog is the best pet to have.

D. Humans breathe.

104. **Which of the following is a fact?**
(Easy) (Skill 34.3)

A. It's going to rain.

B. John is a liar.

C. Joe said he believes John is a liar.

D. The world is going to the dogs.

105. **The quality of sound is the definition of:**
(Rigorous) (Skill 35.1)

A. timbre.

B. rhythm.

C. harmony.

D. melody.

106. **Common percussion instruments include:**
(Average rigor) (Skill 35.2)

A. xylophone, tambourine, and bells.

B. trumpet, trombone, and tuba.

C. oboe, clarinet, and saxophone.

D. viola, cello, and piano.

107. **In the visual arts, works that project a design from the center axis are said to have:**
(Rigorous) (Skill 35.4)

A. Horizontal balance.

B. Radial balance.

C. Symmetrical balance.

D. Asymmetrical balance.

108. **The predominant themes found in the arts of this period include dramatic climaxes of well-known stories, legends and battles, and the grand spectacle of mythology.**
(Rigorous) (Skill 35.6)

A. Mesopotamian.

B. Middle Ages.

C. Egyptian.

D. Baroque.

109. **This area of drama requires management skills to produce and perform an onstage activity.**
(Easy) (Skill 36.2)

A. Acting.

B. Directing

C. Screenwriting.

D. Designing.

110. **It was during this historical time period that dramatic performances were banned.** *(Rigorous) (Skill 36.7)*

   A. Medieval.

   B. Ancient Greece.

   C. Puritan New England.

   D. Roman.

Answer Key

29.	C	57.	A	85.	B
30.	A	58.	C	86.	C
31.	D	59.	C	87.	A
32.	B	60.	A	88.	D
33.	C	61.	A	89.	B
34.	D	62.	A	90.	B
35.	D	63.	D	91.	C
36.	B	64.	C	92.	D
37.	B	65.	B	93.	D
38.	D	66.	A	94.	D
39.	B	67.	A	95.	A
40.	A	68.	C	96.	D
41.	C	69.	D	97.	D
42.	A	70.	D	98.	A
43.	D	71.	B	99.	B
44.	B	72.	A	100.	A
45.	C	73.	A	101.	A
46.	B	74.	B	102.	B
47.	B	75.	D	103.	C
48.	B	76.	D	104.	C
49.	D	77.	D	105.	A
50.	B	78.	C	106.	A
51.	C	79.	C	107.	B
52.	D	80.	B	108.	D
53.	A	81.	D	109.	B
54.	B	82.	D	110.	C
55.	B	83.	D		
56.	D	84.	B		

27. A
28. B

Rigor Table

	Easy	Average Rigor	Rigorous
	20%	**40%**	**40%**
Q #	21, 22, 29, 31, 53, 60, 61, 66, 74, 82, 83, 86, 87, 91, 93, 95, 96, 103, 104, 109	6, 7, 10, 11, 13, 14, 16, 23, 24, 25, 28, 30, 33, 38, 39, 42, 43, 46, 49, 50, 51, 56, 57, 62, 63, 67, 69, 70, 72, 73, 75, 76, 77, 81, 84, 85, 89, 92, 94, 101, 106	5, 12, 15, 17, 18, 19, 20, 26, 27, 32, 34, 35, 36, 37, 40, 41, 44, 45, 47, 48, 52, 54, 55, 58, 59, 64, 65, 68, 71, 78, 79, 80, 88, 90, 97, 98, 99, 100, 102, 105, 107, 108, 110

RATIONALES

1. **Deductive reasoning is:**
    (Average Rigor) (Skill 2.1)

    A. The process of finding a pattern from a group of examples.

    B. The process of arriving at a conclusion based on other statements that are known to be true.

    C. Both A and B

    D. Neither A nor B

Answer: C

Both A and B

Deductive reasoning moves from a generalization or set of examples to a specific instance or solution.

2. **Find the inverse of the following statement: If I like dogs, then I do   not like cats.**
    (Rigorous) (Skill 2.2)

    A. If I like dogs, then I do like cats.

    B. If I like cats, then I like dogs.

    C. If I like cats, then I do not like dogs.

    D. If I do not like dogs, then I like cats.

Answer: D

If I do not like dogs, then I like cats.

When you take the inverse of the statement you negate both statements. By negating both statements you take the opposite of the original statement.

3. **Find the converse of the following statement: If I like math, then I do not like science.**
   (Average Rigor) (Skill 2.2)

   A. If I do not like science, then I like math.

   B. If I like math, then I do not like science.

   C. If I do not like math, then I do not like science.

   D. If I like math, then I do not like science.

Answer: A

If I do not like science, then I like math.

When finding the converse of a statement you take the second part of the statement and reverse it with the first part of the statement. In other words, you reverse the statements.

4. **Which of the following is an irrational number?**
   (Rigorous) (Skill 41)

   A. .36262626262…

   B. 4

   C. 8.2

   D. -5

Answer: A

.362626262626…

Irrational numbers are numbers that can not be made into a fraction. This number cannot be made into a fraction so it must be irrational.

5. **The number "0" is a member of all the following groups of numbers EXCEPT:**
    (Rigorous) (Skill 4.1)

    A. Whole numbers

    B. Real numbers

    C. Natural numbers

    D. Integers

Answer: C

Natural numbers

The number zero is a member of the whole numbers, real numbers, and integers, but the natural numbers (also known as the counting numbers) start with the number one, not zero.

6. **An item that sells for $375 is put on sale at $120. What is the percent of decrease?**
    (Average Rigor) (Skill 4.2)

    A. 25%

    B. 28%

    C. 68%

    D. 34%

Answer: C

68%

In this problem you must set up a cross-multiplication problem. You begin by placing X/100 to represent the variable you are solving for and it being over 100% and then you place 120/375 to represent the new price over the original price. Once you cross multiply you will get 68, which is the percent decrease the item is selling for.

7.   **0.16 is equivalent to:**
        (Average Rigor) (Skill 4.2)

        A. 16

        B. 16%

        C. 16/10

        D. 1.6

Answer: B

16%

0.16 is equivalent to 16% because 16% is 16/100.

8.   **4,087,361 What number represents the ten-thousands place?**
        (Easy) (Skill 4.4)

        A. 4

        B. 6

        C. 0

        D. 8

Answer: D

8

The ten-thousands place is the number 8 in this problem.

9. **What is the greatest common factor of 16, 28, and 36?**
   (Easy) (Skill 4.4)

    A. 2

    B. 4

    C. 8

    D. 16

Answer: B

4

The smallest number in this set is 16; its factors are 1, 2, 4, 8, and 16. 16 is the largest factor, but it does not divide into 28 or 36. Neither does 8. 4 does factor into both 28 and 36.

10. **The order of mathematical operations is done in the following order:**
    (Average Rigor) (Skill 5.1)

    A. Simplify inside grouping characters such as parentheses, brackets, square root, fraction bar, etc.; multiply out expressions with exponents; do multiplication or division, from left to right; do addition or subtraction, from left to right.

    B. Do multiplication or division, from left to right; simplify inside grouping characters such as parentheses, brackets, square root, fraction bar, etc.; multiply out expressions with exponents; do addition or subtraction, from left to right.

    C. Simplify inside grouping characters such as parentheses, brackets, square root, fraction bar, etc.; do addition or subtraction, from left to right; multiply out expressions with exponents; do multiplication or division, from left to right.

    D. None of the above

Answer: A

Simplify inside grouping characters such as parentheses, brackets, square root, fraction bar, etc.; multiply out expressions with exponents; do multiplication or division, from left to right; do addition or subtraction, from left to right.

When facing a mathematical problem that requires all mathematical properties to be performed first, you do the math within the parentheses, brackets, square roots, or fraction bars. Then you multiply out expressions with exponents. Next, you do multiplication or division. Finally, you do addition or subtraction.

11. **Which of the following is an example of the associative property?**
    (Average Rigor) (Skill 5.2)

    A. a (b + c) = ab + bc

    B. a + 0 = a

    C. (a + b) + c = a + (b + c)

    D. a + b = b + a

Answer: C

(a + b) + c = a + (b + c)

The associative property is when the parentheses of a problem are switched.

12. **What is the absolute value of the number -5?**
    (Rigorous) (Skill 6.2)

    A. -5

    B. 10

    C. 1/5

    D. 5

Answer: D

5

The absolute value is how far on a number line the number is from zero.

13.　　$3x + 2y = 12$　　　$12x + 8y = 15$

Solve for x and y.
(Average Rigor) (Skill 6.2)

A. All real numbers

B. $x = 4, y = 4$

C. $x = 2, y = -1$

D. None of the above

Answer: D

None of the above

Multiplying the top equation by -4 and adding results in the equation $0 = -33$. Since this is a false statement, the correct choice is the null set.

14.　　**Two mathematics classes have a total of 410 students. The 8:00 a.m. class has 40 more than the 10:00 a.m. class. How many students are in the 10:00 a.m. class?**
(Average rigor) (Skill 6.4)

A. 123.3

B. 370

C. 185

D. 330

Answer: C

185

Let x = # of students in the 8 am class and x − 40 = # of students in the 10 am class. So there are 225 students in the 8 am class, and 225 − 40 = 185 in the 10 am class, which is answer C.

15. **Three-dimensional figures in geometry are called:**
(Rigorous) (Skill 7.1)

A. Solids

B. Cubes

C. Polygons

D. Blocks

Answer: A

Solids

Three-dimensional figures are referred to as solids.

16. **If a right triangle has legs with the measurements of 3 cm and 4 cm, what is the measure of the hypotenuse?**
(Average Rigor) (Skill 7.3)

A. 6 cm

B. 1 cm

C. 7 cm

D. 5 cm

Answer: D

5 cm

If you use the Pythagorean Theorem, you will get 5 cm for the hypotenuse leg.

17. **What is a translation?**
    (Rigorous) (Skill 7.4)

    A. To turn a figure around a fixed point.

    B. The object has the same shape and same size, but figures face in different directions.

    C. To "slide" an object a fixed distance in a given direction.

    D. The transformation that "shrinks" or "makes it bigger."

Answer: C

To "slide" an object a fixed distance in a given direction.

A translation is when you slide an object a fixed distance, but do not change the size of the object.

18. **If the radius of a right circular cylinder is doubled, how does its volume change?**
    (Rigorous) (Skill 8.1)

    A. No change

    B. Also is doubled

    C. Four times the original

    D. Pi times the original

Answer: C

Four times the original

If the radius of a right circular cylinder is doubled, the volume is multiplied by four because in the formula, the radius is squared. Therefore, the new volume is 2 x 2 or four times the original.

19. **Find the area of a rectangle if you know that the base is 8 cm and the diagonal of the rectangle is 8.5 cm:**
(Rigorous) (Skill 8.1)

    A. 24 cm²

    B. 30 cm²

    C. 18.9 cm²

    D. 24 cm

Answer: A

The answer is choice A because the base of the rectangle is also one leg of the right triangle, and the diagonal is the hypotenuse of the triangle. To find the other leg of the triangle you can use the Pythagorean Theorem. Once you get the other leg of the triangle, that also is the height of the rectangle. To get the area you perform the base times the height. The reason why the answer is A and not D is because area is measured in centimeters-squared, not just centimeters

20. **All of the following are examples of obtuse angles EXCEPT:**
(Average Rigor) (Skill 8.1)

    A. 110 degrees

    B. 90 degrees

    C. 135 degrees

    D. 91 degrees

Answer: B

90 degrees

A 90 degree angle is not obtuse; it is a right angle.

21. **What measures could be used to report the distance traveled in walking around a track?**
(Easy) (Skill 8.2)

A. Degrees

B. Square meters

C. Kilometers

D. Cubic feet

Answer: C

Kilometers

Degrees measure angles, square meters measure area, cubic feet measure volume, and kilometers measure length. Kilometers is the only reasonable answer.

22. **The mass of a cookie is closest to:**
(Easy) (Skill 8.2)

A. 0.5 kg

B. 0.5 grams

C. 15 grams

D. 1.5 grams

Answer: C

15 grams

Science utilizes the metric system, and the unit of grams is used when measuring mass (the amount of matter in an object). A common estimation of mass used in elementary schools is that a paperclip has a mass of approximately one gram, which eliminates choices B and D, as they are very close to 1 gram. A common estimation of one kilogram is equal to one liter of water. Half of one liter of water is still much more than one cookie, eliminating choice A. Therefore, the best estimation for one cookie is narrowed to 15 grams, or choice C.

23. Given the formula d=rt, (where d = distance, r = rate, and t = time), calculate the time required for a vehicle to travel 585 miles at a rate of 65 miles per hour.
(Average Rigor) (Skill 8.3)

   A. 8.5 hours

   B. 6.5 hours

   C. 9.5 hours

   D. 9 hours

Answer: D

9 hours

We are given d = 585 miles and r = 65 miles per hour and $d =rt$. Solve for t hours.

24. In probability, the sample space represents:
(Average Rigor) (Skill 9.1)

   A. An outcome to an experiment

   B. A list of all possible outcomes of an experiment.

   C. The amount of times you must flip a coin.

   D. The amount of room needed to conduct an experiment.

Answer: B

The sample space is all the possible outcomes that you can have for an experiment.

25. Corporate salaries are listed for several employees. Which would be the best measure of central tendency?
(Average Rigor) (Skill 9.2)

    $24,000 $24,000 $26,000 $28,000 $30,000 $120,000

    A. Mean

    B. Median

    C. Mode

    D. No difference

Answer: A

Mean

The median provides the best measure of central tendency in this case, as the mode is the lowest number and the mean would be disproportionately skewed by the outlier $120,000.

26. Permutation is:

    (Rigorous) (Skill 9.3)

    A. The number of possible arrangements, without repetition, where order of selection is not important.

    B. The number of possible arrangements, with repetition, where order of selection is not important

    C. The number of possible arrangements of items, without repetition, where order of selection is important.

    D. The number of possible arrangements of items, with repetition, where order of selection is important.

Answer: C

By definition, permutation is the number of possible arrangements, without repeating items, where the order of the selection is important.

27. Given a drawer with 5 black socks, 3 blue socks, and 2 red socks, what is the probability that you will draw two black socks in two draws in a dark room?
(Rigorous) (Skill 9.5)

   A. 2/9

   B. 1/4

   C. 17/18

   D. 1/18

Answer: A

2/9

In this example of conditional probability, the probability of drawing a black sock on the first draw is 5/10. It is implied in the problem that there is no replacement, therefore the probability of obtaining a black sock in the second draw is 4/9. Multiply the two probabilities and reduce to lowest terms.

28. Suppose you have a bag of marbles that contains 2 red marbles, 5 blue marbles, and 3 green marbles. If you replace the first marble chosen, what is the probability you will choose 2 green marbles in a row?
(Average Rigor) (Skill 9.5)

   A. 2/5

   B. 9/100

   C. 9/10

   D. 3/5

Answer: B

9/100

When performing a problem where you replace the item you multiply the first probability fraction by the second probability fraction and replace the item when finding the second probability.

29.   **The volume is:**
       (Easy) (Skill 10.1)

       A. Area of the faces excluding the bases

       B. Total area of all the faces, including the bases

       C. The number of cubic units in a solid

       D. The measure around the object

Answer: C

The number of cubic units in a solid

Volume refers to how much "stuff" can be placed within a solid. Cubic units is one of many things that can be placed within a solid to measure its volume.

30.   **The following are examples of chemical reactions EXCEPT:**
       (Average Rigor) (Skill 10.1)

       A. Melting ice into water

       B. Dissolving a seltzer tablet in water

       C. Using a fire-cracker

       D. Burning a piece of plastic

Answer: A

Melting ice into water

When you melt ice there is no chemical reaction. Ice and water have the same chemical make-up.

31. **The transfer of heat by electromagnetic waves is called _____:**
    (Easy) (Skill 10.3)

    A. Conduction

    B. Convection

    C. Phase change

    D. Radiation

Answer: D

Radiation

Heat transfer via electromagnetic waves (which can occur even in a vacuum) is called radiation. Heat can also be transferred by direct contact (conduction), by fluid current (convection), and by matter changing phase, but these are not relevant here.

32. **In the following equation, what does G represent?**
    (Rigorous) (Skill 11.2)

$$F_{gravity} = G \frac{m_1 m_2}{d^2}$$

A. The distance between the two masses

B. The universal gravitational constant

C. Coulomb's constant

D. The speed of the object

Answer: B

The universal gravitational constant

The force of gravity is the force that causes objects to fall to Earth. We can feel the force of gravity when we lift something up. The force of gravity also keeps the moon rotating around Earth and Earth rotating around the sun. The universal law of gravity states that there is a gravitational attraction between all objects on Earth determined by the equation:

$$F_{gravity} = G \frac{m_1 m_2}{d^2}$$

where G is the universal gravitational constant and d is the distance between the two masses. Coulomb's constant relates to electrostatic forces between two objects, and speed, or velocity. Finally, statics is the study of physical systems at rest or moving with a constant speed.

33. **The theory of "sea floor spreading" explains _____ (Average Rigor) (Skill 12.1)**

    A. The shapes of the continents.

    B. How continents got named.

    C. How continents move apart.

    D. How continents sink to become part of the ocean floor.

Answer: C

How continents move apart

In the theory of "sea floor spreading," the movement of the ocean floor causes continents to spread apart from one another. This occurs because crustal plates split apart, and new material is added to the plate edges. This process pulls the continents apart, or may create new separations; it is believed to have caused the formation of the Atlantic Ocean.

34. **Which of the following types of rock are made from magma? (Rigorous) (Skill 12.1)**

    A. Fossils

    B. Sedimentary

    C. Metamorphic

    D. Igneous

Answer: D

Igneous

Metamorphic rocks are formed by high temperatures and great pressures. Fluid sediments are transformed into solid sedimentary rocks. Only igneous rocks are formed from magma.

35. **Which statement is true when describing the stratosphere?**
     (Rigorous) (Skill 12.5)

     A. This layer contains a subarea called the ionosphere.

     B. This is the coldest layer.

     C. This layer is closest to the earth's surface.

     D. This layer contains very little water, and clouds are rare.

Answer: D

This layer contains very little water, and clouds are rare. The layer containing the ionosphere is the thermosphere, while the coldest layer is the mesosphere. Finally, the layer that is closes to the earth's surface is the troposphere.

36. **The most abundant gas in the atmosphere is:**
     (Rigorous) (Skill 12.7)

     A. Oxygen

     B. Nitrogen

     C. Carbon dioxide

     D. Methane

Answer: B

Nitrogen

Nitrogen accounts for 78.09 percent of the atmosphere, oxygen 20.95 percent, carbon dioxide 0.03 percent, and methane does not make up any of the atmosphere.

37.   **Which of the following is the best definition for 'meteorite'?**
       (Rigorous) (Skill 12.7)

       A. A meteorite is a mineral composed of mica and feldspar.

       B. A meteorite is material from outer space that has struck the earth's surface.

       C. A meteorite is an element that has properties of both metals and nonmetals.

       D. A meteorite is a very small unit of length measurement.

Answer: B

A meteorite is material from outer space that has struck the earth's surface.

Meteoroids are pieces of matter in space, composed of particles of rock and metal. If a meteoroid travels through the earth's atmosphere, friction causes burning and a "shooting star" (i.e., a meteor). If the meteor strikes the earth's surface, it is known as a meteorite. Note that although the suffix –ite often means a mineral, answer A is incorrect. Answer C refers to a "metalloid" rather than a "meteorite," and answer D is simply a misleading pun on "meter."

38.   **All of the following are natural resources EXCEPT:**
       (Average Rigor) (Skill 12.8)

       A. Trees

       B. Coal

       C. Fish

       D. Paper

Answer: D

Paper

A natural resource is something that is found in nature and though trees are found in nature, paper is not.

39. **Which of the following is the most accurate definition of a nonrenewable resource?**
    (Average Rigor) (Skill 12.8)

    A. A nonrenewable resource is never replaced once used.

    B. A nonrenewable resource is replaced on a timescale that is very long relative to human life spans.

    C. A nonrenewable resource is a resource that can only be manufactured by humans.

    D. A nonrenewable resource is a species that has already become extinct.

Answer: B

Renewable resources are those that are renewed, or replaced, in time for humans to use more of them. Examples include fast-growing plants, animals, or oxygen gas. (Note that while sunlight is often considered a renewable resource, it is actually a nonrenewable but extremely abundant resource.) Nonrenewable resources are those that renew themselves only on very long timescales, usually geologic timescales. Examples include minerals, metals, or fossil fuels.

40. **What cell organelle contains the cell's stored food?**
    (Rigorous) (Skill 13.1)

    A. Vacuoles

    B. Golgi Apparatus

    C. Ribosome

    D. Lysosome

Answer: A

Vacuoles

In a cell, the subparts are called organelles. Of these, the vacuoles hold stored food (and water and pigments). The Golgi Apparatus sorts molecules from other parts of the cell; the ribosomes are sites of protein synthesis; and the lysosomes contain digestive enzymes.

41. **Identify the correct sequence of organization of living things from lower to higher order:**
    (Rigorous) (Skill 13.1)

    A. Cell, Organelle, Organ, Tissue, System, Organism

    B. Cell, Tissue, Organ, Organelle, System, Organism

    C. Organelle, Cell, Tissue, Organ, System, Organism

    D. Organelle, Tissue, Cell, Organ, System, Organism

Answer: C

Organelle, Cell, Tissue, Organ, System, Organism

Organelles are parts of the cell; cells make up tissue, which makes up organs. Organs work together in systems (e.g., the respiratory system), and the organism is the living thing as a whole.

42. **Which kingdom is comprised of organisms made of one cell with no nuclear membrane?**
    (Average Rigor) (Skill 13.2)

    A. Monera

    B. Protista

    C. Fungi

    D. Algae

Answer: A

Monera

To answer this question, first note that algae are not a kingdom of their own. Some algae are in Monera, the kingdom that consists of unicellular prokaryotes with no true nucleus. Protista and Fungi are both eukaryotic, with true nuclei, and are sometimes multi-cellular. Therefore, the answer is A.

43.   **Heterozygous refers to:**
      (Average Rigor) (Skill 13.7)

      A. Having 2 dominant genes

      B. Having 2 recessive genes

      C. Having neither a recessive nor a dominant gene

      D. Having 1 recessive gene and 1 dominant gene

Answer: D

Having 1 recessive gene and 1 dominant gene

Heterozygous means to have 1 recessive gene and 1 dominant gene, so the correct answer is A.

44. **Which of the following is a correct explanation for scientific evolution?** *(Rigorous) (Skill 13.7)*

   A. Giraffes need to reach higher leaves to eat, so their necks stretch. The giraffe babies are then born with longer necks. Eventually, there are more long-necked giraffes in the population.

   B. Giraffes with longer necks are able to reach more leaves, so they eat   more and have more babies than other giraffes. Eventually, there are more long-necked giraffes in the population.

   C. Giraffes want to reach higher for leaves to eat, so they release   enzymes into their bloodstream, which in turn causes fetal development of longer-necked giraffes. Eventually, there are more long-necked giraffes in the population.

   D. Giraffes with long necks are more attractive to other giraffes, so they get the best mating partners and have more babies. Eventually, there are more long-necked giraffes in the population.

Answer: B

Organisms with a life/reproductive advantage will produce more offspring. Over many generations, this changes the proportions of the population. In any case, it is impossible for a stretched neck (A) or a fervent desire (C) to result in biologically mutated baby. Although there are traits that are naturally selected because of mate attractiveness and fitness (D), this is not the primary situation here, so answer (B) is the best choice.

45. **In an experiment measuring the growth of bacteria at different temperatures, what is the independent variable?**
    (Rigorous) (Skill 14.1)

    A. Number of bacteria

    B. Growth rate of bacteria

    C. Temperature

    D. Size of bacteria

Answer: C

Temperature

To answer this question, recall that the independent variable in an experiment is the entity that is changed by the scientist in order to observe the effects (the dependent variable). In this experiment, temperature is changed in order to measure growth of bacteria, so C is the answer. Note that answer A is the dependent variable, and neither B nor D is directly relevant to the question.

46. **Which is the correct order of methodology?**
(Average Rigor) (Skill 14.3)

1. Collecting data

2. Planning a controlled experiment

3. Drawing a conclusion

4. Hypothesizing a result

5. Re-visiting a hypothesis to answer a question

     A. 1,2,3,4,5

     B. 4,2,1,3,5

     C. 4,5,1,3,2

     D. 1,3,4,5,2

Answer: B

4, 2, 1, 3, 5: Hypothesizing a result, planning a controlled experiment, collecting data, drawing a conclusion, and re-visiting a hypothesis to answer a question.

The scientific method is a very structured way to create valid theories and laws. All methodologies must follow this specific, linear plan.

47. **This following formula depicts:**
(Rigorous) (Skill 15.2)

$$s = \sqrt{\frac{(x_i - \bar{x})^2}{n-1}}$$

A. Newton's law of motion

B. Standard deviation

C. Pythagoras' theorem

D. None of the above

Answer: B

Standard deviation

This formula is also called the root mean square deviation, also called the standard deviation, and is defined as in the formula above. Pythagoras' theorem is stated as a2 x b2 = c2; Newton's first law of motion states that an object at rest will remain at rest and an object in motion will remain in motion at a constant velocity unless acted upon by an external force. Newton's second law of motion states that if a net force acts on an object, it will cause the acceleration of the object. The relationship between force and motion is force equals mass times acceleration. (F = ma). Newton's third law states that for every action there is an equal and opposite reaction. Therefore, if an object exerts a force on another object, that second object exerts an equal and opposite force on the first.

48. **Which scientist is credited with launching the Scientific Revolution in the 16th century?**
    (Rigorous) (Skill 16.1)

    A. Roger Bacon

    B. Nicolaus Copernicus

    C. Johannes Kepler

    D. Isaac Newton

Answer: B

Nicolaus Copernicus

Roger Bacon (1224–1294) is considered one of the early advocates of the scientific method. In the 14th century, there was scientific progress in kinematics, but the Scientific Revolution began in the 16th century with the heliocentric theory of Nicolaus Copernicus. In 1605, Johannes Kepler discovered that planets orbit the sun in elliptical, not circular paths. In 1677, Isaac Newton derived Kepler's laws from the second law of motion.

49. **All of the following professions are classified under 'earth sciences' EXCEPT:**
    (Average Rigor) (Skill 16.4)

    A. Geologist

    B. Meteorologist

    C. Seismologist

    D. Biochemist

Answer: D

Biochemist

A geologist, meteorologist, and seismologist all work with phenomena that are earth related. A biochemist deals with objects that are living.

50. **The period of development which includes children learning more complex motor patterns including running, jumping, climbing and balancing describes which stage of motor development?**
(Average rigor) (Skill 17.1)

A. Stage 1

B. Stage 2

C. Stage 3

D. Stage 4

Answer B

Stage 2

In, Stage 1, children progress from simple reflexes to basic movements such as sitting, crawling, creeping, standing, and walking. In Stage 2, children learn more complex motor patterns including running, climbing, jumping, balancing, catching, and throwing. In Stage 3, children learn more specific movement skills. Finally in Stage 4 (during adolescence), children continue to develop general and specific motor skills and master specialized movements.

51. **According to Piaget's stages of development, in which stage is a child thought to be able to utilize logic?**
(Average rigor) (Skill 17.1)

A. Preoperational

B. Formal operational

C. Concrete operational

D. Sensorimotor

Answer C

Concrete operational

The sensorimotor stage is when spatial abilities are developed including reflexes, development of coordination, and development of habits. During the preoperational stage, a child is able to identify an object by a single feature, but cannot sort through objects based on differing features. This egocentric period is crucial for language development as objects and actions begin to be associated with words. During the concrete operational stage, a child is able use logic to solve problems. This stage marks the beginning of major problem solving skills. Finally the formal operational stage builds upon the previous three and is characterized by the ability to think and reason logically, draw conclusions from multiple sources, make value judgments on sources, and think deeply about hypothetical situations.

52. **The alleged benefit of this substance is an increase in muscle mass and strength; however, it produces harmful side effects such as premature closure of growth plates in bones.**
     (Rigorous) (Skill 17.6)

     A. Cocaine

     B. Alcohol

     C. Nicotine

     D. Steroids

Answer D

Steroids

Anabolic steroids are illegal and produce harmful side effects, including premature closure of growth plates in bones can occur if abused by a teenager, limiting adult height. Other effects include bloody cysts in the liver, increased risk of cardiovascular disease, increased blood pressure, and dysfunction of the reproductive system. Drugs produce a variety of effects on the body, abuse of drugs can produce many negative affects, including distortion of memory, perceptions, and sensation. Amphetamines and cocaine give users an inflated sense of performance. The negative effects of too much alcohol include an increased risk of cardiovascular disease, nutritional deficiencies, and dehydration. Alcohol also causes ill effects on various aspects of performance such as reaction time, coordination, accuracy, balance, and strength. Finally, Nicotine, a legal but often abused substance, can increase the risk of cardiovascular disease, pulmonary disease, and cancers of the mouth. Nicotine consumption through smoking severely hinders athletic performance by compromising lung function. Smoking especially affects performance in endurance activities.

53.   **Gross motor development is:**
       (Easy) (Skill 18.2)

       A. the movement of the large muscles of the body

       B. the movement of the small muscles of the body.

       C. an essential skill for learning to write.

       D. A & C.

Answer A

The movement of the large muscles of the body

Gross motor development refers to the movement and development of the large muscles of the body. These movements include running, climbing, and jumping. The movement of the small muscles of the body refers to fine motor skills, and it is these skills that are essential for learning to write.

54.   _____ **is a tough band of fibrous connective tissue that connects muscle to bone or muscle to muscle.**
       (Rigorous) (Skill 18.5)

       A. A joint

       B. A tendon

       C. A ligament

       D. Cartilage

Answer B

A tendon

A joint connects bones to bones, while a tendon connects muscles to bones or other muscles. A ligament connects bones to other bones to form a joint. Finally, cartilage is not a connective tissue.

55. **Target Hearth Rate (THR) is determined by which following formula?**
    (Rigorous) (Skill 18.5)

    A. 220-height multiplied by .75 to .80.

    B. 220-age multiplied by .60 to .80.

    C. 210 – age multiplied by .65 to .90.

    D. 220-age multiplied by .75 to .80.

Answer B

220 – age multiplied by .60 to .80

This is the formula used to determine target hear rate. Multiply by .6 to determine 60% and multiply by .8 to determine 80% of the target heart rate. The 60% - 80% range is best for fitness. The other formulas are incorrect.

56. **The arrangement and relationship of words in sentences or sentence structure best describes:**
    (Average Rigor) (Skill 19.1)

    A. Style

    B. Discourse

    C. Thesis

    D. Syntax

Answer: D

Syntax

Syntax is the grammatical structure of sentences.

57. **All of the following are true about phonological awareness EXCEPT?**
     (Average Rigor) (Skill 19.1)

     A. It may involve print.

     B. It is a prerequisite for spelling and phonics.

     C. Development of phonological skills may begin during the prekindergarten years.

     D. Students have the ability to recognize the sounds of spoken language.

Answer: A

It may involve print.

The key word here is EXCEPT, which will be highlighted in upper case on the test as well. All of the options are correct aspects of phonological awareness except the first one, A, because phonological awareness DOES NOT involve print.

58. **Which of the following is <u>NOT</u> one of the metalinguistic abilities acquired by children from early involvement in reading activities?**
     (Rigorous) (Skill 20.1)

     A. Conventions of print

     B. Word consciousness

     C. Spelling fluency

     D. Functions of print

Answer: C

Spelling fluency

Conventions of print, word consciousness, and functions of print are all learned from children's early involvement with reading. Spelling fluency is learned a little later on in reading and a fluent speller is often good at reading comprehension.

59. **Which of the following is NOT a strategy of teaching reading comprehension?**
(Rigorous) (Skill 20.4)

    A. Summarization

    B. Utilizing graphic organizers

    C. Manipulating sounds

    D. Having students generate questions

Answer: C

Manipulating sounds

Comprehension simply means that the reader can ascribe meaning to text. Teachers can use many strategies to teach comprehension, including questioning, asking students to paraphrase or summarize, utilizing graphic organizers, and focusing on mental images.

60. **Which of the following indicates that a student is a fluent reader?**
(Easy) (Skill 20.5)

    A. Reads texts with expression or prosody

    B. Reads word-to-word and haltingly

    C. Must intentionally decode a majority of the words

    D. In a writing assignment, sentences are poorly-organized structurally

Answer: A

Reads texts with expression or prosody.

The teacher should listen to the children read aloud, but there are also clues to reading levels in their writing.

61. **To decode is to:**
(Easy) (Skill 21.1)

    A. Construct meaning

    B. Sound out a printed sequence of letters

    C. Use a special code to decipher a message

    D. None of the above

Answer: A

Construct meaning

Word analysis (phonics or decoding) is the process readers use to figure out unfamiliar words based on written patterns. Decoding is the process of constructing meaning of an unknown word.

62. **If a student has a poor vocabulary, the teacher should recommend that:**
(Average Rigor) (Skill 21.1)

    A. The student read newspapers, magazines, and books on a regular basis.

    B. The student enroll in a Latin class.

    C. The student write the words repetitively after looking them up in a dictionary.

    D. The student use a thesaurus to locate synonyms and incorporate them into his/her vocabulary.

Answer: A

The student should read newspapers, magazines, and books on a regular basis.

It is up to the teacher to help the student to choose reading material, but the student must be able to choose where he/she will search for the reading pleasure indispensable for enriching vocabulary.

63. **Which of the following is an example of nonfiction literature?**
(Average Rigor) (Skill 22.1)

A. Letters

B. Biographies

C. Journals

D. All of the above

Answer: D

All of the above

All of these are examples of nonfiction literature.

64. **"The use of steroids in professional baseball is ruining the sport." Which of the following does NOT support this thesis?**
(Rigorous) (Skill 22.2)

A. Steroids are performance enhancers and give players who take steroids an unfair advantage.

B. Steroids are physically harmful to the players.

C. Steroids make baseball more exciting because more players hit home runs.

D. Kids in high school and college are taking steroids because they want to give themselves a better shot to make it into the major leagues.

Answer: C

Steroids make baseball more exciting because more players hit home runs.

The thesis speaks negatively about steroids in the sport of baseball, while choice C is a positive statement about steroids. Because of this, choice C does not support the thesis.

65. **Which is NOT a true statement concerning an author's literary tone?** *(Rigorous) (Skill 22.3)*

   A. Tone is partly revealed through the selection of details.

   B. Tone is the expression of the author's attitude toward his/her subject.

   C. Tone in literature is usually satiric or angry.

   D. Tone in literature corresponds to the tone of voice a speaker uses.

Answer: B

Tone in literature corresponds to the tone of voice a speaker uses.

Tone in literature conveys a mood and can be as varied as the tone of voice of a speaker (e.g., sad, nostalgic, whimsical, angry, formal, intimate, satirical, sentimental, etc).

66. **All of the following are examples of transitional phrases EXCEPT:** *(Easy) (Skill 22.4)*

   A. The

   B. However

   C. Furthermore

   D. Although

Answer: A

The

The word "the" is not a transitional word. "However," "furthermore," and "although" are all transitional words.

67. **A sixth-grade science teacher has given her class a paper to read on the relationship between food and weight gain. The writing contains signal words such as "because," "consequently," "this is how," and "due to." This paper has which text structure?**
(Average Rigor) (Skill 22.4)

   A. Cause & effect

   B. Compare & contrast

   C. Description

   D. Sequencing

Answer: A

Cause & effect

Cause and effect is the relationship between two things when one thing makes something else happen. Writers use this text structure to show order, inform, speculate, and change behavior. This text structure uses the process of identifying potential causes of a problem or issue in an orderly way.

68. **All of the following are common types of narratives EXCEPT:**
(Rigorous) (Skill 23.2)

   A. Legends

   B. Short stories

   C. Poems

   D. Memoirs

Answer: C

Poems

Poems are not narratives; however legends, short stories, and memoirs are.

69.   **Which of the following is NOT a characteristic of a fable?**
      (Average Rigor) (Skill 23.2)

      A. Animals that feel and talk like humans

      B. Happy solutions to human dilemmas

      C. Teaches a moral or standard for behavior

      D. Illustrates specific peoples or groups without directly naming them

Answer: D

Illustrates specific people or groups without directly naming them.

A fable is a short tale with animals, humans, gods, or even inanimate objects as characters. Fables often conclude with a moral, delivered in the form of an epigram (a short, witty, and ingenious statement in verse). Fables are among the oldest forms of writing in human history: it appears in Egyptian papyri of c 1500 BCE. The most famous fables are those of Aesop, a Greek slave living in about 600 BCE. In India, the Pantchatantra appeared in the third century. The most famous modern fables are those of seventeenth century French poet Jean de La Fontaine.

70.   **Which of the following is a ballad?**
      (Average Rigor) (Skill 23.2)

      A. "The Knight's Tale"

      B. *Julius Caesar*

      C. *Paradise Lost*

      D. "The Rime of the Ancient Mariner"

Answer: D

"The Rime of the Ancient Mariner"

"The Knight's Tale" is a Romantic poem from the longer *Canterbury Tales* by Chaucer. *Julius Caesar* is a Shakespearian play. *Paradise Lost* is an epic poem in blank verse. A ballad is an *in media res* story told or sung, usually in verse and accompanied by music, and usually with a refrain. Typically, ballads are based on folk stories

71. **Which of the following is an epic?**
    (Rigorous) (Skill 23.2)

    A. *On the Choice of Books*

    B. *The Faerie Queene*

    C. *Northanger Abbey*

    D. *A Doll's House*

Answer: B

The Faerie Queene

An epic is a long poem, usually of book length, reflecting the values of the society in which it was produced. *On the Choice of Books* is an essay by Thomas Carlyle. *Northanger Abbey* is a novel written by Jane Austen, and *A Doll's House* is a play written by Henrik Ibsen.

72. **The children's literature genre came into its own in the:**
    (Average Rigor) (Skill 23.2)

    A. Seventeenth century

    B. Eighteenth century

    C. Nineteenth century

    D. Twentieth century

Answer: A

Seventeenth century

In the seventeenth century, authors such as Jean de La Fontaine and his *Fables*, Pierre Perreault's *Tales*, Mme d'Aulnoye's Novels based on old folktales and Mme de Beaumont's *Beauty and the Beast* all created a children's literature genre. In England, Perreault was translated, and a work allegedly written by Oliver Smith, *The Renowned History of Little Goody Two Shoes*, also helped to establish children's literature in England.

73. **A simile is:**
 (Average Rigor) (Skill 23.3)

   A. A direct comparison between two things.

   B. An indirect comparison between two things.

   C. When human characteristics are applied to things that are not human, such as animals.

   D. Deliberate exaggeration for effect or comic effect.

Answer: A

A simile is when there is a direct comparison between two things. For example: "The boy was as red as a lobster."

74. **A student has written a paper with the following characteristics: written in first person; characters, setting, and plot; some dialogue; and events organized in chronological sequence with some flashbacks. In what genre has the student written?**
 (Easy) (Skill 23.3)

   A. Expository writing

   B. Narrative writing

   C. Persuasive writing

   D. Technical writing

Answer: B

Narrative writing

These are all characteristics of narrative writing. Expository writing is intended to give information such as an explanation or directions; in it, the information is logically organized. Persuasive writing gives an opinion in an attempt to convince the reader that this point-of-view is valid. It also tries to persuade the reader to take a specific action. The goal of technical writing is to clearly communicate a select piece of information to a targeted reader or group of readers.

75.   **Alliteration is a poetic device where:**
      (Average Rigor) (Skill 23.3)

      A. The words used (*Pow, Zap,* etc...) evoke meaning by their sounds.

      B. The final consonant sounds are the same, but the vowels are different.

      C. The vowel sound within a word matches the vowel sound within a   nearby word, but the surrounding consonant sounds are different (Ex.   *June* and *Tune).*

      D. The initial sound of a word, beginning in either a consonant of a vowel, in repeated in succession (Ex. *People* who *pen* poetry).

Answer: D

The initial sound of a word, beginning in either a consonant of a vowel, in repeated in succession (Ex. *People* who *pen* poetry).

Alliteration is the repetition of a consonant or a vowel within poetry.

76.   **Which of the following reading strategies is NOT associated with fluent reading abilities?**
      (Average rigor) (Skill 24.2)

      A. pronouncing unfamiliar words by finding similarities with familiar words

      B. establishing a purpose for reading

      C. formulating questions about the text while reading

      D. reading sentences word by word

Answer: D

Reading sentences word by word

Pronouncing unfamiliar words by finding similarities with familiar words, establishing a purpose for reading, and formulating questions about the text while reading are all excellent strategies fluent readers use to enhance their comprehension of a text. Reading sentences word by word is a trait of a non-fluent reader as it inhibits comprehension as the reader is focused on each word by itself rather than the meaning of the whole sentence and how it fits into the text.

77. **Which of the following is NOT a technique of prewriting?**
    (Average Rigor) (Skill 24.3)

    A. Clustering

    B. Listing

    C. Brainstorming

    D. Proofreading

Answer: D

Proofreading

Proofreading cannot be a method of prewriting, since it is done on already written texts only.

78. **All of the following are correctly capitalized EXCEPT:**
    (Rigorous) (Skill 25.1)

    A. Queen Elizabeth

    B. Congressman McKay

    C. commander Alger

    D. the president of the United States

Answer: C

commander Alger

If the statement read "Alger the commander" then commander would not need to be capitalized; however, because commander is the title it is capitalized.

79. **All of the following are correctly punctuated EXCEPT:**
(Rigorous) (Skill 25.1)

    A. "The book is on the table," said Bill's mother.

    B. "Who would like to sing 'The Star Spangled Banner'?" the teacher asked.

    C. I was embarrassed when Joanne said, "The meeting started an hour ago!"

    D. "The policeman apprehended the criminals last night."

Answer: C

In sentences that are interrogatory or exclamatory, the question mark or exclamation point should be positioned outside the closing quotation marks if the quote itself is a statement or command or cited title. The sentence should read I was embarrassed when Joanne said, "The meeting started an hour ago"!

80. **Orthography is:**
(Rigorous) (Skill 25.2)

    A. The study of word structure.

    B. A method of representing a spoken language through the use of written symbols.

    C. The complete set of related word-forms associated with a given lexeme.

    D. A process of word-formation that involves combining complete word-forms into a single compound form.

Answer: B

A method of representing a spoken language through the use of written symbols.

By definition, orthography is using written symbols to represent spoken language

81. **When students present information orally, they should keep the following in mind:**
    (Average Rigor) (Skill 26.1)

    A. Volume

    B. Pace

    C. Body language

    D. All of the above

Answer: D

All of the above

When students are presenting information orally, they should be aware of the volume of their voice, the pace in which they speak, and their body language.

82. **Which of the following is NOT an advisable strategy for making sense of oral language?**
    (Easy) (Skill 26.1)

    A. Observing body language and other nonverbal cues

    B. Take notes to outline major points

    C. Critique, question, and evaluate others' as well as students' own oral presentations

    D. Ignore prior knowledge of the topic as it does not help understand what is being presented

Answer: D

Ignore prior knowledge of the topic as it does not help understand what is being presented.

Observing body language and other nonverbal cues, taking notes to outline major points, and critiquing, questioning, and evaluating others' as well as students' own oral presentations are all good strategies when listening to an oral presentation. Ignoring prior knowledge of the topic does not help make sense of oral language. Utilizing one's own prior knowledge of a topic allows the listener to bring his or her own set of information to help understand what is being presented.

83.   **Which of the following are examples of research materials that are available to use?**
       (Easy) (Skill 27.1)

       A. Encyclopedias

       B. Internet search engines

       C. Card catalogues

       D. All of the above

Answer: D

All of the above

Encyclopedias, Internet search engines (Google, AOL), and card catalogues can all be used for research purposes.

84.   **The Bill of Rights consists of which Amendments?**
       (Average Rigor) (Skill 28.2)

       A. Amendments 1-5

       B. Amendments 1-10

       C. Amendments 1 and 2

       D. Amendments 1-22

Answer: B

Amendments 1-10

The Bill of Rights consists of the first 10 amendments.

85.   All of the following are examples of why the first known civilizations developed by water EXCEPT:
        (Average Rigor) (Skill 30.2)

        A. Rivers provided water, which both the humans and animals needs.

        B. Rivers allowed the settlers to travel so they could trade goods.

        C. The rivers attracted animals so hunters had a continuous supply of food.

        D. The rivers overflowed, which left a deposit of very rich soil.

Answer: B

Rivers allowed the settlers to travel so they could trade goods.

There is no evidence that the *first* civilizations used water for trading purposes.

86.   All of the following are oceans EXCEPT:
        (Easy) (Skill 30.2)

        A. Pacific

        B. Atlantic

        C. Mediterranean

        D. Indian

Answer: C

Mediterranean

The Mediterranean is a sea, which is smaller than an ocean and surrounded by land.

87. **Which term best defines the customs, traditions, and arts of a group of people?**
    (Easy) (Skill 30.4)

    A. Culture

    B. Democracy

    C. Interdependence

    D. Geography

Answer: A

Culture

When dealing with customs, traditions, and the arts of a group of people only culture A makes sense. The other answers do not refer to people, so they are not logical answers to the question.

88. **Cultural diffusion is:**
    (Rigorous) (Skill 31.1)

    A. The process that individuals and societies go through in changing their behavior and organization to cope with social, economic and environmental pressures.

    B. The complete disappearance of a culture.

    C. The exchange or adoption of cultural features when two cultures come into regular direct contact.

    D. The movement of cultural ideas or materials between populations independent of the movement of those populations.

Answer: D

The movement of cultural ideas or materials between populations independent of the movement of those populations.

By definition, cultural diffusion is the movement of cultural ideas or materials between populations independent of the movement of those populations.

89. **Which one of the following is NOT a reason why Europeans came to the New World?**
    (Average Rigor) (Skill 32.1)

    A. To find resources in order to increase wealth.

    B. To establish trade.

    C. To increase a ruler's power and importance.

    D. To spread Christianity.

Answer: B

To establish trade.

When the Europeans came to the New World they were not concerned to establish trade: they wanted to increase their wealth and influence across seas.

90. **The year 1619 was memorable for the colony of Virginia. Three important events occurred, resulting in lasting effects on U.S. history. Which one of the following is not one of events?**
    (Rigorous) (Skill 32.1)

    A. Twenty African slaves arrived.

    B. The London Company granted the colony a charter making it independent.

    C. The colonists were given the right by the London Company to govern themselves through representative government in the Virginia House of Burgesses.

    D. The London Company sent to the colony 60 women who were quickly married, establishing families and stability in the colony.

Answer: B

The London Company granted the colony a charter making it independent.

In the year 1619, the Southern colony of Virginia had an eventful year, including the first arrival of twenty African slaves, the right to self-governance through representative government in the Virginia House of Burgesses (their own legislative body), and the arrival of sixty women sent to marry and establish families in the colony. The London Company did not, however, grant the colony a charter in 1619.

91. **The belief that the United States should control all of North America was called:**
(Easy) (Skill 32.1)

    A. Westward Expansion

    B. Pan Americanism

    C. Manifest Destiny

    D. Nationalism

Answer: C

Manifest Destiny

The belief that the United States should control all of North America was called Manifest Destiny. This idea fueled much of the violence and aggression towards those already occupying the lands such as the Native Americans. Manifest Destiny was certainly driven by sentiments of nationalism and gave rise to westward expansion.

92. **All of the following were causes of the American Revolution EXCEPT:**
(Average Rigor) (Skill 32.1)

    A. The Tea Act of 1773

    B. The Stamp Act

    C. The colonists were forced to house English troops

    D. The colonists wanted more schools

Answer: D

The colonists wanted more schools

The colonists were not concerned about the number of schools they had, and it was not a factor of the American Revolution.

93. **The English placed taxes on the colonies for two reasons. What were they?**
(Easy) (Skill 32.1)

A. To generate revenue

B. To gain control over the colonists

C. A only

D. Both A and B

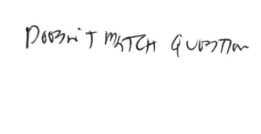

Dobesn't match guestion

Answer: D

Both A and B

The English placed taxes on the colonies to both generate revenue and gain control over the colonists.

94. **The Westward expansion occurred for a number of reasons; however, the most important reason was:**
(Average Rigor) (Skill 32.1)

A. Colonization

B. Slavery

C. Independence

D. Economics

Answer: D

Economics

Westward expansion occurred for a number of reasons, the most important being economic.

95. **Which war took the most American lives in American history?** *(Easy) (Skill 32.1)*

    A. The Civil War

    B. The Revolutionary War

    C. World War I

    D. World War II

Answer: A

The Civil War

In the Civil War, it was Americans fighting Americans, so the casualties were astronomical and more than the Revolutionary War, and both World War I and World War II.

96. **The economic collapse of the United States in 1929 is known as the:** *(Easy) (Skill 32.1)*

    A. Cold War

    B. New Deal

    C. Unhappy times

    D. Great Depression

Answer: D

Great Depression

The economic collapse of the United States in 1929 was known as the Great Depression.

97. **Which civilization invented the wheel?**
(Rigorous) (Skill 33.2)

    A. Egyptians

    B. Romans

    C. Assyrians

    D. Sumerians

Answer: D

Sumerians

The ancient Sumerian civilization invented the wheel.

98. **What is the "Pax Romana"?**
(Rigorous) (Skill 33.2)

    A. Long period of peace enabling free travel and trade, spreading people, cultures, goods, and ideas all over the world

    B. A period of war where the Romans expanded their empire

    C. The Roman government

    D. A time where the government was over-ruled

Answer: A

Long period of peace enabling free travel and trade, spreading people, cultures, goods, and ideas all over the world

The "Pax Romana" was a time when the Roman's were peaceful and wanted to spread their culture all over the world.

99. **Who wrote the *Iliad* and the *Odyssey*?**
     (Rigorous) (Skill 33.2)

     A. Aristotle

     B. Homer

     C. Pythagoras

     D. Herodotus

Answer: B

Homer

Homer is the author of both the *Iliad* and the *Odyssey*.

100. **The "divine right" of kings was the key political characteristic of:**
     (Rigorous) (Skill 33.2)

     A. The Age of Absolutism

     B. The Age of Reason

     C. The Age of Feudalism

     D. The Age of Despotism

Answer: A

The Age of Absolutism

The "divine right" of kings was the key political characteristic of The Age of Absolutism and was most visible in the reign of King Louis XIV of France, as well as during the times of King James I and his son, Charles I. The divine right doctrine claims that kings and absolute leaders derive their right to rule by virtue of their birth alone. They see this both as a law of God and of nature.

101. **Which one of the following would NOT be considered a result of World War II?**
(Average Rigor) (Skill 33.3)

A. Economic depressions and slow resumption of trade and financial aid

B. Western Europe was no longer the center of world power

C. The beginnings of new power struggles not only in Europe but in Asia as well

D. Territorial and boundary changes for many nations, especially in Europe

Answer: A

Economic depressions and slow resumption of trade and financial aid

Following World War II, the economy was vibrant and flourished from the stimulant of war and an increased dependence of the world on United States industries. Therefore, World War II didn't result in economic depressions and slow resumption of trade and financial aid.

102. **The cold war involved which two countries who both emerged as world powers?**
(Rigorous) (Skill 33.3)

A. China and Japan

B. United States and the Soviet Union

C. England and Brazil

D. Afghanistan and the United States

Answer: B

United States and the Soviet Union

After World War II, the United States and the Soviet Union constantly competed in space exploration and the race to develop nuclear weapons.

103. **Which of the following is an opinion?**
(Easy) (Skill 34.3)

    A. The sky is blue.

    B. Albany is the capital of New York State.

    C. A dog is the best pet to have.

    D. Humans breathe.

Answer: C

A dog is the best pet to have.

An opinion is a subjective evaluation based upon personal bias.

104. **Which of the following is a fact?**
(Easy) (Skill 34.3)

    A. It's going to rain.

    B. John is a liar.

    C. Joe said he believes John is a liar.

    D. The world is going to the dogs.

Answer: C

Joe said he believes John is a liar.

The only answer that is a fact is C. Joe said he believes John is a liar. It's a fact that he said it, even though what he said may not be a fact.

105. **The quality of sound is the definition of:**
(Rigorous) (Skill 35.1)

   A. timbre.

   B. rhythm.

   C. harmony.

   D. melody.

Answer: A

Timbre

Answer A is the definition of timbre – the quality of sound. Rhythm refers to the duration of musical notes. Harmony refers to the vertical aspect of music or the musical chords related to a melody. Finally, Melody is the tune (a specific arrangement of sounds in a pleasing pattern).

106. **Common percussion instruments include:**
(Average rigor) (Skill 35.2)

   A. xylophone, tambourine, and bells.

   B. trumpet, trombone, and tuba.

   C. oboe, clarinet, and saxophone.

   D. viola, cello, and piano.

Answer: A

Xylophone, tambourine, and bells

Percussion instruments are those that the musician hits or shakes to make sound. These include the xylophone, tambourine and bells. Both brass and wind instruments make sound as air travels through an air chamber. Trumpets, trombones, and tubas are examples of brass instruments and the oboe, clarinet and saxophone are examples of wind instruments. The viola, cello and piano are examples of string instruments.

107. **In the visual arts, works that project a design from the center axis are said to have:**
    (Rigorous) (Skill 35.4)

    A. Horizontal balance.

    B. Radial balance.

    C. Symmetrical balance.

    D. Asymmetrical balance.

Answer: B

Radial balance

Balance is a fundamental of design seen as a visual weight and counterweight, and radial balance refers to works that project a design from the center axis. Horizontal balance includes works which utilize the picture plane from left to right. Works with symmetrical balance have objects or arrangements on both sides, and works with asymmetrical balance display objects or arrangements on one side or another or are uneven.

108. **The predominant themes found in the arts of this period include dramatic climaxes of well-known stories, legends and battles, and the grand spectacle of mythology.**
(Rigorous) (Skill 35.6)

   A. Mesopotamian.

   B. Middle Ages.

   C. Egyptian.

   D. Baroque.

Answer: D

Baroque

The predominant themes found in the arts of the Baroque period include the dramatic climaxes of legends and battles and the grand spectacle of mythology. During the Mesopotamian period, prayer statues pointed to the theme of polytheism in religious worship. Religion, namely Catholicism themes, dominated the vast time period of the Middle Ages, and finally, the predominance of funerary art from ancient Egypt illustrates the theme of preparation for the afterlife and polytheistic worship.

109. **This area of drama requires management skills to produce and perform an onstage activity.**
(Easy) (Skill 36.2)

    A. Acting.

    B. Directing

    C. Screenwriting.

    D. Designing.

Answer: B

Directing

Directing requires the management skills to produce and perform an onstage activity. This requires guiding and inspiring students as well as script and stage supervision. Acting requires the student to demonstrate the ability to effectively communicate using skillful speaking, movement, rhythm, and sensory awareness. Scriptwriting demands that a leader be able to produce original material and staging an entire production through the writing and designing a story that has performance value. Finally, designing involves creating and initiating the onsite management of the art of acting.

110. **It was during this historical time period that dramatic performances were banned.**
(Rigorous) (Skill 36.7)

    A. Medieval.

    B. Ancient Greece.

    C. Puritan New England.

    D. Roman.

Answer: C

Puritan New England.

The Puritan Commonwealth was ruled by Oliver Cromwell who outlawed dramatic performances and that ban lasted for nearly twenty years.

XAMonline, INC. 25 First St. Suite 106 Cambridge MA 02141

Toll Free number 800-509-4128

TO ORDER Fax 781-662-9268 OR www.XAMonline.com

WEST SERIES

PO#   Store/School:

Address 1:

Address 2 (Ship to other):

City, State Zip

Credit card number_____-_____-_____-_____   expiration_____

EMAIL _____

PHONE   FAX

ISBN	TITLE	Qty	Retail	Total
978-1-58197-638-0	WEST-B Basic Skills		$27.95	
978-1-58197-609-0	WEST-E Biology 0235		$59.95	
978-1-58197-693-9	WEST-E Chemistry 0245		$59.95	
978-1-58197-566-6	WEST-E Designated World Language: French Sample Test 0173		$15.00	
978-1-58197-557-4	WEST-E Designated World Language: Spanish 0191		$59.95	
978-1-60787-138-5	WEST-E Elementary Education 0014		$28.95	
978-1-58197-636-6	WEST-E English Language Arts 0041		$59.95	
978-1-58197-634-2	WEST-E General Science 0435		$59.95	
978-1-58197-637-3	WEST-E Health & Fitness 0856		$59.95	
978-1-58197-635-9	WEST-E Library Media 0310		$59.95	
978-1-58197-674-8	WEST-E Mathematics 0061		$59.95	
978-1-58197-556-7	WEST-E Middle Level Humanities 0049, 0089		$59.95	
978-1-58197-043-2	WEST-E Physics 0265		$59.95	
978-1-58197-563-5	WEST-E Reading/Literacy 0300		$59.95	
978-1-58197-552-9	WEST-E Social Studies 0081		$59.95	
978-1-58197-639-7	WEST-E Special Education 0353		$73.50	
978-1-58197-633-5	WEST-E Visual Arts Sample Test 0133		$15.00	
978-1-60787-141-5	WEST-E History 027		$59.95	
	SUBTOTAL			
	1 book $8.25, 2 books, $11.00, 3+ books $15.00		**SHIP**	
	FOR PRODUCT PRICES VISIT WWW.XAMONLINE.COM		**TOTAL**	